Multicultural Theatre II

Contemporary Hispanic, Asian and African-American Plays

Edited, and with a
critical introduction by

Roger Ellis

MERIWETHER PUBLISHING LTD.
Colorado Springs, Colorado

Meriwether Publishing Ltd., Publisher
PO Box 7710
Colorado Springs, CO 80933-7710

Executive editor: Theodore O. Zapel
Cover design: Janice Melvin

© Copyright MCMXCVIII Meriwether Publishing Ltd.
Printed in the United States of America
First Edition

Library of Congress Cataloging-in-Publication Data

Multicultural theatre II : contemporary Hispanic, Asian, and
    African-American plays / edited and with a critical introduction by Roger Ellis.
-- 1st ed.
        p.   cm.
    Includes bibliographical references.
    ISBN-13 978-1-56608-042-2
    ISBN-10 1-56608-042-8
       1. American drama — Minority authors. 2. Ethnic groups — United States — Drama. 3. Minorities — United States — Drama. 4. Hispanic Americans — Drama. 5. Asian Americans — Drama. 6. Afro-Americans — Drama. I. Ellis, Roger, 1943 May 18-
    PS627.M5M85 1998
    812'.54080920693--dc21   98-28515
                                          CIP
                                          AC

2   3   4   05   06   07

Acknowledgments

Among the many individuals who lent me their assistance with this book, special recognition should be given to Grand Valley State University which provided me with the much-needed funding and release time from teaching to compile and prepare the material. I'm also grateful for the continued support and advice of my editor, Ted Zapel, at Meriwether Publishing. In addition, I'm indebted to the cooperation of numerous theatres across the nation for access to their script libraries and the help of their literary managers. Without the assistance of organizations like the Theatre Communications Group, New Dramatists, and others, several of the plays included here would not have come to my attention. Credit should also be given to all the authors' agents for their patience and cooperation in arranging permission fees and contracts with the playwrights. And last but not least I owe a debt of gratitude I can never repay to all of the actors whose performances enabled me to recognize the power and the grace, the subtlety and theatricality of the plays contained in this anthology.

Contents

Introduction

On the Cultural Politics of Diversity

It is impossible today to assemble a collection like this without at some point engaging the issue of race and ethnicity in contemporary America. Like it or not, cultural diversity has become a flashpoint for American society as we move into the twenty-first century, and many critics would have us believe that it is *the* central social problem facing us at this point in our history.

Thus to pretend to offer a survey of recent multicultural literature either by presenting the plays to readers "objectively," or by editorially sidestepping the political context which surrounds these dramas would probably seem naive to most people, and even fatuous and reactionary to many others. In short, it's very difficult as an editor to present these dramas strictly as works of art without connecting that art to the political ramifications in the back of everyone's mind as they read or see them. "Ars gratia artis" is a mantle only grudgingly draped over the shoulders of playwrights nowadays — if indeed it can exist any longer at all.

The editorial difficulty here is further compounded by the ambiguity of the terminology we would use in addressing the sociopolitical context surrounding these plays. What, in fact, do the terms "multicultural," "intercultural," or "multiethnic" mean? How do we accurately distinguish between "ethnicity," "cultural diversity" or "cultural pluralism"? And who should be singled out as an "ethnic" playwright or excluded from the club? Of course *broad* distinctions readily spring to mind: Lorraine Hansberry is plainly an "ethnic" writer and David Mamet is not. *Ragtime* certainly deals with multicultural issues, at least in part, while *A Chorus Line* does not. But how far does this get us? Any college freshman could observe as much.

Once again, we're forced to concede that the political debate which has raged in the United States since the nineteen-sixties has blurred the important semantic distinctions for us and infused the discussion at every level. Like shapeshifters, our critical terms dissolve in our hands even as we try to use them to pry deeper into the issues and gain the insight, clarity and perspective we all seek.

Finally, there is the question of motive. Modern communications theory has sensitized all of us — critics and editors, artists, audiences and institutions alike — to the biases inherent in any "editorial" process. Waving the banner of ethnocentrism over this very point, dramatist August Wilson would have *only* African-American theatres produce work by African-American writers; and his views are shared by many in the Hispanic and Asian-American communities towards their own plays which they regard as cultural artifacts. At the same time, it's impossible to ignore how many artists of color have become disenchanted by Wilson's claim — artistic director Ricardo Khan, for example, or the playwright Philip Kan Gotanda — feeling that such consignment to some ethnic camp will result in ghettoizing valuable work that should instead speak to *all* races, especially to the culturally pluralistic society that the United States is fast becoming.

Despite such problems surrounding this anthology, there are some constants we should bear in mind as we approach the plays contained here. Setting aside for the moment the predictable tub-thumping rhetoric of partisans on both the left and the right, we might first observe that no single issue has ever stirred up so much controversy in the history of the American stage as has the current debate over "cultural diversity in the American theatre." Neither the damage done to the careers of dramatic artists by Joe McCarthy and his supporters, nor the outrageous (and often illegal) antics of groups like the Living Theatre and San Francisco Mime Troupe during the wild and woolly sixties, nor even the current hullabaloo over government patronage of the arts ever produced such widespread and continuing argument at all levels of the art form.

Secondly, one needs to remember that in the field of dramatic writing, some of the most muscular, inventive and significant plays now being written in the United States — both literarily and theatrically considered — are addressing themselves to the issues of race and culture. And this is very unusual in the history of the American stage, that so many gifted playwrights are turning their attention to a single issue. Ethnic writers like Eduardo Machado and Luiz Valdez, David Henry Hwang and Philip Kan Gotanda, OyamO, August Wilson, and Maria Irene Fornes seem very well established today, and many have already become theatrical household words. Other playwrights who are unaligned with a particular ethnic background have also written plays on ethnic issues for theatres across the country: Emily Mann, Alfred Uhry and David Rabe, to mention but a few.

As an editor I've tried to remain sensitive to what I prefer to call the "cultural politics of diversity" surrounding the writers in this book, without taking sides in the debate. I mean by this that I sympathize with writers who deal today with problems of racism or ethnicity, because they must work in a social climate that is politically charged, and at times restrictive. It's difficult, that is, for a playwright to introduce any one of many ideas about race and ethnicity without feeling the eyes of audiences, critics, other playwrights, etc. trained on their play and conscious of the "social stakes" that are involved.

As an editor, however, it's not my place to seek to resolve that issue here any more than the writers I've selected have sought to do so in any single one of their plays. To fairly present these dramas to readers I've tried to select as broad a cross-section as possible, and to further regard each of them as cultural documents in the most general — dare I even say "anthropological" — sense of that word. As a result, I feel the writers in this collection "hold the mirror up to nature"; and I choose to let their plays speak for them, as I sincerely believe they, too, wish to do.

I've tried to assemble the present collection in the belief that new American plays dealing with ethnic issues can be a vigorous source of insight into our culture. By and large the authors included here are also emerging, although one or two may already be familiar to dedicated theatergoers. And it is these new, often marginalized voices on the issues of race and culture that this anthology seeks to capture and publicize.

About the Collection

In choosing the material for this anthology directed towards young actors and audiences, I've tried to focus upon plays that I feel are the most worthwhile in terms of their dramaturgy, scenic potential, and their treatment of issues. I've seen many of them in performance; others I've located in the script collections of producing theatres and playwrights' labs such as New Dramatists in New York, the Audrey Skirball-Kenis Theatre in Southern California, and others. Some scripts have come to me from agents and playwrights whom I've contacted about the needs of the book; and of course the "Plays in Process" series lately published by the Theatre Communications Group has been invaluable because it summarized and highlighted plays of all kinds produced by our nation's professional theatres. But in addition to my own judgment of the artistic quality residing in a particular script, several other criteria have influenced my decisions on whether or not to include a given play in this collection.

My first guideline in the selection process has been that of currency: I've tried to locate scripts written or first produced within the past fifteen years. In fact, most of the plays included here are even more recent. I've done this because I feel that dramas written about the experience of cultural pluralism in the United States are now entering a new stage by displaying significantly different features and concerns than those written between 1950-1980. Prior to the eighties, ethnic playwrights tended to speak primarily to audiences of their own ethnic persuasion, to concentrate heavily upon domestic situations in their plays, and to rely on a realistic production style which has been, of course, a staple of American drama for many decades. Such authors as Lorraine Hansberry, Wakako Yamauchi or Joseph Walker, for example, typify this phase of ethnic writing.

But more recent plays by Suzan Lori-Parks, Migdalia Cruz or Rick Shiomi, for example, are markedly different in their dramaturgy, thematic concerns and scenic potential. These authors boldly attack white mainstream society's interpretation of American history, or grapple with contemporary forms of American pop culture threatening their cultural identities, as they illuminate their particular ethnic concerns. Also, their work demonstrates very eclectic theatrical influences from Shakespeare to Brecht, from multimedia stagings to modern performance art. And it is this more recent work, closer to our own time, that I'm attempting to highlight.

A second important measure in my selection procedure is that of production: each play here has been "tested" in the crucible of public presentation. In most cases, the dramas have had more than one staging, a process that I believe helps writers to refine their work and editors to validate the quality of what they read. Naturally any editor will have to rely mainly on his or her personal impressions of worth in scripts they peruse; and for each of the plays I've selected, I've rejected ten or twelve others. In doing so, however, I've often found useful the opinions of producers, directors and audiences — those most directly connected with a play's worth in actual performance.

Certainly a third criterion of selection has been a play's suitability for young people. None of the plays represented here were written specifically for young audiences; and by "young" I mean that I've tried to remain sensitive to the needs of theatre students, readers or audiences from middle school through college. I know, for example, that K-12 teachers nationwide have a great need for good, up-to-date writing on themes relating to cultural diversity. Such material is useful in literature and oral interpretation classes, and in forensics or dramatics activities as our schools continue to reflect the increasing cultural pluralism of American society-at-large. I know, too, that theatre producers are strengthening their efforts to bring to the stage works that appeal to more diverse audiences; and plays that can challenge the talents of designers, directors and actors. Finally, as a university professor, I continue to discover more and more benefits from including ethnic material in my curricula, theatre programming and training work. Hence, each of these plays contains a significant number of roles capable of being played by young actors, and especially actors-of-color; and each demonstrates what I feel to be a high quality of writing that is likely to be useful for literary, forensics or theatrical applications with young people.

Finally, a word must be said regarding the umbrella criterion of "ethnic diversity." Readers will note that I've broadly organized these works into "Hispanic," "Asian" and "African-American" categories. This is because many people approaching ethnic writing for the first time seem to understand it only in these general terms. But it should be noted that in each category I've tried to include plays from ethnic subgroups that constitute that broader category. Thus in the section entitled "Plays of Hispanic-American Experience," the reader will find a play dealing with Mexican culture (*The Migrant Farmworker's Son*), Central or South American culture (*Night Train to Bolina*), and Puerto-Rican culture (*Maricela de la Luz Lights the World*). I've tried to follow the same approach in selecting plays for the Asian-American and, to a lesser extent, the African-American categories.

Another more delicate point, however, must be raised with regard to the "ethnic diversity" found in this anthology. Not all these authors are writers-of-color, in the way we customarily understand that term. In fact, two of them are Caucasian playwrights. Certainly lived experience — in terms of gender, religion, race, occupation, etc. — offers many advantages to an author who would write of that subject. But without engaging in a long debate on this issue of whether or not one must have personally experienced ethnic problems in order to write about them, let me defer to the opinion of the South African playwright Athol Fugard. He points out that we *must* grant a playwright the artistic ability to create characters widely different from his or her own background, or else forget about playing the dramatic game altogether. Shakespeare did not have to be an African in order to create a stunning portrait of white racism in the first act of *Othello*. Nor does David Henry Hwang have to be a Frenchman to write insightfully of European power-broking diplomats in *M. Butterfly*; nor David Rabe a Vietnamese in order to create compelling Asian characters in *Sticks and Bones*. In making my decisions for inclusion, I've tried to take account of the heartbeats more than just the color of an artist's skin.

A Reminder About Intellectual Property

In all the anthologies I edit, I feel compelled to remind readers that the plays in the collection are intended for reading *only*. When it comes to performing them, producing them in public readings, or adapting them in any way via the electronic media for other audiences—educational, amateur, or professional—then permission *must* be obtained and royalties paid to the agent or author.

Perhaps this "caution" needs to be restated in this age of the Internet where so much is available online or otherwise reproducible at little or no charge. Readers must remind themselves that plays — like other unique, cultural artifacts — are not equivalent to the "factoids" we slug through and manipulate by the thousands every day. They are the intellectual property of human beings who have spent many years earning, and who therefore deserve, proper acknowledgment and compensation for producing and distributing them to the public.

Bear in mind that I'm attempting in this book to highlight and promote the work of a handful of uniquely talented and very highly motivated artists whose worth, importance and cultural value in our society is already deeply discounted, frequently ridiculed, and even despised. Their plays are their honest work, their "products." Pay for them. Credits appear at the end of this volume; call or write for permission. These artists are not unreasonable in what they expect from us.

Editor's Note

The numerals at the left of the pages of all plays are for convenient, specific reference to lines during a discussion of the work.

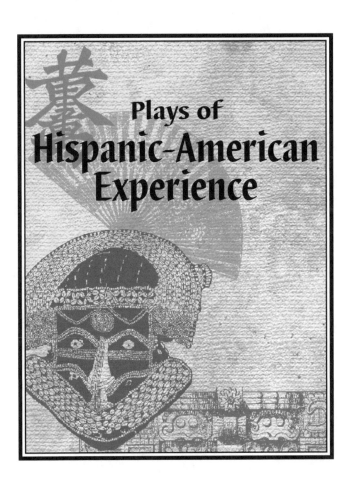

Plays of
Hispanic-American
Experience

Maricela de la Luz
Lights the World
by José Rivera

Commentary by José Rivera

I come from a family of storytellers. None of us but me is a professional — in fact, storytelling in my family is not a job but a way of life. All my siblings do it and my mother as well. So did my *abuelo* and *abuelita*. If you were to ask me to define what it means to be Puerto Rican, I would have to place storytelling near the top of the list. Now, this talent, or gift, is a tricky thing. Sometimes the stories have a funny way of crowding out reality. In fact, I would say that there is often a blurring of the boundaries between reality and fantasy in my family's storytelling talent. Whether they are the stories of my parents' courtship in Puerto Rico told by my mother, or stories of the Persian Gulf War as told by two brothers who fought in that conflict, or the stories I choose to tell my friends — it's sometimes almost impossible to know the difference between the fact and the invention. And I think this is because this tendency to blur the lines happens *in the mind of the storyteller as the story is being told*. It's just a reflex we have: we just forget what's true. We embellish, we lie, we fib, we fabricate, we alter, we amend, we misconstrue, we misremember, we misstate — we do everything a good journalist is not supposed to do — but most of all, we try to entertain. We play for laughs. We milk the moments. We try to get a good hearty rise from our bewitched audiences. It's a great way to spend the time between the moments when true (but often dull) reality demands we pay attention.

It was in this spirit that I started to tell my daughter Adena bedtime stories from the time she was old enough to understand my words. I told them faithfully every night I could. They were long, intricate tales in which, inevitably, a little red-haired girl named Adena saved the beleaguered city of Los Angeles from giants, or witches, or sand creatures, or car-digesting blobs of toxic waste — you get the pattern, right? She loved them. She was the center of the story. The girl hero. The active, engaged little warrior who used her wits and her courage to save an unsavable city from its primitive threats. As Adena got older, I started telling her longer and longer tales until, over a period of months, I told her a continuous, ever shape-shifting story with countless installments and plot twists. When the professional writer in me began to sense that I actually had a viable story that others might share (i.e., I could make some money on this), I would ask Adena, each morning, to tell me the parts of the previous night's episode which she remembered best. Inevitably she remembered the best parts. I would sit at my computer and write what she told me. Eventually these bits and pieces from a child's prodigious memory became the blueprint for the children's play, *Maricela de la Luz Lights the World*.

For Adena and Teo

"...and Alice began to remember
that she was a Pawn,
and that soon it would be time
for her to move."
— Lewis Carroll

This play was commissioned by the Seattle Children's Theatre. Special thanks to Heather Dundas, Deborah Frockt, Linda Hartzell, Vanessa Marquez, Armando Molina, John Michael Morgan, Jessica Hecht, David Wohl, Lauren Tom, Pamela Gordon, Mitchell Anderson, Andrea Stein, Elizabeth Ruscio, Robert Fieldsteel, Shishir Kurup, Paige Leong, Kimberleigh Aarn, Ellis Williams, Lisa Peterson, Len Berkman, the Wilton Project, and the Mark Taper Forum's Mentor Playwrights.

1   MARICELA DE LA LUZ LIGHTS THE WORLD
2   by José Rivera
3
4 *ACT ONE*
5 *(San Diego, California. A week before Christmas. A hot sunny too-*
6 *bright day. An outdoor parking lot of a massive mall. Canned*
7 *muzak — José Feliciano's "Feliz Navidad" — plays. As package-*
8 *laden SHOPPERS scurry to and fro, MARICELA and RICCARDO*
9 *DE LA LUZ, brother and sister, come out of the mall, carrying*
10 *shopping bags full of gifts. MARICELA, 11, has an impish face*
11 *with great dark eyes full of questions and doubts, light brown*
12 *skin, jet black hair. She wears shorts and a T-shirt. RICCARDO, 9,*
13 *is dark-skinned with brown eyes and a smart mouth: shorts, T-*
14 *shirt and Walkman™. RICCARDO comes in holding a big pair of*
15 *sunglasses. MARICELA chases RICCARDO, one hand over her*
16 *eyes, trying to grab the sunglasses.)*
17
18 **MARICELA: My eyes! My eyes! Aaaaaah! They're melting in my**
19   **face! Oozing outta my crusty eye sockets ... !**
20 **RICCARDO:** *(Dodging her)* **Gross as *usual*, Maricela!**
21 **MARICELA: ... 'til they fall to the ground, I *step* on 'em — and**
22   **they go — *splatter!* — eyeball juice everywhere!**
23 **RICCARDO:** *(Looking up at the sky)* **Whoa — look at the sky**
24   **today. It's white. Whoever heard of a totally white sky?**
25 **MARICELA:** *(Shielding her eyes)* ***Oye*, don't start with me: I can't**
26   **even believe it's Christmas next week. Ninety-five degrees**
27   **in the shade. Stupid San Diego! Back in the Bronx it's**
28   **really winter.**
29 **RICCARDO:** *(Mockingly)* **Ho ho ho.**
30 **MARICELA: A white Christmas was so cool. Fists of snow**
31   **smashing the tops of cars. People all civilized for once and**
32   **giving to the street Santas. A little bit of hope. People**
33   **doing hopeful things!**
34 **RICCARDO: Yeah, Christmas even made *you* nice ...**
35 **MARICELA:** *(Trying to hit him)* **We shouldda never left — period!**

1   **RICCARDO:** (*Dodging her*) **Palm trees? Beaches? This is tons**
2   **better'n freezing our faces off in the Bronx. You know**
3   **what your trouble is? You don't know when you're in**
4   **paradise.**
5   **MARICELA: This ain't no paradise, Riccardo. It's a mall.**
6

7   (*There's a brilliant flash of light — the sound of supernatural*
8   *laughter — the color of the sky changes — this climaxes with an*
9   *explosive clap of thunder that makes MARICELA and RICCARDO*
10   *jump. It starts to snow. MARICELA and RICCARDO watch the*
11   *snow dumbfounded as the SHOPPERS, reacting to the snowfall,*
12   *scream in terror, and start running for their Off-stage cars en*
13   *masse. We hear screeching car tires and horns honking.*
14   *(MARICELA and RICCARDO don't yet notice they've been left*
15   *completely alone.)*
16

17   **MARICELA: Is that ... ? Is that ... ?**
18   **RICCARDO: Yeah ... it's ... it's ...**
19   **MARICELA: Snow? Excuse me?!? Hello?!? Can someone explain**
20   **this to me please?!?**
21   **RICCARDO: It *is* winter, you know!**
22   **MARICELA: In Southern California?! It's gotta be computer**
23   **graphics, bro!**
24   **RICCARDO:** (*Sticking out his tongue*) **Tastes like the real thing**
25   **to me. Man! A white Christmas in San Diego! Oooooooo,**
26   **freaky!**
27   **MARICELA: If you're finished having your cosmic moment, I'm**
28   **trying to figure this out?**
29   **RICCARDO: It's just real, Mari'. Surrender to it, girl! You can't**
30   **control the universe, you know!**
31   **MARICELA: If Mami was here she could say if it's real or not!**
32   **RICCARDO:** (*Worried*) **And accumulating. Fast.**
33   **MARICELA:** (*Not listening*) ***Yo no sé*, just last night, I was lying in**
34   **bed wishing for snow – something abnormal and bad falling**
35   **outta the sky to freak Mami out and bring her to her senses.**

1   RICCARDO: *Oye*, maybe I can find out something on the news.
2   *(RICCARDO turns on his Walkman and puts on the*
3   *headphones. MARICELA notices the silence. She looks*
4   *around, worried.)*
5   MARICELA: **Bro, *oyeme*,** has it gotten, like ... really quiet all of
6   a sudden?
7   RICCARDO: *(Listening to radio)* **¡*Mira que cosa!* Mari'!** They're
8   saying there's freezing temperatures all over the city!
9   *(MARICELA notices all the SHOPPERS have disappeared.)*
10 MARICELA: *(Worried)* ... Hey, where'd everybody go, anyway?
11 RICCARDO: *(Whacking Walkman)* **Oh no, stupid batteries!**
12 MARICELA: *(Looking out)* **¡*Ay, Riccardo!*** That's the last car
13 leaving the lot! Heading home as fast as they can! Yo,
14 We're all alone! We might need some help!?
15 RICCARDO: *(Listening)* **...Oh no!** ... the national weather service
16 is expecting four to five feet of snow to fall on the city by
17 tonight!
18 MARICELA: You're making that up, right?!
19 RICCARDO: *(Listening)* It's massive. It's a blizzard. And you
20 wished for it.
21 MARICELA: Wishes don't come true in the real world, tonto!
22 RICCARDO: *(Listening)* The whole system of roads and
23 freeways is gonna be crippled! Scientists at U.C.S.D. have
24 no idea what's up!
25 MARICELA: *(Looking through pockets)* **Mira, creo que tengo**
26 Mami's number at the hotel ...
27 RICCARDO: *(Listening)* The Governor's calling for evacuation
28 of the city!
29 MARICELA: *(Still searching)* ... Mami picked a great weekend to
30 go running off with that moron ...
31 RICCARDO: ... Weird, it don't sound like the Governor!
32 MARICELA: *(Finding it)* ... I shouldda said something last night
33 to her! I was going to! I was *that* close, too! Why didn't I? I
34 know why, 'cause I'm a chicken, that's why!
35 RICCARDO: *(Listening)* **Este,** check this out ... it's ... only

1   snowing on San Diego itself ... the snow ... stops right at
2   the borders of the city. On the other side of the border it's
3   ninety-five degrees.
4   MARICELA: *¡Eso, no lo creo!*
5   RICCARDO: *(Listening)* No — I'm losing the signal ... no, c'mon
6   ... stupid batteries ...
7   MARICELA: *(Looking out)* **Mira.** The street's all white.
8   RICCARDO: *(Listening)* **Wild caribou are roaming the city.**
9   **Downtown is all buried in dirty slush! And the batteries**
10 **are dead!**
11 MARICELA: All right, don't freak, Riccardo, we can't freak,
12 *entiendes?*
13 RICCARDO: I would really like to freak, Maricela.
14 MARICELA: Yeah, well, so would I, but ...
15 RICCARDO: *(Teeth chattering)* ... freezing, freezing ...
16 MARICELA: Focus! OK. We go back in the mall. We call Mami in
17 Vegas. Tell her we're OK. Then we call Ofelia to pick us up,
18 take us home, OK? *(MARICELA and RICCARDO turn*
19 *Upstage. They try to open the mall doors but the doors are*
20 *now locked. MARICELA pounds on them.)* **It's locked! Hey,**
21 **let us in!**
22 RICCARDO: There's no one in there. They all left us. Left a
23 couple of charming children behind.
24 MARICELA: I'm gonna sue every one of them wimps when we
25 get home!
26 RICCARDO: Maybe Ofelia will figure out it's a city emergency
27 and come find us.
28 MARICELA: *(Looking around)* Yeah? Or else she's worried about
29 her own kids and she took off with them. The only city on
30 the planet without telephone booths!
31 RICCARDO: Do you think Mami or Papi know?
32 MARICELA: Mami might, from the news. But if she gets on a
33 plane right now ... she's still hours away.
34 RICCARDO: If the airport is open. And where Papi is — who
35 knows?

1   MARICELA: *(Looking around)* The only city on earth without
2   taxis!!
3   RICCARDO: I don't feel like waiting for Ofelia, do you? We don't
4   live that far, Mari, you know.
5   MARICELA: *(Torn)* And I'm not even sure the way home. What
6   if we get lost?
7   RICCARDO: Oh, man, why did we have to move to this stupid
8   city?
9   MARICELA: You know why!
10 RICCARDO: *(Teeth chattering harder)* ... *más* freezing, *más*
11   freezing ...
12
13 *(MARICELA desperately tears through the gift-wrapped*
14 *Christmas presents in their bags. There are sweaters, jogging*
15 *pants, and scarves in the boxes. She gives them to RICCARDO as*
16 *she puts on a sweater.)*
17
18 MARICELA: *Toma.* You put this on. At least now we won't
19   freeze: we may lose our minds, but we won't freeze.
20 RICCARDO: *(Putting on clothes)* You're an optometrist.
21 MARICELA: *(Putting on clothes)* **Optimist.** Hardly. *(A huge*
22   *POLAR BEAR enters, happily frolicking in the snow.)*
23 RICCARDO: *Este* ... don't look now ... but there's a polar bear
24   walking around the mall!
25 MARICELA: It — escaped from *el* zoo?
26 RICCARDO: Just like those plucky penguins over there ... !
27 MARICELA: What're penguins doing in Southern California?!
28 MARICELA AND RICCARDO: Ice skating!
29 MARICELA: *(Deciding)* Okay! *Nos vamos.* We're going. We just
30   explain to Ofelia we couldn't stay here and be devoured
31   raw by a polar bear and a penguin and we explain to Mami
32   it was your idea.
33 RICCARDO: Yes! Adventure!
34 MARICELA: *(Getting up her courage)* We know this element. We
35   grew up in it. We can survive a short walk in this.

1
2   *(MARICELA and RICCARDO take a step forward. Lights change*
3   *dramatically. The POLAR BEAR exits. It stops snowing.*
4   *MARICELA and RICCARDO look at the strange street, wary.)*
5
6   **RICCARDO: I give up, how lost are we?**
7   **MARICELA: It ain't even funny how lost we are.**
8   **RICCARDO: Why're the houses all boarded up?**
9   **MARICELA: I had bad dreams looked like this place. It's like we**
10   **slipped into some alternating universe, bro!**
11 **RICCARDO: Guess everyone heard the Governor and split.**
12 **MARICELA: Does the snow feel weird? Feeling real funny**
13   **under my feet. Vibrating.**
14 **RICCARDO: Electrical. Pulsing. Like it's ... alive ...**
15
16 *(Suddenly RICCARDO chases MARICELA around the stage,*
17 *roaring like a monster. MARICELA mock-screams. RICCARDO*
18 *grabs MARICELA and they laugh — but it's a nervous laugh that*
19 *thinly conceals their real fear. Silence. Interrupted by howling*
20 *wind.)*
21
22 **MARICELA: Wow, thanks, that was a blast.**
23 **RICCARDO: Let's go back to the mall and try again, OK?**
24 **MARICELA: *Muchacho,* we took so many little U-turns an' stuff,**
25   **I don't know the way ...**
26 **RICCARDO: You really messed up, Mari'. Mami's gonna to be**
27   **mad. We shouldda waited for Ofelia. It's your fault — *tú!***
28 **MARICELA: Shut up or I maim your face!**
29 **RICCARDO: (*Looking around*) I just wanna go back to where I**
30   **know what everything means.**
31 **MARICELA: *Yo no sé.* I get the feeling things won't never mean**
32   **what they used to.**
33
34 *(XBALANQUE [Sha-ba-lan-koo-a], a young Mayan Moon God,*
35 *comes running across the stage. XBALANQUE is dressed in ornate*

1 *feathers and a jaguar skin. He is barefoot, handsome, muscular.)*

2

3 **XBALANQUE:** *(Running)* **Brother! Brother! Brooooooo-**

4 **theeeeeeer!** *(XBALANQUE is gone. MARICELA and*

5 *RICCARDO, stunned, look at each other.)*

6 **MARICELA: You see that?**

7 **RICCARDO: What was that?**

8 **MARICELA: Maybe it's help.**

9 **RICCARDO: Why is help dressed like that?** *(XBALANQUE runs*

10 *back On-stage. MARICELA and RICCARDO nearly tackle him*

11 *to make him stop. XBALANQUE looks at MARICELA and*

12 *RICCARDO in shock.)*

13 **MARICELA: Excuse me *señor*!**

14 **XBALANQUE: Who are you? Why are you touching me? Do you**

15 **know who you're touching?**

16 **MARICELA:** *(Fast) Yo soy Maricela de la Luz.* **This is my brother**

17 **Riccardo. We're children. Our Mami went to Las Vegas**

18 **with her new boyfriend this weekend and our father's**

19 **stationed in Korea and they're divorced and he don't**

20 **know she's blowing all her money gambling with this total**

21 **loser and leaving us with this dimwitted baby-sitter Ofelia**

22 **who dropped us off at the mall for a couple of hours but**

23 **then it started to snow, as you can see, and everyone**

24 **freaked out 'cause they're all wussies in California *and***

25 **they closed the mall *and* – .**

26 **XBALANQUE: Get your impure, unclean hands *off* me!**

27 *(MARICELA lets go of XBALANQUE.)*

28 **MARICELA: Sorry, bro, but we're lost big time, we need a lift**

29 **home, I can pay you for gas –**

30 **XBALANQUE: What's gas?**

31 **MARICELA: Gas, *tú sabes,* what you put in a car –**

32 **XBALANQUE: What's a car?**

33 **RICCARDO: You must be new to California, stranger.**

34 **XBALANQUE:** *(Frustrated)* **I don't have time to talk to crazy**

35 **people. A terrible thing has happened. And I must take**

1   care of it right now!

2 MARICELA: *(Confused)* Look, are you, like, a cross-dressing,
3   unemployed actor?

4 XBALANQUE: My brother is missing! Do you hear that? Do you
5   know what that implies for the fate of the universe?

6 RICCARDO: Sounds serious! I like it!

7 XBALANQUE: What planet are you people from? He's my twin
8   — and he's gone! Missing in action! One minute he was
9   shining down on us, great and glorious, the
10   next...*(XBALANQUE clasps his hands in prayer and looks up
11   to the sky.)* Sovereign Plumed Serpent! Heart of Sky!
12   Thunderbolt Hurricane! Listen to me, you ancient gods of
13   the Maya. If you have stolen my brother from the sky, I
14   will avenge him! I will or my name isn't Xbalanque!

15 MARICELA AND RICCARDO: *(Mangling it)* Shabalu — coolly —
16   que?

17 XBALANQUE: *(Correcting them)* Xbalanque. Means "Little
18   Jaguar Sun." You may refer to me, however, as the "Full
19   Moon" — brother of the missing Hunahpu. We are the twin
20   sons of One Hunahpu our father, and Blood Woman our
21   mother — though we never call her Blood Woman, we call
22   her Mommy, Mamacita, Big Mama, *Yo* Big Mama ...

23 RICCARDO: Your brother *who*?

24 XBALANQUE: Hunahpu. Mayan Sun God. I am the Moon God.
25   We're a set. You don't get one without the other. Don't you
26   know anything? Don't you read about us in school?

27 MARICELA: Never.

28 XBALANQUE: *(In despair)* Quite, quite forgotten! Worse than I
29   thought!

30 MARICELA: *(Losing patience)* *Señor*, we gotta get home!

31 XBALANQUE: Something's up. Some maverick God has stolen
32   my brother. I sense a great cosmic battle about to start.
33   The Forces of the Sun versus the Forces of Ice!

34 RICCARDO: A god battle? That's the bomb!

35 XBALANQUE: Yes and in every battle, you need soldiers to throw

1   those bombs. Somebody willing to risk everything for a
2   great cause! If somebody – say, you two, for instance ...
3 MARICELA: No, no, don't get us mixed up with you. I think
4   you're a nutcase! I think it's wrong of you to lie to
5   children. I think –
6 XBALANQUE: Ahhhhhhhhhhhh! *(With a cry of frustration and*
7   *despair, XBALANQUE runs off again.)*
8 MARICELA: Whoa, man, we need you! Come back here! *(They*
9   *watch XBALANQUE disappear.)*
10 RICCARDO: Mari'? He said he's a god?
11 MARICELA: He's not, he's some con artist –
12 RICCARDO: But if the Sun God got kidnapped, that explains
13   the snow ...
14 MARICELA: Are you cracked? You don't explain one mystery
15   with another, bro!
16
17 *(The lights change again. The air is filled with the sounds of*
18 *chimes and wind. A TWO-HEADED WOMAN enters. This is*
19 *OFELIA, Goddess of the U.S.-Mexico border. The hair on both*
20 *OFELIA's heads is long, wild, down to her waist and it's filled with*
21 *barbed wire, broken hearts, and other debris. OFELIA wears a*
22 *long, diaphanous gown of stunning colors. The gown is covered*
23 *in icicles and slabs of ice. OFELIA'S faces are blue. Icicles hang*
24 *from her arms. She shivers. She looks very, very cold.)*
25
26 OFELIA: You have to help me. I'm cold!
27
28 *(Holding out her arms like Frankenstein, OFELIA takes several*
29 *quick steps toward MARICELA and RICCARDO. The kids scream,*
30 *make snowballs, and stare at her in fear and wonder. OFELIA*
31 *lowers her arms. All her movements are difficult, painful. She*
32 *tries to smile. Both heads speak in unison.)*
33   I know, I know ... it must be hard to understand what
34   happened to you today. One minute you're in San Diego,
35   Christmas shopping, the next minute, you're cowering in

1 a snowdrift talking to a frozen border goddess! All pretty
2 weird! But the truth is, everything has turned upside-
3 down and some of us are in real danger. So we have to
4 materialize, come forward and try to get some help! We
5 have to make contact across the gulf separating the
6 natural from the supernatural, the visible from the
7 invisible!
8 MARICELA: *(To Riccardo)* Let's run. *(MARICELA and RICCARDO*
9 *start to back away from OFELIA.)*
10 OFELIA: Please don't go! Please don't! Please! I need you! I'm
11 freezing! I'm dying! I need your help! I really do! *(OFELIA*
12 *cries. MARICELA and RICCARDO stop. They get closer to*
13 *her.)*
14 MARICELA: Who are you people?
15 OFELIA: I am Ofelia, Goddess of the U.S.-Mexico border.
16 MARICELA: The border's got a goddess?! Yeahright! *¡Vayamos,*
17 *Riccardo!*
18 OFELIA: Open your eyes children! Every street in this city has
19 its gods and goddesses. There's a God of the 5 Freeway!
20 Nymphs protect Chula Vista. There's the Supreme
21 Goddess of Automobiles and the Minor Gods of Mass
22 Transit. Don't they teach you this in school?
23 MARICELA: *(Sarcastic)* Is there a Goddess of Reality? May I
24 please speak to the Goddess of Give Me a Break?
25 OFELIA: *(Ignoring her sarcasm)* Now, I wasn't always a goddess.
26 I came to the West Coast long ago to be an actress. But I'm
27 half-Latina and there wasn't any work for a Latina actress.
28 So I quit the business and decided to take up meditation
29 and I meditated all day long – until! – I was transformed
30 utterly! I became a goddess and started protecting the
31 U.S.-Mexico border as it cut through the continent. Now
32 half of me looks north and the other half looks south: and
33 my heart loves both sides. Once upon a time I dreamed of
34 being a free passageway – like a door between two rooms
35 of the same house. I dreamed of access and peace!

1   *Ranchera* and rock-n-roll! But lately forces beyond my
2   control have turned me into a wall, armed and dangerous,
3   where people risk their lives and sometimes die. It makes
4   me so sad! Look at my hair! Filled with barbed wire and
5   broken hearts! Very upsetting! But I persevere! I pray for
6   better times and follow and protect my darling border as
7   if it were life itself! *(A short silence. MARICELA starts to*
8   *walk away.)*
9   MARICELA: First a guy in feathers, now a couple of maniacs in
10   drag! Everyone's gone quietly nuts today ...
11   RICCARDO: *(Shocked)* Mari'! Don't be rude to the goddess!
12   MARICELA: *(To Ofelia, angry)* We're a couple of lost kids, we're
13   cold, hungry – get a grip on your life, you two!
14   RICCARDO: *(To Ofelia, re Maricela)* She's really stressed out –
15   MARICELA: I'm telling you, all the adults in the Universe are
16   flipzoid! These two think they're a goddess. My Mami
17   thinks she was reincarnated eight times! My *abuelito*
18   thinks he's a witch! My *tío* thinks he's an alien – from
19   outer space! I don't believe in any of this!
20   RICCARDO: *(To Ofelia)* Ever since our parents broke up, she –
21   MARICELA: I believe in food. In words. In arithmetic. In
22   gravity. In answers. I believe you only live once. You only
23   get one chance to do all this and after you die that's it. *It.*
24   So your job while you're living is to know as much of
25   reality and life as possible, meaning the things you touch
26   with your hands ...
27   OFELIA: *(Taking her hand)* I understand; I do ...
28   MARICELA: *(Pulling away)* Yeahright! *Oye*, I'm facing sixth
29   grade next year – like if I ever get home! *Mira*, I'm half
30   Puerto Rican, half Swedish. Facing a world where people
31   wanna know, "baby, on what side of the race line are you?"
32   Half Latina, half Anglo, half east coast, half west coast,
33   half girl, half teen – divorced parents – and you wonder
34   why I think you grownups are all cracked? *Venga,*
35   *Riccardo; nos vamos –*

1   OFELIA: *(Stubborn)* I think something – or someone – in the
2   mythic world has stepped out of line – cracked the thin
3   pale shell separating the so-called real world from the
4   mythic world and creatures and strangers and chaos and
5   mayhem have tumbled through – so now both worlds are
6   out of balance ...
7   MARICELA: *(Trying to pull Riccardo Off-stage)* Uh-huh. Good
8   one.
9   RICCARDO: *(Resisting)* That's what Shu-be-du said, Mari'!
10 OFELIA: ... and the situation in San Diego is getting worse! Half
11   the gods and goddesses have left town. If somebody – say,
12   *you two* for instance ...
13 MARICELA: *(Pulling him)* Riccardo, you waste ...
14 OFELIA: ... if you could bring back the sunlight, you could
15   restore the heat, life could return, and you'd be heroes!
16 RICCARDO: *(Resisting)* I think we gotta listen to her – them!
17 OFELIA: And I'll tell you something else ... in some places, the
18   snow has started to ... come alive ...
19 MARICELA: *¿Qué?*
20 OFELIA: The snow is gathering together ... forming little
21   shapes ... animal shapes ... snow-squirrels, snow-rats ...
22 MARICELA: You're just trying to scare us!
23 OFELIA: You better be scared! It's scary being a hero. So who
24   would blame you if you decided to do nothing? Doing
25   nothing is the easiest way to go. But evil flourishes when
26   good people do nothing. Remember that! What's your
27   name?
28 RICCARDO: I'm Riccardo de la Luz. That chicken is Maricela de
29   la Luz.
30 OFELIA: De la Luz! *¡Qué nombre!* That's a name full of power –
31   voltage – electrons! Don't be afraid. Search your
32   imaginations ... somewhere in the dark hemispheres
33   where dreams are formed ... a hero will appear. Now
34   listen. Just after the snow started I saw a little creature ...
35   he was wearing a Viking helmet and flying around with a

1   blue glowing crystal in his hand. **I have a powerful feeling**
2   **that little creature is none other than the notorious,**
3   **noxious, horrible and really insane God of Ice, Lo-Lo-Lo ...**
4   *(Distant thunder. OFELIA stops talking. She's frozen solid.*
5   *MARICELA and RICCARDO stare.)*
6   **MARICELA:** *Ay Dios mío,* **they're frozen!**
7   **RICCARDO: That mean she's dead?**
8   **MARICELA:** *¡Señora!* **Ofelia!**
9   **RICCARDO:** *(Taking her pulse)* **She's still alive, Mari'.**
10   **MARICELA: Man, we can't carry her, them, nowhere ...**
11   **RICCARDO: We can't leave her here.** *(MARICELA takes off one of*
12   *her sweaters and puts it on OFELIA.)*
13   **MARICELA:** *(To Ofelia)* **We'll find you some help.** *(Louder)* **We'll**
14   **find you some help!**
15   **RICCARDO:** *(To Ofelia)* **There's gotta be a house!**
16   **MARICELA:** *(Shouting to Ofelia)* **Try not to die or something 'til**
17   **we get back!**
18   **RICCARDO:** *(To Ofelia)* **Then the three of us can team up and**
19   **find that guy with the helmet and the crystal and kick his**
20   **butt!** *(The sound of distant thunder. Suddenly MARICELA*
21   *jumps up, yelps.)*
22   **MARICELA: Ow! It bit me! The snow bit me! This snow's got teeth,**
23   **Riccardo! Snow's not supposed to chew people! Let's go!**
24
25 *(MARICELA and RICCARDO take a step forward. Lights change.*
26 *OFELIA exits. A volcano is brought On-stage. MARICELA and*
27 *RICCARDO can't believe what they see. They approach cautiously.*
28 *They hold their noses.)*
29
30   **RICCARDO: Stinky.**
31   **MARICELA: Sulphur.**
32
33 *(The ground starts to rumble and shake. MARICELA and*
34 *RICCARDO run from the edge of the volcano and hit the ground,*
35 *covering their heads with their hands. From deep underground*

1   *comes the saddest voice human ears have ever heard.)*

2

3   **CYCLOPS'S VOICE: Oh I am truly the most unhappy creature**
4   **that ever lived!**

5

6   *(The rumbling hits a peak and from the depths of the volcano*
7   *comes a giant of a man with one eye. The CYCLOPS is really ugly:*
8   *there's a big black hole on his face where his other eye used to be.*
9   *His face is covered in scars and his teeth are gnarled. MARICELA*
10   *and RICCARDO scream when they see the CYCLOPS, who*
11   *doesn't immediately notice them. The CYCLOPS speaks to the*
12   *stars.)*

13

14   **RICCARDO:** *(Sotto to Maricela)* **Now do you believe your eyes?**
15   **MARICELA:** *(Sotto)* **Oh my poor brain!**
16   **CYCLOPS: Why am I here? Why was I born? Unhappy me!**
17   **Unattractive, vulnerable, helpless, living in substandard**
18   **housing, surrounded by unfriendly magma – discarded,**
19   **demeaned, deleted, defaced, depressed! Why should there**
20   **exist a beast whose only reason for living is to**
21   **demonstrate a supreme example of abject misery? And**
22   **why should that monster be me? If there's only one me in**
23   **the world – one! – why does that me have to be me?! And I**
24   **can't see anymore! My one eye was made for darkness: for**
25   **the deep caverns and rococo labyrinths of the volcano,**
26   **where there's no green, no life, no sunshine, nothing to**
27   **see but the hard numbing monotony of rock. Up here,**
28   **where there should be life in abundance – dear, deaf**
29   **stars, my only audience! – hideous snow covers**
30   **everything: and the snow is too bright for my massive**
31   **pupil and I am blinded by the glare!**
32   **RICCARDO:** *(Sotto to Maricela)* **Maybe we can help this guy's**
33   **self-image and bring him back to help Ofelia and team up**
34   **and help the Moon God and ...**
35   **MARICELA:** *(Scared)* **No, forget him, he's too gross ...**

1   RICCARDO: But evil flourishes when good people do nothing,
2   Maricela!
3   MARICELA: I think I'm starting to hate that line!
4   CYCLOPS: *(Hearing them)* Who's there? I know you're there!
5   *(MARICELA and RICCARDO tentatively step forward.)*
6   MARICELA: Travelers. Simple, unarmed, not-very-digestible.
7   CYCLOPS: People? At my doorstep?
8   RICCARDO: *Sí.* Harmless. Very small.
9   CYCLOPS: Oh! You've come to do something bad to me! To steal
10   my big, fat horde of silver coins, diamond earrings, gold
11   ankle bracelets, and double tax-free mutual funds!
12 MARICELA: *Este,* no, no, big, gentle cyclops, we're not here to
13   steal nothing ...
14 CYCLOPS: Ah, you've come to take Polaroids™ of me! To
15   capture me on film so you can show the rest of the world
16   how odious I am! So you can sit around your rumpus
17   rooms and laugh at me!
18 MARICELA: *(Sarcastic, to herself)* Yeahright, you want our
19   friends to throw up?
20 RICCARDO: Mari'!
21 MARICELA: Uh, no, *señor*, we're not here to take your amazing
22   likeness!
23 CYCLOPS: No? I wish I could believe you. A Cyclops has a
24   fabulous heart, you know! My heart is the biggest organ in
25   my body! It's very easy to break!
26 MARICELA: So, we ... actually ... OK ...
27 CYCLOPS: *(Not hearing)* But no – maybe – this is my lucky day!
28   Maybe it's wrong to be so cynical! Yes! You really are here
29   to be my friends, I feel it in my bones!
30 MARICELA: *Este,* truth to tell ...
31 CYCLOPS: Friends! At long last! Friends to comfort me! To ease
32   my existential torment. My gloom! Friends to stick by me
33   when all others flee my indescribable ugliness and bad
34   breath! Friends to relieve the eternal homelessness of my
35   soul ...

1   **MARICELA:** *(Determined)* *¡Esperate!* **We did come here for**
2   **something, for help, not to be friends with you ...**
3   **CYCLOPS:** *(As if stabbed)* **Oh! Oh me! Unhappy, trusting, soft-**
4   **hearted Cyclops!**
5   **RICCARDO:** *(Sotto to Maricela)* **Dude needs major therapy ...**
6   **CYCLOPS: Why should I help you? What has the world done for**
7   **me? When has any person had a kind word for the**
8   **Cyclops? My own father, the Sky God, rejected me! DA-DA-**
9   **DADDYYYY!**
10 **MARICELA:** *(Sympathetic)* *¡Ay bendito!* **Look! We're in the**
11   **middle of a massive problem!**
12 **CYCLOPS: Don't even think about it: don't even breathe your**
13   **problems in my direction! Problems? You wanna hear**
14   **problems? When I was just a baby Cyclops, all the nymphs**
15   **took one look at me and ran off to Tijuana ...**
16 **RICCARDO: Maricela, this could take forever!**
17 **MARICELA: Gentle, handsome Cyclops, what if we ... gave you**
18   **– something to make you less depressing – I mean,**
19   **depressed. Could that convince you to help us out?**
20 **CYCLOPS What do you have? I already have a treasure! You**
21   **have something better than money?**
22 **RICCARDO:** *(Sotto)* **Yeah, what do we got?**
23 **MARICELA:** *(Feeling her pockets)* **Well, we got, uhm ...** *tenemos*
24   **... something so much better than mere cash ...** *(She finds*
25   *her sunglasses in her pocket.)* **... it's just the thing you're**
26   **looking for, Cyclops! You said you couldn't see 'cause the**
27   **snow makes you blind. Well, what if ... you had a pair of**
28   **special cool designer top-of-the-line Cyclops sunglasses ...**
29   *(MARICELA breaks off one of the lenses of the sunglasses.*
30   *She hands the CYCLOPS her broken sunglasses. The*
31   *CYCLOPS puts them on. Something resembling a smile*
32   *seems to happen to his face.)*
33 **MARICELA: You're happy?**
34 **CYCLOPS: I'm happy! I'm happy! I'm happy!**
35 **MARICELA: Good. Focus. It snowed. We met a Moon God. His**

1 brother the Sun God is missing. He said there's a god
2 battle going on. Then we met a goddess. She's frozen solid.
3 But she told us a little guy in a Viking helmet, with a
4 glowing crystal, might be the reason ...
5 CYCLOPS: *(Suddenly afraid)* Oh. Sounds like Loki. Crazy Loki!
6 *(There's a crack of thunder. The CYCLOPS shakes with fear.)*
7 MARICELA: You know him?
8 CYCLOPS: No! Never heard of him!
9 RICCARDO: But you said —
10 CYCLOPS: Far too much already! Sorry! That's tonight's report:
11   thank you — this is Señor Cyclops signing off, crawling
12   back into my safe little hole!
13 RICCARDO: *Pero*, we need you to help Ofelia, so we can track
14   down this Loki, so we can help this Moon God, so life
15   could go back to normal — *(Thunder. CYCLOPS starts to go*
16   *down his hole.)*
17 CYCLOPS: Love the shades! Thanks a heap!
18 MARICELA: Don't you know that evil flourishes when — ?
19 CYCLOPS: Don't you know how handsome I am? I'm gonna go
20   out right now to find me a wife! *¡Adiós!*
21 MARICELA: If you're scared to —
22 CYCLOPS: You're my heroes! Thanks for the eyesight!
23 MARICELA: No, don't leave — *(Before MARICELA can stop him,*
24   *the CYCLOPS is down the volcano and gone forever.*
25   *MARICELA runs to the edge of the volcano and looks down*
26   *into it.)* C'mon — come back! Get back here you big loser!
27   Chicken! Chicken! Chicken! *(Frustrated MARICELA*
28   *suddenly gets tears in her eyes. She sits on the floor, buries*
29   *her face in her hands, and tries not to cry. RICCARDO*
30   *watches her.)*
31 RICCARDO: You all right?
32 MARICELA: Nothing ... get lost ...
33 RICCARDO: Tell me.
34 MARICELA: I don't want to. Okay. When I was little? Mami and
35   Papi used to sit on my bed at night ... they told me dumb

1   stuff ... stories they made up ... didn't matter what they
2   were about ... the *telling* was what I liked ... but they
3   stopped ... Papi went bye-bye ... I can hardly remember
4   them like that ...
5 RICCARDO: Your mind works in mysterious ways.
6 MARICELA: *(Smiles, wipes her eyes.)* Big solace I am, huh? Yeah,
7   totally good in a crisis! Who you gonna call? Maricela! The
8   big jellyfish ...
9 RICCARDO: It's cool.
10 MARICELA: It's just ... I like to wake up from my bad dreams,
11   *entiendes*? When I don't ... Mami and Papi always got me
12   through the nightmares. I thought I didn't need them for that.
13 RICCARDO: Can't live in the past, *hermana.*
14 MARICELA: I just wish Mami wasn't a total slave to that
15   boyfriend. You know she's paying off his car?! We're
16   gonna get lumps of coal for Christmas 'cause he's sucking
17   up all her cash.
18 RICCARDO: *(Wanting to change the subject)* But hey ... you're
19   doing a, *tú sabes,* adequate job.
20 MARICELA: *(Trying to smile)* Liar.
21 RICCARDO: Well, I'm not technically starving to death ... and
22   you haven't gotten us killed ... *(There's the distant howling*
23   *of WOLVES.)* ... yet... *(The WOLVES howl again. The howling*
24   *sounds distorted, bloodless, almost supernatural. Nearby*
25   *there's heavy wolf breathing. MARICELA is on her feet,*
26   *wiping her eyes.)*
27 MARICELA: Yo, this ain't funny! *(As the WOLVES continue to*
28   *howl, RICCARDO sees something far out on the horizon.)*
29 RICCARDO: Maricela. There's a boat. Out on the harbor. A boat
30   with people!
31 MARICELA: *(Looking)* People? I like people!
32 RICCARDO: Boat says "Argo."
33 MARICELA: *¿Estás seguro?* Argo was the ship Jason and the
34   Argonauts sailed to find the Golden Fleece. *(The WOLVES'*
35   *howling is closer.)*

1 **RICCARDO: Run!** *(MARICELA and RICCARDO run to the edge of*
2   *the harbor.)*
3 **MARICELA: We're in luck, bro! That's a ship full of heroes. Big**
4   **bulky hairy guys from antiquity.**
5 **RICCARDO:** *(Waving his arms)* **¡Mira! Over here! Yo, antique**
6   **hero guys, over here!**
7 **MARICELA:** *(Looking)* **They see us!** *(From several sides of the*
8   *stage a pack of SNOW-WOLVES appears. The WOLVES are*
9   *made of ice and snow. All the features that make natural*
10   *wolves terrifying — their snouts, their teeth, their cold*
11   *intelligent eyes — are greatly exaggerated.)*
12 **RICCARDO: The wolves are made of snow, including the teeth!**
13 **MARICELA: And we're lookin' really tasty!**
14
15 *(WOLVES howl. They surround MARICELA and RICCARDO. At*
16 *the edge of the harbor an ancient Greek ship, the Argo, appears.*
17 *The prow of the Argo is a wooden statue of a WOMAN with two*
18 *large removable WINGS. Around the Argo, if possible, icebergs*
19 *abound. On the Argo are three Argonauts. Their leader is JASON,*
20 *a tall, handsome youth with the body of a Greek statue. ORPHEUS*
21 *is introspective, dressed in black, holding a lyre. HERCULES is a*
22 *big, muscle-bound hulk dressed in the skin of the Nemean Lion*
23 *and a Panama hat. HERCULES is fast asleep. He snores. Loud.*
24 *WOLVES howl and salivate as JASON helps MARICELA and*
25 *RICCARDO get on board. The WOLVES disperse, the howling*
26 *fades.)*
27
28 **MARICELA: Thank you, uh, *señor* ...**
29 **JASON: Jason. Of Jason and the Argonauts. That's Orpheus.**
30   **Hercules. And you're very lucky. We're not supposed to be**
31   **rescuing people today.**
32 **MARICELA: *Pues, lo siento, pero,* we got a lot of work for you**
33   **hero guys! *Mira,* there's a frozen goddess, and a missing**
34   **Moon God, and a city under the snow ...** *(JASON laughs,*
35   *grabs a bottle of suntan lotion and puts it on.)*

1   JASON: Miss, we're on vacation. We're sailing to sunny Spain!
2   Land of enchantment! Gypsies! Lorca! And pretty
3   theñoritath!
4   RICCARDO: Ain't you *un poquito* off course?
5   JASON: Yes. Things were going fine. It was hot and sunny, with
6   cool Mediterranean breezes coming in from the
7   southwest – when suddenly – it was like some demon tore
8   a hole through the atmosphere – we were sucked into a
9   void – and spit out into this harbor!
10   MARICELA: That's 'cause, yeah, big nasty garbage is mangling
11   the cosmos and you gotta help us make it right –
12   JASON: Kids, kids, please. The wolves have disappeared.
13   They're off chasing a snow-moose. We're gonna turn
14   around now.
15   MARICELA: *(Stunned)* You're not gonna help us?
16   JASON: That's what it means!
17   MARICELA: But – ain't you guys card-carrying heroes?
18   JASON: Good luck and have a nice day!
19   MARICELA: Didn't you risk your life to find that cool sheepskin
20   ... didn't Orpheus go to hell for his girlfriend ...?
21   ORPHEUS: Oh, don't remind me!
22   JASON: Please don't remind him!
23   MARICELA: ... but heroes don't turn their backs on children ...!
24   JASON: Look, girl, in this day and age definitions change,
25   things are flexible, the lines are blurred, you know? A
26   hero means something else in this day and age.
27   MARICELA: But you're not *from* this day and age! You're from
28   mythology!
29   JASON: Hey, don't start that mythology thing on me. I have a
30   hard enough time trying to figure out if I exist or not.
31   Like, what am I – fiction? I mean, don't you think it gets a
32   little boring battling the demons of the collective
33   unconscious year after year?
34   ORPHEUS: *(Sad)* **Viva** Spain. *(ORPHEUS starts to cry. He strums*
35   *the lyre. The lyre music is sad. Everyone starts to cry.)*

1   JASON: *(Crying)* **Poor Orphy. A thousand hours of therapy and**
2   **he's still pining away for his old girlfriend! Tell me he**
3   **doesn't look like a man who needs a vacation! And**
4   **Hercules over there! Twelve labors and he's a physical**
5   **wreck!** *(HERCULES snores. His snore shakes the ship.)*
6   MARICELA: *(Crying)* **Pero ... uhm ...**
7   JASON: **Besides, you people from the present, your problems**
8   **are just too darn big. We're old fashioned heroes. We fight**
9   **with dinky swords. Give the average guy in your world an**
10   **Uzi and he could wipe out all of Troy in one afternoon!**
11   **You, Maricela, you could've won the Trojan War single-**
12   **handedly!**
13   ORPHEUS: **Or. In your time. The monsters are subtle. Too hard**
14   **to see. They look like people. When they talk they make**
15   **sense. Or the monster is something you love. Or it's a little**
16   **evil voice in your heart.**
17   JASON: **How can you tell the good guys from the bad guys in**
18   **your time? Naw. You gotta dump us and come up with**
19   **some new heroes of your own.**
20   MARICELA: **You guys – *por favor* – don't you know? ...** *(She*
21   *looks at RICCARDO.)*
22   MARICELA AND RICCARDO: **... evil flourishes when good**
23   **people do nothing?!** *(ORPHEUS stops playing. He and*
24   *JASON look uncomfortable.)*
25   JASON: **Well, yeah, we know that.**
26   ORPHEUS: **All the great heroes of antiquity know that.**
27   JASON: **It's like a secret password. We hear those words and we**
28   **leap into action.**
29   MARICELA: **You do? So you'll help us?**
30   JASON: **Don't have alotta *choice* do I?**
31   MARICELA: **Ay, qué bueno, qué great! Now, the only thing we**
32   **know is that some little creature named, uh, Louie –**
33   RICCARDO: **Loki!** *(Thunder. The Argo begins to rock violently.)*
34   JASON: *(Very afraid)* **Loki? He's a trickster god. He's very bad.**
35   **He's a liar. A coward. He loves chaos and trouble-making.**

1   He's completely destructive and absolutely immoral! I
2   don't wanna mess with that! Time for you to get off the
3   boat!
4
5   *(Thunder and lightning. HERCULES' snores shake the boat.*
6   *Suddenly from the depths of the reservoir, a huge SEVEN-*
7   *HEADED HYDRA appears. Each of the creature's heads is a*
8   *different monster: Medusa, Frankenstein, Kali, Nixon, Godzilla,*
9   *Nosferatu, and Hitler.)*
10
11   **HYDRA'S HEADS:** *(Maniacal laughter)* **HA HAHAHA HA HA HA**
12   **HAHAHA!!** *(The HYDRA advances on the Argo as the*
13   *children scream:)*
14   **MARICELA AND RICCARDO:** *UGGLYYYYYY!!*
15
16   **BLACKOUT**
17
18   **END OF ACT ONE**
19
20
21   **ACT TWO**
22
23   *(The HYDRA gets closer and closer to the Argo, jaws opening and*
24   *closing, long necks writhing, eyes blazing, as MARICELA,*
25   *RICCARDO, JASON, and ORPHEUS look on in amazement.*
26   *HERCULES sleeps.)*
27
28   **MARICELA:** I give up, what is that?!
29   **JASON:** Major pain is what it is. It's the Seven-Headed Hydra.
30   **MARICELA:** Can we, you know, reason with it? Can we talk to it?
31   **JASON:** It spurns reason. It lives to create chaos and terror.
32   **MARICELA:** *¿Qué podemos hacer?*
33   **JASON:** *(To Hercules)* Yo, Hercules! Wake up! We're in kind of a
34   huge mess here! I think we could really use your help!
35   *(JASON, MARICELA, and RICCARDO go to HERCULES. They*

1   *try everything to wake him up, but nothing works.)*

2   MARICELA: *(To Riccardo)* **Remember when Papi used to fall**

3   **asleep like this and no one could wake him — 'cept me?**

4   *(MARICELA pulls out one of HERCULES's chest hairs.*

5   *HERCULES wakes up with a shout.)*

6   HERCULES: *OUUUEWWW!!* **Who did that?! Where am I? Is this**

7   **a boat? I am on a boat. Hello, I am Hercules —**

8   MARICELA: *¡Hola!* **I'm Maricela de la Luz and we're in a major —**

9   HERCULES: **I am big and strong. I am a hero. Are you a hero**

10   **too? I was asleep and now I am awake. Are you a**

11   **theñorita? Is that the perilous and deadly Seven-Headed**

12   **Hydra coming our way?**

13   JASON: **Herk. Focus. We're in a mess.**

14   HERCULES: **I want to sleep. I am tired. I work too hard. I**

15   **thought we were going on vacation. Not fair. Just because**

16   **I am big and strong, I get no rest. My chest hurts. Ouuuu.**

17   MARICELA: *Señor* **Hercules, you're such a great man. You, uh,**

18   **cleaned some really stinky horse stables. Got some**

19   **important gold apples from someplace. You held up the**

20   **whole sky for that big Titan guy!**

21   HERCULES: **I did those things. I am big and strong. My muscles**

22   **are round like apples. No, like watermelons.**

23   MARICELA: **You gotta protect us from that thing!** *¡Ahora!*

24   HERCULES: **It is a burden being big and strong. Sometimes I**

25   **want to paint watercolor still lifes. Or write pop songs.** *(The*

26   *HYDRA screams. Everyone but HERCULES covers their ears.)*

27   **Being a hero does not mean to be big and strong. An animal**

28   **can be big and strong. Is that a hero? I do not know. Let me**

29   **think about these questions while I snooze ...**

30   HYDRA'S HEADS: **Chaos is my Hero!**

31   **Madness is my Home!**

32   **Nightmares are my Children!**

33   **Destruction is my Garden!**

34   **Death is my Flower!**

35   JASON: *(Panicking)* **What're we gonna do? What're we gonna**

1   do? **Think of something Maricela! Please!**

2   **MARICELA: Me? Why me?** *(One of the HYDRA heads tries to take*

3   *a big bite out of MARICELA. She screams and jumps away.*

4   *She looks at the long boat and gets an idea.)* **Ricky!** *– este –*

5   **go to that part of the boat!** *(RICCARDO runs to one end of*

6   *the Argo while MARICELA runs to the other end.)* **All right.**

7   **Now – tell them to come eat you!**

8   **RICCARDO: Excuse me?**

9   **MARICELA: *¡Hagalo! ¡Así!* Yo, Hydra! You big, ugly floating**

10   **piece of iodine-infested seaweed! Come get me! I'm over**

11   **here!**

12   **RICCARDO:** *(Terrified)* **Maricela! *¡Por Dios!***

13   **MARICELA: *¡Ahora – hagalo!***

14   **RICCARDO:** *Este* **... hey Hydra, man – uhm – yo – lunchmeat!**

15   **MARICELA: Don't listen, Hydra, I'm your lunch! Come to this**

16   **side of the boat and eat me!**

17   **RICCARDO:** *(Getting it)* **No, no, come to this side and eat me!**

18

19   *(The HYDRA is torn. Half the heads want to go to MARICELA, the*

20   *other half to RICCARDO. The heads begin fighting among*

21   *themselves. Before long the Hydra's heads are in a hopeless*

22   *writhing tangle of twisted necks and confused looks. Sadly it*

23   *looks at the Argo and sinks impotently into the water. All the*

24   *stunned heroes look at MARICELA and RICCARDO.)*

25

26   **JASON: You saved us.** *(MARICELA and RICCARDO run to each*

27   *other and high-five. MARICELA turns to JASON.)*

28   **MARICELA: Now you owe us, buddy. You turn around and hit**

29   **land. We're gonna help Ofelia, then the Moon God, then**

30   **we're gonna kick Loki's –** *(Thunder and lightning shake the*

31   *Argo again. Then a thick FOG rolls in engulfing the Argo.*

32   *JASON takes a deep breath.)*

33   **JASON: Oh ... what a sweet-smelling fog ...**

34   **RICCARDO:** *(Enjoying the smell)* ***Sí, me gusta ...***

35   **MARICELA:** *(Suspicious)* ***Yo no sé*** **... I don't like it ...** *(MARICELA*

1   *instinctively covers her mouth with her hand.)*

2   **HERCULES:** *(Smelling)* **It smells like flowers!**

3   **MARICELA: Since when does fog smell like flowers?**

4   **JASON:** *(Intoxicated, yawning)* **Oh give it a rest, Maricela! You're**

5   **so...so...parochial...**

6   **MARICELA: ... *paranoid* ...** *(HERCULES yawns. Soon JASON,*

7   *ORPHEUS, and HERCULES are asleep. The heroes snore in*

8   *unison. MARICELA looks at them.)* **Guys? Guys? Ugh —**

9   **Useless! Riccardo — cover your nose and mouth! This fog!**

10   **It's put them to sleep!** *(RICCARDO covers his nose and*

11   *mouth.)*

12   **RICCARDO: How do we sail this thing? There's icebergs all over**

13   **the place! We hit one, we're sunk!**

14   **MARICELA: What a titanic pain in the butt this is turning out**

15   **to be!** *(We hear the VOICE of the FOG. The mouth of the*

16   *WOODEN WOMAN on the prow moves up and down.)*

17   **FOG: Sleep, my children! Sleep!**

18   **MARICELA: Who is it?** *¿Quién me habla?*

19   **FOG: I am the Voice of the Fog!**

20   **MARICELA: Great — now the weather's talking!**

21   **FOG: You're in treacherous waters. There are whirlpools, sea**

22   **monsters and metaphors here. Don't fight them! Fall**

23   **asleep! Give in!**

24   **MARICELA: We're not gonna fall asleep. We're gonna sail this**

25   **thing to shore!**

26   **RICCARDO:** *(To the FOG)* **Can you show us how?**

27   **FOG: I am made of air. My body is a mist. I have no will. The**

28   **currents in the wind are my muscles. I go where I am told.**

29   **When I'm too dense, I rain. Feels good!**

30   **MARICELA:** *(Sotto to Riccardo)* **I don't trust that voice for one**

31   **minute! Grab the — thing — the helm.** *(RICCARDO grabs*

32   *the helm. MARICELA stands on the prow and tries to see*

33   *through the thickening fog.)* **Riccardo — Left! Left!**

34   *(RICCARDO tries to steer the ship to the left. He yawns.)*

35   **RICCARDO: You know something, Maricela ... ?**

1 MARICELA: *(Not listening)* **Doing good! I see the shore!**
2 RICCARDO: *(Yawns)* ... **I'm, you know, I'm ... starting to forget**
3   **things ... whoa – I can't remember what Papi looked like!**
4   **Did he go to Korea yet? Is he still in the army?**
5 MARICELA: **Don't let yourself go, Riccardo.**
6 RICCARDO: **I remember him** *muy alto*, **tall. But maybe he**
7   **wasn't.**
8 MARICELA: **Left! Left! Right!**
9 RICCARDO: **I don't remember Mami's laughter. She used to**
10   **laugh so much when Papi was around.**
11 MARICELA: **Papi's five foot eight. Mami's five four. She loves**
12   **José Feliciano.**
13 RICCARDO: **All I want to do is forget ...**
14 FOG: **Forget!**
15 MARICELA: *(To the FOG)* **Go away and leave us alone!**
16 RICCARDO: **... forget and sleep ...**
17 FOG: **Sleep!**
18 MARICELA: **No!**
19 FOG: **Dream!**
20 RICCARDO: **... on a boat ... through the sweet-smelling clouds ...**
21   **I could be dreaming right now ...**
22 FOG: **If you dream, Riccardo, I could take you to some beautiful**
23   **places. Where people are always fun. There's no work to do.**
24 RICCARDO: **... sounds cool ...**
25 MARICELA: **You don't wanna live in a dream!**
26 FOG: **There are strawberry sunrises ... food music ... birds teach**
27   **you to breathe underwater ... angels teach you to dance on**
28   **the head of a pin ...**
29 RICCARDO: **... awesome ...**
30 MARICELA: **It's an illusion. A mirage. You're you. I'm me. We**
31   **can't sleep now! We can't get taken to places, no matter**
32   **how pretty they look!**
33 FOG: **... and if you want to play, we'll play. There are battles.**
34   **And riddles. And monsters to fight. Gold and glory to win:**
35   **and cool sound effects ...**

1   **RICCARDO:** (*Getting very sleepy*) ... **did I have a sister?**

2   **MARICELA: If we fall asleep now, in these waters, it's *over!***

3   **RICCARDO:** ... **let someone else save the world** ...

4   **FOG:** ... **in the world we're going to, sweetheart, parents never**

5   **split up, childhood is simple, school is peaceful, grown-**

6   **ups are wise, work is play, everyone eats, and cable is free.**

7

8   (*RICCARDO falls asleep and snores. MARICELA looks around the*

9   *ship for something that will help her out of this dilemma. She*

10   *finds JASON's sword and pulls it out of its sheath. She stabs the*

11   *FOG.*)

12

13   **MARICELA: Take that, Fog! And that! And that!** (*The sword does*

14   *nothing but make the FOG laugh sinisterly. MARICELA*

15   *throws down the sword.*) **Think, Maricela. You don't need a**

16   **weapon. You need to be smarter** ... (*MARICELA spies the*

17   *big WINGS on the prow of the ship. She runs to them. She*

18   *straps the wings on her arms, remembering what the FOG*

19   *had said:*) **The winds are your muscles** ... ? (*MARICELA*

20   *flaps her wings. Instantly wind begins to blow.*)

21   **FOG: Hey cut that out! I'm not through yet! He needs me!**

22   **MARICELA: He don't need you – he needs his Mami and Papi –**

23   (*MARICELA flaps again and again.*)

24   **FOG:** (*Angry*) **You're just scared** ... **you're a selfish, scared little**

25   **girl!** (*The wind blows harder and harder until the FOG is*

26   *completely gone. MARICELA starts to float off the ground as*

27   *she flaps.*)

28   **MARICELA: Hey eat this!**

29   **FOG: No ... no ... no ... no ...** ! (*As the FOG lifts, stars twinkle in the*

30   *clear night sky above the Argo. Galaxies appear. Comets.*

31   *Supernovas explode. MARICELA looks around and smiles.*

32   *Then she realizes she's several inches off the ground.*)

33   **MARICELA: Riccardo! ¡*Mira!* Check me out!** (*MARICELA*

34   *continues to flap until she is high above the Argo.*

35   *RICCARDO wakes up, blinks, looks around. JASON,*

1   ORPHEUS, *and* HERCULES *come out of their dreamy sleep.)*

2   **RICCARDO:** *(Looking up)* **What're you doing?**

3   **MARICELA: I wonder if I could go** *un poquito* **higher.**

4   **RICCARDO:** *(Worried)* **Higher?**

5   **MARICELA:** *(Laughing)* **This feels so great! I bet I could go as**
6   **high as I want! I bet I could file my nails on the rough**
7   **rings of Saturn! Yeah! Swim in a supernova! Ride the**
8   **galaxies like surfboards! It's in our name, Riccardo — "de**
9   **la Luz" — "of the light" — that means I belong up here,**
10   **higher than all the lights of the Milky Way, Riccardo!**
11   **Bigger and brighter and better than anything, Riccardo!**

12 **RICCARDO: Maricela! No! Don't go too close to those galaxies!**
13   **They're too hot!**

14 **MARICELA: But I'm one of them now! I'm a diamond! I'm an**
15   **explosion!**

16 **RICCARDO: You're not! You're Maricela, remember? You are**
17   **you and I am me!**

18 **MARICELA: But I want to see where it all ends... what's at the**
19   **edge of the edge of space...?** *(MARICELA goes higher and*
20   *higher getting brighter and brighter. Desperate, RICCARDO*
21   *looks around, trying to find a way to bring MARICELA back.*
22   *He quickly jumps overboard, landing in the frigid water.)*

23 **RICCARDO: Cold! Cold! Cold!** *Cold! Cold!* **COLD!** *(JASON and*
24   *ORPHEUS notice RICCARDO, who is flailing around in the*
25   *water.)*

26 **JASON: I can't swim!**

27 **ORPHEUS: Neither can I!**

28 **JASON AND ORPHEUS: Hercules!** *(The Argo starts to slowly float*
29   *away from the flailing RICCARDO as JASON and ORPHEUS*
30   *vainly attempt to wake the sleeping HERCULES.)*

31 **RICCARDO: Maricela, help me!**

32 **MARICELA:** *(Not looking down)* **Yo, can't you see I'm busy being**
33   **fabulous?!**

34 **RICCARDO: Maricela, you jerk, I'm drowning!** *(MARICELA*
35   *looks down at RICCARDO flailing around in the water. She*

1   *sees the Argo drifting away, leaving the stage.)*
2   **MARICELA:** *(Realizing)* **Swim to shore, Riccardo — swim to**
3   **shore!**
4
5   *(As RICCARDO swims to shore, the lights change. MARICELA flies*
6   *down and lands on the stage. The Argo is completely gone.*
7   *RICCARDO crawls onto the shore, coughing, shivering.*
8   *MARICELA quickly takes off her wings, and goes to the prostrate*
9   *RICCARDO as he continues to cough and shiver. She holds him,*
10 *rubbing his arms, trying to make him warmer.)*
11
12 **MARICELA: You OK? Talk already!**
13 **RICCARDO:** *(Weakening, coughing)* **Mari' ... Mari' ... did you**
14 **think I was gonna die?**
15 **MARICELA:** *(Trying not to cry)* **Man, I thought if anything**
16 **happened to you Ricky, *la verdad* bro, I'd never live with**
17 **my damn self.**
18 **RICCARDO: That's nice to know, *porque ... tú sabes* ... I was only**
19 **kidding! I was only kidding! I was only kidding!**
20 *(RICCARDO immediately gets up and prances around the*
21 *stage, chanting "I was only kidding!")*
22 **MARICELA: I hate you.**
23 **RICCARDO:** *(Chanting)* **You thought I was dying! You do have a**
24 **heart!**
25 **MARICELA:** *(Smiles despite herself.)* **We ever get outta this mess,**
26 **I'm gonna completely distress you!** *(RICCARDO dances*
27 *around the stage, not watching where he is going.*
28 *RICCARDO falls into a large sinkhole.)*
29 **RICCARDO: AAAAHHHHH!** *(RICCARDO is gone. MARICELA*
30 *isn't looking at RICCARDO. From underground we can hear*
31 *RICCARDO calling.)* **Mari — cel — aaaaaaa! — Help Meeeeee!**
32 **MARICELA:** *(Not looking)* **Yeahright.**
33 **RICCARDO'S VOICE:** *(Underground)* **I fell in a sinkhole! I'm**
34 **underground! Help me!**
35 **MARICELA:** *(To herself)* **How stupid does he think I am?** *(She*

1   *looks around and realizes RICCARDO is nowhere to be*
2   *seen.)* **Riccardo?**
3   **RICCARDO'S VOICE: MariceLaaaaa!** *(MARICELA runs to the sink*
4   *hole and looks down.)*
5   **MARICELA: Just great, homey, just great!** *(MARICELA closes her*
6   *eyes and jumps in.)* **AHHHHHHHHHHHHHHHHHH!**
7   *(Blackout. Slowly, lights come up. The light deep*
8   *underground is brown and amber. Tree roots poke out*
9   *through the dirt and into this dusty, rocky tunnel.*
10   *MARICELA is alone, dusting off her clothes, trying to peer*
11   *into the darkness.)* **Ricc** − **aaaaaaa** − **aaa** − **aaa** − **ar** −
12   **doooooooo!** *(RICCARDO suddenly appears behind her. He*
13   *taps her on the shoulder. She screams. He screams. She*
14   *screams. He throws his arms around her.)*
15   **RICCARDO: Maricela! ¡Hermanita!**
16   **MARICELA:** *(Annoyed, pushing him away)* **Don't get in my face**
17   **with that!**
18   **RICCARDO: I'm not kidding − I saw something really weird.**
19   **MARICELA: Uh-huh.** *Pobrecito.* **Let's get outta here.**
20   **RICCARDO: No, really, you have to see this. It's right around**
21   **the corner. It's a face. A face. I saw a face. There's a face in**
22   **there. It's got a hand. A face and a hand!** *(RICCARDO tries*
23   *to pull MARICELA toward the yet unseen face.)*
24   **MARICELA: I ain't going in there!**
25   **RICCARDO: But the hand's in there ... it's holding a blue crystal ...**
26   **MARICELA: So?**
27   **RICCARDO: So didn't Ofelia say something about seeing a blue**
28   **glowing crystal right after it started to snow? Maybe this is it.**
29   **MARICELA: Okay. You need to turn around, go back in there,**
30   **and talk to the face.**
31   **RICCARDO: Oh, don't make me talk to the face −**
32
33 *(MARICELA pushes RICCARDO into a new space. When*
34 *RICCARDO and MARICELA enter this space the rising light*
35 *reveals the wall of a cave. Embedded in the wall are two FACES.*

1 *Each FACE has a HAND next to it. One FACE is a man's SMILING*
2 *FACE. The other is a woman's FROWNING FACE; her eyes are*
3 *closed. The SMILING FACE looks at MARICELA and RICCARDO*
4 *and smiles wider.)*
5
6 **SMILING FACE: Adriana! Adriana, look! Visitors from another**
7 **world! They look so weird! Let me describe them to you,**
8 **Adriana dear! They have bodies like ours. But below their**
9 **bodies are strange appendages. Long, wide, fleshy**
10 **growths ...**
11 **MARICELA:** *(Touching her chest)* **These are bodies.**
12 **SMILING FACE: ... and on the sides of the fleshy growths are**
13 **tuberous growths with hands on either end! Hands that**
14 **look like ours!**
15 **MARICELA: Arms.**
16 **SMILING FACE: And below ... are two more tuberous growths,**
17 **terminating in roundish pedestals ...**
18 **MARICELA: Legs. Feet.**
19 **SMILING FACE: Adriana! Dearest! This is the most amazing**
20 **night! First a nervous little creature in a strange horned**
21 **helmet throws a bright star through the sky which**
22 **bounces along the floor of the world and lands in my**
23 **hand! Next, sky creatures from a distant world come down**
24 **to visit us! And they speak English!**
25 **RICCARDO: We're not from another planet. We're from San**
26 **Diego.**
27 **SMILING FACE: Adriana, tell our visitors, they are welcome to**
28 **our planet. Tell them we are a friendly people. And we**
29 **hope that the sky creatures from this planet called San**
30 **Diego are also friendly.**
31 **MARICELA:** *Este.* **Adriana — tell your friend, my brother and**
32 **me ...**
33 **SMILING FACE: Adriana. Fair wife! Eternal flower! Tell our**
34 **intergalactic visitors that my name is Adriano.**
35 **MARICELA: Adriana ... tell Adriano ... it's cool to be visiting his**

1   really lovely world ... and, *este* ... that glowing crystal he's
2   holding in his hand ... might help us solve a problem that's
3   befallen our once vibrant planet ...
4 SMILING FACE: Adriana! Kind heart! Tell our spunky star
5   people that I don't give two shakes of a shrew's tail for the
6   problems of their universe! I like this dazzling blue star
7   and I'm not giving it to anyone!
8 MARICELA: Adriana! Nice lady! Tell Adriano we gotta have that
9   crystal!
10 SMILING FACE: Adriana! Tell this rude creature to forget it!
11 MARICELA: Adriana! Tell Adriano not to be so stubborn!
12 SMILING FACE: Adriana! Tell it to go away!
13 MARICELA: Adriana! Tell him we're not leaving this boring
14   place without that crystal!
15 SMILING FACE: Adriana! Explain to our uninvited interlopers
16   how neither of us have been able to eat in all the years
17   we've been under this spell. That this blue gem is the only
18   thing I've gotten my hand on in years – and I intend to eat
19   it right now!
20
21 *(The SMILING FACE puts the crystal in his mouth. He says to*
22 *MARICELA "What do you think of that?", but it comes out:*
23 *"Rmhyphrmythmmmmmhrrruhhhmyuryhhffffft!?")*
24
25 RICCARDO: *(To Maricela)* Spell?
26 MARICELA: ¡*Esperate!* Adriana! Tell Adriano ... what if ... we
27   found a way to take the spell off you? Would Adriano give
28   us the crystal then? *(The SMILING FACE takes the crystal*
29   *out of his mouth.)*
30 SMILING FACE: Adriana! Tell our loquacious visitors ... it's a
31   deal!
32 MARICELA: ¡*Vaya!* We'll do it! We'll break the spell!
33 SMILING FACE: Adriana! Sad, silent wife! The hour of our
34   liberation is near! Tell our new friends they must walk
35   down that dark tunnel over there ...

1 RICCARDO: (*Looking down tunnel*) **That one?**
2 SMILING FACE: **... and all they have to do is bring back the**
3 **Golden Tuning Fork.**
4 MARICELA: **That's it? That's easy!**
5 SMILING FACE: **Adriana! Tell our adventurous arrivals — yes!**
6 **Bring back the Golden Tuning Fork, strike it against the**
7 **wall of the cave, and the spell will be broken!**
8 MARICELA: *Vayamos,* **Riccardo!**
9
10 (*MARICELA and RICCARDO start going down the dark tunnel.*
11 *Lights up in the tunnel reveal an enormous YELLOW SNAKE with*
12 *a golden tuning fork in its mouth. MARICELA and RICCARDO see*
13 *the snake — and scream. The YELLOW SNAKE looks at MARICELA*
14 *and RICCARDO and its jeweled eyes glisten. The YELLOW SNAKE*
15 *strikes the tuning fork against the cave wall. A beautiful note plays*
16 *— a note that mutates into other notes, creating an eerie, ethereal,*
17 *death-like melody. The YELLOW SNAKE sleepily closes its eyes.*
18 *When the note ends the YELLOW SNAKE opens its evil eyes and*
19 *stares at MARICELA and RICCARDO. MARICELA gets closer to*
20 *the YELLOW SNAKE. The YELLOW SNAKE opens its mouth and*
21 *reveals its huge fangs.*)
22
23 RICCARDO: **Careful!**
24 MARICELA: *Oye* **... it likes music ... do something musical: sing!**
25 RICCARDO: **You want me to sing? I can't sing! I couldn't even**
26 **make chorus —**
27 MARICELA: **Sing or I break your legs! Make it up! Do**
28 **something! Sing something Mami likes!** (*RICCARDO sings*
29 *à la José Feliciano.*)
30 RICCARDO: **¡***Feliz Navidad!* **¡***De de de de!* **¡***Feliz Navidad!* **¡***De de*
31 *de de!* **Feliz Navidad, Prospero Año, y felicidad!** (*As*
32 *RICCARDO sings, the YELLOW SNAKE's eyes seem to get*
33 *heavy. It lowers its head until it's almost even with*
34 *MARICELA. MARICELA stands on the YELLOW SNAKE's*
35 *huge body. RICCARDO stops singing.*) **Maricela!**

1

2 *(The YELLOW SNAKE snaps out of its mysterious stupor. It sees*
3 *MARICELA standing close by and quickly coils its huge body*
4 *around her. MARICELA screams. RICCARDO runs to the*
5 *YELLOW SNAKE, beating it with his fists.)*

6

7 **MARICELA: Go back and sing ... !**
8 **RICCARDO: No!**
9 **MARICELA: ¡... hagalo, por favor ... !** *(The YELLOW SNAKE*
10 *squeezes MARICELA tighter. She lets out a strangled cry.)*
11 **God, if I ever get out of this, I'm gonna eat veggies every**
12 **day, never talk back, get straight As, and volunteer at a**
13 **soup kitchen!**
14 **RICCARDO: I wanna wish you a Merry Christmas! I wanna**
15 **wish you a Merry Christmas!** *(The YELLOW SNAKE*
16 *instantly relaxes. MARICELA wiggles free as the YELLOW*
17 *SNAKE's droopy diamond eyes close. MARICELA slowly,*
18 *slowly reaches for the tuning fork in the YELLOW SNAKE's*
19 *mouth.)* **I wanna wish you a Merry Christmas from the**
20 **bottom of my he-art!** *(MARICELA puts her hand down the*
21 *snake's long throat, and grabs the golden tuning fork.*
22 *MARICELA strikes the tuning fork on her hand. The*
23 *beautiful note plays.)*
24 **MARICELA:** *(Sotto to Riccardo)* **... OK ... stop that horrible**
25 **singing and let's go now ...**
26

27 *(MARICELA and RICCARDO, hitting the tuning fork over and*
28 *over again, creating successive waves of beautiful notes, start to*
29 *leave the YELLOW SNAKE. Overcome by the bombardment of*
30 *music, the YELLOW SNAKE falls asleep. Lights down on the*
31 *YELLOW SNAKE. MARICELA and RICCARDO embrace. She's*
32 *trying not to cry.)*
33

34 **MARICELA: *Gracias, Riccardo* ...**
35 **RICCARDO: You're totally outta control, girl ...** *(MARICELA and*

1   *RICCARDO walk back to the two FACES.)*
2   **MARICELA: Adriano! Adriana! We got it! Now what do we do?**
3   **SMILING FACE: Hit it, baby, just hit it!**
4
5   *(MARICELA strikes the tuning fork. The beautiful note fills the*
6   *theatre and changes and changes. The FROWNING FACE's eyes*
7   *open. The frown turns into a smile. Suddenly the two FACES*
8   *begin to separate themselves from the cave wall. Necks, torsos,*
9   *arms, and legs appear. In moments two full grown people —*
10 *ADRIANO and ADRIANA — stand before us. ADRIANO and*
11 *ADRIANA look at each other and embrace.)*
12
13 **ADRIANO: Adriana! I thought I lost you, Adriana!**
14 **ADRIANA: Adriano! I thought I lost you, Adriano!**
15
16 *(As ADRIANO and ADRIANA hold each other, MARICELA gingerly*
17 *takes the crystal from ADRIANO's hand. ADRIANO barely notices as*
18 *he and ADRIANA continue to kiss. Lights down on ADRIANO and*
19 *ADRIANA. MARICELA and RICCARDO hold the crystal, looking at it.)*
20
21 **MARICELA AND RICCARDO: Oooooooooooooooooooooooo.**
22 **MARICELA:** *(Looking in)* **There it is. The sunshine. The barbecues.**
23   **The cactus, the beaches, all the electrical energy of the city.**
24   **Trapped.**
25 **RICCARDO:** *(Looking in)* **The Mayan Sun God! He's waving at**
26   **us! ¡Hola!**
27 **MARICELA:** *(Not sure)* **Bueno. Let's get out of this hole and back**
28   **up to the mall and pray to the High God of Happy Endings**
29   **that we're not too late.**
30
31 *(Lights change. MARICELA and RICCARDO are back in the mall*
32 *parking lot. Nearby are SNOW PEOPLE, large round Frosty the*
33 *Snowman figures, coming in and out of the mall. There's*
34 *something silly and sinister about them. Upstage is a SNOW*
35 *WOMAN with a Viking helmet, watching.)*

1
2 RICCARDO: *(Looking around)* **Completely changed ...**
3 MARICELA: **Those snow-creatures ... are people. Snow people**
4   **shopping at the mall!**
5 RICCARDO: **Are we too late?**
6 MARICELA: *Looking at the crystal)* **No way.**
7 RICCARDO: *(Smiles.)* **Yeah. Smash it!** *(MARICELA is about to*
8   *throw the crystal on the ground.)*
9 SNOW WOMAN: **Wait a minute, children!**
10 MARICELA: **Who said that?**
11 SNOW WOMAN: **I did.**
12 RICCARDO: *Hagalo, Maricela, hagalo ...*
13 SNOW WOMAN: **I'm a snow woman. Look at me. I can talk, I**
14   **can breathe! My blood is very cold. But it's my blood. My**
15   **heart beats softly. But it's my heart. I'm alive.**
16 MARICELA: *(To Snow Woman) Oye,* **we have to do this ...**
17 SNOW WOMAN: **Don't you see? It's too late —**
18 RICCARDO: **No it's not, Maricela —**
19 SNOW WOMAN: **This city is frozen now. Everything you knew**
20   **here is frozen. And look. See those snowy mounds over**
21   **there, looking at us? My family. My snow children. And**
22   **there? Another snow family. All of us are here now. We are**
23   **here now. We like it here.**
24 MARICELA: **But this is our home ...**
25 SNOW WOMAN: **Was your home. There's been a change of**
26   **management!**
27 MARICELA: **Are you telling me — everything I did, I did for**
28   **nothing?**
29 SNOW WOMAN: **Not for nothing. You can be one of us. You and**
30   **your brother. You can be part of the snow. You can be**
31   **frozen with us, live a new life with us, it's easy.** *(It starts to*
32   *snow only on MARICELA and RICCARDO.)*
33 MARICELA: **But I wanted to save ...**
34 SNOW WOMAN: **You wanted. You. It always seems to be about**
35   **you. It doesn't work like that. I'm a hero here. Why?**

1   Because being a hero is about "us," "we." A hero gives up
2   everything for a greater cause. And that's what you have to
3   do. Give up everything for a greater cause. My cause.
4   RICCARDO: Wait a minute ...
5   MARICELA: *(Starting to freeze)* Riccardo! I'm cold!
6   RICCARDO: I recognize that voice, Maricela ...
7   MARICELA: I can feel my heart slowing down ... *mí sangre* — my
8   blood — it's freezing ...
9   SNOW WOMAN: Good!
10   MARICELA: ... but I can't give in ... I had an adventure ... I was
11   a hero on that adventure ...
12   SNOW WOMAN: What's a hero? Huh? A spoiled, selfish little girl
13   who goes out to fight Seven-Headed Monsters?
14   RICCARDO: ... that voice ... the Governor's, the Hydra's, the
15   Fog's!
16   SNOW WOMAN: Well, I'll tell you something. There are no such
17   things as Seven-Headed Monsters in the real world! Some
18   hero! A hero with nothing to do!
19   MARICELA: *(Getting colder)* ... not true ... there are monsters ...
20   SNOW WOMAN: On TV?
21   MARICELA: Inside. In our hearts and minds. Monsters of
22   apathy. Of cowardice. Of ignorance. Of hate.
23   SNOW WOMAN: Oh barf! Why don't you give me that crystal
24   before you hurt yourself, kid?
25   MARICELA: *(Weakening)* Riccardo, I can't fight anymore ...
26   RICCARDO: You have to ...
27   MARICELA: I'm too cold ... *(The SNOW WOMAN reaches for the*
28   *crystal.)*
29   RICCARDO: *(Weak)* Are you a good person who does nothing ... ?
30   MARICELA: I don't remember ...
31   RICCARDO: *Are you a good person who does nothing ... ?!*
32   MARICELA: No ... I'm not ...
33   RICCARDO: Then do it, Mari ...
34   MARICELA: No I'm not ... !
35

1 *(RICCARDO grabs the hand in which MARICELA holds the*
2 *crystal. He lifts her hand and, together, they throw the crystal to*
3 *the ground. MARICELA and RICCARDO shield their eyes as the*
4 *stage is blasted with light.)*
5
6 **MARICELA AND RICCARDO: Aaaahhhh!** *(Thunder crashes.*
7   *Wind. Music. Suddenly the Mayan Sun God HUNAHPU,*
8   *XBALANQUE's twin brother, appears in all his solar*
9   *radiance. He screams with joy and runs across the stage.)*
10 **HUNAHPU: Freeeeeeddoooooommmm!**
11
12 *(The terrified SNOW PEOPLE start running away. HUNAHPU goes*
13 *to the SNOW WOMAN and rips apart the outer shell of snow,*
14 *revealing an androgynous looking little creature in a Viking*
15 *helmet. This is the trickster god LOKI. HUNAHPU reappears high*
16 *above the stage. Sunshine has returned to San Diego. LOKI howls*
17 *with rage, falls to the ground, and covers his head. SHOPPERS*
18 *again come in and out of the mall.)*
19
20 **RICCARDO:** *(Exhausted, overwhelmed)* **Look, Maricela. It's home.**
21 **MARICELA: ¡*El sol esta en el cielo!* It's bright, like before. Feel**
22   **how warm!**
23
24 *(MARICELA and RICCARDO shed their extra layers of clothing.*
25 *They notice LOKI lying on the ground, small, defeated. They*
26 *approach LOKI tentatively.)*
27
28 **LOKI: Go away.**
29 **MARICELA: Did you do this?** *(LOKI struggles to stand up. Wipes*
30   *the dust off his body. Straightens his Viking helmet. Tries to*
31   *look dignified.)*
32 **LOKI: I can't believe this. Everyone evacuated San Diego as**
33   **soon as the snow hit – everyone – except for you two!**
34 **MARICELA: *Pero*, who are you, Loki?**
35 **LOKI: See? That's the problem! Worst thing that could happen to**

1   a myth is to be forgotten! I wanted to be remembered! To
2   make a comeback. Stage a little demonstration of my
3   power. Set up a beachhead. Conquer some territory. Terrify
4   the other gods! Figured if I could take bright, hot,
5   steaming San Diego on the first try – me, Loki, a snow god!
6   – I could take anything! Oh, it would have been so
7   beautiful here! The cold is life itself! Snow is the dearest
8   substance in the world! Before the world was made there
9   was a swirling vortex of ice and snow and from that
10   primordial chaos the world was made! You and I are made
11   from the same substance: from snow! And it bothers me to
12   see a place where there is never any winter, where snow is
13   forbidden and even on Christmas day, the crown jewel of
14   winter, even on Christmas there are no snow covered
15   fields, no way for snowmen to live and thrive: to get
16   married and have cute little snow babies! Every year, on
17   this day, I've been tempted to do it, to take the heat of the
18   city away forever ... and every year I change my mind and
19   spare the city ... but this year, I heard you talking about
20   missing the snow and it made me brave and I did it! And
21   that was just the beginning: the tip of the iceberg, as it
22   were: I wanted the world worshipping me instead of the
23   Sun: to sing praises to the New Ice Age, Loki's Ice Age!
24 MARICELA: Dang. Guess you lose, bro!
25 LOKI: Oh, listen to her! Thinks she's bad now! Thinks she can
26   take me on! Ha!
27 MARICELA: Before I met you, I'd never done anything. Now
28   I've done something. Ricky and me. And we can't be the
29   same again.
30 LOKI: I ain't listenin' to this naïve puke!
31 MARICELA: And now we're more a part of this city than ever.
32   It's not perfect. There are more demons and monsters in
33   this city than the imagination can hold. But you know
34   what? It's different now. It's got me to deal with now.
35   *(Punching RICCARDO's arm.)* Me and stupid.

1   **RICCARDO:** (*Laughs, punching her arm*) *¡Tú!*

2   **MARICELA:** This place is my place. This time is my time. This

3   place is part of me and I am part of it. And I have you to

4   thank for that.

5   **LOKI:** Yeah? Well, I'm not finished. In fact I haven't even

6   started. You wait. I still have a few more tricks to pull,

7   Maricela de la Luz and Riccardo de la Luz. You punks win

8   this one. But, you wait, as soon as I get my strength, I'll be

9   back!

10

11   (*LOKI sticks out his thumb and starts limping Off-stage, hoping to*

12   *hitch a ride out of town. MARICELA and RICCARDO look at the*

13   *busy SHOPPERS who go about their business, oblivious.*)

14

15   **MARICELA:** I give up, how come no one's congratulating us for

16   saving the world an' stuff?

17   **RICCARDO:** Maybe they don't know what happened.

18   **MARICELA:** OK, cool – what did happen?

19   **RICCARDO:** I don't know, but you looked pretty stupid sticking

20   your hand in that snake!

21   **MARICELA:** And you looked pretty stupid singing to it! *¡Tonto!*

22   *¡Malcreado!* (*MARICELA and RICCARDO walk Downstage.*

23   *HUNAHPU disappears and turns into XBALANQUE. The*

24   *lights change, until it's a starry night — clear, peaceful, and*

25   *beautiful.*)

26   **RICCARDO:** What do you want to do now? We saved San Diego.

27   You wanna save San Clemente?

28   **MARICELA:** I just wanna ... sit down with Mami ... and tell her

29   I think she's losing her personality to her android

30   boyfriend and I'm not gonna let her do it. She can hate me

31   if she wants, but I have to tell her the truth.

32

33   (*OFELIA, the CYCLOPS, HERCULES, JASON, XBALANQUE, and*

34   *LOKI appear — unseen by MARICELA and RICCARDO. OFELIA's*

35   *long dress is free of icicles, it's blue, pure, like flowing water.*

1   *RICCARDO senses the presence of the unseen gods and*
2   *goddesses.)*
3
4   **RICCARDO: Wow! I just got this really weird, freaky feeling,**
5   **Maricela.**
6   **MARICELA: Like what?**
7   **RICCARDO: Like invisible people are watching us. Lots and lots**
8   **of them. All weird shapes and sizes.**
9   **MARICELA: That's just your imagination, *hermano*. Just your**
10   **imagination.**
11
12 *(XBALANQUE comes forward, holding tiny lights and goes to*
13 *MARICELA and RICCARDO. He puts lights in their hair and on*
14 *their hands, arms, and legs. When lights go to black, the lights on*
15 *MARICELA and RICCARDO make them look like living*
16 *constellations. They blend into the starry night. Blackout.)*
17
18 **END OF PLAY**
19
20
21
22
23
24
25
26
27
28
29
30
31
32
33
34
35

The Migrant Farmworker's Son

by Silvia Gonzalez S.

Perhaps the most poignant area of concern for playwrights dealing with multicultural subjects today is that of the family: the "culture shock" that occurs when a family's traditional ethnic culture and values collide and seek to merge with mainstream American society. And this collision is often ongoing. For example, Asian-American writers like Philip Kan Gotanda or Wakako Yamauchi have traced in their plays the generational problems faced by the newly-arrived "issei" immigrants, the struggle for social acceptance by the second-generation "nissei," and finally the search for personal identity among their present-day descendants.

Nowhere does this question of the family's domestic problems become more acute than in the impact of cultural assimilation upon immigrant children. The young, of course, seem to adapt most quickly to American society, eagerly adopting the language, dress codes, musical tastes and other features of their peer groups in schools and on playgrounds as they seek to win acceptance and an entrée into American youth culture. But in this process of acculturation, many children find themselves restricted, threatened and even embarrassed by the ethnic values and customs of their parents and older family members. They find themselves torn between the demands of an older society — frequently one which they may only dimly remember — and the compelling, seductive cultural attractions of contemporary America.

This painful situation lies at the center of the following drama by Silvia Gonzalez S. But even as the father-son conflict between the values of old Mexico and pop culture '90s America threatens to tear the migrant farmworker's family apart, we slowly come to realize that "culture shock" is not the real culprit here. Culture clash seems only a catalyst, a pressure cooker within which the father's more universal, human problems can be suddenly illuminated and then examined. And only when that point is reached, can the process of reconciliation and healing begin.

Silvia Gonzalez S. is an Oregon dramatist who has earned wide recognition for her work over the past eight years. Her plays include *I Can't Eat Goat's Head* (1995), *¡Fiesta!* (1995), *La Llorona Llora* (1994), *U Got the Look* (1994), *The Migrant Farmworker's Son* (1994), *Waiting Women* (1993), *Los Matadores* (1992), *Boxcar* (1991), and others. They have been produced at the Kennedy Center, the Portland International Theatre Festival, and by such groups as INTAR, Chicago's Body Politic and Victory Gardens Theatres, the Whole Art Theatre, the South Coast Rep, and several others. Among her numerous grants and awards are a Lila

Wallace/Reader's Digest Grant, a Rockefeller Grant, and the Lee Korf Playwriting Award.

The Migrant Farmworker's Son first appeared in workshop form at the Chicago Dramatists' Workshop in 1991.

Characters:

HENRY: High school student, Hispanic. Rambunctious, attempts to lighten even the gloomiest of moments. Uses rap for tension release.

OLIVERIO SANTOS: A farmworker, Mexican-American. Loves poetry. Passionate about nature. His words are loaded with meaning. He is humorous and never didactic.

DAD: Mexican national, thirties, buried in his misery. He is a good man, but constantly fails in his attempts for betterment. A good heart, but not sophisticated. Tormented by memories. His lack of English understanding causes friction with his very American teenage son.

MOM: Mexican national, thirties. A good mediator. Quick-witted. Extremely adaptable. Has plans for self-betterment.

GIRL: Mexican-American, very young. Six to eight years old. She wears white ribbons and her dress is filled with ruffles. Spunky girl. A father's joy.

GROUP OF MEXICAN PEASANTS: With blue skins, and gray, bluish clothes (three to five).

Place:
A rural community in Yuma, Arizona.

Times:

Act One, Scene One	1970
Act One, Scene Two	1972
Act One, Scene Three	1985 (Early days of rap)
Act One, Scene Four	Late that evening
Act One, Scene Five	Next day
Act One, Scene Six	Late at night
Act One, Scene Seven	Next day
Act One, Scene Eight	Two days later
Act One, Scene Nine	Later that day
Act One, Scene Ten	Same day
Act One, Scene Eleven	Same day
Act One, Scene Twelve	Next day
Act One, Scene Thirteen	A few days later
Act One, Scene Fourteen	Next day
Act Two, Scene One	Three months later
Act Two, Scene Two	Same day
Act Two, Scene Three	That evening
Act Two, Scene Four	Next day
Act Two, Scene Five	That evening
Act Two, Scene Six	Same evening
Act Two, Scene Seven	Two months later
Act Two, Scene Eight	That evening

1 **ACT ONE**
2 **Scene One**
3
4 *Eerie blue light. Sounds of a tractor going across a field.*
5 *Silhouette light, chest up, on OLIVERIO looking blankly out.*
6 *BLUE MEXICAN PEASANTS cut lettuce off the ground and bag*
7 *them. (This is like a dance with pantomime.) MOM and DAD also*
8 *work the ground. (They are younger.) After a few moments, rough*
9 *sounds from a tractor trying to stop in the distance are heard.*
10 *Lights dim out on OLIVERIO. The PEASANTS look in the opposite*
11 *direction. In awe, MOM and DAD and the PEASANTS start to*
12 *move towards the sound, then stop. Then, a sound of a tractor*
13 *losing control, followed by music.*
14
15 **BLUE MEXICAN PEASANT:** *(Religious)* **Aye, Dios mío.** *(The men*
16 *take off their hats and the women cover their heads with*
17 *their rebozos and turn away sadly.)*
18
19 *Eerie light*
20 **SLOW BLACKOUT**
21 **END OF SCENE**
22
23 **ACT ONE**
24 **Scene Two**
25
26 *A young GIRL enters in a ruffled dress and hair in braids. She is*
27 *playful and full of charm. The light is slightly on her. Purple*
28 *shadows behind her. She is talking to a baby in a crib, but it is not*
29 *seen.*
30
31 **GIRL: Bay-bee. Leetle baby-bee. Cahm here leetle baby. That's**
32 **how mommy called you . . . I'm going to sing you a little**
33 **song. Itzy Bitzy spider, went up the water spout. Down**
34 **came the rain and... But Daddy, I learned the song in**
35 **school. Down came the rain and washed the spider out...**

1   **Daddy, I like to... It's pretty... Out came the sun and...** *(Long*
2   *pause)* **Don't daddy, please.**
3
4 **END OF SCENE**
5
6 **ACT ONE**
7 **Scene Three**
8
9 *DAD enters with a crate of oranges. He's wearing field clothes and*
10 *is quite weathered. He puts the crate aside. Then exits and enters*
11 *with a Nintendo™ game. He sets it up to play. MOM enters. She*
12 *has already changed from working in the fields. She has a nice*
13 *clean appearance. She is drying her hair.*
14
15 **MOM: What's that?**
16 **DAD: Nintendo™.**
17 **MOM: Where's the telephone? What did I say to do after work?**
18 **DAD: It's for Enrigue.**
19 **MOM: Henry?**
20 **DAD: Enrigue. His name is Enrigue. You keep forgetting your**
21   **own son's name.**
22 **MOM: What about the telephone?**
23 **DAD: Look how they put a game in the TV and you can play.**
24   **Right here on the sofa. It's new. Everybody is getting one.**
25 **MOM: How much did that cost?**
26 **DAD: Practically nothing. Beto had to get rid of it. He was**
27   **getting too addicted to it. It was taking all his beer time.**
28   **We all forced him to sell it to me.**
29 **MOM: So the money is gone? Last time you were supposed to**
30   **get a new carburetor, and instead, you gave the money to**
31   **your brother.**
32 **DAD: He needed it to pay rent.**
33 **MOM: Does he return favors?** *(Dad looks at her with extreme*
34   *sadness. Then he returns to the game.)*
35 **DAD: He did one time.**

1   **MOM:** (*Long moment and softly*) **Play your game.**

2   **DAD:** (*Recuperating well*) **They say Mario is Italian, but I think**

3   **he's a Mexicano.** (*Pause.*) **Aye, Mario hit a wall.** (*HENRY*

4   *enters with headphones. HENRY is much like a boy of today,*

5   *in manners and dress. The clash of the cultures is obvious.*

6   *HENRY will attempt to make lighter many moments until a*

7   *certain point.*)

8   **HENRY: Wow! Dad bought a Nintendo™. Alright! Give me the**

9   **controls.**

10 **DAD: No.** *Todavía* **no.** (*MOM exits.*)

11 **HENRY: Hey, Mom? What's the matter with her?**

12 **DAD: Ah! She's mad at me.**

13 **HENRY: For what?**

14 **DAD: Nothing.** *Women.*

15 **HENRY: Yeah,** *Women.*

16 **DAD: Don't let a woman work. She'll think she's wearing the**

17   **pants in the house.**

18 **MOM:** (*Off*) **I do. And I'm a harder worker than you in the fields.**

19 **DAD:** (*Yelling back*) **You are working there because you want to.**

20   (*To HENRY.*) **If we lived in Mexico, they would shame me**

21   **for letting her work. A real man doesn't allow that.**

22 **HENRY: Then why do you cook, Dad?**

23 **DAD: Sh! That's a family secret. Never tell anyone what goes on**

24   **in this house. Understand? I told you that before. It's not**

25   **the way.** (*Back to Nintendo™.*) **Look at that funny guy. He's**

26   **a cartoon.**

27 **MOM:** (*Enters with a basket of clothes.*) *You're* **a cartoon.**

28 **DAD:** (*Still to Henry*) **She wouldn't talk like that to me if we lived**

29   **over there. And your Spanish would be better.** (*Pause*) **I'm**

30   **ready to go tomorrow to get my dignity back.**

31 **MOM: They already stepped on it and tossed it out into the**

32   **gutter. You know I am not going back. And you're not**

33   **going back either. Your dad's been talking like this for**

34   **fifteen years.** (*HENRY hasn't been listening. He is wearing*

35   *his Walkman™.*)

1   **DAD: Are you making fun of me?**

2   **MOM: You're not going back. You would die of starvation over**

3   **there.**

4   **DAD: I don't believe it.**

5   **MOM: Why do you think you're here?**

6   **DAD: There's death in this dirt.** *(MOM turns away. HENRY looks*

7   *as if he is used to this situation, even though he's not sure*

8   *what they are talking about. There is silence for awhile.)*

9   **MOM: Henry wouldn't make it over there. And why should I go**

10   **back?**

11 **DAD: Is there another man?**

12 **MOM: What?**

13 **DAD: Do you have a man to take care of you already?**

14 **MOM: You don't need a man in the United States.**

15 **DAD:** *(To HENRY)* **See that. She's becoming more *gringa* every**

16   **day.** *(HENRY is not listening. DAD knocks HENRY's*

17   *headphones off.)* **Want to go with me to Mexico?**

18 **HENRY: Of course not.**

19 **DAD: Why not?**

20 **HENRY: Like you said, I don't speak Spanish well.**

21 **DAD: You used to speak Spanish when you were a child. Why**

22   **did she have in her head you would do better in life with**

23   **only English? Now look at you. You don't understand half**

24   **the things I say. This is a conspiracy to take you away from**

25   **me and from the mother country.**

26 **HENRY: Dad, I like everything the way it is.**

27 **DAD: Ah. What do you know?**

28 **MOM: I'm his mother and I look after his education.**

29 **DAD: You took my son away.** *(Silence.)*

30 **HENRY: I'm not like you, Dad. We're different. Sorry.**

31 **MOM: That's not what's bothering him. You don't like it that I**

32   **am learning too.**

33 **DAD: *Basta.***

34 **MOM: I like to learn.**

35 **DAD: It's a waste of time for a woman to learn.**

1 HENRY: Dad, you got to stop living in the stone age.

2 DAD: *¿Qué?*

3 HENRY: Let her be. (*DAD looks at HENRY with inexplicable rage.*

4   *He often does this.)*

5 MOM: Go, Henry. I'll take care of this.

6 DAD: Come here, pocho. *("Po-show" is a slang term for being*

7   *neither Mexican, nor American. DAD motions for HENRY to*

8   *approach. DAD touches his belt as a threat to HENRY, but*

9   *MOM doesn't see this action.)*

10 HENRY: We live in America, Dad. You can't do that.

11 DAD: You must respect your father.

12 HENRY: Who is going to respect *me? (MOM directs HENRY out*

13   *to get his DAD a beer. MOM stares at DAD.)*

14 DAD: *(Softening)* I did the same to my father. He is growing up.

15 MOM: And what did he do?

16 DAD: Enrigue's very first words, between his crying and

17   pooping his pants, was *"Hola papá."*

18 MOM: It was *"Hola mamá." (HENRY re-enters.)*

19 HENRY: And before that I was a one-cell swimmer.

20 DAD: You didn't swim. You were born here. *(HENRY sits.)*

21 HENRY: You don't understand, dad. Can I play the game now?

22   *(Long pause.)* Thanks. *(Sounds of Nintendo™ game, All stare*

23   *at the screen.)*

24 HENRY: Where did you get the money for this?

25 MOM: He used some of the money for the telephone

26   connection.

27 HENRY: Man, no phone? Messed up.

28 DAD: Not everything. I sold his bike.

29 HENRY: What? Mom!

30 DAD: What do you need a bike for? You're too old for it.

31 HENRY: How will I get around?

32 DAD: You have two feet.

33 HENRY: I can't believe this. Without asking me?

34 DAD: Respect me. Respect me. *(HENRY looks at him with so*

35   *much anger he can't take it.)* In the ranch, we had *nothing*.

1   **And you *cry for a bike?* (HENRY** *rushes out of the house. A*
2   *long silence between MOM and DAD after HENRY goes.*
3   *MOM has an understanding expression on her face even*
4   *though she disapproves greatly of what DAD did. DAD looks*
5   *at her and becomes a little boy. He is really not the pillar of*
6   *strength he tries to be. Softening)* **You know I love him.**
7   **MOM: Then tell him.**
8   **DAD: Who told me?** *(DAD goes to the Nintendo™ game and starts*
9   *playing. He glances at MOM several times. MOM exits.)*
10
11   **END OF SCENE**
12
13
14   **ACT ONE**
15   **Scene Four**
16
17   *HENRY is by himself in a field. OLIVERIO is watching him from*
18   *a distance. MOM approaches HENRY. OLIVERIO disappears.*
19
20   **MOM: Henry.**
21   **HENRY: Mom.**
22   **MOM: Don't be angry with your father.**
23   **HENRY: I can't stand him.**
24   **MOM: Now God will punish you for saying that.**
25   **HENRY: We don't go to church.**
26   **MOM:** *(Pause)* **He's had a hard life.**
27   **HENRY:** *I've* **had a hard life.**
28   **MOM: I'll get your bike back.**
29   **HENRY: Forget it mom. I think I just saw some kid riding it and**
30   **he looked too happy.**
31   **MOM: You'll drive the car then.**
32   **HENRY: That piece of crap. I'd be embarrassed.**
33   **MOM: That's a way of life for a lot of people. There's nothing**
34   **wrong with being poor.**
35   **HENRY: I want to be alone, Mom.**

1   **MOM: No, you don't. You don't want to be alone. No one does.**

2   **HENRY: Yes, I do.** *(MOM hesitates, then leaves quietly. HENRY*

3   *sits there. Cross-fade to DAD near a canal in the background.*

4   *He sits there staring at the water. He looks across and sees*

5   *GIRL smiling at him. She then disappears.)*

6   **DAD: Why did you go, *hija*? I don't like being alone.**

7

8   **BLACKOUT**

9   **END OF SCENE**

10

11

12   **ACT ONE**

13   **Scene Five**

14

15   *DAD enters the house. He is covered with mud from the canal.*

16   *MOM is trying to play Nintendo™.*

17

18   **DAD: I saw her.**

19   **MOM: You didn't see anybody.**

20   **DAD: I see her every time I clean out the canals.** *(Silence. DAD is*

21   *distraught again.)*

22   **MOM: I don't know why I listened to you. No pictures, no**

23   **talking about her. As if she was never alive. You even made**

24   **me bury her far away.**

25   **DAD: I wanted her in Mexican soil.**

26   **MOM: This was once Mexican soil.**

27   **DAD: I have no worth here, so she couldn't stay.**

28   **MOM: Tell Henry about her now.**

29   **DAD: No. You know how I get. He'll think I'm weak.** *(HENRY*

30   *enters. DAD stares at HENRY. HENRY eyes DAD's muddy*

31   *appearance.)*

32   **HENRY: How come when I come in that dirty, I get in trouble?**

33   *(Silence. HENRY looks around.)* **The silent treatment.**

34   **MOM: I'll get some towels.** *(MOM exits. HENRY and DAD stare at*

35   *each other.)*

1   HENRY: Hi, Pop.
2   DAD: Pop? What happened to Papá?
3   HENRY: Yeah, what happened to you?
4   DAD: What do you got in that bag?
5   HENRY: Fish.
6   DAD: From where?
7   HENRY: The canal.
8   DAD: I told you not to go to the canals.
9   HENRY: Dad, this toxic waste could be dinner.
10 DAD: Don't go over there.
11 HENRY: OK. I won't go there . . today.
12 DAD: What did you say?
13 HENRY: *(Puts his Walkman™ headphones on.)* **Rap with me.**
14 DAD: **I'll rap your face. Stop that!** *(HENRY keeps dancing.)* *¡Ya!*
15   *(DAD grabs HENRY.)* **I want you to say thank you for**
16   **breaking my back for you.** *¡Dilo!* **For a roof over your head,**
17   **for food on the table. Give me appreciation for all that I do**
18   **for you!**
19 HENRY: Is it Father's Day or something?
20 DAD: *¡Dilo!*
21 MOM: *(Re-enters)* *¡Dejalo!*
22 DAD: *¡Diga!*
23 HENRY: Thanks, Dad.
24 DAD: *¡Papá!*
25 HENRY: Thanks *Papá*!
26 DAD: The rest!
27 MOM: Stop it, you two.
28 HENRY: I know you work hard.
29 MOM: **Leave him alone.** *(DAD lets go of HENRY. HENRY goes to*
30   *sit on the table and picks up a hardened tortilla. He then*
31   *breaks the tortilla.)*
32 HENRY: Look, I'm abusing a tortilla.
33 DAD: What did he say?
34 MOM: He's being funny.
35 DAD: Being funny while we work in the fields.

1 **MOM: Get your father a beer.**
2 **HENRY: Gladly.** *(HENRY puts his headphones back on to escape.*
3 *He starts moving to the beat. He gets the beer from the*
4 *refrigerator and continues dancing with a beer in hand,*
5 *absentmindedly. MOM and DAD are unaware of his*
6 *movement with the can of beer for they are talking quietly*
7 *with each other. Then HENRY stops to adjust his*
8 *headphones, and DAD looks up.)*
9 **DAD: You have my beer?**
10 **HENRY: Here, Dad.**
11 **DAD:** *(Correcting him)* **Papá.** *(He opens the beer and it squirts all*
12 *over his face. DAD runs after HENRY and catches him by the*
13 *ear.)*
14 **MOM: Stop it!**
15 **HENRY: Ow! Dad, you're making a Van Gogh out of me.**
16 **DAD: Hear that! He told me to go! No respect!** *(HENRY breaks*
17 *away.)*
18 **HENRY: *Van Gogh*. He lost an ear. Well, he cut it out.**
19 **MOM: Go out, Henry.**
20 **HENRY: Glad to.** *(He exits to the bedroom.)*
21 **DAD: He has no respect for me. The children born here are**
22 **spoiled.**
23 **MOM: We came here to spoil our children.**
24 **DAD:** *(Softens)* **Not like this.**
25 **MOM: You are jealous of your own son.** *(HENRY enters and*
26 *heads for the front door.)*
27 **HENRY: I don't need this.**
28 **MOM: Henry!**
29 **HENRY What?!**
30 **MOM: Come back here.**
31 **HENRY: When you stop arguing!**
32 **MOM: Who's arguing? This is how we make love.**
33 **HENRY: Funny, mom. I'm not in the mood.**
34 **MOM: Talk to your son! *Andale.***
35 **DAD: You'll never do what I do. Never will you cut lettuce or**

1   pick from the trees, or anything.

2 HENRY: No problem!

3 DAD: Understand? Understand?

4 HENRY: Who's going to pick the oranges in the tree out back? A

5   **wetback like you, Dad?** *(DAD is about to reach for his belt*

6   *when several BLUE MEXICAN PEASANTS restrain him. The*

7   *BLUE PEASANTS are only seen by the audience. The BLUE*

8   *MEXICAN PEASANTS finally let DAD go and exit with*

9   *HENRY.)*

10 DAD: *(Softening)* If I had all the money in the world, I would

11   give that boy everything. I would give my wife the world.

12   *(Pause)*

13 MOM: *(Softly)* Don't work in the canals, anymore. It brings bad

14   memories. It turns you into this monster.

15 DAD: Sometimes, bad memories makes the monster happy.

16

17

18 END OF SCENE

19

20

21 ACT ONE

22 Scene Six

23

24 *Night time. Stars in the sky. OLIVERIO stands in a field. White*

25 *doves fly around him. He is smiling and enjoying the stars. He*

26 *then starts shoveling dirt. HENRY walks by holding his ear.*

27 *OLIVERIO notices.*

28

29 OLIVERIO: Something in your ear? Hey! I'm talking to you.

30   Something in your ear like your finger? Then take your

31   finger out.

32 HENRY: I thought it was bleeding.

33 OLIVERIO: *El corazón sangra* . . . *(Waits for a response.)* Only the

34   heart bleeds, idiot.

35 HENRY: My Spanish isn't that good.

1   OLIVERIO: Pity. Where are you going?

2   HENRY: Nowhere.

3   OLIVERIO: Then you are in the right place.

4   HENRY: You work here?

5   OLIVERIO: I work all the time. And you?

6   HENRY: I don't work all the time. I'm too young.

7   OLIVERIO: I started working when I was this high. I had a rifle

8   at the age of seven.

9   HENRY: To protect yourself?

10 OLIVERIO: To shoot my food. Jack rabbits. Sometimes a

11   squirrel. Whatever came my way. I was sent off to herd the

12   sheep and fend for myself. Sometimes it was months

13   before I saw another person. Sometimes I forgot what I

14   looked like. No mirror in my pocket. And I should have

15   had one. I was very good-looking. Well, I needed to remind

16   myself of that.

17 HENRY: You killed for your own food, at *seven*?

18 OLIVERIO: Or eight years old. I can't remember now. Once I ate

19   a 'possum. It tasted very good. The tail wasn't good. Felt

20   like a snake in your mouth. The eyes were good. Well,

21   when you are in the middle of nowhere and you are not

22   sure you'll get a chance to kill for food again, everything

23   tastes good.

24 HENRY: Would you eat 'possum again?

25 OLIVERIO: Eh, no . . . What's your name?

26 HENRY: Henry.

27 OLIVERIO: Mine's Oliverio. Like Oliver, but only better.

28   *El señor de la tierra*

29   *El señor de poesías*

30   *El señor muy amable*

31   *Con poesías mas allegres que tú.*

32 HENRY: What are you doing here?

33 OLIVERIO: Look at that one. Don't you see it? Staring at the

34   stars cleanses the soul. You should try it. Maybe it'll clean

35   out that ear of yours. Look, there's the North star.

1   HENRY: Great, I'm standing here with an old man that stares at
2   stars.
3   OLIVERIO: And I'm standing with an idiot who holds his ear. I
4   recognize that look on your face . . . Once, I picked up a
5   lemon from the ground and put it in my pocket. It came
6   from a man who was selling them. He saw the bulge in my
7   pocket and rushed me to my father by the shirt collar. My
8   father beat me up so much. Everyone saw him whipping
9   me in the street. He wanted to teach me a lesson I would
10   never forget.
11   HENRY: You didn't steal the lemon. You just picked it up.
12   OLIVERIO: And put it in my pocket. Same thing. My father was
13   very determined I learn respect for the hard working
14   man.
15   HENRY: My father is a hard working man. Hard at work in
16   smacking me.
17   OLIVERIO: Maybe you deserved it.
18   HENRY: I didn't deserve that. Did you? *(Pause)*
19   OLIVERIO: See that star? That one is mine. And that one over
20   there. That one. That belongs to your family. Do you want
21   a star to give away?
22   HENRY: A what?
23   OLIVERIO: Humor me.
24   HENRY: Alright. Then, that one belongs to my girlfriend. Well,
25   the one girl I really like.
26   OLIVERIO: Oh, you have a girlfriend. That's nice. Much too
27   young to fall in love. Don't you know what love does to
28   you? It makes you love more. It makes you hurt more. It
29   makes you horny. Of course I've forgotten that part.
30   HENRY: *Qué viejito.* What else do you have to amuse me, you
31   old fart.
32   OLIVERIO: Fart? It was the dog. *(He smiles, then picks up some*
33   *dirt and lets it sprinkle to the ground slowly.)* **Look at this.**
34   This is my family. All of them. My uncles, my aunts, my
35   father, mother, brothers, sisters, and my grandparents,

1   and all the greats before them. But not the grandchildren
2   or my wife. They are still alive and live well enough.
3   HENRY: Where are your children?
4   OLIVERIO: Lost. Like you.
5   HENRY: And the rest of the family is dirt?
6   OLIVERIO: The darker ones are mud. They're dust. Don't say
7   dirt, sounds impersonal. Say dust. Say it like this, *Dust.*
8   HENRY: OK, *"Dust."*
9   OLIVERIO: Dust. We are all simply dust. *Muchacho,* look at
10   your shoes. You've been stepping on my mother. And that
11   right there sticking to your pants, is one of my ancestors.
12   She was an Aztec Indian. OK. Take them home and
13   introduce them to your family. *(HENRY starts to exit.)* So
14   soon? Then go. But come back again.
15   HENRY: I should stay. I'll probably get my other ear smacked.
16   OLIVERIO: *(Looks at the stars.)* No you won't.
17
18   END OF SCENE
19
20
21   ACT ONE
22   Scene Seven
23
24   *BLUE MEXICAN PEASANTS enter. From their bags they take out*
25   *tomatoes, onions, and some oranges and put them on the kitchen*
26   *table. One BLUE PEASANT puts a carton of eggs and a package of*
27   *tortillas by the stove. Another PEASANT opens one end of the*
28   *tortilla package. Another goes to the shelf and gets the corn oil*
29   *and sets it near the stove and then picks up a dollar bill he knows*
30   *is payment and puts it in his pocket. DAD enters and starts dicing*
31   *up the ingredients for Migas. He tears the tortilla into bits and*
32   *throws it in with the tomato and onion to fry. He then adds eggs.*
33
34   DAD: *(While cooking happily)* **Migas, migas, migas, Qué**
35   **sabrosas. Tomate, cebolla, y huevos. ¿Y qué más?** *(He looks*

63

1   *into the refrigerator and pulls out beans to put in the*

2   *mixture. GIRL appears. DAD accepts her presence.)* **Hija.**

3   GIRL: Hi, daddy.

4   DAD: *Qué bonita te miras.*

5   GIRL: *(Curtseys)* Thank you daddy.

6   DAD: *Papá.* Remember what I told you. *Papá.*

7   GIRL: OK, daddy.

8   DAD: *¿Tienes hambre, mija?*

9   GIRL: Yes, Daddy.

10 DAD: *Diga, sí papá.*

11 GIRL: *Sí, papá.*

12 DAD: *Muy bien. Tengo migas. Qué sabrosas. ¿Te gustan?*

13   *Huelelas.*

14 GIRL: Smells good, daddy.

15 DAD: *(Correcting her)* *Papá.*

16 GIRL: Daddy.

17 DAD: *Sí, mona.*

18 GIRL: I want to take my bike out. Can I borrow your keys?

19 DAD: Keeyz?

20 GIRL: Yeah. The keys. I need the keys to take my bike out of the

21   shed. You locked it in there. So I want the keys.

22 DAD: The keeyz?

23 GIRL: Yeah. The keys.

24 DAD: OK. *(DAD puckers up and makes a smoochy kiss noise.)*

25   There.

26 GIRL: No, not a kiss, the keys.

27 DAD: Oh, I thought you said a keeyz.

28 GIRL: You do that all the time. OK, *las llaves. Presteme las*

29   *llaves.*

30 DAD: *Mejor. Aquí estan. (He takes the keys out of his pocket.)*

31   *¿Otra cosa?*

32 GIRL: Can I have a quarter?

33 DAD: Me no speak English.

34 GIRL: Daddy!

35 DAD: *Cuando hables Español. (GIRL exits as HENRY enters.)*

1   HENRY: Hey, Dad. I want to borrow the car. Can I borrow the keys?

2   DAD: Keeyz?

3   HENRY: Yeah. I want to see my friends over at the high school.

4   I won't be long.

5   DAD: Yule want the keeyz?

6   HENRY: Yea. That's what I said. Can I have the keys?

7   DAD: OK. *(DAD puckers up to make a smoochy kiss noise.)*

8   HENRY: Oh, Dad! Not a kiss, the keys!

9   DAD: Oh . . . No.

10 HENRY: Ah, come on. There's going to be a pep rally.

11 DAD: A what?

12 HENRY: A pep really. *Cheerleaders* will be there.

13 DAD: Girls?

14 HENRY: Yeah.

15 DAD: *(Thinks)* You go.

16 HENRY: The keys, dad. You sold my bike.

17 DAD: All right. One hour.

18 HENRY: One hour! That's not enough.

19 DAD: Then give me back the keeyz.

20 HENRY: Man . . . What can I do to stay out a bit longer? Get you

21   a beer?

22 DAD: Respect me.

23 HENRY: I do, dad.

24 DAD: No you don't. You don't know what it means.

25 HENRY: *Por favor.*

26 DAD: Go for an hour and a half.

27 HENRY: Dad, listen. It's exciting. There's dancing, music.

28   Everyone is happy. It's fun, Dad. Want to go?

29 DAD: Me? No. You go. Go for two hours. Maybe three.

30 HENRY: *Gracias, Papá.*

31 DAD: You should learn Spanish. It's good for you. If you forget

32   the language, you'll be lost. You'll never know yourself, or

33   your history.

34 HENRY: *No hablo español.*

35 DAD: ¡*Vete!*

1   **HENRY:** (*Laughing*) ***Adíos, Papá.*** (*Exits.*)

2   **DAD:** (*Under his breath*) **Go kill yourself.**

3

4   **SLOW BLACK OUT**

5   **END OF SCENE**

6

7

8   **ACT ONE**

9   **Scene Eight**

10

11 *DAD and MOM are sitting at the table with bills and statements*

12 *scattered about. MOM does the bill paying as DAD watches. Then*

13 *MOM puts money in an envelope and that in a Ziplock™ bag. She*

14 *then puts it in a secret place: a hole in the wall under the sink.*

15

16 **DAD: My friend's children speak the language so beautifully. I**

17   **understand them. They have respect. I don't understand**

18   **Enrigue.**

19 **MOM: Henry will do better with −**

20 **DAD:** (*Overlapping on "better"*) **Enrigue.**

21 **MOM: Henry.**

22 **DAD:** (*Pause*) **Mothers and sons always stick together and gang**

23   **up on the father.**

24 **MOM: Why don't you go to school and learn English yourself?**

25   **That's the secret to success.**

26 **DAD: Why waste my time? I'm going to die in Mexico.**

27 **MOM: You're not going back.**

28 **DAD: Yes, I am. I have to be buried in the soil that speaks my**

29   **language. If I don't, then I'll truly feel like a foreigner.**

30 **MOM: You don't feel anything when you're dead.**

31 **DAD: I will.**

32 **MOM:** (*Pause*) **You want that boy to succeed, you let him speak**

33   **the language of this country. You'll see that I am right. The**

34   **schools here—**

35 **DAD:** (*Overlapping on "here"*) **Help families lose their children.**

1   He talks to me about things I don't know. Like pep-to,
2   pepto bees-mo.
3   MOM: What?
4   DAD: He invited me to go to the school for the pepto-*algo*. I
5   don't know. The girls, cheerleaders.
6   MOM: Oh, the pep rally.
7   DAD: Yes. How did you know that's what it's called?
8   MOM: If we both take a class, we would learn English very well.
9   And you would understand your son better.
10 DAD: Take a class to understand my son? I refuse to be made an
11   idiot in public.
12 MOM: It's a school. You go there because you are an idiot. *(DAD*
13   *looks at her. Long moment. Softly.)* Do you like Salinas
14   better?
15 DAD: In Salinas I can forget about her. Here, I think I see her all
16   the time.
17 MOM: Try to forget. Then the misery will leave you. *(MOM exits.*
18   *DAD sits silently. A blue arm opens the kitchen window and*
19   *slips several school books onto the sink counter. Moments*
20   *later DAD takes one of the books and tries to read it. He*
21   *covers one eye in an attempt to better see the page. He then*
22   *puts the book down and exits.)*
23
24 **END OF SCENE**
25
26
27 **ACT ONE**
28 **Scene Nine**
29
30 *Near a canal HENRY is assembling a fishing pole. DAD enters.*
31
32 HENRY: Dad. Ah, there's a bunch of fish in there. I saw them
33   swimming. I borrowed the fishing pole and . . . Are you
34   mad?
35 DAD: What are you doing here?

1   HENRY: Fishing?

2   DAD: *¿Cómo?*

3   HENRY: With a fishing pole.

4   DAD: Ah. You don't need a fishing pole. In the ranch, all you

5   needed was some line and a hook. *Mira.* I'll show you. Get

6   this fishing line and wrap it around something. A rock, or

7   a little stick. Then put a hook at the end. *Aquí.* Now put it

8   in the water. This end with the stick, you put in your

9   pocket, but first twist the middle of the line around the

10   button of your *camisa. Así.* When you feel your shirt

11   moving, you got a fish.

12   HENRY: You can catch a fish that way?

13   DAD: *Pescados grandes.*

14   HENRY: Get out of town. You won't catch a thing.

15   DAD: (*DAD waits for the fish. Suddenly, his shirt tugs and a fish*

16   *splashes up.*) *Vamos aver.*

17   HENRY: I don't believe it.

18   DAD: Watch it. Watch it. *Aye.* You let it get away! *Bueno.* That's

19   what it's all about.

20   HENRY: That's totally amazing. I've never seen anything like

21   that. Cool. So utterly cool. (*GIRL appears from across the*

22   *canal. DAD's mood becomes somber.*) Let's do it again over

23   here. Kind of embarrassing in a way, but who cares. We're

24   catching fish. Dad, let's . . . Dad? What's the matter? Dad?

25   Papá? Hey Come on. Don't stop, now. This is the best fun

26   we've had in a long time. Dad? (*DAD is staring at GIRL*

27   *smiling at him. HENRY can't see GIRL.*)

28   DAD: (*Slowly*) I miss Mexico.

29   HENRY: Dad. It's not too far.

30   DAD: *Vamanos.*

31   HENRY: Dad. Geesh. (*Under his breath*) Man, get it together.

32   (*DAD exits. GIRL watches HENRY gather the fishing gear and*

33   *start to go.*)

34

35   **END OF SCENE**

1 **ACT ONE**

2 **Scene Ten**

3

4 *MOM is listening to a "Learn the English Language" tape.*

5

6 **TAPE:** I am hungry.

7 **MOM:** I am hungree.

8 **TAPE:** I am hungry.

9 **MOM:** I am hungry.

10 **TAPE:** Repeat. I am hungry.

11 **MOM:** Repeat I am hungry.

12 **TAPE:** What would you like to eat?

13 **MOM:** Apple pie and coffee.

14 **TAPE:** I am not hungry.

15 **HENRY:** *(Enters)* Mom.

16 **MOM:** Sh!

17 **TAPE:** I am not hungry.

18 **HENRY:** Mom. *(MOM turns off the tape.)*

19 **MOM:** I'm practicing my English. You're bothering me. Making

20   me nervous.

21 **HENRY:** You speak good enough.

22 **MOM:** Oh no. People stare at me when I talk. I have to get rid of

23   the accent.

24 **HENRY:** It's all right Mom.

25 **MOM:** I want to speak properly. No accents.

26 **HENRY:** Mom, even in the English language there are different

27   accents.

28 **MOM:** That's not true.

29 **HENRY:** Yes it is.

30 **MOM:** Well, then, it all sounds the same to me.

31 **HENRY:** But it isn't. Listen to me. Here's one accent. *(Southern*

32   *California accent)* Killer dude. Totally awesome. Freakster.

33   And here's another one. *(Boston accent)* Where's da ca? Or

34   this, *(Chicago south side accent)* Hey, I'a breaka your face.

35 **MOM:** It all sounds the same to me.

1   HENRY: Ma. I'm sure it's like that over there. Regional Spanish?

2   MOM: Well, yes. Different accents. But I liked the first one. I'll

3   speak like that. That accent sounded good.

4   HENRY: The California talking?

5   MOM: Keeler doode. I like that. What does that mean?

6   HENRY: Nothing.

7   MOM: How can something mean nothing?

8   HENRY: Put the tape away.

9   MOM: No. I want to be educated. You can be educated.

10 HENRY: I have enough skills to make it in life.

11 MOM: That's not good enough. Go to college.

12 HENRY: We've talked about this before and you said you'd stop.

13   I want to rap.

14 MOM: Then go rap and I'll study. *(Pause)* You're stubborn like

15   your father.

16 HENRY: Where is he?

17 MOM: He went his way and I went mine. *Hombre tan sonso.*

18 HENRY: Most would leave, Mom.

19 MOM: I can't leave my husband. I'm Catholic. Besides, we were

20   taught not to leave a man if he has some good in him.

21   Anyway, I have to help him.

22 HENRY: Help him do what?

23 MOM: *Nada.*

24 HENRY: What's wrong with him? Is he sick?

25 MOM: No. Go rap.

26 HENRY: What's the matter, then?

27 MOM: I have to listen to my tape. Go. I'll study for the both of us.

28 HENRY: Mom. I'm old enough to know what's going on.

29 MOM: No, you're not. *(Pause.)* Go. You're making this hard on

30   me.

31 HENRY: Sure. I don't want to be a burden. *(HENRY exits. MOM sits*

32   *there quietly for a long moment. She then turns on the tape.)*

33 TAPE RECORDER: *(MOM's voice)* Everyone is a burden. Even

34   memory becomes a burden. The memory of it brings you

35   down. Tears you to pieces. Best to forget and remember only

1   **when you are alone. If the mind was more powerful you**
2   **could tell it to erase things. Then record a different message**
3   **over it. And play what you want to hear again and again.**
4   **TAPE: I am thirsty.**
5   **MOM: I am thirstee.**
6   **TAPE: I am thirsty. Repeat.**
7   **MOM: Repeat.**
8

9   *(MOM turns off the recorder, but it still continues. We hear*
10   *"repeat, repeat, repeat" in a strange way for a while longer. Then*
11   *the "repeat" fades away. MOM walks over to a shoe box. Inside the*
12   *shoe box are several ruffled hair ribbons that belonged to GIRL.*
13   *There is also a small school picture of GIRL. MOM stares at the*
14   *picture. MOM then goes to the refrigerator. As she opens the door,*
15   *a BLUE MEXICAN PEASANT's face is inside and looks out. MOM*
16   *takes a beer and closes the refrigerator door. She then takes some*
17   *paper out of the shoe box and walks over to the trash can. As she*
18   *is ready to toss the paper, a blue arm reaches out of the trash can*
19   *and takes the paper, then crumbles it and disappears into the*
20   *trash can with it. Moments later MOM goes to the sink and slices*
21   *a lime. Outside of the window are several BLUE MEXICAN*
22   *PEASANTS looking miserable. They stare at MOM. She doesn't see*
23   *them. She goes to the table and squeezes the lime slice into the*
24   *beer. She continues to look at the picture. She licks her side wrist,*
25   *sprinkles salt on it and licks the salt off. She then drinks her beer.*
26   *A group of BLUE MEXICAN PEASANTS enter and surround her.*
27   *They have devastated looks on their face. MOM continues looking*
28   *at the picture. She starts to cry and the BLUE MEXICAN*
29   *PEASANTS back off. MOM quickly regains control of herself, and*
30   *the BLUE PEASANTS approach again. They stare at her as if to tell*
31   *her something, but then give up and exit.)*
32

33   **CROSS FADE TO DARKNESS**
34   **END OF SCENE**
35

1 **ACT ONE**

2 **Scene Eleven**

3

4 *GIRL is at the window. She opens it and looks in. Moments later*

5 *HENRY walks past. He then exits. A bit later, DAD enters, gets his*

6 *boots, and exits. MOM then enters and sits at the table to sew a dress.*

7

8 **GIRL: Mommy. Mommy, can you hear me? Mommy! Mommy,**

9 **why don't you open the door. I was out there and you**

10 **didn't even hear me. Where did Dad go? He can hear me.**

11 **You're too busy to hear me. Daddy always hears me. He**

12 **really listens when I speak Spanish. What are you doing?**

13 **Mommy! I'm talking to you. I know, I know, you're too**

14 **busy.** *(Pause)* **Why do you and Daddy fight? It's no good to**

15 **fight. Why do you let him be mean to my brother. You're**

16 **not mean.** *(Pause)* **Mommy, don't go to Salinas without me**

17 **again. I have to stay here all by myself when you go. I get**

18 **scared. I get so scared. Mommy, you never listen to me.**

19 **Listen to me. Listen to me. I hate you. I hate you.** *(MOM*

20 *starts to cry.)* **I'm sorry Mommy. Don't cry. I'll be good. I'll**

21 **be quiet. I'll go outside to play. I'm so sorry.** *(MOM stops*

22 *crying. GIRL feels better.)*

23

24 **CROSS FADE**

25 **END OF SCENE**

26

27 **ACT ONE**

28 **Scene Twelve**

29

30 *DAD enters with a few cantaloupes in his arms. He then turns on*

31 *the radio and hears rap music. He quickly changes it to a Spanish*

32 *radio station. He then listens for a moment and then slices a*

33 *cantaloupe. MOM enters.)*

34

35 **DAD:** *Aye querida.*

1 MOM: You're in a good mood.

2 DAD: I am. Look. I want to talk to you. Have some of this.

3 MOM: What is it?

4 DAD: *¡Melon!*

5 MOM: I know. What do you want to tell me?

6 DAD: Guess.

7 MOM: You quit smoking.

8 DAD: No.

9 MOM: Well, you should. You stink up the house.

10 DAD: Guess again.

11 MOM: You quit drinking.

12 DAD: No.

13 MOM: Then it's not good news.

14 DAD: I got a job.

15 MOM: You got a job?

16 DAD: A better one than the fields.

17 MOM: Is that why you left so early?

18 DAD: I had to.

19 MOM: They were asking me where you were. I told them you

20   were urinating. You still didn't come back so I told them

21   you had infection on your "***pito***." *(pronounced "peet-to")*

22 DAD: Why did you tell them that?

23 MOM: I had to.

24 DAD: Anyway, I did go to urinate, then I saw Julio.

25 MOM: Julio!?

26 DAD: He's starting a business.

27 MOM: *(Suspicious)* What kind of business?

28 DAD: A restaurant. He wants me to be a partner.

29 MOM: He wants you to put all the money in. You know I don't

30   trust him.

31 DAD: Neither do I, but it's a chance.

32 MOM: A chance for what? To lose what you already have?

33 DAD: What do I have? I have nothing. How can I lose nothing?

34   The Salvadorians are taking the field work from us. They

35   do the work for practically nothing. Soon they'll be doing

1   all the work. There's so many of them who are trying to

2   survive like us.

3   MOM: What are you going to do in that restaurant, wash

4   dishes?

5   DAD: I did that before. This time, I get to be in charge. I'll be the

6   boss. If I only give Julio money today to —

7   MOM: (*Overlapping on "money"*) We have no money.

8   DAD: We have some hidden.

9   MOM: That's not ours.

10   DAD: We'll use a little and then replace it.

11   MOM: It's not ours. We're giving it to Henry when he decides to

12   go to college.

13   DAD: It came from our suffering. Think about our future. He

14   will benefit from it.

15   MOM: I didn't come to this country to steal from my child.

16   DAD: He doesn't know he has it. He's not serious about school.

17   He won't be for a long time and by that time, I'll have

18   replaced it two times over.

19   MOM: No. My son means more to me than that stupid

20   restaurant.

21   DAD: (*Overlapping on "than"*) Than me?

22   MOM: Than that restaurant.

23   DAD: What about me? What about me? (*Long tension-filled*

24   *silence. DAD goes to the shoe box. He throws out the*

25   *contents and holds a picture of GIRL.*) Do it for her!

26   MOM: Julio will make you eat dirt.

27   DAD: Give it to me.

28   MOM: He's not doing anything for you. Only for himself.

29   DAD: It's a chance! . . . It's a chance. Listen to me, *querida*. We

30   have to work together the way the Koreans do. You know

31   when they come to this country they have nothing. Just

32   like us, nothing. Then all the members of the family put

33   their money together and buy one store. They all work it,

34   bumping into each other, day and night, saving all the

35   profits, until they pay for the store. Then they buy another

1   store, and together work that one until they have enough
2   to buy another one, then another one, then another one.
3   Finally, all the members who put their money in for the
4   first store, get their own store at the end. They do this all
5   the time. That's how they have all the grocery stores. And
6   we're grateful for at least they are selling tortillas.
7 MOM: (*Pause*) None of those Koreans went into partnership
8   with Julio. It's with their own families they do such
9   things. No one cheats a family member and if they do, the
10   whole family tells him to go to hell.
11 DAD: My family is all over and they are more miserable than
12   me! That is why I am going to use the money with Julio.
13 MOM: No, you're not.
14 DAD: Yes, I am.
15 MOM: No, you're not.
16 DAD: *Querida*. This time you are wrong.
17 MOM: Our son is our only chance for self-respect.
18 DAD: Because I didn't give it to you?
19 MOM: We are immigrants to this country. I didn't come with
20   high expectations. It's foolish to have —
21 DAD: (*Overlapping on "foolish"*) Foolish to have high
22   expectations of this country, or me.
23 MOM: Not with my son's college money.
24 DAD: Then with what? (*MOM covers her ears to avoid listening.*
25   *DAD looks at her wedding ring. She notices this, and after a*
26   *long moment slips off the ring and gives it to DAD. DAD then*
27   *starts to exit.*) You are a strong woman for doing this.
28   (*Pause*) Julio also thanks you. (*He exits.*)
29 MOM: Julio is a *pinche cabron*. And so are you.
30
31 **END OF SCENE**
32
33
34
35

1   ACT ONE

2   Scene Thirteen

3

4   *OLIVERIO is pushing a wheelbarrow across the field. DAD walks*

5   *by holding a plastic bag with money inside.*

6

7   OLIVERIO: *Estrellas, estrellas, estrellas. Muchas estrellas.*

8   *(HENRY sneaks up to scare OLIVERIO.)* **Ep-pa.**

9   HENRY: Scared you.

10   OLIVERIO: Scared me like a ghost.

11   HENRY: I got good news. Remember that girl I told you about?

12   OLIVERIO: No.

13   HENRY: Yeah, you remember, old man. She's going to Mesa

14   College. It's a good way to get the hell out of here if you got

15   the money.

16   OLIVERIO: Those *gringos* like to use Spanish names for

17   everything now. One time, everything here, was named in

18   Spanish. They changed them to English, and now back to

19   Spanish to sell it as high real estate. Ha-ci-en-da Heights,

20   ugh. La Play-zza di May-you, ehh. Yor-ba Lin-da. Es yerba

21   linda. Such a travesty to corrupt a beautiful language. At

22   least their gardeners say the names correctly. Ah! A

23   beautiful night. Oh, look. Isn't that beautiful? Let's see

24   how smart you are. What is it?

25   HENRY: A star.

26   OLIVERIO: What is it really?

27   HENRY: A meteorite?

28   OLIVERIO: No. It's a mass with gas. That's what we are. And, we

29   are all the same. Should be no names, no labels, no

30   political affiliation. All those things make war.

31   Understand? *(No answer)* Someday you will. *(They see a*

32   *falling star.)* See that one going down? . . . Has a lot of gas.

33   Too many tacos. *(HENRY's not amused.)* What's the matter?

34   Life can be fought with a smile and a little joking. For that

35   matter, death. When you're my age, you won't care about

1   too many things. Too much effort. Will give you ulcers.

2   *(Burps.)*

3 **HENRY: How old are you?**

4 **OLIVERIO: Why do you want to know? Isn't it enough to see the**

5   **gray hair and the wrinkles running into each other?**

6   *(Smiles.)* **Did you know that the tears of the clown are so**

7   **true.**

8 **HENRY: What?**

9 **OLIVERIO: He cries.**

10   **There's tears painted on his face, but he cries.**

11   **He cries from what he feels inside.**

12   **"*Las lágrimas*"**

13   **It's painted on the face**

14   **But he smiles**

15   **Do you know why he smiles? . . .**

16   **He smiles because he learned that he has to face a**

17   **situation,**

18   **with the opposite.** *(No response)*

19   **I've learned that true wisdom comes with death.** *(No*

20   *response)* **Your girlfriend is going to college? Go yourself.**

21   **Maybe what I learned in the fields someone with a degree**

22   **can teach you.**

23 **HENRY: Money problems, *hombre.* Plus why should I? Where's**

24   **it going to take me?**

25 **OLIVERIO: At least to show that some dirt can mix with the**

26   **white sand. Look my boy, someday you'll find that money**

27   **doesn't make you happy. It's the work. If you like what you**

28   **do, then you'll care less about the money and the things**

29   **you can get with it.**

30 **HENRY: That's what you're trying to tell me? My parents are**

31   **picking for me? Give me a break.**

32 **OLIVERIO: No. They're picking for everybody.** *(HENRY looks at*

33   *OLIVERIO for a long moment, then exits. At that moment,*

34   *GIRL appears. OLIVERIO sees GIRL and goes to her.)* **Are**

35   **you ready?**

1   GIRL: In English?
2   OLIVERIO: Will you interrupt?
3   GIRL: I don't know.
4   OLIVERIO: You always do. All right. Ready? In the eyes of a
5   child.
6   GIRL: The child sees so much.
7   OLIVERIO: Rainbows never pass without mention.
8   GIRL: Ooohh. I liked that one.
9   OLIVERIO: The face brightens
10   in peaceful acknowledgment of the colors
11   The cheeks of a child
12   soft, soft
13   soft pillows of joy
14   When pressed against a parent's face
15   Brings more colors of happiness
16   and even more joy.
17 GIRL: Can I sing?
18 OLIVERIO: And from the tenderness of the lips
19   A voice so pure exists
20   Making all who have saddened
21   A temporary haven
22   One that will only continue
23   If you insist
24   The baby cries
25   And sounds so demanding
26   Deciding quickly what the child needs
27 GIRL: *(Interrupts on "child")* I have a little brother. His name is
28   Enrigue
29   That's what my father said was his name.
30   I told you teacher. Enrigue. His name is Enrigue.
31   She said "Henry. His name is Henry."
32   Your name is Henry.
33 OLIVERIO: He needs everything. Mother, father, soil
34   All the tools to begin.
35 GIRL: I'm going to teach him English. So they don't make fun

1   of him. He'll be good in school, like me.

2   **OLIVERIO: Pity those who don't understand.** *(OLIVERIO exits*

3   *as a group of MEXICAN BLUE PEASANTS enter and sit*

4   *around GIRL.)*

5   **GIRL: OK everyone. Are you ready? Itzy bitzy spider, went up**

6   **the water spout. Down came the rain and washed the**

7   **spider out.** *(The PEASANTS then gently grab GIRL. She goes*

8   *limp. They toss her in the movement of water going through*

9   *an irrigation canal. In this stylized dance of water rushing*

10   *they exit with GIRL. DAD enters and runs toward them. He*

11   *doesn't reach GIRL in time.)*

12   **DAD:** *¡HIJA!*

13

14

15   **END OF SCENE**

16

17

18   **ACT ONE**

19   **Scene Fourteen**

20

21   *Lights up on HENRY. He is watching DAD in the distance. They*

22   *are both being watched by the BLUE MEXICAN PEASANTS. DAD*

23   *drops to his knees. Cross fade to OLIVERIO and HENRY.*

24

25   **HENRY: You like to pick?**

26   **OLIVERIO: I like the life on the farm.**

27   **HENRY: It's degrading.**

28   **OLIVERIO: To you maybe, but to me, it's wonderful. Seeing**

29   **how God makes a seed grow from a soil that is black like**

30   **hell.**

31   **HENRY: It's hell all right.**

32   **OLIVERIO: Feeling the sun that can silently peel your skin**

33   **from its intense rays.**

34   **HENRY: I only tan on a beach.**

35   **OLIVERIO: From water that comes all the way from the**

1   mountains in the north, then through these canals.
2   Canals that hold life. They can also hold death. Are you
3   afraid to die?
4 HENRY: No.
5 OLIVERIO: Death is a blanket. It stops life, yet it's the
6   beginning of something else. Go home now. Your parents
7   need you.
8 HENRY: Maybe I will go away. Just leave with twenty cents in
9   my pocket and make a life.
10 OLIVERIO: Sounds familiar.
11 HENRY: My dad said he did that.
12 OLIVERIO: I had ten cents in my pocket. Will you follow your
13   father's footsteps?
14 HENRY: What do you think?
15 OLIVERIO: I think you made up your mind. Go then.
16 HENRY: (*Hesitates.*) I will.
17 OLIVERIO: Get what you need for the road, but travel light.
18   Good luck.
19 HENRY: I'm going. Don't rush me.
20 OLIVERIO: What kind of work will you find?
21 HENRY: What do you mean, what kind of work?
22 OLIVERIO: You have to survive. I worked in the fields for
23   money to pay for food. Don't tell me you have an American
24   Express card?
25 HENRY: I'll rap.
26 OLIVERIO: (*Confused*) How much they pay you?
27 HENRY: Thousands of dollars if you're good. That's the
28   profession I want. I want to feel important.
29 OLIVERIO: The oldest profession in the world is just as
30   important.
31 HENRY: The oldest profession in the world?
32 OLIVERIO: Without it, there would be no population.
33 HENRY: The oldest profession in the world is —
34 OLIVERIO: Farming. That's the oldest profession in the world.
35   Think about it.

1   HENRY: I will. *(HENRY walks to his home. DAD is there waiting*
2   *for him.)*
3   DAD: Enrigue. I'll need your help in the restaurant.
4   HENRY: What restaurant?
5   MOM: Your father bought a partnership with Julio.
6   HENRY: He's a drunk, Dad.
7   DAD: I'll be running the business. You work as a busboy.
8   HENRY: No way.
9   DAD: *¿Por qué no?*
10 HENRY: *(Hesitates.)* 'Cause, I'm going to school.
11 DAD: What school?
12 HENRY: The junior college. Mesa College.
13 MOM: I want you to go to the state college.
14 DAD: You're not even serious about life. How are you going to
15   go?
16 HENRY: What if I get a scholarship?
17 MOM: This is wonderful. I knew it. Henry, I want to show you
18   something. Oh, your father and I worked hard for this.
19   We've managed to scrape up some money for you. I've been
20   sewing for ladies to add to it. I hope you'll appreciate it. We
21   obligated ourselves to save it for you. So your life would be
22   better. It's not that much, but at least you can pay for a few
23   classes, books and — *(As she speaks she reaches for the*
24   *envelope in the hole. The BLUE MEXICAN PEASANTS look*
25   *through the window. MOM doesn't find the Ziplock™ bag*
26   *with the envelope of money. She turns to DAD.)* You took it!
27 DAD: Julio needed more. I had to do it. No more dirt on my
28   fingers. No more getting my hands moist from the
29   *"canales de muerte."* You know how I hate working *los*
30   *canales*, as well as the fields.
31 MOM: He's our only hope.
32 DAD: What about me? You're married to me, not to him.
33 MOM: You took the money that belonged to him. *(HENRY runs*
34   *out. OLIVERIO catches him and they embrace.)*
35 DAD: Everything that comes into this house is mine. I can do

1 **whatever I want with it.** *(MOM and DAD stare at each other*
2 *as the lights turn blue, then exit. Then the BLUE MEXICAN*
3 *PEASANTS enter wearing skull masks. They strip the house*
4 *of all its furniture. They place a microwave in the room. "Itzy*
5 *Bitzy Spider" is heard faintly in the distance.)*
6
7
8 **END OF ACT ONE**
9
10
11 **ACT TWO**
12 **Scene One**
13
14 *The room is bare. There is a microwave in the kitchen. MOM is*
15 *chopping oranges in strong strokes that pattern her anger.*
16
17 **HENRY: Mom. Mom. Have you used the microwave? I was**
18 **lucky. I won it at the school raffle. I never win anything**
19 **and I got it. I wanted the bike, but the microwave was the**
20 **second prize. You can cook tortillas in it.** *(DAD is cursing in*
21 *the other room.)* **What's his problem?** *(No answer)* **You two**
22 **keep things from me. I wish I had a sibling to team up**
23 **with me against you two. Sibling. What a funny word.**
24 **Sounds like chicken.**
25 **MOM:** *(Stunned, then threatens to strike)* **I'm going to break your**
26 **mouth.**
27 **HENRY: Why? What did I do?**
28 **MOM: Get out of my sight, you snake in the grass.** *(About to*
29 *strike HENRY but he grabs her arm.)*
30 **HENRY: I'm not a snake! Call me anything, but that.**
31 **MOM: Oh, my God. I'm turning into your father.**
32 **HENRY: Some kind of compulsion. Beat the kid.**
33 **MOM: Enrigue. He stopped it, didn't he? I told him *no more* of**
34 **that behavior.** *(HENRY starts rapping with sound effects.*
35 *DAD enters.)*

1   DAD: *¿Qué está pasando aquí? Tú sabes qué no me gusta* rap.

2   MOM: *(Exploding)* You said Julio knew what to do.

3   DAD: He had the place rented for two months.

4   MOM: He strings people along.

5   HENRY: How much did Julio take you for?

6   MOM: Even your own son knows about Julio.

7   HENRY: Everyone knows about Julio. He stands in front of the
8   school waiting to gyp someone. If he thinks you got
9   something, he goes after you. When I was coming home
10   with the microwave, he tried to give me a ring for it. I told
11   him to get lost.

12 MOM: Did you see the ring?

13 HENRY: No. He said he had it in a safe place.

14 DAD: Why didn't you tell me this before?

15 HENRY: Because you never asked. *(Silence. HENRY then goes to*
16   *the refrigerator and gets three beers. He gives one to MOM*
17   *and DAD, and gets one for himself. He pops open his beer.)*

18

19 **SLOW BLACKOUT**

20 **END OF SCENE ONE**

21

22

23 **ACT TWO**

24 **Scene Two**

25

26 *In the fields. A glimmer of stars. The BLUE MEXICAN PEASANTS*
27 *walk across holding baskets of fruit, a baby bundle, and a television*
28 *set. A somber MOM follows them with the shoebox. They exit.*
29 *Much later, OLIVERIO enters to see the stars. HENRY then enters.*
30 *He sees OLIVERIO, but wants to walk past, avoiding him.*

31

32 OLIVERIO: Where are you coming from and where are you
33   going? Come on. Relax. Soon life will be over and all that
34   has preoccupied you will not be that important anymore.
35   Ignoring me? Fine. Then I'll talk to myself. I'll make up a

1   poem right here as you walk away.

2   *El espíritu te envia*

3   *El corazón se enternece*

4   *La vida se va*

5   *Sin todos los muebles*

6 HENRY: What does that mean?

7 OLIVERIO: How the hell should I know.

8 HENRY: But you said it.

9 OLIVERIO: I only speak from the heart. A lot of times I don't

10   know what it means.

11 HENRY: That doesn't make sense.

12 OLIVERIO: Oh, but it does. It's much later when I figure them

13   out. But by that time, it's too late. I've already lost the

14   original feeling of the poem and feel something else. Then

15   there comes a new poem, and I have to figure that out, too.

16   It gets to be too much, but I write a lot of poems that way.

17   I meant it. Where are you going?

18 HENRY: I don't know. I have to get away.

19 OLIVERIO: From what?

20 HENRY: From everything. From my parents. I'm going crazy

21   with them. I don't know who they are or what they want

22   from me. You know, I don't always understand the way

23   they talk. How come they don't talk like you?

24 OLIVERIO: Poetry?

25 HENRY: No. In simple English so I can understand. I get bits

26   and pieces and I know I miss the rest. They know too, but

27   say nothing.

28 OLIVERIO: Henry. Language doesn't mean a thing. It's what's

29   here, in the heart, that speaks. *(Long moment)* There's

30   your girlfriend's star. Have you seen her lately?

31 HENRY: Yeah. She made me mad by touching my arm. So I hit her.

32 OLIVERIO: Oh boy. You're a handful. Why I got you, I'll never

33   know.

34 HENRY: What?

35 OLIVERIO: Look at that star.

1   HENRY: I have no more stars to look at.

2   OLIVERIO: Then look at the moon. The moon looks so

3   innocent, and at times it realizes it's not. So it goes away

4   for awhile to think things out. And then it returns to try

5   again. Each time it fails, but it keeps coming back to try

6   again. A new poem.

7   *La luna no sabe*

8   *Como todos la miran*

9   *Ella siempre va y viene*

10   *Para qué todos la admiran*

11   HENRY: What the hell does that mean?

12   OLIVERIO: I just recite them, I don't explain them. Anyway, if I

13   did tell you, it would lose its mystery. It's not what the

14   words mean. It's how the language makes you feel. If you

15   feel the meaning, then why do you need to know the

16   words?

17   HENRY: Because, if you don't know the words, you get hit.

18   OLIVERIO: There's meaning even behind that. Don't always

19   listen to the sounds of the whip. Feel the meaning behind it.

20   HENRY: I'll never understand you, or them!

21   OLIVERIO: You will always think about us. Even when you are

22   far away. Even if you run away up here, you'll think about

23   us. See those stars. You think about them even when you

24   don't see them, especially on those foggy nights. You'll

25   think, "Where are the stars? I know they are there."

26   Another poem.

27   *¿Dónde están las estrellas?*

28   *Los guiero con toda mí alma*

29   *Brillan orgullosas*

30   *Aun cuando nos dormimos* (HENRY exits.)

31   Where are the stars

32   I love them will all my life

33   They shine with pride

34   Even when we sleep.

35

1   Boy, that sounds like crap in English

2   *(With some passion)*

3   *Cuando ellas brillan*

4   *Mí tristeza resultan*

5   *Y mís lagrimas caen*

6   *Quiero decirle a mí gente*

7   *Qué no sé vayan muy lejos*

8   *Y siempre recuerdan*

9   *de las mañanitas allegres*

10

11 END OF SCENE

12

13

14 ACT TWO

15 Scene Three

16

17 *HENRY is at the kitchen table doing his homework. DAD enters*

18 *and stands there, staring at HENRY.*

19

20 HENRY: Dad, I have homework to do. *(No response. Still more*

21   *staring)* Dad, leave me alone. I'm doing *tarea.*

22 DAD: *Tarea. ¡Digalo bien!*

23 HENRY: *Tengo ser me tarea. Adesso.*

24 DAD: *Adesso? Eso es Italiano.*

25 HENRY: I like Italian. And for your information, that's where

26   I'll go if I'm going to travel. *There,* or Egypt. See, I already

27   know about Mexico.

28 DAD: No, you don't. I thought I knew everything about the

29   United States, and when I came here, I was mistaken.

30   Where's your mother?

31 HENRY: She went to class.

32 DAD: I told her not to go.

33 HENRY: Give her a break.

34 DAD: She's planning to leave me. *(Long pause.)* In this house,

35   *vamos hablar puro Español, des de ahora.*

1 HENRY: Speak in Spanish only? Not in our life.

2 DAD: You're going to write your homework in Spanish. And if
3   you don't, out you go.

4 HENRY: I'll go! *(HENRY gets up, but DAD grabs him and throws*
5   *him on the chair.)* I'll fail if I write this in Spanish.

6 DAD: I failed, too! *Comiensa su tarea en Español.*

7 HENRY: Dad!

8 DAD: *¡En este momento! ¡Andale!* *(DAD pushes HENRY off the*
9   *chair.)*

10 HENRY: Go to hell! *(DAD pulls out his belt. A BLUE MEXICAN*
11   *PEASANT appears. He is holding a belt and watches the*
12   *action.)*

13 DAD: *Venga aquí. Lloron.* You baby.

14 HENRY: Baby? I saw you near the canal, crying! *Crying!* You are
15   a grown man who cries near the canal! Macho, macho,
16   macho.

17 DAD: I'm going to kill you.

18 HENRY: Go ahead and do it! It just doesn't hurt me anymore!

19 DAD: If your mother could hear you talking to me in this way.

20 HENRY: If I told her you never stopped, she'd leave you! And
21   you would be solo! *Muy solo.*

22 DAD: So you think I'm an animal?

23 HENRY: No dad. I think you're crazy. *(DAD is about to strike*
24   *HENRY, but HENRY protects himself by picking up a basket*
25   *of laundry and throwing it towards DAD.)*

26 DAD: You run from *su Papá*, and I'll beat you harder.

27 HENRY: *¡Tú no eres mí papá!*

28 DAD: *Venga aquí.*

29 HENRY: No. You're going to hit me.

30 DAD: I'll hit you harder if you don't come *en este momento.*

31 HENRY: You'll hit me anyway. *(DAD stares at HENRY for a long*
32   *time. HENRY weakens to his DAD's authority. He then*
33   *approaches DAD, stops, and turns around to get hit.)*

34 DAD: I'll kill you.

35 HENRY: Go ahead. Being dead is better than this.

1   **DAD:** *En Español.*

2   **HENRY: No.** *(DAD raises the belt and at the top, freezes. The BLUE*

3   *MEXICAN PEASANTS start swinging belts in slow motion*

4   *during HENRY's monologue. HENRY will be stoic as he*

5   *speaks, staring straight out.)* **See, Dad. It was bound to**

6   **happen. I got used to it. I got used to all the beatings. Ever**

7   **wonder if that would happen? This is not how you get**

8   **respect. If only I had brothers and sisters to share in this**

9   **delightful activity. If only they'd been here to either take**

10   **it with me, or help me in telling you how wrong you are in**

11   **doing this. Ever since I was little I had to cover what you**

12   **did to me. I had to have a smile on my face and pretend**

13   **nothing happened. So no one would suspect. Never see my**

14   **shame. Never let anyone know what happens in this**

15   **house. Keep hitting me, dad, if it makes you feel better.**

16   **After all, this is your house. I am a snake in the grass for**

17   **not understanding you. For being too young and stupid to**

18   **know why you hurt. I will always remember the beatings**

19   **with pity for you, because the scars of this will be a lot**

20   **deeper for you.**

21   **DAD:** *(Unfreezes)* **¡Llora! ¡Llora!** *(As he unfreezes, the PEASANTS*

22   *stop whipping the air. They express silent pain. DAD ends*

23   *his swing.)* **Ya. You will respect your father.** *(HENRY exits.*

24   *DAD stands there staring at the belt for a long time. He then*

25   *goes to the refrigerator for a beer. Mexican waltz music as*

26   *GIRL enters. DAD sees her and they come together to dance.*

27   *DAD is enjoying his dance with his daughter. They continue*

28   *dancing on the next lines.)*

29   **GIRL:** *Papi.*

30   **DAD:** *Sí, mija.*

31   **GIRL: Love me?**

32   **DAD: With all my heart.**

33   **GIRL: Love Enrigue?**

34   **DAD:** *(Breaks down)* **Sí.** *(They continue dancing. Then GIRL stops*

35   *and exits. Softly)* **No! Come back. Come back to me!**

1   (*Sobbing.*) *Aye, hija.* Why do you keep leaving me? Why do
2   you go? I miss you so much. I missed you when I was at
3   work. I missed you when you started to grow from a baby.
4   You were so independent. Strong like your mother. Nothing
5   could hurt you. Then you started to mistreat me by learning
6   a language I couldn't understand. You came home to sing
7   songs that had no meaning to me. I couldn't understand. In
8   my own home I couldn't understand your voice. I couldn't
9   learn. I was too busy in the fields. You don't talk to anyone
10 when you work the fields. You have no time. As each day
11 passed, you became a stranger to me. I gave you life.
12 (*Attempting to be in control*) It would have been nice if you
13 said a few words in *español* before you . . . Forgive me for
14 punishing you on the day you died. I will never lose that
15 guilt. (*DAD turns to see MOM and HENRY in a light in the*
16 *background. HENRY is covered with large bruises.*) I hit him
17 only because I need to make a man out of him. It's true,
18 Henry. (*MOM takes a breath.*) I'm preparing him for what
19 will happen out there. (*Lights fade out on MOM and HENRY.*)
20 Is everyone leaving me? Is everyone leaving this man who
21 has nothing? Nothing but misery? You think the devil is me?
22 I'll wrestle with the devil. I'll take him by the neck and force
23 him to get away from me. At night, he comes and tells me
24 what a failure I am. I wake up and see that he is right. (*BLUE*
25 *MEXICAN PEASANTS enter. They are wearing hideous masks.*
26 *The one wearing the devil mask coaxes DAD to fight with*
27 *him.*) I drink so I'd be too drunk to go with you. I know why
28 you do this to me. No matter how foolish my decisions are,
29 I'm a good man, and you can't stand that. (*Pause*) It's not my
30 fault. This is what I was taught. To make them good. She
31 didn't listen to me, and dirtied her dress. The dress her
32 mother and I worked so hard to buy. I hit her for dirtying
33 her dress. She ran to the canal to wash it, and then, she fell.
34 She ended up washing her dress with tears. And my tears
35 have never stopped.

1   **SLOW BLACK OUT**

2   **END OF SCENE**

3

4

5   **ACT TWO**

6   **Scene Four**

7

8   *HENRY has the rap music on very loud, and is on the furniture*

9   *dancing to it. The BLUE MEXICAN PEASANTS are dancing, too.*

10 *MOM enters after a few moments, not too surprised for his acting*

11 *out his frustration. She's frustrated too. The MEXICAN*

12 *PEASANTS exit.*

13

14 **MOM: Henry, get down.**

15 **HENRY: No.**

16 **MOM: Don't punish me, get down.** *(He won't.)* **Henry. Henry.**

17   **Henry.**

18 **HENRY:** *(With the rap)* **I'm black and blue. I'm black and blue.**

19 **MOM: Stop it.**

20 **HENRY: Don't you get it, Mom? It's an English expression.**

21 **MOM: Stop it.**

22 **HENRY: You just don't get it. I'm black and blue!**

23 **MOM:** *(She turns off the music.)* **Stop it, Enrigue.**

24 **HENRY: No, I'm E.B.J.**

25 **MOM: No, you are my son and I want you to sit down. I want to**

26   **explain something to you.**

27 **HENRY: Explain what to me? Why I get beat?**

28 **MOM: Henry! He only gets this way when he's frustrated.**

29 **HENRY: I'm frustrated. I'm suffering here worse than that**

30   **tearful Madonna. And what have you done? Stand there**

31   **while it was happening – You closed your eyes mom, and**

32   **I can't forgive you.**

33 **MOM: I didn't close my eyes. I've told him to stop.**

34 **HENRY: He didn't, Mom.**

35 **MOM: He said he would.**

1   HENRY: He didn't.

2   MOM: Then why didn't you tell me?

3   HENRY: Because I thought I loved you.

4   MOM: Henry.

5   HENRY: What?

6   MOM: *(Losing her temper)* Don't talk to me like that. Don't you
7   talk to me like that. I'm your mother. You don't know what
8   I do for you. Both of you blaming me!? I'm stuck between
9   two stubborn boys who are fighting. Don't you think I get
10   tired of this? Do you think I'm made of stone? Don't you
11   see how I mourn for the way you two behave? I'm sick and
12   tired of going between you and your father. Never
13   appreciation from the two of you. You think I'm on your
14   father's side when I ask you to have pity for him. He
15   thinks I'm on your side when I ask him to let you be a
16   teenager. It is impossible to be both judge and lawyer. The
17   two of you have been spoiled by my understanding
18   attitude. Let me make this clear today and at this moment.
19   I'm finished with protecting you from each other. At this
20   point, I could care less if you kill each other. Go ahead. I
21   don't have a family. I lost it a long time ago. I have animals
22   living in here and I've had it! *(She exits.)*

23 HENRY: *(Starts rapping sounds.)* Now you know,
24   Now you know, Now you know
25   Why I'm black and blue. *(Ends with rapping sounds.)*

26

27 **END OF SCENE**

28

29

30 **ACT TWO**

31 **Scene Five**

32

33 *HENRY is in the field rapping. OLIVERIO hears him and goes to*
34 *him.*

35

1   **HENRY:** Yo

2   And my name is Eee

3   E.B. Jay

4   I'm here to find the only way

5   To tell you who, who I really am

6   But first,

7   I'm no fool

8   Stop messing with my mind

9   Or I'll give you a fight

10   Yo

11   Word to your mother. Olé.

12   **OLIVERIO:** *Dios mío.* If this is poetry, I'm getting out of town.

13   **HENRY:** I am. As soon as I get my act together, I'm gone. *Hasta*

14   *la vista.* Word to your mother.

15   **OLIVERIO:** You're stepping on her. If you need help with your

16   poetry, you knew I was here.

17   **HENRY:** I need no help from you.

18   **OLIVERIO:** What is E.B.J.? Sounds like some disease you get

19   from mosquitoes. You need help with the words. Right

20   now, it sounds like you put them together with spit. I put

21   the words together with dust.

22   **HENRY:** Stop with the dust business. I'm bored of it. Alright?

23   **OLIVERIO:** So you want to be a poet.

24   **HENRY:** A rapper.

25   **OLIVERIO:** A clapper?

26   **HENRY:** A *Rap-per.* Get out of here, man.

27   **OLIVERIO:** Your verse stinks.

28   **HENRY:** Go away.

29   **OLIVERIO:** What's the first line?

30   **HENRY:** What?

31   **OLIVERIO:** To that ugly thing you were singing.

32   **HENRY:** Damn. I think I said "yo."

33   **OLIVERIO:** Yo?

34   **HENRY:** Yo. It's not Spanish.

35   **OLIVERIO:** What does it mean?

1   HENRY: It's how you say it.

2   OLIVERIO: *Las palabras dicen mucho.*

3   HENRY: What are you doing?

4   OLIVERIO: *Pero lo qué dicen, no es todo la verdad.*

5   HENRY: (*Translating reluctantly*) The words say a lot. But it's not

6   what they say that is, that is, happening.

7   OLIVERIO: *Cuando me siento mal.*

8   HENRY: (*More into it*) But when I feel very sad.

9   OLIVERIO: *Necessito su paciencia.*

10   HENRY: All I really want is your patience. Patience? Shit, when

11   I'm black and blue.

12   OLIVERIO: People share their hopes and pains. That's part of

13   life. Don't expect things to change so fast. Unnatural when

14   it does. Are you going to be a clapper?

15   HENRY: You mean a rap-per? I don't know. (*OLIVERIO picks up*

16   *a clump of grass.*)

17   OLIVERIO: You got to be patient. Sometimes the plant takes its

18   time. Other times, the weeds choke it. But the plant still

19   sucks water from the ground, pollinates, and feeds the

20   people. That's a beautiful plant for you. Look. A worm is

21   hiding in between the roots. Get out little fellow. Find

22   another place to rest your body. Then come back and

23   nourish the soil. Go. Go churn the ground with your

24   friends so it's ready for the seeds.

25   HENRY: A bird is going to eat that worm.

26   OLIVERIO: It has to take his chances.

27   HENRY: (*Pause*) Maybe he needs a star. (*OLIVERIO disappears*

28   *and MOM enters. She gives HENRY the picture of GIRL.*)

29   MOM: Go to your father. He's finally ready to explain her to you.

30   (*HENRY looks at the picture then at MOM. He exits.*)

31

32   **END OF SCENE**

33

34

35

1   **ACT TWO**

2   **Scene Six**

3

4   *HENRY enters and sees DAD. HENRY is outraged. He holds out the*

5   *picture of GIRL. DAD drops his head in pain.*

6

7   **HENRY: Who is she, Dad?** *(DAD won't look at the picture.)* **Who is**

8   **she? She's someone you're ashamed of? Someone you've**

9   **been hiding? I get it. I get the whole picture. It comes as a**

10   **shock, Dad, but I should have figured it out. You had a**

11   **child from some other woman, and the guilt has been**

12   **eating you up inside.** *(DAD is silent. He is almost suffocating*

13   *with grief.)* **Come on! Come on!** *(DAD won't move. He is*

14   *frozen. Finally HENRY pulls out his belt and is about to*

15   *smack DAD with it when the MEXICAN BLUE PEASANTS*

16   *enter and shake their index fingers and heads "no." GIRL*

17   *enters and DAD and her eyes meet.)*

18   **GIRL: Daddy?**

19   **DAD: *Mija.*** *(GIRL exits.)* **No!**

20   **HENRY: *Who is she?!*** *(DAD looks all around for her and can't find*

21   *GIRL. In desperation, he grabs the picture and then looks at*

22   *HENRY with the belt. They look at each other for a long time,*

23   *then DAD turns away, and HENRY drops the belt after seeing*

24   *the look in DAD's eyes.)*

25   **DAD:** *(Softly)* **If you ever want to kill me, I give you permission.**

26   **Why would I want to live anyway? I'm no good. I hurt the**

27   **people I love. I can't give you a better life. I am ashamed of**

28   **myself at every turn. I make mistakes every single day.**

29   **The picture is the next beautiful thing to your mother. I**

30   **never wanted to tell you about this because I didn't want**

31   **you to suffer like me . . .** *(Pause)* **You and your mother have**

32   **a connection I envy. We wanted two children. A son for her**

33   **and a daughter for me. We had made plans to spoil each**

34   **one in our own private way. Then she went away . . . I had**

35   **the love of a daughter and she went away. She is your**

1   sister. One year after you were born, she was taken away
2   from me. From your mother and I. I have not been able to
3   forget her. Do you know what kind of pain is in your
4   stomach when you see a child you've given life to sink to
5   the bottom of the water? . . . . No. You don't understand
6   my pain. No one does. Your mother is a strong woman
7   and she let God have her fifteen years ago. But I couldn't
8   let her go. I want to hold her every day. I want to touch
9   her hair and the ruffles on her dress. I didn't get a chance
10   to love her! . . . To think she would have been married by
11   now. *(HENRY has been retreating.)* I blame myself. I am a
12   stupid man . . . Come back here with your belt and *"dame*
13   *shingasos."* I deserve it for what I have done to you. I let
14   misery take me away. This house and the one in Salinas
15   have had misery imprinted on the walls. It's time to wash
16   it away. *(Silence)*
17 HENRY: Dad. You have a son left. *(They hesitate, then hug.)*
18
19 **END OF SCENE**
20
21
22 **ACT TWO**
23 **Scene Seven**
24
25 *In back, rap music is playing loudly. Light on a sofa chair. DAD is*
26 *sitting there listening to the rap music. The expressions on his*
27 *face alternate from: "Rap isn't too bad," "I'll give it chance," "It's*
28 *OK," "There's some good in it," etc. HENRY enters, wearing*
29 *glasses and holding a book bag.*
30
31 HENRY: Dad? Dad! You like that?
32 **DAD:** *(Nods his head with the beat, then)* I like it. I like rap.
33   Spanish, English, whatever. *(HENRY smiles as he watches*
34   *his DAD's head nod up and down with the beat. He starts to*
35   *exit and passes MOM. MOM has huge pieces of paper stuffed*

1   *in her ears. HENRY waves to her and she waves back smiling.*
2   *He exits.)*
3
4   **END OF SCENE**
5
6
7   **ACT TWO**
8   **Scene Eight**
9
10   *OLIVERIO is in the field staring at the stars. HENRY enters.*
11
12   **HENRY: Hey.**
13   **OLIVERIO: Hello.**
14   **HENRY: Where've you been?**
15   **OLIVERIO: Where've you been?**
16   **HENRY: No place. Just doing a little studying, and . . . Hanging**
17   **out with my dad. Can you believe it?**
18   **OLIVERIO: What about the clapping?**
19   **HENRY: Rapping? Nothing . . . I came to tell you that –**
20   **OLIVERIO:** *(Overlapping on "you")* **I already know.** *(HENRY*
21   *smiles and turns to leave.)* **You ever get the chance, stop at**
22   **a field that is about to get picked. Look at all the vegetables**
23   **and tell them you respect them. Then, come and watch**
24   **the pickers, and tell them you respect them. Doing those**
25   **two things is like thanking the guy above.**
26   **HENRY: I came to say –**
27   **OLIVERIO: Good-bye? I already said good-bye.**
28   **HENRY: You did?**
29   **OLIVERIO: You say good-bye everyday.**
30   **To the dust. To the stars,**
31   **HENRY: – To the moon . . .**
32   **To the worms.**
33   **To the vegetables**
34   **picked by my father and mother**
35   **Their sweat**

1   to give us fruit to eat

2   **Their sacrifice**

3   **For the love of their son**

4   **Their dreams**

5   **a small step**

6   **towards happiness.**

7 **OLIVERIO: Not bad.** *(Challenging)* **Children of the dust.**

8 **HENRY: Following the crops of their parent's frown**

9 **OLIVERIO: Families canvassing the land of land**

10 **HENRY: Walking across patches of striped earth**

11 **OLIVERIO: Green, beige and brown**

12 **HENRY: Heavy boots, callused hands**

13 **OLIVERIO: Machetes swinging on tough plants**

14 **HENRY: Children watching parents work**

15   **From the trailers with broken doors.**

16 **OLIVERIO: Very nice. I like how you say it.**

17 **HENRY: Oliverio, where do you live?**

18 **OLIVERIO: I live nowhere, and I live here on the field.**

19 **HENRY: How poetic.**

20 **OLIVERIO: "Yo." You better believe it.** *(OLIVERIO smiles and*

21   *waves good-bye to HENRY. HENRY turns to go home. The*

22   *BLUE MEXICAN PEASANTS enter. They smile and walk up*

23   *to OLIVERIO.)* **You don't have to force me to go with you.**

24   **I've known all my life. I only do what I can to change the**

25   **pain. So I laugh as you all finally smile.** *(GIRL appears.)*

26   **And I hold the hand of the most precious gift there is. The**

27   **love of a child.** *(OLIVERIO and GIRL exit. HENRY enters his*

28   *home and sees MOM and DAD in the kitchen. DAD hands*

29   *HENRY an envelope filled with money.)*

30 **DAD: For your school.**

31 **MOM:** *(Sing-song)* **Julio will kill you for it.**

32 **DAD: I would kill for my family.**

33 **MOM: What about the ring?** *(DAD nods no.)* **Julio is a crook.**

34 **HENRY: I can't take the money. I'll work for it myself.**

35 **MOM: Take the money, before your father spends it again.**

1   **HENRY: I'd even work in the fields for extra money. It would be**
2   **good for me, so I'd respect.**
3   **DAD: No. You saw your parents pick, you have enough to be**
4   **humble about.**
5   **HENRY:** *La luna no sabe*
6   *Como todos la miren*
7   *Ella siempre va y viene*
8   *Para qué todos la admiren* (MOM and DAD stare at HENRY.)
9   **MOM: Where did you learn that?**
10 **HENRY: It's one of Oliverio's poems.**
11 **MOM: Whose poem?**
12 **DAD:** *Era de Oliverio.*
13 **MOM:** *(To DAD)* **What does this mean?**
14 **HENRY: He doesn't explain them. He only recites them.**
15   *(HENRY smiles, then looks out the window.)* **Hey. Look at**
16   **the stars. Aren't they beautiful. Mind if I go outside and**
17   **take a look? Come out and see them with me.** *(HENRY goes*
18   *out the door. He looks at the stars. There is a sense of hope.*
19   *MOM and DAD stare at each other in bewilderment.)*
20 **DAD: Oliverio used to recite them when he was . . . alive.**
21 **MOM: It can't be. He rolled over in the tractor fifteen years ago.**
22   **He's dead.**
23 **DAD: Yes, but the spirit never dies.**
24 **MOM: We must tell Henry.** *(DAD smiles and is about to nod "no"*
25   *when a BLACKOUT happens.)*
26
27 **END OF PLAY**
28
29
30
31
32
33
34
35

Night Train to Bolina

by Nilo Cruz

Unlike the other plays in this collection, *Night Train to Bolina* does not deal with the experience of immigrants adjusting to life in the United States: its setting is Latin America, and its central characters are two children who are not yet teens. But it does define the experience of millions of Latin Americans who, like the young girl Talita, look forward to the prospect of traveling to the United States where a new life, perhaps a new family, and certainly new opportunities are all possible. This play can help remind us that many in our culturally-diverse nation today are not just descendants of immigrants, they're immigrants themselves; and their unique backgrounds in widely different cultures is an important key to understanding them.

And for understanding ourselves. What has drawn, and still today draws so many to our shores is often something that those of us who live in the United States take for granted: basic freedom. The freedom to live in a place safe from terrorism and persecution, or the freedom to say what one thinks are high on the list of benefits for many immigrants. And certainly freedom of opportunity appeals to many others today, just as it did for many of our forefathers who arrived in the United States over the centuries. All these values are found here in Nilo Cruz's play about young Clara and her friend Mateo.

What is especially poignant about this play, however, in light of the play's socio-political context outlined above, is the fact that Mateo and Clara are not, in fact, going to the United States. They are to remain in Latin America where they will have to fend for themselves as best they can. Perhaps it is a form of cultural arrogance which assumes that life in the United States would certainly be better than a life in their own country. Nonetheless, Nilo Cruz does seem to imply that here, if only because of the strong character contrasts that he establishes towards the end of the drama.

Characters:

CLARA: A young girl of eleven

MATEO: A young boy of ten

TALITA: A young girl of fourteen

SISTER NORA: A woman in her late thirties, early forties

DOCTOR MARTIN: A man in his late forties

PASSENGERS ON TRAIN: To be played by the actors who perform the roles of Talita, Doctor Martin, Sister Nora and even the Stage Manager.

Time and Place:
Latin America. The present.

Set:
There is a large scrim on the back of the stage on which colors are projected, representing the mood of the scenes. The scrim is also used to project slides, old photographs for the cemetery scenes. To the left of the stage there is a stack of old wooden chairs, a basket of linen and a few hand-loomed rugs. In the second act squares of light and objects define the given locales.

Note:
The roles of Clara and Mateo are to be played by actors from ages fifteen to twenty-four.

1 **CARING FOR HIS BRUISES**

2 **SCENE ONE**

3

4 *Sound of wind. In a field. MATEO sits on the ground. He is*

5 *mending his paper kite. CLARA comes running to him. She holds*

6 *a small paper bag. She opens it and looks inside. She closes the*

7 *bag. She opens it again and looks at him.*

8

9 **CLARA: I brought you alcohol for your bruises. You got new**

10   **bruises?**

11 **MATEO: Yes.**

12 **CLARA: I thought you would. Let me see.**

13 **MATEO: Not now.**

14 **CLARA: Come on, let me see.**

15 **MATEO: Not now, I'm fixing this. Later.**

16 **CLARA: They hurt?**

17 **MATEO: Yes.**

18 **CLARA: They hurt less when you don't pay them any mind.**

19 **MATEO: I know that.**

20 **CLARA: They hurt less if you don't scratch them. Did they form**

21   **into scabs?**

22 **MATEO: Yeah.**

23 **CLARA: Ha! You probably have an infection.**

24 **MATEO: What do you know?!**

25 **CLARA: The scabs! That's the door . . . That's the door to**

26   **infection. It lives there.**

27 **MATEO: You don't know anything about it.**

28 **CLARA: I'm leaving** (*Takes the bag and starts to leave.*)

29 **MATEO: Wait.**

30 **CLARA: What do you want?**

31 **MATEO: Stay. Help me to finish fixing it. It almost got lost**

32   **yesterday. It was twirling in whirlwind. It was already going**

33   **real high up there. My Papa says that when kites get lost, they**

34   **go to Bolina. It's where kites come undone and disappear.**

35   **Where they fly loose and die. That's where they go to die.**

1   **CLARA: Like the cemetery.**

2   **MOTHER:** *(Voice heard offstage)* **Mateo . . . . . . Mateo . . . . . .**

3   **MATEO: She's calling me. Every time she calls for me, I freeze.**

4   **I start to think she's coming after me to hit me. That's all**

5   **she does, hit me. Yesterday, she threw a bucket of water at**

6   **me. And all because I brought flowers into the house. I**

7   **can never make her happy. At first she smiled, 'cause she**

8   **hadn't seen flowers since the drought. Then she threw the**

9   **bucket of water at me . . . Like that . . . Bushhhhh . . . And**

10   **all because I told her that I jumped on the train and went**

11   **to the cemetery . . . And I got the flowers from there. Then**

12   **she started crying 'cause that was the last bucket of water**

13   **we had. So, I went to my hiding place and started crying**

14   **too. Mama is so worried about the drought. I told her it's**

15   **going to rain. You watch and see. All we need is one cloud**

16   **over the house. Just one cloud, and we can fill all the**

17   **buckets with water. And we can go on the rooftop and take**

18   **a shower. Shshshshshhhhhhhhhhhhh . . .** *(Pretends to*

19   *shower. CLARA climbs on his back and does the same. He*

20   *spins her around.)* **Mama says that if we continue going to**

21   **the sea to take a bath, we're going to turn into fish.**

22   *(MATEO spins her around again.)*

23 **CLARA: Did I tell you I got a new hiding place?**

24 **MATEO: Where?**

25 **CLARA: In my Grandma's armoire.**

26 **MATEO: They'll hit you more if they find you there.** *(MATEO*

27   *spins her around one more time. She giggles.)*

28 **CLARA: Grandma doesn't use it. She always wears the same old**

29   **dress.**

30 **MATEO: I used to hide in my Grandma's armoire. But it was**

31   **always too stinky there, 'cause Grandma don't wash her**

32   **clothes. She pees in her bloomers every time she laughs.**

33 **CLARA: She can't hold it in?**

34 **MATEO: No. She sticks socks inside her panties to soak up the**

35   **pee pee. She was stealing all my socks until I caught her.**

1   But I told her I wouldn't tell Mama. Otherwise, Mama will
2   give her a beating too.
3   **CLARA: Your Grandma?** *(MATEO and CLARA walk towards each*
4   *other as he winds up the kite's string on a spool.)*
5   **MATEO: My mother hits everybody. She'll hit you too, if you**
6   **lived in my house.** *(Lifts his shirt.)* **See this mark here.**
7   **That's from the last beating I got. She hit me with my**
8   **Papi's belt. She said I was stealing my father's socks to**
9   **give it to my dog Pricila. Every time Pricila goes crazy, she**
10   **bleeds all around the house and breaks things . . . And**
11   **Mama gives her my Father's old socks and underwear . . .**
12   **But I didn't take his good socks. I told Mama it was**
13   **Grandma who took his socks . . . She takes everybody's**
14   **socks. — So you see this one here . . .** *(He lifts his shirt again*
15   *to show her another bruise.)* **Not the one on top. The one on**
16   **top is from telling Papa that it was Grandma who took his**
17   **socks . . . He hit me and started saying, "You respect your**
18   **Grandma . . . Respect her."** *(Pause)* **That's what I get for**
19   **being honest. For telling the truth. Let me see your**
20   **bruises. You got any new ones?**
21   **CLARA: No. They don't hit me no more. They just make me**
22   **kneel down in front of the virgin. They make me repent**
23   **for what I've done wrong. Sometimes they leave me there**
24   **for hours, and my knees start to hurt. Ever since that**
25   **witch came to my house, she gave Mama new ideas.**
26   *(Mockingly)* **She said, "You have to educate this child."**
27   **Every time she sees me, she puts me to read.**
28   **MATEO: Who's that?**
29   **CLARA: My Grandma's sister. I heard her tell my Grandma,**
30   **"That's what I do to the girls in my school." So my**
31   **Grandma told Mama. I bet you Mama will tell your Ma'.**
32   **MATEO: Don't say that.**
33   **CLARA: I bet you it's going to be big here, when everybody**
34   **hears about it. In every house they're going to start doing**
35   **that . . . And they're not going to let you wear long pants,**

1   even when you're thirteen, so you can feel the floor real

2   hard on your knees.

3 MATEO: *(Slaps her.)* That's mean. Don't say that. Don't ever say

4   that again.

5 CLARA: Why did you hit me?

6 MATEO: 'Cause you said mean things.

7 CLARA: How can you hit me? I never hit you. I thought we

8   made a promise never to hit each other. How can you

9   break that promise? I'm not going to talk to you anymore.

10   I'm leaving.

11 MATEO: I'm sorry.

12 CLARA: I'm sorry is not enough.

13 MATEO: I'm sorry! I'm sorry! I'm sorry! *(There is a pause.)* Are

14   you still my friend?

15 CLARA: *(There are tears in her eyes.)* I brought you alcohol and

16   everything. I brought you iodine and cotton for your

17   bruises . . . And . . . And . . .Look at what you do to me. You

18   hit me. I could get yelled at for stealing the alcohol. They'll

19   put me on my knees again, if they catch me. *(Pause)*

20   Grandma thinks this stuff is like gold. She treats it like

21   holy water. She says we have to start thinking that

22   everything we have is the last of its kind, so we can treat it

23   with respect, so we don't waste things. All she knows how

24   to say is, "We have to ration this. We have to ration that."

25   Ration! Ration! Ration! But what does ration mean?

26 MATEO: I don't know. It's probably a new word.

27 CLARA: But what is it?

28 MATEO: It's probably something that looks like that. Like a

29   ration. Like a machine. . . Like a . . . Like a radio . . . *(Pause)*

30   Are you still mad at me?

31 CLARA: No. Lift up your shirt.

32 MATEO: I'm hungry. *(Lifts up his shirt and turns his back*

33   *towards her.)*

34 CLARA: I brought you a piece of bread. *(Gives him bread.)*

35 MATEO: How come your family has bread and mine doesn't?

1   **CLARA: 'Cause my family prepared themselves for the drought.**
2   **Papa filled the house with bread.** *(CLARA swabs the*
3   *wounds.)*
4   **MATEO: Aaaaahhh! That hurts.**
5   **CLARA: I'm sorry.**
6   **MATEO: Your family wants to see us starve.**
7   **CLARA: I don't want to see you starve.**
8   **MATEO: I don't mean you. I mean your father, and the rest of**
9   **the people around here. Ever since my Aunt Julia set her**
10   **house on fire and ran out naked, they think the rest of us**
11   **are like Aunt Julia.**
12   **CLARA: Why did she do that?**
13   **MATEO: Her husband left her and moved to the city. Poor aunt**
14   **Julia. They keep her in the crazy house now.**
15   **CLARA: I'll set my house on fire if you leave. Promise me you'll**
16   **never leave.**
17   **MATEO: I promise. And if I leave, I'll fly my kite real high, so**
18   **you'll always know where I am.**
19   **CLARA: But don't leave.** *(MATEO kisses her face. He lies back on*
20   *the ground. He leans forward and looks at her.)*
21   **MATEO: Lie on top of me. Pretend I'm your bed.**
22   **CLARA: No.**
23   **MATEO: Just to hold each other.** *(CLARA looks around to see if*
24   *there's anybody watching. She positions herself slowly on*
25   *top of him. MATEO embraces her.)*
26
27   **LIGHTS FADE TO BLACK**
28
29
30   **FEEDING AN ANIMAL**
31   **SCENE TWO**
32
33
34   *CLARA places a few hand-loomed rugs on the ground and beats*
35   *them with a stick. MATEO enters from the right of the stage.*

1
2 CLARA: Go away! Go away! And keep away! I'm being punished.
3   They put me to beat the rugs because of you. They put me
4   to do this, for stealing the alcohol. They put me to sweep
5   the floor and dust the furniture. I can't talk to you. It's
6   because of you, they have me doing this. Go away! They'll
7   make me beat the rugs again. They'll put me on my knees,
8   if they see me talking to you. You bring me nothing but
9   trouble. *(MATEO starts to walk away. He runs back to the*
10   *rugs and stomps on them.)* Stop it . . . Stop it . . . Stop it . . .
11   *(CLARA struggles with him, trying to pull him away from*
12   *the rugs. He falls to the ground.)* You stay away . . . I'm
13   punished . . . And what do you want anyway? I haven't seen
14   you in two days.
15 MATEO: I was hiding. I'm hungry.
16 CLARA: I can't get you any bread. I'm being punished. See, they
17   have me doing this.
18 MATEO: Come play with me.
19 CLARA: I can't.
20 MATEO: I didn't come to see you 'cause I was hiding.
21 CLARA: And what did you do this time?
22 MATEO: Nothing.
23 CLARA: What did you do?
24 MATEO: I said nothing.
25 CLARA: I kept looking for your kite.
26 MATEO: I buried it.
27 CLARA: Why?
28 MATEO: 'Cause I got mad.
29 CLARA: Well, I'm mad at you.
30 MATEO: Why?
31 CLARA: 'Cause . . . 'Cause I'm mad. You disappeared!
32 MATEO: I'll pee on your rugs, if you don't stop being mad.
33   *(Starts to unfasten his fly.)*
34 CLARA: Mama . . . Mama . . .
35 MATEO: *(Takes a hold of her and covers her mouth.)* Are you

1   going to stop? I'll leave if you don't want to play.

2   CLARA: No. Stay. Are you going to get your kite back?

3   MATEO: I told you I buried it. I took it to the cemetery and

4   buried it. I don't want Ma' to find me. She went around

5   the room with her finger pointed like this . . .She was

6   pointing at everyone in the house. She was asking us,

7   "What are you going to give the pig to eat? What are you

8   going to give the poor animal, huh?" – She says he's going

9   to die if we don't give him something. He's got nothing to

10   eat, and we need to make him fat. It's all dry out there. We

11   don't even have food for ourselves. But she stood right

12   there, telling us we have to give him something. Like the

13   time we didn't have food for the goats . . . She went around

14   the room asking the whole family for something, to make

15   a stew for those stupid animals. Grandma gave her pillow

16   away . . . Grandpa gave a pair of shoes . . . I gave those goats

17   my favorite toy. My blue car. I closed my eyes and I threw

18   it right in the pot. Mama stirred the stew and I never saw

19   it again. That was it. It was gone. And you know

20   something? . . . Somehow, I always knew I was going to get

21   it back, 'cause later Mama killed all the goats and we ate

22   them. Except I don't know if I ate the goat that chewed up

23   my car . . . But sometimes, when I get real hungry, like

24   now, my stomach makes noises, like my car used to make.

25   So I know I ate the right goat. And my car is in there,

26   somewhere riding in one of my veins. Like in a tunnel.

27   You want to hear it?

28   CLARA: (*Walks towards him and listens to his stomach.*) You

29   better go to the hospital and have them pull out that car.

30   MATEO: Uh-uh. If nothing happened to the goat, nothing's

31   going to happen to me. Grandma says she's going to give

32   her fan for the pig's stew. That's all she's got left, since the

33   hurricane took her house and wiped out all her things.

34   CLARA: But pigs don't eat fans.

35   MATEO: I know. That's why Mama turned green yelling at

1   Grandma. Mama knows that Grandma can't think
2   straight . . . And . . . And she still yelled and screamed at
3   her. Poor Grandma . . . Just to shut Mama up, she said she
4   would give the pig her yellow canary. But she don't know
5   my sister Flora ate it already. I bet that with all the hunger,
6   Grandma sees visions, and still thinks the canary is inside
7   the cage.
8   CLARA: What's your Grandpa going to give for the stew?
9   MATEO: He's got nothing to give. Mama said she would throw
10 him out of the house, if he didn't give something. He's got
11 nothing but his tired old body. Thank God Pricila ran
12 away from home or he would've thrown her in the stew.
13 Then I would've killed Grandpa.
14 CLARA: Don't say that. You can't kill your Grandpa.
15 MATEO: I didn't mean it. I'm so hungry my mind is leaving me.
16 *(CLARA brings him close to her. He rests his head on her*
17 *shoulder.)*
18 CLARA: Shshshshsh . . . . . . I'll bring you some bread.
19 MATEO: Grandpa said he's got nothing to give for the stew. He
20 said he's just going to cut his arm and throw it in the stew.
21 CLARA: His arm?
22 MATEO: Uhn-huh. That's what he said. He's got to give
23 something. And Aunt Ursula, she's got nothing to give . . .
24 So, she's going to give her hips away for the stew . . ..
25 CLARA: You're lying. You're imagining things.
26 MATEO: *(Speaks rapidly.)* No, I'm not. No . . . No . . . Aunt Ursula
27 doesn't want them she said. She says that men come to her
28 side all the time because of her hips . . And she doesn't
29 want no more men. She's tired of them. My brother
30 Nelson said he was going to give away his left ear. And . . .
31 And Mama crossed her arms, until he said his right one
32 too. That's good, 'cause he don't have to hear Mama
33 scream no more. *(Starts to run as if shocked. Stops and takes*
34 *a hold of himself.)* Then when Mama pointed at me, I
35 started trembling. I said I was going to give my eyelashes,

1   and Mama hit me. Then I said, my eyelashes and my
2   eyebrows, and she hit me again. Then I said my hair, and
3   she started hitting me like a machine gun. *(Does motions*
4   *as if he were hitting someone.)* And . . . And I didn't know
5   what to say . . . I didn't know what to do. I thought of my
6   finger . . . And Mama kept on saying, "Come on, I'm
7   waiting. Come on." When I raised my finger 'cause I
8   couldn't talk, my sister pulled out her tongue at me, and
9   called me copycat. So. . .So, I didn't say anything . . . And I
10   thought of my foot. But how can I walk with just one foot?
11   I thought of my eyes, my nails . . . And I can't give a stupid
12   animal a piece myself . . . I can't . . . Then I called Mama to
13   the side 'cause I couldn't decide on anything. And . . And
14   just before Mama could hit me, Grandpa winked at me
15   and pointed to down there . . . And all of a sudden I said,
16   my pee pee. Everybody in the room started laughing at
17   me. So I ran out . . I ran as fast as I could, so no one could
18   catch me. *(He moves away from CLARA. He holds his crotch.*
19   *He turns to her.)* Would you kill the pig with me? Would
20   you come with me? *(CLARA is motionless.)*
21 CLARA: We're not strong enough. It takes a big person to kill a
22   pig. Someone who has an ax or a gun.
23 MATEO: If we don't kill it, they'll turn me into a girl. They'll put
24   me in a dress, and I'll be a girl just like you. *(Pause)* Would
25   you love me if I become a girl?
26 CLARA: Of course I will. I'll love you even more, 'cause we'll
27   always be together. And you'll let your hair grow. And
28   when it gets long, I'll comb it and braid it. *(CLARA touches*
29   *his hair. MATEO rests his head on her shoulder. The sound*
30   *of a train is heard in the distance.)* And we'll clean the
31   dishes and wash clothes together. And we'll iron together.
32   And we'll play with my doll, and dance together. *(The*
33   *sound of the train is heard louder.)* Come on, let's go wave
34   to the train. *(CLARA pulls him by the arm.)* Let's go . . . The
35   train is coming . . . Come on . . .

1   MATEO: I don't want to go.

2   CLARA: Let's go . . . We'll miss it . . . Let's see who gets there first

3   . . . Let's go. *(They both run to see the train.)*

4

5   **LIGHTS FADE TO BLACK**

6

7

8   **DRESSING LIKE A GIRL**

9   **SCENE THREE**

10

11   *MATEO tries on a white dress. He faces Upstage. CLARA has her*

12   *eyes covered.*

13

14   CLARA: One . . . Two . . . Three . . . Four . . . I'm waiting . . . One . . .

15   Two . . . Three . . . Four . . . Five . . . what's taking you so long?

16   MATEO: I'm not finished. Look around you. Is there anybody

17   coming?

18   CLARA: No.

19   MATEO: Look to the right. I don't want anybody to see me.

20   CLARA: No, I don't see anybody.

21   MATEO: To the left.

22   CLARA: No nobody. *(Goes to get a mirror.)*

23   MATEO: What was that sound?

24   CLARA: Nothing. Just me walking. There's no one here.

25   MATEO: All right, I'm ready. Are you sure there's no one out

26   there?

27   CLARA: Come out and let me see you.

28   MATEO: I'm embarrassed.

29   CLARA: You look beautiful. Turn around. You'll make a

30   beautiful girl. I won't let you look in the mirror yet. First

31   you have to learn how to walk. Like this . . . *(Positions a*

32   *basket of linen on top of her head.)*

33   MATEO: What's that supposed to be, a hat?

34   CLARA: No. My sister taught me this. It's to keep your balance.

35   *(Demonstrates walk.)* Women have to let their hips move

1   ahead of them, when they walk. Let the hips lead the
2   walk. As if the hips know where they're going. See, they
3   know where they want to go. The hips go, pim, pom, pim,
4   pom, pim, pom . . . The arms go, bim, baum, bim, baum. .
5   . The shoulders go terracata, terracata, terracata. . . *(Speaks*
6   *rapidly.)* Pim, pom, bim, baum, terracata, terracata. . . Pim,
7   pom, bim, baum, terracata, terracata. . . Then comes your
8   behind. The behind goes, boom, boom, boom, boom. . .
9   That's the most important part of the walk. You got to
10   move your behind. Look at the cows how they move their
11   tails. *(Goes to put basket on top of his head.)*
12 MATEO: I can't do that.
13 CLARA: Why not?
14 MATEO: You don't walk like that.
15 CLARA: I forget. But that's the way you got to walk.
16 MATEO: I can't. Let me look in the mirror. Just let me look in
17   the mirror. *(He looks at himself. He throws the mirror*
18   *against the floor. He takes off the dress and starts to rip it to*
19   *shreds.)* I'll kill the pig. . . I'll kill him. . . I'll cut its head. . .
20   *(Clara tries to hold him.)* I'll kill him. . .
21 CLARA: You can't, he's stronger. . .
22 MATEO: I'll cut his head. . .
23 CLARA: You can't, he'll bite you. . .
24 MATEO: I'll kill him. . .
25 CLARA: He's stronger than you. . . Mama. . . Come help me. . .
26   Mama. . .*(MATEO starts to run away. CLARA tries to hold*
27   *him. He gets away. CLARA picks up her dress. There are tears*
28   *in her eyes.)* My dress . . . *(CLARA starts to gather the*
29   *carpets.)*
30
31 LIGHTS FADE
32
33
34
35

1 **A PRAYER**
2 **SCENE FOUR**
3
4 *CLARA and MATEO are kneeling in squares of light. MATEO's*
5 *hand is bandaged.*
6
7 **CLARA: Through all my mother's prayers, my father's, my**
8 **sister's, my grandmother's, and my grandfather's prayers,**
9 **I remain untamed. They say I'm a sheep who's gone**
10 **astray. Should I stay here awake all night and pray for my**
11 **sins?** *(CLARA prays rapidly.)*
12 **MATEO: I know, God. I know. I've been told. They were only evil**
13 **thoughts. I didn't kill.** *(Raises his hand.)* **And this is what I**
14 **got for my evil thoughts. That pig bit me because of my**
15 **evil thoughts. Please forgive me. I promise to be good.**
16 *(MATEO prays rapidly.)*
17 **CLARA: I try to hear your voice, but I can't hear your words.**
18 **Should I burn my knees with candles of the virgin? Talk to**
19 **me. Tell me I'm not bad.**
20 **MATEO: I will erase all evil thoughts within me. Like what**
21 **Grandma said, "Evil thoughts are like weeds that grow in**
22 **the garden of the heart and soul. They're like the insects**
23 **that come in the summertime and eat our fruits." She says**
24 **evil thoughts are like the winds of the hurricane that took**
25 **her house away. I know, Grandma told me. I know. I know.**
26 **CLARA: I'll mend my dress. It's torn but I'll mend it. I'll take**
27 **care of my clothes. Mateo and I were only playing. Please**
28 **help me to be obedient, so my family won't be ashamed of**
29 **me. Guide my steps. Don't let me fall, for I have fallen**
30 **before. Send me an angel to guide my footsteps. . . And**
31 **send one for Mateo . . .**
32 **MATEO: Evil thoughts are like dirt. The dirt that sticks to my**
33 **skin. The dirt in my fingernails. The rocks that break the**
34 **soles of my shoes. It's what Mama calls grime, unwashed,**
35 **unclean. . . What Aunt Ursula calls vile and foul . . .**

1   Impure, rotten . . . What my brother Nelson calls garbage
2   . . . And my sister Flora calls caca . . . I want to call it
3   something too, Lord. So when an evil thought comes to my
4   mind, I can call it by its name and make it go away.
5   *(MATEO gives her a small piece of paper and a pencil.)* **Here**
6   . . . Start writing. Write down that we want to escape. That
7   we want to escape from here.
8   CLARA: I don't know how to write escape.
9   MATEO: Write something else.
10   CLARA: What?
11   MATEO: Write: Dear God, we want to leave this place. Write
12   that we want to leave soon.
13   CLARA: I don't know how to write that word either.
14   MATEO: Then write that we want to run away.
15   CLARA: Another word.
16   MATEO: You don't know how to write.
17   CLARA: I do. I can write house, light, father, mother. My name
18   your name . . .
19   MATEO: It's not going to work.
20   CLARA: I can draw a picture. He'll understand. A picture of you
21   and I.
22   MATEO: He doesn't want to look at a picture. God knows how to
23   read.
24   CLARA: *(Draws rapidly.)* The tombs in the cemetery have
25   pictures of the dead people. They have pictures with their
26   names, so God will know who they are. I can draw a
27   picture. And . . . And. . . I can put our names. Look, like
28   this. And I can draw wings on our back, like if we want to
29   fly away from here. Fly away from this place. Then I can
30   draw a house with no windows. With no doors. No
31   chimney. A falling house. So God will know that we can't
32   come back here. Like this, look. See the house. No one can
33   live in a house like this.
34   MATEO: Let me look at it. *(Takes the paper from her.)* **This**
35   doesn't look like us.

1   **CLARA: Yes, he's skinny like you. And this is me. See me with**
2   **my dress. We go to the cemetery, we get your kite and tie**
3   **the message to the string, then we let it fly to the clouds.**
4   **We just have to make sure we send the message on the**
5   **right day. My mother says that on Mondays and Tuesdays**
6   **are good days to pray because after resting on the**
7   **weekend, God has a clear mind. That Wednesdays and**
8   **Thursdays are good days for cleaning your ears, because**
9   **God speaks from above.**
10 **MATEO: What's today?**
11 **CLARA: The day for cutting your hair.**
12 **MATEO: I don't mean that. Forget it. It's not going to work.**
13 *(Tears the paper.)*
14 **CLARA: Let me have it. Give it back! Give me back my paper.**
15 **MATEO: No!** *(Runs from her. CLARA runs after him.)*
16 **CLARA: Give it here.** *(MATEO gives her the torn paper. CLARA*
17 *moves away from him and looks up.)* **I know that God will**
18 **understand. He'll understand what we're trying to tell**
19 **him.**
20

21 **CHANGE OF LIGHT**
22

23

24 **BOXES AND THE NIGHT TRAIN**
25 **SCENE FIVE**
26

27 **MATEO: Look at it fly . . . That's how we're going to be, free . . .**
28 **Free . . . We're going to be free when we escape.** *(Waves to*
29 *the kite.)*
30 **CLARA: Let him go . . . Break the string.**
31 **MATEO: No, let him fly higher.**
32 **CLARA: Just let him go.** *(MATEO cuts the string with his teeth.*
33 *The kite disappears. They wave to the kite in silence.)*
34 **MATEO: Now he can fly and take the message, then he can go to**
35 **die where he belongs.**

1 CLARA: I want to go to my house.
2 MATEO: You can't go back, and neither can I. I can't go back. I
3   told you my sister Flora heard me talk in my sleep last
4   night. She heard me talk about our escape. That's why
5   Mama tied my leg to the kitchen table, 'cause Flora told
6   Mama I was talking in my sleep about going to the city. I
7   cut the rope with my teeth. Ha! They thought I couldn't get
8   away. Let's go play with the dead people. This is going to
9   be the last time we play with them, then they'll never see
10   us again. Come on! Let's play pretend. I'll be the man who
11   died in October. You be the woman who died in July. You
12   remember the photograph on her tomb? Let's go look for
13   her.
14 CLARA: No.
15 MATEO: You don't like her? You can be another dead woman, if
16   you want. How about the woman who died in 1949? You
17   remember the picture on her tomb? What was her name?
18 CLARA: Rita.
19 MATEO: Come on . . . You pretend to be Rita. I'll pretend to be
20   the man who died in October. *(Reaches for her hand.)* Come
21   on let's go look for their tombs.
22 CLARA: I'm not going to the city, Mateo.
23 MATEO: I thought we had it all planned. Look at me, we jump
24   on the train, I get in this box, you get inside the other box.
25   No one will see us. *(Gets inside the box.)*
26 CLARA: I'm afraid. In the city there are soldiers. They'll take us
27   away.
28 MATEO: Nothing's going to happen. When the night train
29   comes, we jump on it. I know which wagon to get on. The
30   one with the luggage. We hide in the boxes . . . Come on . . .
31   In the city we can sell cigarettes. Like my brother Luis.
32   Five cents each. I know how to do it. We'll make money.
33   And I will buy you a little ring with the money I make. And
34   you can sell fruits and beans on the sidewalk. When I
35   make more money, we can get a table. Like the ones in the

1   market. And we can put all the merchandise on top of the
2   table, like real vendors.
3   CLARA: And where are we going to live?
4   MATEO: We could live on the church steps. I've seen people
5   living there.
6   CLARA: I can't go. I made a promise to be good.
7   MATEO: If you don't come with me I'll die.
8   CLARA: Don't say that.
9   MATEO: All of me will break into little pieces. And I'll be dead.
10   Dead! Watch. . . I'll stop breathing. *(Covers his mouth.)*
11 CLARA: Don't do that! Stop it!. . .*(MATEO continues to hold his*
12   *breath. He runs away from her. CLARA runs after him.)* **Stop**
13   **it. . . You're scaring me. . . Stop it Mateo.**
14 MATEO: If you don't come with me, I'll die. . . If you don't come
15   with me, I'll die. . . *(Runs faster around the stage.)*
16 CLARA: Stop it! You're going to get sick. . .*(MATEO falls to the*
17   *ground. He pretends to be dead.)* **Mateo . . . Mateo . . . Wake**
18   **up . .. Don't play dead . . . I know you're not dead.** *(MATEO*
19   *doesn't respond.)* **Mateo . . . Oh God! Wake up, Mateo!**
20   **Mateo . . . Please wake up . . . Wake up! Wake up . . . I'll go**
21   **with you . . . I promise to go with you . . . Please wake up .**
22   **. . I promise.** *(MATEO opens his eyes.)* **You scared me.**
23 MATEO: You promise to go with me?
24 CLARA: Yes . . . Yes . . . I'll go with you.
25 MATEO: Tonight.
26 CLARA: Yes.
27 MATEO: Good . . .So let's play with the dead people one last
28   time. Come on... Let's play...I'm the dead man who died in
29   October. My name is Faro. My tomb is right there.
30 CLARA: I'm the dead woman who died in July.
31 MATEO: Hello!
32 CLARA: Hello!
33 MATEO: What's your name?
34 CLARA: Rita. My tomb is back there. My tomb has an angel with
35   a horn. He plays music for me.

1 MATEO: My tomb has a cross and a wreath of laurel leaves. I
2   was a soldier.
3 CLARA: Soldiers are mean. They kill and steal children.
4 MATEO: Not me. I was a good soldier.
5 CLARA: All soldiers are bad. I don't talk to soldiers.
6 MATEO: (*Runs around the stage to look for another tomb.*) All
7   right, then I'll be this man, right here.
8 CLARA: What's your name?
9 MATEO: I can't read his name. But they call me Pipiolo like my
10   uncle. What's your name?
11 CLARA: I'm still Rita. I'm beautiful like her. I was a singer.
12 MATEO: I was a barber.
13 CLARA: Would you comb my hair?
14 MATEO: I lost my comb.
15 CLARA: Well, find your comb and your scissors. I'm going to
16   sing tonight and I want my hair combed. See that tomb
17   right there, that's my stage.
18 MATEO: I'll charge you twenty-five cents.
19 CLARA: I don't have any money. I can give you the flowers on
20   my tomb.
21 MATEO: I want twenty-five cents.
22 CLARA: I don't have any money. The soldiers stole my money.
23 MATEO: The soldiers took my comb. Hide. They'll kill you if
24   they find you. (*Both children run around the stage.*) Ay! Ay!
25   My hand hurts. It hurts a lot.
26 CLARA: Let me look at it. (*CLARA unbinds the bandage.*)
27 MATEO: Ay!
28 CLARA: Your hand is purple. It's swollen.
29 MATEO: No, it's not.
30 CLARA: It's infected.
31 MATEO: It's not infected.
32 CLARA: We have to put something on it. Alcohol.
33 MATEO: No. Leave it like that. There's nothing wrong with it.
34   Leave it like that.
35 CLARA: Let me wrap it again.

117

1 MATEO: In the city you can learn to be a nurse. You could work
2   in a hospital and wear a white uniform.
3 CLARA: Me?
4 MATEO: Yes. And you can learn to give injections. And you can
5   be my nurse when I get sick. *(CLARA kisses him on the*
6   *forehead.)*
7
8 **FADE TO BLACK**
9
10
11 **A BRIDGE TO THE CITY**
12 **A BRIDGE TO EACH OTHER**
13 **SCENE SIX**
14
15 *Soft music plays "Gymnopedie" by Satie. CLARA and MATEO*
16 *wear paper hats. They appear on the stage with four chairs. They*
17 *walk on the chairs lifting them up every time they take a step.*
18 *They place each chair in a line. The chairs face the left of the stage.*
19 *CLARA and MATEO establish a game by walking on top of the*
20 *chairs as if it was a bridge. They each take turns to walk on top of*
21 *the chairs. CLARA invents another game. She runs to the basket*
22 *and gets a sheet. She spreads it on the ground. She gets a dress*
23 *from the basket and holds it in front of her body. She looks at*
24 *MATEO. She walks holding the dress, as if she was wearing it. She*
25 *looks at MATEO as she walks around the sheet. There's seduction*
26 *in all of CLARA's movements. She takes the dress and places it on*
27 *top of the sheet. The dress represents her lying down. MATEO*
28 *takes notice of her game. He runs to the basket and takes a pair of*
29 *pants. He looks at her. He follows her game of seduction and*
30 *places the pair of pants by the dress. The pants represent him*
31 *lying close to her. CLARA walks around the sheet with her eyes*
32 *fixed on MATEO. He follows her. Suddenly, she pulls the sheet*
33 *and makes it into a bundle. She runs away with it. MATEO runs*
34 *after her. The music fades. The steaming sound of a train fills the*
35 *stage. The sound of a conductor's whistle is heard. Several*

1   *passengers appear on the stage with luggage and sit in the given*
2   *chairs. A train whistle is heard. CLARA and MATEO appear on the*
3   *stage hiding inside the boxes. The two boxes are seen walking*
4   *slowly across the stage. The steaming sound of the train fills the*
5   *stage. There is smoke.*
6
7   **LIGHTS FADE TO BLACK**
8
9
10
11
12
13   **ACT II**
14
15   **A NEW FRIEND AT THE MISSION**
16   **SCENE ONE**
17
18   *At the hospice. There are two beds on the stage. CLARA stands to*
19   *the right of the stage. TALITA lies in bed to the left of the stage.*
20
21   **TALITA: When the little stick points to seven and the big stick**
22   **points to twelve, that's the time the bell rings. That's seven**
23   **o'clock. That's the time we have to wake up. Sister Nora**
24   **taught us how to tell time. Have you ever seen a cuckoo**
25   **clock? It goes cuckoo . . . cuckoo. . . And a little bird comes**
26   **out to the clock. Sister Nora has one in her classroom.**
27   **Right around this time the bell rings. When the bell rings**
28   **it's time to go to sleep.** *(The bell rings and lights dim.)*
29   **CLARA:** *(Frightened)* **What happened to the lights?**
30   **TALITA: It's time to go to sleep. The cuckoo clock must be going**
31   **cuckoo . . . cuckoo . . Are you afraid? Nothing's going to**
32   **happen to you. I used to be afraid like you. Natalia, the girl**
33   **who used to sleep in your bed was afraid too. She was**
34   **always afraid the roof would cave in at night and soldiers**
35   **would come in here.**

1 CLARA: I want to leave the place. I want to get out.
2 TALITA: You can't. They won't let you.
3 CLARA: Why not?
4 TALITA: Because this is where you belong. Who brought you
5   here? Was it your father?
6 CLARA: No.
7 TALITA: Who did?
8 CLARA: A man from the city. He was cleaning the church steps,
9   and I told him my friend was sick. He took us into a little
10   room inside the church. He gave my friend medicine.
11   Then he took us to the hospital in a car. But they didn't
12   want us in the hospital, because there were no beds. So he
13   brought us here, me and my friend. You know where the
14   infirmary is?
15 TALITA: Yes.
16 CLARA: That's where they took my friend. He's sick.
17 TALITA: Was he dying? Did a soldier shoot him?
18 CLARA: No. His hand is infected.
19 TALITA: I clean the floor of the infirmary. I see people die
20   everyday. When I used to live at the Santa Rosa mission I was
21   sick in the infirmary and I saw a boy die next to my bed.
22 CLARA: He's not going to die! Don't say he's going to die!
23 TALITA: Shshhhhhhh . . . They'll hear you outside. We're
24   supposed to be sleeping. See, I hear someone coming.
25   Someone's coming this way, pretend that you're sleeping.
26   *(SISTER NORA enters the room. She goes over to TALITA's*
27   *bed and covers her. Then proceeds to CLARA's bed and does*
28   *the same. When SISTER NORA exits both girls open their*
29   *eyes..Whispering.)* **Run to the door and see if she's gone.**
30 CLARA: You do it. *(TALITA runs to the door and sees if the nun*
31   *has left.)*
32 TALITA: She'll be back later. She's Sister Nora. She's nice. When
33   I can't sleep, because I have bad dreams she tells me
34   bedtime stories. Except she always falls asleep, instead of
35   me. Then she starts snoring. One time she took us to the

1   zoo and I saw a monkey called Nunu. He was sitting like
2   this. *(Sits on CLARA's bed and crosses her legs.)* Like a little
3   man with his legs crossed. He wasn't a boy. He was a
4   woman. Not a woman. A monkey mother. Her little
5   monkey was sleeping and she came to me and looked into
6   my eyes like this. *(Moves her head from side to side.)* Then
7   she went like this with her lips. *(Makes monkey sounds.*
8   *Does monkey movements and spins around.)*
9 CLARA: *(Laughs.)* Do it again.
10 TALITA: Good. I made you laugh. *(CLARA becomes serious*
11   *again. TALITA repeats motions.)* The little monkey would
12   put her hand to her nose, like if she was going to sneeze.
13   Like if she had a cold. Like this. *(Places hand on her nose,*
14   *breathes in and out through her mouth and spins. Laughs.)*
15   She looked like she wanted to be my mother. *(Pause. Faces*
16   *forward.)* I don't have a mother. I used to have two
17   mothers. I used to. Not anymore. One lives in America and
18   one disappeared from home. My Papi says she was
19   kidnapped by soldiers. Do you know what kidnap means?
20   *(CLARA shakes her head.)* It means that they steal you. The
21   soldiers that come to our village, they come and do bad
22   things. They put people in bags of rice and take them
23   away. Then they throw them into a pit. Were you at the
24   Santa Rosa Mission? *(CLARA shakes her head.)* That's
25   where my father took me, so my American mother can
26   come for me. I'm going to be her daughter. If I show you a
27   secret, promise not to tell anybody. *(CLARA nods.)* Stand
28   there and close your eyes. I don't want anybody to know
29   where I hide my secret. Come on, close your eyes and
30   stand there. Go on over there. *(CLARA closes her eyes and*
31   *walks away from TALITA. TALITA pulls out a bundle from*
32   *under her bed cushion.)* Open your eyes. And don't tell
33   anybody I showed these to you. *(TALITA takes out a pair of*
34   *shoes from inside a pillowcase.)* My mother in America sent
35   them to me in a letter. In a little box. They didn't fit me

1   when I got them. So my mother gave them to my sister,

2   because she had bigger feet. Now they are small on me,

3   because my feet got big. Try them on. they'll fit you. You

4   have small feet. *(CLARA tries them on.)* Aren't they

5   beautiful. But you see my sister scratched them. She never

6   took care of them. She was going to break them and get

7   them dirty, so I took them away from her. She was

8   sleeping one night and I took them from under the bed. I

9   put them inside a sack, I dug a hole and buried them

10   inside the ground, so she wouldn't wear them again. Wait.

11   Let me see if someone's coming. *(Runs to the door and*

12   *takes a peek. She runs back to CLARA.)* The next day

13   everybody in my house was looking for the shoes. And I

14   didn't tell. I didn't say anything. I used to go out at night

15   and dig them out of the ground and wear them for a little

16   while. Even if they were big on me. Then I would polish

17   them with my nightshirt and dab a bit of saliva to make

18   them shine. They would shine so much you could see the

19   bright moon reflected on them. Go see if someone's

20   coming. *(CLARA goes to the door.)*

21 CLARA: No one's out there.

22 TALITA: She'll make her round again. Then she'll sit by the

23   door and fall asleep. Let me wear the shoes.

24 CLARA: But they don't fit you.

25 TALITA: It doesn't matter. *(Places shoes on top of her head.)* One

26   day I will melt them into a hat. My grandma had her gold

27   tooth melted into a wedding band. I could do the same

28   with my shoes. And I'll have a hat. Maybe a purse. *(Holds*

29   *them by the strap, as if they were a purse.)* Maybe a pair of

30   gloves, like the ones rich ladies wear to church.

31 CLARA: Keep them how they are.

32 TALITA: When I look at them, I remember the smell of back

33   home. Walking on the moist grass. The moon shining on

34   my shoes. My Grandma's face.

35 CLARA: You miss your Grandma.

1   TALITA: Sometimes.

2   CLARA: I miss Mateo. When will I see him again?

3   TALITA: Pretend you're sick. They'll take you to the infirmary

4   to see a doctor, then you can see him.

5

6   **BLACKOUT**

7

8

9   **A BROKEN HAND A BROKEN LIE**

10 **SCENE TWO**

11

12 *This scene takes place in an X-ray room and a doctor's office. The*

13 *lights accentuate back and forth the dialog between the given*

14 *spaces. MATEO sits in a chair to the left of the stage. CLARA stands*

15 *to the right of the stage.*

16

17 MATEO: What are you going to do to me?

18 DOCTOR MARTIN: I'm going to take an X-ray of your hand. Do

19   you know what this is? It's a picture of your bones. It's not

20   going to hurt. It's just like standing in front of a camera.

21   *(Positions MATEO for the X-ray. Lifts his right hand.)* **The**

22   photographer tells you, "Look at the pretty bird." And . . .

23   "*Voila*" he takes a picture of you. — Again with the pretty

24   bird . . . And . . . "*Voila*"

25 MATEO: What does *voila* mean?

26 DOCTOR MARTIN: What does it mean? It means there it is.

27   There you go. *(Stands away from MATEO.)* "Pretty bird one

28   more time." . . . And . . . "*Voila*" . . . *(Freeze.)*

29 SISTER NORA: *(Writes and reads rapidly on a chart.)* Clara Maria

30   Prago, eleven years old, complains of abdominal pain and

31   nausea. The child defines the pain or discomfort, as an ill-

32   defined mass in the epigastrium. *(Stops reading from the*

33   *chart.)* Do you feel pain now?

34 CLARA: Yes . . . yes . . . Right here by my ribs. The pain doesn't

35   let me breathe sometimes. It goes all the way to my chest

1   and my throat. Like if something was hitting me there
2   with a hammer. More like a knife.
3 SISTER NORA: Like a sharp pain.
4 CLARA: Yes.
5 SISTER NORA: Does the pain extend to your back?
6 CLARA: Sometimes.
7 SISTER NORA: Where on your back?
8 CLARA: It goes all over. It's like a car inside my body. But more
9   like an airplane.
10 SISTER NORA: Why an airplane?
11 CLARA: Because the pain goes up and down. It's like a balloon.
12   It's flying inside me. It wants to get out and it gets trapped
13   inside my ribs. *(Freeze.)*
14 DOCTOR MARTIN: I want you to open and close your hand.
15 MATEO: It hurts when I do that.
16 DOCTOR MARTIN: I want you to try and do it.
17 MATEO: I tell you it hurts.
18 DOCTOR MARTIN: It's going to hurt, but you've got to do it. I'll
19   give you a pill and the pain will go away.
20 MATEO: No. I can't do it. It hurts.
21 DOCTOR MARTIN: Try. *(MATEO Lifts his arm and closes his eyes.*
22   *He is in pain. He opens and closes his hand.)* Good. Very
23   good. Now I'm going to pull back your fingers, just a little.
24 MATEO: Aaahhhh . . . Aaaaayyyyyyyyyyhhhhhhh . . . *(Freeze.)*
25 CLARA: That sounds like Mateo's voice. Is he next door? I want
26   to see him.
27 SISTER NORA: There are many children here. I don't think
28   that's your friend.
29 CLARA: But it sounds like him. I know his voice.
30 SISTER NORA: You must miss your friend very much.
31 CLARA: Yes, I want to see him.
32 SISTER NORA: He's sick. You know he's sick. When he's better
33   you can see him. Come on, let's listen to your heart. I want
34   you to take a deep breath. *(Places the stethoscope on*
35   *CLARA's stomach.)*

1   CLARA: Aaaaaaaaaaaaahhhhhhhhhhhh . . . *(Freeze.)*

2   DOCTOR MARTIN: I want you to try one more time. Open and

3   close your hand. *(Pulls back his hand.)*

4   MATEO: Aaaaahhhhh . . . Aaayyyyyhhhh . . . Ahhhh! Ah!

5   Aaaaahh!

6   CLARA: That's Mateo. I know that's him. *(Stands up on the chair*

7   *and calls in a loud voice.)* Mateo . . . Mateo . . .

8   SISTER NORA: Sit down . . . Sit down . . . Pay attention.

9   CLARA: Mateo . . . .

10 SISTER NORA: Clara!

11 CLARA: I want to see you , Mateo . . .

12 MATEO: Come see me. *(Stands on the chair.)*

13 DOCTOR MARTIN: Sit down.

14 SISTER NORA : Sit down, Clara.

15 CLARA: I can't come see you. They won't let me. *(To SISTER*

16   *NORA)* Please let me see him. I feel better. I feel better.

17 SISTER NORA: Get down from that chair. *(Tries to pull her*

18   *down.)*

19 CLARA : What are they doing to you?

20 MATEO: Nothing. I'm fine.

21 DOCTOR MARTIN: Stop yelling across the room.

22 SISTER NORA: Now Clara listen to me, you can see your friend

23   when he's better. And stop yelling across the room.

24 CLARA: Please let me see him. I feel much better.

25 SISTER NORA: Get down from that chair. I said get down. You'll

26   see him some other time.

27 MATEO: Clara . . . Clara . . . *(There is a pause. CLARA lowers her*

28   *head.)*

29

30 LIGHTS FADE

31

32

33

34

35

1 **CHORES FOR THE DAY**
2 **SCENE THREE**
3
4 *Daytime. CLARA sits on a chair to the center of the stage. SISTER*
5 *NORA stands behind her braiding her hair. CLARA is braiding*
6 *TALITA's hair, who is kneeling in front of her.*
7
8 SISTER NORA: There used to be a time when the needs of this
9   place were fulfilled, and children like you spent the whole
10   day in classrooms, learning how to read and write. Now
11   there's not enough of us and this place is falling apart.
12   Everything smells of mold. As when things become moldy
13   and moth-eaten. There used to be a time when this
14   building was airy and sanitary, because we had time to
15   scrub our walls and floors. We had time to maintain our
16   gardens, to cut down the branches from our trees and let
17   in the fresh air. And in the summertime we used to throw
18   buckets of water on the floor, flooding the mission up to
19   our ankles, so the tiles could retain the cool and moist and
20   soothe the heat. Our walls were painted and there were no
21   leaks on our roofs. Then things changed. No missionaries
22   wanted to come here to work. And others left frightened of
23   danger. Afraid of getting killed or lost in our jungles, to end
24   up mangled or mutilated by guerrillas or soldiers. So now
25   if the alms box needs to be painted, we take a brush and
26   paint it. All you children have to help us. If there's no one
27   to mend the altar cloths, we take a needle and thread and
28   mend them. Do you know how to sew, Clara?
29 CLARA: No.
30 SISTER NORA: I'll teach you. You know how to sweep and dust?
31 CLARA: Yes.
32 SISTER NORA: Good. You can sweep and dust the parish. Take
33   a broom and duster from the room next to the vestry.
34   Talita, you take her there and show her where they're
35   kept. Show her how to sweep under the prayer stools. To

1 get underneath the stools with the broom. Dirt
2 accumulates down there. And show her how to polish the
3 pulpit and the altar rails. The altar cloths are washed on
4 Mondays. The candles are also changed on that day. I like
5 to change them on Mondays, because Mondays are dull
6 and somber. New candles brighten up the church and
7 bring clarity. When you clean the saints use soap and
8 water. Not too much soap or you'll get too much foam.
9 Then it will take you forever to rinse them. Make sure you
10 dry them well with the cloth I set aside for them. Talita
11 will show you. You know, that's one thing I always liked
12 doing, washing the saints and angels. I like to bathe them
13 as if they were my children. Clean their ears and elbows
14 real good, as I would do a baby. And talk to them. They like
15 it when you talk to them. They like to listen.
16
17 **BLACKOUT**
18
19
20 **TAKE ME TO HER**
21 **SCENE FOUR**
22
23 *MATEO sits to the left of the stage. He plays with shoes, bottles*
24 *and cans he has taken out of a box. He lines the objects as if they*
25 *were a battalion of soldiers. DOCTOR MARTIN has fallen asleep*
26 *by his bed.*
27
28 MATEO: If you can't bring her to me, take me to her. You can
29   march through the hallways until you get to the girls'
30   dormitory. That's where she's at. I described her to you.
31   Her name is Clara. First you can take my eyes and put
32   them by her pillow. Take my eyebrows and lie them by her
33   night table. Then you can take my hands, and hang them
34   on a nail until I get there. Then you can take my knees and
35   put them behind the door. Take my arms and fly them to

127

1   the ceiling. Take my whole face and hide it in her pitcher
2   of water. Leave the rest of my body in a corner of the
3   room. I'll take my feet and walk there. *(A bottle from the*
4   *battalion falls to the side. The DOCTOR wakes up from the*
5   *sound.)*
6   DOCTOR MARTIN: What are you doing? What are you doing up
7   from bed?
8   MATEO: I want to go home.
9   DOCTOR MARTIN: You're not going anywhere. Get back in bed.
10   MATEO: Where's my friend Clara?
11   DOCTOR MARTIN: What's all this stuff? What's this mess? Get
12   back into bed. Come on . . . *(The DOCTOR tries to get him*
13   *up. MATEO moves away. Pause.)* Listen, we're not here to
14   hurt you. Now, do as I say. *(MATEO goes back to bed.)* I'll get
15   you your pills. It's time for your medicine. *(MATEO gets up*
16   *and hides the objects under the bed. A bell rings.)*
17
18   LIGHTS CHANGE
19
20
21   THE CONFESSION
22   SCENE FIVE
23
24   *An armoire is placed to the center of the stage. CLARA and*
25   *TALITA stand to the left of the armoire. A square of light defines*
26   *the room.*
27
28   TALITA: Here's a broom and a duster. Let's go to the parish.
29   CLARA: Why can't I work in the infirmary like you do?
30   TALITA: Because in order for you to work in the infirmary you
31   have to be prepared. You wouldn't like it there. I make the
32   beds with Sister Nora. Me on one side of the bed and Sister
33   Nora on the other side. How would you like to see bloody
34   sheets, bullet holes on people's skin. Burnt skin. You
35   know why I prefer to work here? I'll show you. *(Opens the*

1   *armoire which is full of white communion garments.)*
2   **Communion dresses. See the veils. Just like wedding veils.**
3   **CLARA: Can I try one on?**
4   **TALITA: No.**
5   **CLARA: Why not?**
6   **TALITA: Because you're not ready for communion.** *(Tries on the*
7   *veil.)* **See, I look like a bride.**
8   **CLARA: Let me wear it?**
9   **TALITA: No, I'm going to be the bride. You're not old enough to**
10   **be a bride. I have breasts. Look at my breasts.** *(Opens her*
11   *blouse and shows CLARA her breasts.)* **Your breasts have to**
12   **grow like mine. They have to get bigger.**
13   **CLARA: I'll give you my slice of sweet bread at snack time.**
14   **TALITA: You can't wear one until you do confession. You have**
15   **to confess your sins.**
16   **CLARA: How do I do that?**
17   **TALITA: You have to kneel down and tell me your sins. Come**
18   **here.** *(TALITA takes CLARA and positions her on the other*
19   *side of the open door of the armoire. TALITA positions*
20   *herself opposite to CLARA, as if the door was a confessional.)*
21   **Go down on your knees. Tell me a secret.**
22   **CLARA: I don't have secrets.**
23   **TALITA: Everybody has secrets. You know what a secret is?**
24   **CLARA: Of course.**
25   **TALITA: Sister Nora says that secrets are sins. What we're doing**
26   **is a secret, a sin. My breasts are a secret. A sin. They are**
27   **dirty.**
28   **CLARA: You don't wash them?** *(SISTER NORA enters from the*
29   *right side of the stage and notices the girls. She remains*
30   *quiet to listen to their conversation.)*
31   **TALITA: They are dirty because they were touched by a man. A**
32   **soldier. A soldier touched them and bit them, like if they**
33   **were food. Like if he was going to eat them. He made them**
34   **dirty. My mouth is dirty because he kissed me, my neck,**
35   **my shoulders. Are you dirty too? Did a soldier touch you?**

1   **CLARA:** No.

2   **TALITA:** Then you're not dirty.

3   **CLARA:** I'm not dirty. But someone touched my body.

4   **TALITA:** Who?

5   **CLARA:** Not a soldier.

6   **TALITA:** That still makes you dirty. Who was it?

7   **CLARA:** His hands weren't dirty. His hands were clean.

8   **TALITA:** I know who it is.

9   **CLARA:** You don't.

10   **TALITA:** Then I won't let you wear the veil. You have to tell me.

11   That's what confession is for.

12   **SISTER NORA:** What are you girls doing? What are you doing?

13   **TALITA:** We're playing. We are just playing.

14   **SISTER NORA:** What is it you don't want to tell her? What is it?

15   **TALITA:** It's just a game, Sister Nora.

16   **SISTER NORA:** Who were you talking about, Clara?

17   **TALITA:** She was probably talking about a soldier. But she

18   doesn't want to tell.

19   **SISTER NORA:** Leave us alone, Talita. *(TALITA exits.)*

20   **SISTER NORA:** Why don't you tell me, Clara? Why don't you talk

21   to me? It's not good to keep things inside.

22   **CLARA:** I'm not dirty, Sister Nora. I'm not dirty. I'm clean! I'm

23   clean! *(Runs out of the room.)*

24

25   **LIGHTS FADE**

26

27

28

29   **SOLDIERS AND HEARTS WITH TONGUES**

30   **SCENE SIX**

31

32   *A cart full of boxes is rolled to the center of the stage. SISTER*

33   *NORA and DOCTOR MARTIN stand to the left of the cart. SISTER*

34   *NORA holds a writing pad and a pencil. A square of light defines*

35   *the room.*

1
2   DOCTOR MARTIN: Four boxes of evaporated milk, two boxes of
3   canned goods, two bags of rice. A box of soap. I don't know
4   what's in here. *(Opens the box.)* Another box of used
5   clothes. Do you want to go through this box?
6   SISTER NORA: We might as well.
7   DOCTOR MARTIN: One pair of pants.
8   SISTER NORA: Those will fit Alfonso.
9   DOCTOR MARTIN: A blue sweater.
10   SISTER NORA: Keep that for Luz Maria, she needs a sweater.
11   DOCTOR MARTIN: A white shirt.
12   SISTER NORA: That will fit Tato. Let me look at it.
13   DOCTOR MARTIN: It's kind of small. *(Hands her the shirt.)*
14   SISTER NORA: It will fit him.
15   DOCTOR MARTIN: Another pair of pants.
16   SISTER NORA: Those will fit Otilio.
17   DOCTOR MARTIN: A dress.
18   SISTER NORA: That's pretty. We'll give it to Leandra. She could
19   use a new dress.
20   DOCTOR MARTIN: A pair of shoes.
21   SISTER NORA: What size?
22   DOCTOR MARTIN: Size five.
23   SISTER NORA: Those will fit Marita.
24   DOCTOR MARTIN: *(Takes out a pair of pants.)* The military
25   stopped us on the way here, just as we were entering the
26   village. They were exhibiting the clothes of the guerrillas
27   who had died.
28   SISTER NORA: *(Annoyed. Tries to avoid subject.)* Give me those.
29   They'll fit Francisco.
30   DOCTOR MARTIN: *(Takes out a blouse.)* The militiamen made
31   us get out of the bus. They were doing demonstrations.
32   SISTER NORA: That will fit Victoria. *(Takes the blouse from him.)*
33   DOCTOR MARTIN: They started to take prisoners out of a
34   truck. Some prisoners could hardly walk, they were so
35   badly beaten. The soldiers forced them to stand in line

1   and face us. They had cut off parts of their skin. Others
2   had their ears missing.
3 **SISTER NORA:** *(With contained anger)* They're a bunch of wild
4   dogs! I've never killed. But sometimes I want to take a
5   rifle and shoot the first armed man I see in front of me,
6   whether he's a guerrilla fighter or from the military.
7   Sometimes I wish . . . I feel this thing in my chest. They'll
8   come here and demonstrate. I know they will. As if we
9   need to see another demonstration. There's no need to see
10   soldiers mangling and torturing people.
11 **DOCTOR MARTIN:** *(Takes out a pair of shoes)* Will these fit
12   Angelo?
13 **SISTER NORA:** What size are they?
14 **DOCTOR MARTIN:** Four and a half.
15 **SISTER NORA:** Those will fit Mateo. I made him a little ball so
16   he could exercise his hand. I made it out of yarn. He's
17   healing quite well. Clara is the one who worries me. She
18   seems anxious. She doesn't want to eat. She draws these
19   little hearts. Little hearts everywhere. I had to take the
20   pencil from her. She was drawing on the altar cloths, the
21   windowsill of her room, on her pillowcase and sheets. You
22   want to see what they look like? I tell you, all these little
23   hearts everywhere. *(Takes out a piece of paper from her*
24   *pocket and gives it to him.)* See, some of them have crying
25   eyes. Other drawings show bleeding hearts. Look at this
26   one with the tongues. Look at the shape of the tongues.
27   The sexual form of the hearts. You know these hearts lead
28   me to believe that this child was sexually active with her
29   friend. We have to be careful with them. We should keep
30   them apart. *(DOCTOR MARTIN looks at her. He turns back*
31   *to the paper to examine the hearts.)*
32
33 **LIGHTS FADE TO BLACK**
34
35

1 **SCENE SEVEN**
2
3 *CLARA stands to the right of the stage speaking to her doll. She*
4 *sits on a bed. MATEO sits on the floor to the left of the stage.*
5
6 CLARA: Your body is clean, mine is dirty. I wish I didn't have a
7   body, like the dead people in the cemetery. If only I could
8   take a bucket of water and wash away all that is bad. Then
9   Sister Nora will see me clean. She's mad at me, because
10   I'm dirty. They put us in this room because they don't like
11   us here. If we were back home, we would all be together,
12   Mateo, you and I. You would like it there. If we were back
13   home, we could be playing in the cemetery with the dead
14   people. They're so alone inside the ground. Those dead
15   people liked it when we played with them.
16
17 "INCANTATION"
18 **SCENE EIGHT**
19
20 CLARA: Mateo, can you hear me! Mateo . . . Come play in the
21   cemetery . . . Mateo . . .
22 MATEO: *(As if hearing her voice)* Clara . . .
23 CLARA: Come play with me . . .
24 MATEO: Clara . . .
25 CLARA: *(Feeling his presence)* Mateo . . .
26 MATEO: I can see you . . . *(Old photographs of a man and a*
27   *woman are projected on the scrim. CLARA runs to meet*
28   *MATEO on the center of the stage. They both walk*
29   *symmetrically around imaginary tombs.)*
30 CLARA: Mateo when I die you take a picture of me. I'm going to
31   die first, so you take a picture of me.
32 MATEO: Look at her. What do you think her name was?
33 CLARA: A . . . ma . . . li . . .a. Amalia.
34 MATEO: That's a pretty name. If I had a canary, I would name
35   it Amalia.

1   CLARA: She's looking at us. See how she looks at us. *(They walk*
2   *in different directions, as if to hide from the photographs.)*
3   MATEO: She wants to be here with us.
4   CLARA: But she can't. She's dead. She doesn't live anymore.
5   MATEO: Why don't you let her live in your body? You can
6   pretend to be her. I'll pretend to be this man. What's his
7   name? Can you read his name?
8   CLARA: I think it's Agustin.
9   MATEO: All right, I'll be Agustin. You be Amalia.
10 CLARA: Hello.
11 MATEO: Hello.
12 CLARA: Where do you come from?
13 MATEO: From the sky. Where do you come from?
14 CLARA: I was living in a star.
15 MATEO: What star?
16 CLARA: A blue star.
17 MATEO: What's the name of the star?
18 CLARA: Pilar.
19 MATEO: Would you invite me to your star? Would you invite me
20   to dinner?
21 CLARA: Yes. What do you want me to cook for you?
22 MATEO: What dead people eat. Flowers.
23 CLARA: You want carnations?
24 MATEO: No.
25 CLARA: You want jasmine?
26 MATEO: No.
27 CLARA: I can cook you a bowl of chrysanthemum . . . A dish of
28   petunias with morning glory. How about tulips?
29 MATEO: I had tulips last night.
30 CLARA: How about lilies, gardenias, orchids? That's all I have
31   in my kitchen.
32 MATEO: I want to eat violets.
33 CLARA: I don't have violets. How about dahlias, geraniums,
34   water lilies, hibiscus. How about hibiscus, Mateo . . .
35

1   Hibiscus . . . You like hibiscus? Mateo? *(CLARA freezes in a*
2   *pool of light.)*
3
4   **LIGHTS CHANGE**
5
6   **TALITA WITH FIREFLIES AND PLANS TO ESCAPE**
7   **SCENE NINE**
8
9   *MATEO sits in a chair. He throws up and down the little ball made*
10 *out of yarn. SISTER NORA and TALITA are making his bed.*
11
12 TALITA: You think I'll have a big bed in America?
13 SISTER NORA: I'm sure you will. And even if you get a small bed,
14   you should be grateful. What matters is that you'll have a
15   bed where you can rest, and a house where you'll be safe.
16 TALITA: I used to sleep in a little bed like this one. The same
17   size. My father made it out of palm leaves and corn husks.
18   Sister Nora, what does it mean when a firefly comes into a
19   room?
20 SISTER NORA: I don't know. Why do you ask?
21 TALITA: My mother used to say that when a big fly gets inside
22   the house, it means we're going to have visitors. And when
23   a dragonfly gets inside, it means the devil is going to visit
24   the house.
25 SISTER NORA: That's superstition, Talita.
26 TALITA: Last night I let a firefly get inside my mosquito net.
27   You know what I thought when I saw it flying my way?
28   That someone is coming for me.
29 SISTER NORA: Maybe. You'll find out in a couple of days.
30 TALITA: Are you trying to tell me something? Is someone really
31   coming to visit me?
32 SISTER NORA: We'll see in a couple of days.
33 TALITA: Is my mother coming?
34 SISTER NORA: Well, I didn't want to tell you until she got here.
35 TALITA: Oh! Sister Nora, you make me happy. Will she arrive

1   during the day or at nighttime?

2   **SISTER NORA:** I don't know.

3   **TALITA:** Sister Nora, can I go into the patio at night?

4   **SISTER NORA:** What for?

5   **TALITA:** To look for fireflies and catch them. I could catch

6   them with my hands and tie them to a thread, and make

7   myself a necklace. That way when my mother comes, I can

8   look beautiful, bright and shining.

9   **SISTER NORA:** *(Kisses her forehead.)* Sure. But I have a better

10   idea. We'll make you a flower necklace instead. We don't

11   want to kill the fireflies.

12   **TALITA:** I won't kill them. I'll let them fly free, once my mother

13   sees me.

14   **SISTER NORA:** Finish sweeping the floor. I'll get more linen for

15   the other beds. *(SISTER NORA exits.)*

16   **TALITA:** Did you hear what she said? My mother is coming for

17   me. When are they coming for you?

18   **MATEO:** I don't know.

19   **TALITA:** I know who you are. I know how you got that on your

20   hand. A pig bit you. Your friend told me. She told me how

21   you both escaped on the train.

22   **MATEO:** Clara.

23   **TALITA:** She sleeps next to me.

24   **MATEO:** Where?

25   **TALITA:** She doesn't anymore. You want to see her?

26   **MATEO:** I'm not allowed to see her.

27   **TALITA:** You can go see her at night, when the bell rings.

28   **MATEO:** How? *(DOCTOR MARTIN enters and proceeds to undo*

29   *MATEO's bandage. TALITA continues sweeping.)*

30

31   **LIGHTS FADE**

32

33

34

35

1 **PLAYING WITH DEATH**
2 **SCENE TEN**
3
4 *CLARA stands to the right of the stage playing with her doll.*
5 *MATEO sits on the floor to the left of the stage.*
6
7 **CLARA: I wish I were dead. They don't let us do anything here.**
8 **They took away my pencil so I can't draw any more hearts.**
9 **Well, they can all go away and leave me alone. They can**
10 **take away my pencil.** *(Shrugs her shoulders.)* **I can draw a**
11 **heart with something else. I can pull this little scab on my**
12 **elbow and bleed. And with my blood I can paint my**
13 **hearts.** *(With her right elbow she draws the shape of a heart*
14 *in midair.)* **With my saliva and the dust form the floor I can**
15 **draw hearts.** *(Dabs saliva on her fingers and draws the*
16 *shape of a heart. She spins around several times, stomping*
17 *her feet out of anger.)* **My hearts pull out their tongues at**
18 **them! If only I could be a soul. A spirit. The people in the**
19 **cemetery live without a body, invisible. If I were dead**
20 **right now, Mateo could come for me and dig me out of the**
21 **earth with his bare hands. He would have to be dead too.**
22 **But not gone away. Just dead.** *(Lies on the floor.)* **Just dead**
23 **to be with each other. Mateo . . . Mateo . . .**
24
25
26
27 **ESCAPING WITH SOLDIERS**
28 **SCENE ELEVEN**
29
30 *MATEO stands to the left of the stage. He continues to play with*
31 *the objects he has lined up. He gives orders to his battalion. By the*
32 *end of the speech he proceeds to find CLARA.*
33
34 **MATEO: The girl said to cross the patio and make a left. To go**
35 **through the hallway. You follow me. I'll be watching out**

1   for you. I'll open the doors and see if the coast is clear.
2   When I get to the laundry room, I'll signal you. You can
3   hide behind the old furniture. The helicopters can hide
4   behind the lamps and the light bulbs. I'll find a place for
5   myself. When I tell you to march on, you follow me. When
6   we find the staircase, we'll climb up to the second floor.
7   The third room, that's where she's at. I'll run to the door.
8   You stay outside and keep guard. If anybody comes you
9   shoot. Did you hear me? Shoot. *(Holds an imaginary rifle*
10 *and shoots.)* **Pooooooooommmmmmmm . . .**
11
12
13 YOU CAN FIND ME
14 SCENE TWELVE
15
16 *CLARA lies on the floor. SISTER NORA walks towards CLARA and*
17 *puts her to bed and exits. The bell rings and lights dim. CLARA*
18 *sits up in her bed, making a wish.*
19
20 "INCANTATION"
21
22 CLARA: Mateo . . . Find me in the cemetery. I'm this dead
23   woman right here. You can find me if you look for me.
24 MATEO: Clara . . . Clara . . . I can feel you.
25 CLARA: Mateo . . . I can almost see you . . . I'm this dead woman
26   right here. I'm turning into a spirit. I'm flying like your
27   kite. You can find me outside this room on the rooftop.
28 MATEO: Clara I can hear you. I can sense you.
29 CLARA: You can find me through the hallways. You can find me
30   in the zoo with the monkeys.
31 MATEO: You can find me in the zoo with the zebras.
32 CLARA: You can find me in the zoo with the giraffes.
33 MATEO: You can find me if you look for my kite.
34 CLARA: You can find me in the clouds.
35 MATEO: You can find me where kites go to die. Clara, where are

1   you? I can't find you. Clara? Clara . . . I'll find you. *(CLARA*
2   *closes her eyes as if trying to make herself into a spirit.)*
3   **CLARA: I'm this dead woman right here.** *(MATEO walks around*
4   *the stage looking for CLARA's room.)*
5   **MATEO: I'm this dead man right here.**
6   **CLARA: I'm this dead woman right here.**
7   **MATEO: I'm this dead man right here.**
8   **CLARA: I'm this dead woman right here. Mateo . . .**
9   **MATEO: Clara . . .**
10   **CLARA: Mateo . . . You're getting closer . . . I'm the woman who**
11   **died in July.**
12   **MATEO: I'm the man who died in October.**
13   **CLARA: I'm the woman with the pretty smile.**
14   **MATEO: I'm the man with a mustache.**
15   **CLARA: I was a singer.**
16   **MATEO: I was a baker.**
17   **CLARA: I was a seamstress.**
18   **MATEO: My name is Manolo.**
19   **CLARA: My name is Paquita.**
20   **MATEO: I'm Antonio.**
21   **CLARA: I'm going to turn into a man.**
22   **MATEO: Then I'll be this woman.**
23   **CLARA: Then I'll be the man who died in March.**
24   **MATEO: January . . .**
25   **CLARA: September . . .**
26   **MATEO: I had a pretty hat.**
27   **CLARA: I had a necklace . . .**
28   **MATEO: Pst . . . Pst . . . Clara.** *(Stands to the right of CLARA's bed.)*
29   **CLARA: Mateo . . .** *(Turns to him.)*
30   **MATEO: Shshshhhhhhh . . . I think someone's coming.** *(MATEO*
31   *hides under her bed. CLARA covers herself with a sheet and*
32   *pretends to be sleeping. SISTER NORA enters the room and*
33   *makes sure CLARA is well covered with the sheet. SISTER*
34   *NORA exits. CLARA peeks under her bed. MATEO looks up*
35   *at her. They both giggle.)* **I'm going to live under your bed.**

1   **CLARA: You've been gone for so long.**

2   **MATEO: I'm here now.** *(CLARA runs to the center of the stage.*

3   *MATEO runs to her side. She closes her eyes. MATEO does*

4   *the same. They express joy and excitement.)*

5   **CLARA: I'm this dead woman, right here.**

6   **MATEO: I'm this dead man, right here.**

7   **CLARA: I'm this dead woman, right here.** *(The voices become*

8   *faint. Sound of wind.)*

9   **MATEO: I'm this dead man, right here. I'm invisible like air.**

10   **CLARA: I'm invisible like smoke.**

11   **MATEO: I'm invisible like a spirit.** *(The voices become whispers*

12   *as the sound of wind fills the stage.)*

13

14   **LIGHTS FADE**

15

16   **END OF PLAY**

17

18

19

20

21

22

23

24

25

26

27

28

29

30

31

32

33

34

35

Plays of
Asian-American
Experience

Letters to a Student Revolutionary

by Elizabeth Wong

This play is unusual within the body of work represented in this collection. It does not deal with the subject of "culture clash" experienced by people of color trying to adapt to modern American society — a topic that occupies the attention of so many of our contemporary ethnic playwrights like Silvia Gonzalez S., Nadine Graham, and others. Nor does it celebrate the national cultures of people whose relatives and friends have migrated to the United States in hopes of a better life, as do the plays here by Charles Smith, for example, or Nilo Cruz. Instead, Ms. Wong deals with the great gulf in understanding separating those of us who live in the United States from those who enjoy far fewer personal and political freedoms, advantages and opportunities. Elizabeth Wong reminds us that beneath the political rhetoric and media hype surrounding problems with immigration laws and with human rights here and abroad, there are real, painful, and terribly important human issues that we often overlook or take for granted, and that we can ignore only at our peril.

Bibi, an American mall-rat, valley-girl, and beach-baby Asian-American from southern California comes face-to-face with Karen, a young Chinese girl swept up in the intoxication of Western ideas that would lead to the tragedy of Tiananmen Square in 1989. On the surface it would seem the two have nothing in common. The American youth subculture, long decried as shallow, self-obsessed, and ignorant — and yet representing one of our nation's most popular cultural exports — might appear at first glance to be one of the least likely "sounding-boards" for voicing important statements about ethnic issues. But in Ms. Wong's masterful handling of these two women's lives over a span of ten years, and with her brilliant command of epic theatre stage techniques, an unforgettable story unfolds that illuminates the vastly different experiences and societies of both women, raising many questions as it does so.

Not all of the plays in this collection conclude on an optimistic note; and even those that do — *The Migrant Farmworker's Son*, for example, *The China Crisis*, or *The Magic Kingdom* — tend to leave more than a few scars in their wake as the curtain rings down. But the last image in this play — Bibi alone On-stage in a solitary shaft of light after the raucous newsbites, after the letters, after the chaos and the gunfire and the contact have all stopped — presents us with one of the most moving portraits of human suffering the contemporary American theatre has produced.

The play was originally produced in New York by Pan Asian Repertory Theatre on May 7, 1991.

Characters:

BIBI: 20s, a Chinese-American woman

KAREN: 20s, a Chinese woman

CHORUS: A Chorus of four, (Three men and one woman), in the
    following multiple roles:

CHARLIE/LU YAN/CHORUS ONE

BROTHER/FATHER/INS OFFICER/CHORUS TWO

SOLDIER/BOSS/CAT/JONATHAN/CHORUS THREE

MOTHER/MEXICAN LADY/CHORUS FOUR

Place:

China and the United States

Time:

One decade, 1979 - 1989

There is no intermission.

Production Notes:

The play is stylistic and presentational, but also grounded in the art and act of letter writing. The audience is an important part of the play, and any address or appeal to them should be personal and direct.

Set:

The set is divided into two separate areas representing China and the United States. However, the center space must be a neutral territory wherein the rules of time and geography are broken. Minimal props suggest occupation and/or location. Chairs may be black or red. Otherwise, a black and white color scheme is preferred. Reference to the mechanics of the theatre itself are desirable.

Chorus:

The chorus must remain on stage throughout. Their presence is necessary, even if action does not involve them directly. Choral movements are militaristic — crisp and spit polish.

Costumes:

Clothes are suggested by the text. The Chorus wears uniforms of drab loose-fitting garments similar to the Mao jacket and trousers. Both garments must match. Color should be left to the personalities of the two main characters. Karen's clothing, at first, must be simple and a reflection of the choral costume. Bibi is a clothes horse — stylish, with a splash of anti-fashion accents. Her clothes are a chronicler of time, and they must mark her growth as a character as well.

Special Effects:

Slides of the Tiananmen Square Massacre; of Democracy Wall/or Chinese calligraphy; of a shopping mall.

Playwright's Special Note:

Stage directions are few, but significant. Please heed.

1   *(The CHORUS stand impassively together, Upstage. BIBI is*
2   *Downstage.)*
3   **BIBI: Postcard. Day thirty-five. Ain't no peanut butter. No**
4   **cheese. No toast. And I'm sick of jook. Jook is no joke. Jook**
5   **for breakfast - yesterday, today, and tomorrow. What is**
6   **jook, you ask?**
7   **CHORUS ONE:** *(Offers a bowl)* **Rice porridge.**
8   **CHORUS: It's good for you.**
9   **BIBI: Boring. That's it. I've had it.** *(To AUDIENCE.)* **I rebelled**
10   **against breakfast. I pushed myself away from the table.**
11   **The chair went flying, what a clatter, over there, like an**
12   **hockey puck on ice. I struck a definitely defiant Bette**
13   **Davis pose, thank you very much.** *(To CHORUS ONE)* **"Get**
14   **that slop away from me, you . . . you pit!"** *(To AUDIENCE)*
15   **My parents were appalled at my behavior. I was**
16   **impossible. But I couldn't help it. The ghost of James**
17   **Dean. Heavy sigh. So, for thirty-five days, wherein I**
18   **wished I was sunning in the Bahamas instead, I was**
19   **Kunta Kinte of the new roots generation – touring China**
20   **with mom and dad.** *(Chinese opera music clangs. BIBI*
21   *smiles a bit too broadly.)* **Loved the music. Also, loved the**
22   **toasting of the honored guests, including me . . .**
23   **CHORUS** *(ALL):* ***Gom bei!***
24   **BIBI:** *(To CHORUS)* ***Gom bei!*** *(To AUDIENCE)* **Oh sure, I loved**
25   **the endless tours – the jade factory, brocade factory,**
26   **carpet factory. But how could I appreciate it without some**
27   **proper grub. John Wayne wouldn't stand for it, he'd shoot**
28   **the cook, who was probably a Chinese anyway.** *(CHORUS*
29   *ONE offers the bowl again.)* **Cheerios?**
30   **CHORUS ONE: Jook.**
31   **BIBI: What a nightmare!** *(BIBI abruptly runs Upstage. She, not*
32   *the Chorus, sets the scene. Playwrights' note: The Chorus*
33   *should not be individuated, nor should they be illustrative*
34   *of any particular attitude or action.)* **I took to the streets of**
35   **Beijing. Wandered into Tiananmen Square – a hungry**

1 look in my eyes, a vain hope in my heart. *(To CHORUS*
2 *FOUR)* You there, sweeper. Could you please tell me where
3 I might locate a golden oasis of fast food? *(To CHORUS*
4 *TWO)* Hey there Mr. Chicken man, spare an egg for a
5 simple sunnyside up? *(To AUDIENCE)* Someday, right next
6 to that rosy-faced mug of Chairman Mao, there'll be a
7 golden arch and a neon sign flashing — billions and
8 billions served. No place is truly civilized without Mickey
9 D and a drive-up window. *(Runs back Upstage, to CHORUS*
10 *THREE)* 'Scuse me Mr. Soldier, can you possibly direct me
11 to the nearest greasy spoon? *(CHORUS THREE slowly turns*
12 *to look at BIBI, upon whom dawns the idea that she is*
13 *intimidated.)*

14 **CHORUS ONE:** *(To AUDIENCE)* **Summer 1979. Tourism was still**
15 **so new in China.** *(KAREN enters, pushing an old coaster*
16 *bicycle.)*

17 **KAREN:** *(To AUDIENCE)* **I am on my way home from the factory.**
18 **End of the graveyard shift. Is this the correct phrase? Yes,**
19 **I think so. Graveyard shift. This morning, there is much**
20 **mist. But it is already hot like hell. Do I say that right? Yes,**
21 **I think so.**

22 **CHORUS FOUR:** *(To AUDIENCE)* **I sweep. I sweep. Everything**
23 **must be clean.** *(But CHORUS FOUR does not move.)*

24 **KAREN: The square is very crowded, very many people**
25 **everywhere. But I see a girl. She looks like me. But her**
26 **hair is curly like the tail of a pig. She wears pink, lavender,**
27 **indigo. She is a human rainbow.** *(KAREN steps towards*
28 *BIBI. But . . .)*

29 **CHORUS FOUR:** *(To KAREN)* **I sweep you if you become**
30 **unclean. Watch out for contamination!** *(Whispered, to*
31 *CHORUS ONE.)* **You, you there waiter!**

32 **CHORUS ONE**: *(Overlapped whisper, to CHORUS TWO)* **Watch**
33 **out! You, you there butcher!**

34 **CHORUS TWO:** *(Overlapped whisper, to KAREN)* **Watch out! You,**
35 **you there.** *(Intimidated, KAREN backs away from BIBI.)*

1 CHORUS FOUR: *(To Audience)* My duty to sweep all day. My
2   duty to sweep all night. My back hurts. But I have duty to
3   perform.
4 KAREN: What harm is there to practice a little English?
5 CHORUS THREE: *(To KAREN)* I am watching her, and . . . *(To*
6   *AUDIENCE)* I am watching you.
7 BIBI: *(To AUDIENCE)* Oh look. Grandmothers with ancient
8   faces, pushing bamboo strollers like shopping carts. Let's
9   peek. *(She does.)* Ahhhh, sweetest little babies with wispy,
10   fuzzy, spiky hair.
11 KAREN: *(To AUDIENCE)* Look, there is a butcher I know. He
12   carries chickens upside down, hurrying to market. He
13   does not see me.
14 BIBI: *(To AUDIENCE)* Talk about ego. Check these pictures,
15   bigger than billboards on Sunset Boulevard. And what's
16   playing? That's the Mao matinee. That's Lenin. Stalin. Is
17   that guy Marx? Yup. Give the girl a piece of the pie.
18 KAREN: *(To AUDIENCE)* There, a big strong worker shoulders
19   his load of bamboo for scaffolds. He helps to build a
20   hospital. He is too busy to notice me.
21 BIBI: *(To Audience)* Bricklayers push a cartful of bricks. A man
22   carries a pole balanced with two hanging baskets, filled
23   with live fish. Great smell! I think I'm going to faint.
24   Bicycles everywhere in the square.
25 CHORUS ONE: Yes, a busy morning in the square. *(The*
26   *CHORUS, one by one, build an impenetrable HUMAN WALL*
27   *between KAREN and BIBI.)*
28 CHORUS FOUR: *(To AUDIENCE)* I am not you and I am not me.
29   I am a good citizen of the state.
30 CHORUS TWO: *(To AUDIENCE)* With so much going on, so many
31   people, who pays attention to an inconsequential girl on a
32   bicycle?
33 KAREN: I will go up to her and speak to her. We will make
34   beautiful sentences together.
35 CHORUS FOUR: *(To AUDIENCE)* I am watching too. Watching

1   everything. It is my duty as a good citizen of the state.

2   *(KAREN tries to penetrate the wall.)*

3   **CHORUS THREE:** *(To AUDIENCE, overlapping)* **Anarchy will not**

4   **be tolerated.**

5   **CHORUS TWO:** *(Overlapping)* **Even a spark of spirit will be**

6   **squashed.**

7   **CHORUS ONE:** *(Overlapping)* **Wild behavior will not be**

8   **permitted.**

9   **CHORUS THREE:** *(Overlapping)* **Wild thinking will not be**

10   **permitted.**

11   **CHORUS ONE:** *(Overlapping)* **Any messes will be cleaned up.**

12   **CHORUS TWO:** *(Overlapping)* **That is what a broom is for.**

13   **CHORUS FOUR: This is my sword. My broom.**

14   **CHORUS: (ALL):** *(To AUDIENCE)* **We must have cleanliness. The**

15   **state will insist.**

16   **KAREN:** *(Softly)* **Hello.**

17   **BIBI:** *(Ignoring her)* **Like in "Vertigo." Jimmy Stewart climbing**

18   **the steps, looking down from the tower. Or is it Orson**

19   **Welles with the funhouse mirrors in "Lady From**

20   **Shanghai?" Well, anyway, like everything going round and**

21   **round in a woozy circle.** *(BIBI examines each member of*

22   *the CHORUS.)*

23   **BIBI: I see me and I see me and I see me. But not really, you**

24   **know. I don't fit in, not at all.** *(KAREN breaks through the*

25   *wall, crosses over to BIBI.)*

26   **KAREN:** *(Tentatively)* **Hello.** *(BIBI doesn't hear. KAREN steps*

27   *closer. The CHORUS steps into line, turning their backs to*

28   *the AUDIENCE.)*

29   **KAREN: Please excuse.**

30   **BIBI: Oh, hello.**

31   **KAREN: Please. Not so loud.** *(Beat)* **Are you?**

32   **BIBI:** *(Whispers)* **I am. How can you tell?**

33   **KAREN: Ahh.** *(Pause)* **Your hair.**

34   **BIBI: Completely unnatural, I know. It's called a permanent.**

35   **Why something's called permanent when you have it**

1   redone every six months I'll never know. More like a
2   temporary, if you ask me. Go figure.
3   KAREN: Go to figure.
4   BIBI: Right. It's like every time I go to the salon, they want to
5   give me the same old, tired thing — the classic bob and
6   bangs, exactly like yours. So I plead, "Please do something
7   different." Understand? But every time, without fail, I end
8   up with . . . you know . . . *(Indicates KAREN's hair.)* that —
9   bland and boring, like breakfast.
10   KAREN: Like breakfast.
11   BIBI: Right. They tell me, "But oh no, you look so cute. A little
12   China doll, that's what you are." Make me puke. So I say,
13   "Aldo baby darling, perm it. Wave it. Frizz it. Spike it.
14   Color it blue." So if you look in the light. See? Not black,
15   but blue with red highlights, tinged with orange. It's
16   unusual, don't you think?
17   KAREN: You want haircut like me? That easy. Very simple. I do
18   it for you.
19   BIBI: Sorry. I know I talk too fast. I'm what is known as an
20   energetic person. I have so much energy, I sometimes
21   think I'll leap out of my clothes.
22   KAREN: No, I'm sorry. My comprehending is very bad. My
23   English is too stupid. But I wish to practice. I would like to
24   have hair curly like yours. Can you do that for me?
25   BIBI: Sure, you come to California. And I'll set you up with
26   Aldo. But I warn you, he'll poof and pull and snip, and you
27   think you're going to be a new woman, but you get banged
28   and bobbed every time. *(KAREN starts to touch BIBI's
29   sleeve; then withdraws shyly.)*
30   KAREN: Here we have only a few colors. Grey and blue and
31   green.
32   BIBI: Grey and blue and green are good colors.
33   KAREN: May I ask what is your name?
34   BIBI: Bibi. My name is Bibi. *(They reach to shake hands, but
35   before they touch, BIBI and KAREN freeze. The CHORUS*

1   *speaks to the AUDIENCE.)*
2   **CHORUS THREE: It was nothing. Conversation lasted two,**
3   **three minutes tops.**
4   **CHORUS FOUR:** (*Overlapping*) **Anything can happen in two,**
5   **three minutes. Did they touch?**
6   **CHORUS ONE:** (*Overlapping*) **Was there a connection?**
7   **CHORUS TWO:** (*Overlapping*) **Did they touch?**
8   **CHORUS ONE:** (*Overlapping*) **Did she have a newspaper?**
9   **CHORUS THREE:** (*Overlapping*) **A book?**
10 **CHORUS TWO:** (*Overlapping*) **Was there an exchange?**
11 **CHORUS FOUR:** (*Overlapping*) **Did they touch?**
12 **CHORUS THREE:** *(Overlapping)* **Did they touch?**
13 **CHORUS TWO:** (*Overlapping*) **Watch her very closely. Such**
14   **encounters might be dangerous.**
15 **CHORUS FOUR:** (*Whispered*) **Dangerous.**
16 **CHORUS ONE:** (*Overlapping, whispered*) **Dangerous.**
17 **CHORUS THREE:** (*Overlapping, whispered*) **Dangerous.**
18 **BIBI:** (*To AUDIENCE*) **Our conversation lasted about two, three**
19   **minutes tops. It was a fleeting proverbial blink of the eye.**
20   **We didn't have a pencil or even a scrap of paper.** (*The two*
21   *women move away from each other. Shouts.*) **That's Los**
22   **Angeles, California. U.S.A. 90026. Can you remember all**
23   **of that?** *(KAREN nods vigorously.)*
24 **KAREN:** (*To self*) **Yes, I will remember. Yes. Yes, I remember it.**
25 **BIBI:** (*To AUDIENCE*) **She didn't even tell me her name.** (*The*
26   *CHORUS all sound like television newscasters.*)
27 **CHORUS THREE: The girl pedaled away.**
28 **CHORUS TWO: Merged with the other bicycles merging together.**
29 **CHORUS ONE: Bibi couldn't distinguish one rider from the**
30   **other.**
31 **BIBI: I went back to the hotel, hamburgerless.**
32 **CHORUS FOUR: Then Bibi and her parents boarded the train**
33   **to Hong Kong.**
34 **CHORUS ONE: Where she ate a fish fillet at the McDonalds™ on**
35   **Nathan Road.**

1   **CHORUS TWO: Where she also found a Pizza Hut™.**
2   **CHORUS ONE: She stopped in every store and she shopped**
3   **from dawn 'til dusk.**
4   **BIBI: Now that's freedom. Shopping from dawn 'til dusk.**
5   **CHORUS (ALL):** *(Whispers)* **There is no you and there is no me.**
6   **There is no you and there is no me.**
7   **There is no you. There is no me.**
8   **BIBI:** *(To AUDIENCE)* **But China is changing.**
9   **KAREN: But China is changing.**
10 **CHORUS THREE: Nowhere is a hint of anarchy tolerated.**
11 **CHORUS (ALL): Not here, nor there. Not anywhere.**
12 **CHORUS TWO: Bibi went back home to California, U.S.A. And**
13   **that is the beginning.**
14 **CHORUS THREE:** *(To CHORUS TWO)* **The beginning of what?**
15 **CHORUS ONE:** *(To AUDIENCE)* **The beginning of a most**
16   **uncomfortable correspondence.** *(KAREN in her bedroom)*
17 **KAREN:** *(Writes)* **Summer 1979. My dear American friend . . .**
18   *(Scratches out, starts again.)* **My dear new friend. Greetings**
19   **from Beijing.** *(KAREN sits back, stares into space. BIBI on*
20   *the beach)*
21 **BIBI:** *(To AUDIENCE)* **Summer, 1979. This is Venice Beach. I**
22   **have my chair, hunkered down in the sand, positioned for**
23   **maximum good tanning rays. The pier to my left. The**
24   **muscle boys to my right. The surfers in their tight black**
25   **wet suits. Happy sigh. Life can't get better than someone**
26   **muscular in a tight black wet suit.** *(CHARLIE, a virile*
27   *young man, brings on a blaring radio playing "Good*
28   *Vibrations" by the Beach Boys. He's a nice guy. To*
29   *AUDIENCE)* **Speaking of which, my friend. A cross between**
30   **Frankie Avalon and Louis Jordan, which I guess makes me**
31   **a cross between Annette Funicello and Leslie Caron.**
32 **CHARLIE:** *Limon? Ma cheri* **Gidget Gigi?**
33 **BIBI:** *(To AUDIENCE)* **Not bad. But temporary. I mean this guy**
34   **thinks "Casablanca" is a fine wine. He does try though,**
35   **and he brings me lemonade. So here we are, me and**

1   Casanova under an umbrella of blue sky, hoping for a
2   beach blanket bingo state of mind. But I admit, I've been
3   a bit preoccupied. *(BIBI shows a letter to the AUDIENCE.)*
4 CHARLIE: *(To BIBI)* Preoccupied nothing. You've been
5   downright morose. Whatsa matter punky pumpkin? You
6   been bluesy woozy all day.
7 BIBI: Turn that thing off.
8 CHARLIE: OK dokey, cupcake. *(She resumes reading the letter.)*
9   My lady Cleopatra, Queen of the Nile, command me. I live
10   to serve.
11 BIBI: Oh, put a lid on it. *(To AUDIENCE)* Like I said. He does try.
12   *(To CHARLIE)* Caesar, look on this. *(BIBI shows him the*
13   *letter. He takes it, examines it.)*
14 CHARLIE: Nice stamp. *(KAREN continues. Reads.)* Summer
15   1979. Dear Bibi, greetings from China. Do you remember
16   me? I am the girl with whom you have shared a
17   conversation. *(To BIBI.)* Looks like you've got a pen pal. I
18   think it's very sweet.
19 BIBI: Keep reading.
20 CHARLIE: Read. All right. "I met you in Tiananmen Square, I
21   write to you from my little room . . . "
22 KAREN: *(Overlapping)* . . . Tiananmen Square. I write to you
23   from my little room. There is no window, but I have a big
24   picture of a map to show me wondrous sights of America.
25   The Grandest Canyon and OkayDokey Swamp. I share my
26   room with my brother who teaches English at the high
27   school. *(Her BROTHER steps from the CHORUS.)*
28 BROTHER: Hey ugly, turn out the light!
29 KAREN: I would like to get a new brother. Is that possible in
30   America? I think anything is possible where you live. *(A*
31   *CAT steps from the CHORUS, sits at KAREN's feet.)*
32 CAT: *(To AUDIENCE)* Meeooww.
33 BROTHER: *(To KAREN)* And get that hairball out of the room.
34   Or I'll make kitty stew!
35 KAREN: *(To BROTHER)* You wouldn't!

1 BIBI: *(To CHARLIE)* In China, cats are not kept as pets.
2 KAREN: *(To BIBI)* She is not a pet. I do not own her. She is a free
3   cat.
4 BROTHER: *(To AUDIENCE)* Cats are functional. They eat rats.
5   *(To KAREN)* Or they are to be eaten. Which is it?
6 KAREN: *(To AUDIENCE)* I put the cat outside. *(To CAT)* I say, "I
7   am sorry kitty cat. So very sorry, little kitty. Go on now, go
8   to work and catch some micey mousies." *(To AUDIENCE)*
9   And then, she say in extreme irritableness . . .
10 CAT: Meeoow.
11 KAREN: *(To AUDIENCE)* I pretend to go to sleep. And when my
12   brother starts to snore, I get up and write to you, my dear
13   friend Bibi.
14 BIBI: Here it comes.
15 CHARLIE: Bibi, you may sound like a tough cookie, but only I
16   know what a soft, mushy cupcake you are.
17 BIBI: Oh yeah? Well, read on, cupcake.
18 KAREN: *(To AUDIENCE)* It is a happy feeling I have . . . to have
19   you for a secret friend, a special friend. I have such
20   stupidity since I realized I never told you my name. How
21   do you like my name? Do you think this is a good name?
22 BIBI: *(To KAREN)* Karen? Yes. I think Karen is a good name.
23 KAREN: *(To BIBI)* Good. I am so glad for this. *(To AUDIENCE.)*
24   I chose my new name in secret. This is my choice. Only
25   my best friend knows about this secret. We call each
26   other, Debbie and Karen. Where you live, you can be
27   open about such matters. But here we must do
28   everything in secret.
29 CHARLIE: This is a very nice letter, Bibi. Hardly appropriate of
30   you to be so provoked about it, cupcake. *(Provoked by the*
31   *belittling endearment, BIBI takes the letter from CHARLIE.)*
32   Hey!
33 BIBI: You aren't helping. And don't you cupcake me anymore
34   . . . stud muffin. Stop patronizing me, categorizing me,
35   objectifying me, labeling me like some damned jar of jelly.

1   CHARLIE: Why so miffed, love bun?

2   BIBI: There you go again.

3   CHARLIE: I just . . .

4   BIBI: You just what? A lot you know. This, for one, is not a nice

5   letter. This just sounds like a nice letter.

6   CHARLIE: Cupcake, not everybody has ulterior motives. Not

7   everyone is suspect. Have a little faith in human nature.

8   Not everyone is out to use and abuse.

9   BIBI: You are not listening. This letter, stud muffin, is crafted

10   on two predictable emotions– guilt and more guilt. I will

11   *not* be made to feel responsible before my time.

12   CHARLIE: Are we not our brothers' keeper?

13   BIBI: No, we are not. Look here, silver spoon white boy. I have

14   lived in every ghetto slum in Los Angeles. Mom and Dad

15   slaved so I could squander their hard work on college. And

16   on top of everything, they got annoying letters like this.

17   KAREN: Bibi, you have such freedom.

18   BIBI: *(Overlapping)* Bibi, you have such freedom. *(To CHARLIE)*

19   Mom calls them "Ailment-of-the-month" letters. Dear Mr.

20   and Mrs. Lee, my dear very rich American relation, could

21   you send us some money since life here is so bad, and you

22   have it so good.

23   KAREN: I have no freedom. None whatsoever. Is it my

24   misfortune to be born in my country and you were born

25   in yours? I look at you and it is as if I look at myself in a

26   glass.

27   CHARLIE: *(To KAREN)* You mean mirror.

28   KAREN: Thank you for this correction. *(Beat)* Yes, I look in the

29   mirror, yes. I think, "You are me." I was meant to be born

30   in the United States, to live in freedom like you. Do you

31   understand? *(Beat)* Two days after I met you, my boss at

32   the factory where I am in the accounting department,

33   asked to speak to me. *(The CAT gets up, and with an abrupt*

34   *turn becomes the smiling BOSS, who approaches KAREN.)*

35   My boss has a kind voice, but a frown is in his heart. I am

1   taken to a small room in the basement. This is not a good

2   sign.

3 BOSS: Please sit down.

4 CHARLIE: *(To KAREN)* Then what happened?

5 KAREN: I sat down.

6 BOSS: *(Kindly, as if to an errant child)* You were seen talking to

7   an American. An American student. Now, you mustn't be

8   worried. Don't be afraid. You may talk to Westerners now.

9 CHARLIE: *(To BIBI)* I read about this. China is relaxing some of

10   its policies.

11 BOSS: We are more relaxed under the new policies. But you

12   must not listen to what they say. You must not get any

13   ideas. *(Recites by rote.)* Good citizens have only ideas that

14   also belong to The State. The State is your mother. The

15   State is your father. The State is more than your mother or

16   your father. Do you understand?

17 KAREN: I said, "Yes." But in my heart, I do not understand. I

18   have never understood why I cannot speak my opinions. I

19   only speak of my opinions to my friend, my only friend

20   Debbie. Never to anyone else, not even my father, not even

21   my brother. My boss talks to me as if I am but a child. I

22   want to say, "I can think for myself. You are not my

23   mother. You are not my father. I already have a mother. I

24   already have a father. I do not need you." *(Resignedly)* But

25   this is China. *(Beat)* I ride my bicycle home. But then . . . I

26   see something . . . something very strange, a curious event

27   is occurring. I must disembark my bicycle to see what

28   occasion takes place. *(The CHORUS, in a semi-circle, turns*

29   *its back to the AUDIENCE. Slides of Democracy Wall)* Very

30   many people assemble in the street. A big man stands in

31   my way. I cannot see. What is there to see? Something,

32   something . . .

33 CHARLIE: Extraordinary?

34 KAREN: No. Something . . .

35 BIBI: Momentous?

1   CHARLIE: Catastrophic?

2   KAREN: No . . . no. Something . . .

3   BIBI: Important.

4   KAREN: Yes, important. I try to see for myself. I want to be a

5   part of history. So, when a man got in my view, I used my

6   bicycle to scrape him a little on the leg. He moved aside.

7   Look! Look, Bibi! Do you see? A man with wire-rimmed

8   glasses put a piece of paper with big writing on the wall. A

9   newspaper. A poster. Many words I am shocked to read.

10   BIBI: *(To CHARLIE)* Democracy Wall.

11   CHARLIE: *(To BIBI)* I know, I'm not uninformed.

12   KAREN: *(To AUDIENCE)* Very brave to write these words, very

13   brave to read these words. These . . . these . . .

14   CHARLIE: *(To KAREN)* Criticisms.

15   KAREN: Yes. I do not stay to read these criticisms, or else my

16   boss would have some more to say to me. I was a little

17   afraid. Do you understand? To be afraid of words in such

18   a public place. I go home, thinking of freedom. How good

19   freedom must be. What I see in the square makes me feel

20   brave enough to write to you.

21   BIBI: *(To KAREN)* But why me?

22   CHARLIE: *(To BIBI)* Stop wiggling the paper. I'm trying to read

23   the rest.

24   KAREN: *(To AUDIENCE)* I think, Bibi, I want to be having

25   freedom like you. I think maybe I deserve a little of this

26   freedom. So I find my pencil and a bit of paper. I try and

27   try. I have my dictionary from a present my brother made

28   me last year. But, I make many mistakes. Bibi, I think you

29   must be helping me. You are my only friend.

30   CAT: *(Annoyed)* Meeow!

31   CHARLIE: Now that's what the American spirit is made of.

32   Bring me your tired, your poor . . . et cetera, et cetera, uh

33   you know . . . yearning to breathe free.

34   BIBI: I'm so glad you are such a patriot. Because she's all yours.

35   CHARLIE: What?

1 KAREN: I am thinking to accept your invitation to come to live
2   with you in California.
3 CHARLIE: Ooops!
4 BIBI: Bingo!
5 KAREN: Perhaps you, Bibi, will pay $10,000 for my airplane
6   ticket and my living in California. Once I get to live in
7   California, I will work and work and work and pay you
8   back. Does this make sense? What do you think of my
9   idea? I know this letter is my first letter to you and I am
10   asking you for bringing an improvement to my life. But I
11   know Americans have a great opportunity . . . do I say this
12   correctly . . . for making money and for helping other
13   people. I look forward to your favorable response. Your
14   friend, Karen.
15 BIBI: Well?
16 CHARLIE: O.K. Maybe I was wrong. No matter, 'cuz Bibi
17   cupcake, I think you will make an adorable guardian
18   angel.
19 BIBI: This isn't funny, Charlie.
20 CHARLIE: You're her sweet savior. Her fondest hope. Her
21   nearest future.
22 BIBI: I mean it. She's nothing to me and I'm nothing to her.
23   Have you known me to ever be political?
24 CHARLIE: No.
25 BIBI: Exactly. And I could care less. I'm not political. I've never
26   been political. And I resent that she is trying to make me
27   responsible for her freedom. I'm barely responsible for
28   my own. *(Beat)* This is not the Promised Land and I do not
29   have the muscle to be Moses.
30 CHARLIE: You most certainly do not have his beard. Kiss me.
31 BIBI: *(Ducking him)* Oh, that will solve everything.
32 CHARLIE: Forget the ten commandments. How about Burt
33   Lancaster?
34 BIBI: What?
35 CHARLIE: Enough foreign policy. Let's forget about breathing

1　　free. How about a little heavy breathing. I mean, we have
2　　the beach. The waves are crashing. You are Deborah Kerr,
3　　or is that Donna Reed? I forget.
4　BIBI: What about my letter?
5　CHARLIE: So headstrong and optimistic and naive – the true
6　　blue American character. Stubborn in all the right places.
7　　Naive in all the cutest spots. Hopeful sexy neck. I'm sure
8　　you'll think of something diplomatic. Now will you kiss
9　　me? *(BIBI debates quickly. Then tosses aside the letter. In*
10　　*other words, she pounces on him. Lights out. KAREN at*
11　　*home)*
12　KAREN: I have no one else to tell, so I might as well tell you, my
13　　furry friend. You are my best friend. Did you catch any
14　　mice today, Debbie? You better earn your keep, or else.
15　CAT: Meeeoow.
16　KAREN: In America, kitty cats are friends. But we are not in
17　　America but you are my friend anyway, aren't you Debbie?
18　　My good friend Debbie. Look, a letter from the United
19　　States of America. Do you want to open it, or shall I? I will
20　　read it to you? Yes? Yes, I read it to you. Come sit near me.
21　　Now we begin. January 1980. Dear Karen . . . *(BIBI at home)*
22　BIBI: *(Overlapping)* January 1980. Dear Karen, how are you? I
23　　am fine. How's the weather? *(To AUDIENCE)* Too
24　　conventional. *(Resumes.)* Dear Karen, Happy New Year. I
25　　went to a party last night to ring in the new year 1980.
26　KAREN: Imagine a party in America, Debbie. *(BIBI continues.*
27　　*The CHORUS goes to a party – a tableau of drunkenness and*
28　　*revelry.)*
29　BIBI: I drank tequila shots, and someone ended up on the floor
30　　wiggling like a cockroach, and someone pulled up the rug
31　　and danced underneath it, the Mexican Hat Dance.
32　　Temporary Terry, the military guy from Camp Pendleton,
33　　ate the worm. *(To AUDIENCE)* Nope. Too decadent. Bad
34　　first impression. *(BIBI scratches out the paragraph. Writes*
35　　*anew.)* Dear Karen, I am so sorry it's taken me nearly six

1   months to write you back. *(To AUDIENCE, resolutely.)*

2   Honest and direct.

3   KAREN: *(To CAT)* We didn't think she would write us, did we

4   Debbie?

5   BIBI: I hope the new year will bring you much happiness. I

6   would have answered you sooner, but I was unsure about

7   how to respond to your letter. It really packed a wallop.

8   KAREN: What means wallop, Debbie? Do you know?

9   CAT: Meeoow.

10   KAREN: Oh.

11   BIBI: Karen. I don't know what possessed me. But two months

12   ago, I did go to the office of the Immigration and

13   Naturalization Service. Have you ever seen that movie,

14   "Mr. Smith Goes To Washington"? Well, we have this

15   problem in America. It's called bureaucracy.

16   KAREN: Don't I have a good eye for choosing friends, Debbie?

17   CAT: Meeow.

18   KAREN: Oh, don't be jealous. *(The CHORUS queues up at the*

19   *Office of Immigration and Naturalization. The CAT joins the*

20   *CHORUS.)*

21   BIBI: There were a lot of people there. Long lines. I waited in

22   one line and they sent me to another and another and

23   then another. It's been like that all day. Lines at the

24   checkout stand, lines at the bank, so of course, lines at the

25   good ole' I.N.S. I got very frustrated.

26   KAREN: What did they say?

27   BIBI: A lady from Mexico in front of me. Bewildered, but

28   sweetest face. She was holding up the line, you know. Her

29   English was poor, and she didn't have the right forms.

30   KAREN: What did they say about me?

31   CHORUS THREE: Hey, what's holding up this line? I've been

32   here for four hours.

33   CHORUS ONE: Hey, what's holding up this line?

34   BIBI: *(To CHORUS ONE)* Shush . . . be nice.

35   INS OFFICER: You've got the wrong form. This is an L1

1   Intracompany transfer I-21-B. I doubt, lady, you are an
2   intracompany transfer.
3   MEXICAN LADY: *Pero eso esque lo me han dicho. El hombre*
4   *alla . . no se.* (But this is what they told me. The man over
5   there . . . I don't know.)
6   INS OFFICER: Well, he gave you the wrong form. Look, you
7   have to fill out another form. You want to file for
8   permanent status? *Sí?* To stay in this country? Right? No
9   deportee to the border?
10   MEXICAN LADY: Huh? *No, no, no. No es para mi. Es apra mi*
11   *hermana.* (No. No. Not for me. For my sister.)
12   INS OFFICER: For your sister? Why didn't you say so? I haven't
13   eaten all day, lady. And my feet hurt.
14   MEXICAN LADY: *Sí, Sí.* For my sister in Mexico. *Mi hermana*
15   *quiere* (kee air eh) *vivir aqui.* (My sister wants to come to
16   live here.)
17   INS OFFICER: Yea, right. Everybody wants to live in America.
18   Look, just fill this out Petition I-130, to start immediate
19   relative status. Next!
20   MEXICAN LADY: *Mande usted, como?*
21   INS OFFICER: Lady, look at this line. You are holding up all
22   these people.
23   BIBI: Hey, why don't you just answer the lady's question?
24   INS OFFICER: Do you wanna be next or do you wanna see the
25   back of the line?
26   BIBI: *Senora, este tipo es un pendejo.*
27   CHORUS THREE: What'd she say?
28   CHORUS ONE: She called him an asshole, asshole.
29   BIBI: *Este es el formulario de la Peticion E-ciento trenta.*
30   MEXICAN LADY: *Oh, si.*
31   BIBI: *Lo tiene que llenar para ereclamar a su hermana.* To
32   claim your sister, understand? *Espere usted en esa fila.*
33   Then you stand in line over there, *por favor.*
34   MEXICAN LADY: *Gracias, senorita. Muchas gracias.*
35   BIBI: *De nada.* (To INS OFFICER) Please and thank you. You

1   should try adding them to your vocabulary. *(The INS*
2   *OFFICER mimes closing the window.)*
3   CHORUS: (ALL): The sign says, "Closed for lunch." *(The*
4   *CHORUS groans with annoyance. BIBI mimes opening the*
5   *window.)*
6   BIBI: Wait a minute, sir. We've been here in line for hours.
7   INS OFFICER: Hey, I'm entitled. What a day. My back is killing
8   me. Go to the next window. *(INS OFFICER closes the*
9   *window. BIBI reopens it.)*
10   BIBI: Look you. Some of these people can't speak up for
11   themselves. But they deserve your respect, and if not your
12   respect, then at least some courtesy. I want to see your
13   supervisor. *(THE INS OFFICER closes the window.)*
14   KAREN: Bibi, did you talk about me?
15   BIBI: *(To KAREN)* Can't you see I'm trying to prove a point here?
16   INS OFFICER: I thought you people were the quiet ones. *(INS*
17   *OFFICER exits.)*
18   BIBI: *(Shouts.)* Hey, you want quiet! I can be very very quiet! I
19   said, everybody deserves to be treated with respect.
20   CHORUS ONE: Look what you did. Now we all suffer.
21   CHORUS (ALL): Look what you did. Now we all suffer.
22   BIBI: *(To AUDIENCE)* You gotta stand up for yourself, or else
23   your face is a doormat.
24   CHORUS (ALL): We're used to it.
25   BIBI: Well I'm not.
26   CHORUS ONE: Well, get used to it, Chinita. *(The line dissolves.*
27   *The CHORUS moves Upstage. The CAT returns to KAREN.)*
28   KAREN: Will you help me, Bibi? Will you help me?
29   BIBI: Karen, the government told me I was not a suitable
30   sponsor. To be a sponsor, I have to prove I can support you
31   as well as myself. Karen, I'm just starting out in life. I
32   don't have much in the way of money, just my prospects
33   like you.
34   KAREN: So when you are rich, you can sponsor me, yes?
35   BIBI: Karen, I really don't think I can do more. I mean, I don't

1   even know you. I mean, we're not even related. I'm sorry.
2   Sincerely, Bibi.
3   KAREN: *(To CAT)* Then she must get to know me. Isn't that
4   right, Debbie? She must get to know me, and when she
5   will get rich in America, she will send for me, and I will go
6   to live in California.
7   CAT: Meeow.
8   KAREN: I know she will help me, when she gets to know me.
9   Then I will go, but you mustn't be sad or jealous, Debbie.
10   CAT: Meeow.
11   KAREN: No kitty cats on boats to America. But I will send you
12   letters? Yes? Many, many letters.
13   CAT: Meeoow.
14   BIBI: Well, that's the end of that. *(The CHORUS steps forward.)*
15   CHORUS (ALL): Wrong!
16   CHORUS TWO: Karen continued to write to Bibi.
17   CHORUS ONE: Long letters about her life in China.
18   CHORUS FOUR: Her longings for America.
19   KAREN: While Bibi wrote detailed accounts about her new job
20   as a newspaper reporter. Going to sewer commission
21   meetings, the planning board.
22   BIBI: Karen would bring up the subject every now and then.
23   CAT: Karen is very "purrr"sistent.
24   CHORUS FOUR: Bibi tried to ignore the subject.
25   CHORUS THREE: But finally Bibi got fed up.
26   BIBI: Winter 1980. Dear Karen, You may ask me if you wish.
27   But please do not bring my parents into this. They are not
28   rich. The streets here are not paved with gold. They are
29   paved with concrete, sweat, hard work and struggle. My
30   mother and father struggle every day.
31   KAREN: *(Reads.)* Bibi says her mother works in a sewing factory
32   in the downtown. Debbie, are you paying attention? *(The*
33   *CAT sleeps. BIBI's MOTHER steps from the CHORUS, and*
34   *into the bedroom.)* Bibi says her mother brings home a big
35   canvas bag filled with pieces of a shirt. Collars for five

1   cents each and sleeves for three cents American money.
2   BIBI: In my mother's bedroom, there is a big, worn-out sewing
3   machine.
4   KAREN: *(Reading)* Her mother is sewing, sewing, sewing. Bibi
5   says this is the only time they have chance to talk to each
6   other. *(BIBI joins her MOTHER.)*
7   BIBI: *(To AUDIENCE)* My mother hands me a wooden
8   chopstick. I use the chopstick to poke these collars,
9   making a point in the tip, you see? Oh, I'm sorry, I made
10   another hole. Damn.
11   MOTHER: If you are tired, go to bed. And watch your mouth.
12   BIBI: Mommy, no, you quit for the night. You look really tired.
13   MOTHER: I have a few more to go, OK? *(They work in silence.*
14   *Then . . .)* Bibi, why don't you quit the newspaper? Get a
15   respectable job!
16   BIBI: Gosh, look at that pile. We'll be up all night. That Sam is
17   a lecherous old dwarf, and he's a slave driver.
18   MOTHER: Always running around late at night. Ladies do not
19   chase bad people, asking them why why why. People who
20   do bad things might do bad things to you.
21   BIBI: That lovesick Sam still chasing you around, pinching you
22   on your . . .
23   MOTHER: I do what I have to do. When you are a mother, then
24   you will understand what mothers do for their children.
25   *(Beat)* Sam says he's going to finally put everybody on
26   insurance. He better. *(Points to a collar.)* Do that one over.
27   *(Beat)* Plan for the future, Bibi. You are too wild. What if
28   something happens? I'm not getting any younger. I might
29   die tomorrow, then what do you do?
30   BIBI: I hate it when you talk like that. Nothing's gonna happen
31   to you. You are still young. Forty is the prime of life. Why
32   do you put up with that slimy toad? He's all talk. Just get
33   another job where they have insurance.
34   MOTHER: Who will hire me? I'm too old. Who wants someone
35   with no education?

1   BIBI: You could go to night school like you did before. Stop
2   working all these jobs. Three jobs is for three people, not
3   one.
4   MOTHER: I was much younger before.
5   BIBI: Mommy, you're still young. Look in the mirror. *(Both look*
6   *into AUDIENCE, as if into a mirror.)* You got old Sam
7   running circles around you, the old lech. Mommy, you're
8   still pretty. You still are. *(A short pause.)*
9   MOTHER: Before I had my children, I had more choice. Now
10   everything seems grey and broken. No, my life all set. I live
11   for you now. That's why I live. For you. *(Beat)* Watch what
12   you are doing, you made another hole.
13   BIBI: *(Pause, thoughtfully)* Before you had your children? Are we
14   your regrets, Mommy? Would it have been better if . . . if I
15   wasn't around? Would you have worked less? Lived more?
16   MOTHER: *(Disgustedly)* Aiiii! *(MOTHER and CAT rejoin*
17   *CHORUS.)*
18   BIBI: Of course, my mother cares about me. She doesn't mean
19   it. All that about her life being ruined . . . but when I think
20   about all she's given up just because of . . . I sometimes . . .
21   sometimes Karen, I wish . . . then maybe she'd be free. Got
22   anything in the way of a razor blade?
23   KAREN: Bibi, you make abundant jokes, but I know you are
24   feeling upset and sad. *(Beat)* Bibi, we do not choose to be
25   born. In China, as in America, this is not a choice we have.
26   BIBI: Sleeping pills in large quantities, however, is an equal
27   opportunity. This is America.
28   KAREN: In China, we have only few freedoms. There is a
29   saying. Do you know it? *(In Chinese: Death can be as heavy*
30   *as the biggest mountain, or as light as a feather.)* We may
31   choose when to die, how to die and for what we will die.
32   Yes, I think there are times for such a choice. But this is
33   not a good choice for you, especially if you are going to
34   help me.
35   BIBI: *(Choral tone)* Spring 1981.

1   KAREN: You asked about my mother. My mother is dead.

2   BIBI: When did she die?

3   KAREN: When I was very young. Near my house, next to the pig

4   pens, there is a rice field. Yes, a warm day in the rice field.

5   Many mosquitoes. I am raw from the bites. *(Pause)* My

6   mother is in the field. She has long black hair, just like

7   mine. I see her. I run to her. I'm running and so happy.

8   The water from the field splashes up. The ground grabs,

9   holds my feet as I run.

10 BIBI: *(To KAREN, softly)* Watch out. The sheaves of rice are

11   sharp.

12 KAREN: Yes. The rice cut my legs as I run. Blood trickling down

13   my legs. But I don't care. I brought my mother her lunchbox.

14   *(Waves.)* **MaMa!** *"Bao Bao gay ni dai fan lai!"* *(Your baby*

15   *brings you your lunch. Beat)* Wait! Who is that? It is the

16   commissaire! He is the man who reports everything.

17 BIBI: I see him. He's very tall.

18 KAREN: He is shaking my mother. He's shaking her. Why is he

19   doing that? Where is he taking her? MaMa! MaMa! Where

20   are you going? MaMa! MaMa! *(Pause)* I fell in the rice, and

21   I was wet from the water. I just watched my mother as

22   they took her away. *(KAREN's BROTHER steps from the*

23   *CHORUS.)*

24 BROTHER: It was my duty.

25 KAREN: She was our mother.

26 BROTHER: I do not apologize. People must reform their

27   thinking. I miss mother as much as you. But wrong

28   thinking and wrong action must be made into right action

29   and right thinking.

30 KAREN: My brother . . . the little red guard.

31 BROTHER: *(Overlapping)* . . . is a good citizen of the state. The

32   individual is not important.

33 CHORUS *(ALL. Whispers)* When the dust settles, the wolf stands

34   alone.

35 BROTHER: The people have spoken. The individual is dead.

1   KAREN: Yes, our mother is dead.

2   BIBI: I'm sorry. *(KAREN and BROTHER speak dispassionately.)*

3   KAREN: Why?

4   BIBI: Something bad happens and someone should apologize

5   for it.

6   KAREN: The cat eats the mouse. He doesn't apologize for doing

7   what is in his nature to do.

8   BROTHER: My mother took property that belonged to someone

9   else. She was punished. She stole food to feed us.

10 BIBI: She sacrificed her life to make sure you had something in

11   your stomach.

12 BROTHER: To steal from The People is wrong thinking.

13 BIBI: That was too severe a punishment. Punishment should

14   fit the crime.

15 KAREN: She was punished. Not for stealing, but for resisting. If

16   the mouse struggles, the cat grips tighter first with one

17   paw then with two. The only thing the mouse can do is

18   escape, run away. As fast as you can. If you can.

19 BROTHER: And if you cannot, you'll be executed. Crimes

20   against The State.

21 KAREN: A common occurrence. Public execution is part of our

22   daily lives, part of our education process. It is the one

23   activity my brother and I do together. *(Beat)* Lu Yan, a

24   friend who is a teacher from the high school where my

25   brother works, often came with us. *(LU YAN joins KAREN*

26   *and the BROTHER center stage. The following scene must be*

27   *devoid of sentimentality.)*

28 BIBI: I covered an execution once. But from afar. I mean I

29   made some phone calls to the parole board, part of a

30   series of articles on capital punishment. And there was

31   the time I did a piece on the Ku Klux Klan. *(Beat)* You

32   know Karen, I keep thinking that if I write about this

33   stuff, maybe something would . . . I don't know . . . what

34   the hell, I'm not sure we're any different. I mean I'm a

35   lowly reporter, a spectator, a witness, I mean, bad things

1   that happen aren't my fault. I mean that's the best I can
2   do, right? Right? Yeah, that's right.
3   KAREN: In the street, there is a truck.
4   BIBI: We have the electric chair. The cyanide capsule . . .
5   LU YAN: Soviet made. Flatbed.
6   BIBI: We have death by hanging. No guillotine though, that's
7   barbaric, right? And firing squads are definitely passé.
8   BROTHER: See him there. The enemy of the people.
9   KAREN: Which one?
10 LU YAN: He is the man wearing all white.
11 BROTHER: There, down his back. See it?
12 KAREN: Yes.
13 BIBI: What does it say?
14 LU YAN: Can't read it.
15 BROTHER: Nature of crime. Name. A marker to identify the
16   body.
17 KAREN: What is he being executed for?
18 BROTHER: He is an enemy of the people.
19 BIBI: Karen, do something! How can you just sit there?
20 CHORUS: *(Whispers.)* This is what happens. This is what
21   happens when wolves do not stay. In the group. In the
22   pack. This is what happens.
23 KAREN: We all follow the truck to the stadium.
24 LU YAN: The man is taken out of the truck. He stands in the
25   middle of the stadium. A loudspeaker announces his
26   crime. Does he renounce his crime?
27 CHORUS (ALL): Do you renounce your crime? *(A gunshot)*
28 CHORUS ONE: Karen continued in the accounting firm at the
29   import/export factory.
30 CHORUS FOUR: Bibi got a job at a newspaper in the desert,
31   hated the desert. Then she got another newspaper job and
32   moved to the beach. Got another job, moved to the East
33   Coast. *(BIBI at airport)*
34 BIBI: Summer, 1982. I'm writing this quick note at a press
35   conference at an airport, actually the National Guard

1   **Armory in Windsor Locks, Connecticut. Look on your map**
2   **under . . .** *(CHORUS moos.)* **. . . near a cow pasture.** *(The*
3   *CHORUS in a tableau, as eager members of the media)* **Air**
4   **Force One is about to touch down and when it does the vice**
5   **president is going to get a whiff of what rural America**
6   **smells like. The wind has definitely shifted to the right. My**
7   **dress is going up over my head, no one notices, which**
8   **depresses me greatly, as I'm doing a very good Marilyn**
9   **Monroe impression.** *(BIBI freezes in a demure Monroe pose.)*
10 **KAREN: Lu Yan, who is this Marilyn Monroe?**
11 **LU YAN: She was the looker with the great gams.**
12 **KAREN: Do I have great gams?**
13 **LU YAN: Maybe. Read to me the rest of the letter from Bibi.**
14 **KAREN: She says here her father received an illness recently,**
15   **and that why . . .**
16 **LU YAN:** *(Correcting)* **. . . and that IS why . . .**
17 **KAREN: . . . that IS why she has not . . . she did not write to me.**
18 **BIBI: My father owns a grocery store on Hope Street. I know**
19   **that's corny, but it's true. It's called The Little Golden Star**
20   **Market, corner of Hope and California streets in a place**
21   **called Huntington Park. It's too small to be on your map.**
22   *(BIBI's FATHER steps from the CHORUS and joins BIBI. He*
23   *sings a few bars from "The Yellow Rose of Texas.")*
24 **FATHER: The yellow rose of Texas, ta da ta da ta da, ta ta da ta**
25   **da da . . . she's the only girl for me . . .** *(Tickles BIBI.)*
26 **BIBI: I'm done with the price tags.**
27 **FATHER: Good. Did you . . . ?**
28 **BIBI: I counted the register.**
29 **FATHER: Good. And the . . . ?**
30 **BIBI: I swept front and back. Can I go now?**
31 **FATHER: You know Bibi, I think you are gaining weight. Smart**
32   **is one thing, but I want a pretty rose, not a balloon for a**
33   **daughter, o.k.?** *(Tickles BIBI again.)* **Hey, no long face.**
34   **Smile, smile.**
35 **BIBI: Daddy, please. I'm a big girl now.**

1   FATHER: Yes. Too much ice cream. *(Tickles her again.)*
2   BIBI: Stop that. Karen, this is my father. He likes to sing.
3   KAREN: He's standing in the middle of his store. Look at all the
4   shelves. Soy sauce, oyster sauce, spaghetti sauce. So much
5   food. So many vegetables . . .
6   LU YAN: Cigarettes. American cigarettes. I would like to smoke
7   those Marlboro™ cigarettes and wear a big hat from Texas.
8   FATHER: *(Stops singing.)* I feel funny. I feel a little woozy. Must
9   have been your mother's bird nest soup. I think I'm going
10   to sit down right here. Whoops, watch out. Look Bibi, I fell
11   down. Isn't that funny? *(FATHER collapses.)*
12   BIBI: Dad, you don't look so good. Daddy?
13   KAREN: Bibi, what's happening?
14   BIBI: My father, Karen. *(Pause)* My father is on the floor. Daddy,
15   wake up. Stop playing around. Daddy? I put his head in my
16   lap. What's this? What is this? Blood all over me.
17   KAREN: Yes, I know the blood.
18   BIBI: On my legs. On the floor.
19   KAREN: Yes, the blood on my legs. Yes, the blood turned the
20   water warm.
21   BIBI: Wake up, Daddy. No fooling now. You see Karen, my
22   father doesn't mean to hurt me. He likes to joke around.
23   He's forever making a joke. I'll lose weight, Daddy, really I
24   will. Daddy? *(BIBI gives her father a little shake.)*
25   KAREN: Is he all right?
26   BIBI: My daddy works all the time. He's always at work.
27   Sometimes, he says things, and it would hurt me, and I'd
28   wish he'd just go away and die. But I don't mean it. I don't.
29   I didn't really want you to die, Dad.
30   KAREN: Are you all right? Bibi? *(Pause)*
31   BIBI: He's always at work.
32   KAREN: Is everything all right?
33   BIBI: He likes to call me his little yellow rose. He worked all the
34   time. I didn't really know my father, I was so busy, you see.
35   He liked to call me his little yellow rose. I'm your little

1   yellow rose. I'm my Daddy's little yellow rose. *(Lights out*

2   *on BIBI. A short pause. The CHORUS steps forward.)*

3   CHORUS ONE: Bibi and Karen continued their correspondence,

4   but sporadically. About once or twice a year.

5   CHORUS FOUR: Bibi took her father's death very badly.

6   CHORUS THREE: In 1983, "Death of a Salesman" came to China.

7   CHORUS TWO: Biff. Happy. Linda. Willy Loman.

8   CHORUS ONE: Willy Loman didn't know who he was. He had

9   all the wrong dreams.

10   CHORUS THREE: I have those same dreams.

11   CHORUS FOUR: I don't know who I am.

12   BIBI: I don't know who I am. I'm looking though, real hard.

13   CAT: Meeoow.

14   CHORUS THREE: In late winter, 1984. Debbie died. She choked

15   on a mouse.

16   CAT: Meeow. *(Cough)*

17   BROTHER: Shhh. Cats from the grave know too much. Yes. It

18   was me. I turned in my mother. I confess it, but I do not

19   apologize. *(Beat)* I didn't tell anyone about my sister or her

20   letters. I don't know why. Things seem a little different

21   now. More relaxed.

22   CHORUS FOUR: It is Spring 1985.

23   CHORUS THREE: Yes, Spring 1985. By now, economic reforms.

24   Farmers sell their surplus in the markets and keep the

25   profit. Unheard of.

26   CHORUS ONE: But the more China changes, the more

27   discontented I become.

28   CHORUS TWO: The more western China becomes, the

29   unhappier I feel.

30   KAREN: Summer 1985. Thank you Bibi for the fashion magazines.

31   Someday I hope to make such pretty dresses for sale.

32   BIBI: Fall 1985. You're welcome.

33   MOTHER: Spring 1986. Bibi, you not a grasshopper. Stick to

34   your job.

35   BIBI: But mother, I don't like my job.

1   MOTHER: Who likes job? If you quit, *"naw mmn yein nay"* (I
2   don't know you.)
3   KAREN: Summer 1986. Dear Bibi, I took my first trip to the
4   mountains. In China, you must get a permit for travel
5   anywhere. Five years ago, I asked for permission, and now
6   it has arrived. My brother and Lu Yan are coming with me.
7   *(The BROTHER, LU YAN and KAREN are lying on a plateau*
8   *on a mountainside.)* Look at that sky. I see a dragon coiling
9   ready to spring. I see a water buffalo. There's a big, fat
10   lumbering pig. That's you.
11   BROTHER: I feel restless. It's funny to feel so restless.
12   LU YAN: Ask Bibi to send us a copy of this Bill of Rights.
13   BROTHER: What is this "pursuit of happiness?" Even if I were
14   to have it, I would not know how to go about this "pursuit
15   of happiness."
16   LU YAN: I think to be on Lotus Mountain is what is meant by
17   "Life, liberty and the pursuit of happiness."
18   KAREN: *(To BROTHER)* It means even YOU would count for
19   something, you good for nothing.
20   BROTHER: Oh? Who is lazy and who is not? I have written a
21   novel.
22   LU YAN: So why do you hide it?
23   BROTHER: Because I am a bad novelist.
24   KAREN: Well then, your book will be very popular.
25   LU YAN: I think I will be a teacher in a great university. I have
26   already applied for a transfer.
27   BROTHER: Impossible.
28   LU YAN: Maybe.
29   KAREN: If only I could leave my job. I hate accounting.
30   LU YAN: You do?
31   BROTHER: I didn't know that.
32   KAREN: Bibi sends me many fashion magazines. Only Bibi
33   knows how I wish to be a designer of great fashion for very
34   great ladies.
35   BROTHER: Burlap sacks for old bags.

1   KAREN: Lace, all lace and chiffon.

2   LU YAN: You would look beautiful.

3   KAREN: (*Shyly*) Not for me. For the people. I would be a dress

4   designer and go to . . .

5   LU YAN: Paris?

6   BROTHER: London?

7   KAREN: New York City.

8   LU YAN: People would clap and say, "Ahhh, of course, a Karen

9   original."

10 BROTHER: People will say, "How ugly. I will not wear this in a

11   million years."

12 KAREN: I would have a name. Then once I am famous as a

13   clothes designer, I will quit and I would do something

14   else. Maybe be a forest ranger.

15 BROTHER: Or a fireman.

16 LU YAN: Or an astronaut.

17 BROTHER: Or a member of the central committee.

18 LU YAN: Hah! You must be very old to be a member of the

19   central committee.

20 KAREN: Yes, a fossil. (*Beat*) Is it possible to be a somebody?

21 BROTHER: Yes, I am a grain of sand!

22 KAREN: A piece of lint.

23 LU YAN: Those old men on the central committee. What do they

24   know about us? Perhaps we should all take up our books

25   and stone the committee with our new ideas.

26 BROTHER: Lu Yan thinks he can change the world. But I'm

27   telling you if we are patient, all things will come.

28 KAREN: Oh, my brother is a philosopher. I think change must

29   start from within. We need to have a personal revolution,

30   as well as a political one.

31 BROTHER: Oh Karen, these old fossils will never change. Only

32   things that die allow new things to grow and flourish.

33 LU YAN: Yes, he is right. They will die off and leave us with a

34   nation of students. No politicians. Just you and me and

35   Karen.

1 KAREN: Three wolves on the mountainside, sitting in the sun.
2 BROTHER: Change is sure to come.
3 LU YAN: Only if we insist on it.
4 KAREN: Well, this is changing me. *(KAREN waves a small pile of*
5   *books.)*
6 LU YAN: *(Looks at the titles.)* Hemingway. Martin Luther King.
7   Jean Paul Sartre.
8 KAREN: Bibi sent them to me. And this. *(KAREN turns on a tape*
9   *recorder. The MUSIC is Karen Carpenter's "We've Only Just*
10   *Begun." They listen.)*
11 BROTHER: Ugh, not this song again. That's it. I'm leaving. I will
12   go for a walk now. *(The BROTHER rejoins the CHORUS.)*
13 LU YAN: No good citizens of the state anywhere I can see.
14 KAREN: What?
15 LU YAN: Only clouds above and insects below to watch.
16 KAREN: Watch what?
17 LU YAN: This. *(LU YAN leans in to kiss KAREN — it's a very short*
18   *awkward peck on the cheek. Lights out. BIBI at home.)*
19 BIBI: *(To AUDIENCE)* Fall 1986. The anniversary of my father's
20   death. Today, my mother made tay and we went to sit at
21   his grave. We bowed three times. I don't even know what
22   that means, bowing three times. But I do it because my
23   mother says this is how we remember our ancestors. She
24   says it's important to remember.
25 KAREN: That's funny. On the anniversary of my mother's
26   death, I try to forget.
27 BIBI: Mmmm. *(Beat)* You know what, Karen?
28 KAREN: Mmmm.
29 BIBI: Sometimes, I wish someone would tell me. This is what
30   you are good at Bibi, so go and do it. This is the man who
31   is good for you Bibi, marry him.
32 KAREN: You wouldn't listen anyway, and you know it.
33 BIBI: No, I probably wouldn't. *(To Karen)* How is . . . ?
34 KAREN: Lu Yan?
35 BIBI: Yes, Lu Yan. Lu Yan sounds like a very nice guy.

1   KAREN: Lu Yan is the only guy I've ever . . . how you say? . . .

2   BIBI: Slept with?

3   KAREN: No . . . he is the first man I ever dated. Yes, that's the
4   word, dated. Only one to ask, only one go out with,
5   understand? Not much choice here in China, even though
6   we are very many millions of people.

7   BIBI: Choice! Talk about choice. Shall I regale you with tales
8   from the darkside? Dates from hell? By my calculations,
9   since I was a late bloomer, having lived at home
10   throughout my college career, but making up for it like a
11   fiend. After I moved out of the house, I would say I've met
12   a total of, or had a disastrous dinner or ahem, et cetera et
13   cetera, with at least 127 different men — and that's a
14   conservative estimate. Indeed, 127 men of assorted
15   shapes and sizes and denominations. And colors. Don't
16   forget colors.

17 KAREN: I am getting married next year. During the Mid-
18   Autumn Festival. Yes, I am getting married. I'm not sure I
19   want to be married. I want to do and see so much, but my
20   world is so small.

21 BIBI: Here in America, we are free, free to choose our lovers
22   and make our own mistakes. The most wonderful thing
23   about freedom, Karen, is you get plenty of rope in which
24   to hang yourself. Wait! Backspace. Did I hear correctly?
25   Did you say getting married? Getting married.

26 KAREN: Mmmmm.

27 BIBI: How wonderful. It is wonderful, right?

28 KAREN: Mmmmm.

29 BIBI: I think I'm feeling . . . wow, what a novel concept! I think
30   I'm actually jealous.

31 CHORUS THREE: Lu Yan and Karen were married in the fall of
32   1986.

33 CHORUS FOUR: Lu Yan's family gave as a dowry to Karen's
34   father and brother — two live chickens, eight kilos of pig's
35   intestines, five hundred steamed buns, a sea lion bicycle,

1   twenty kilos of fish, and ten cartons of American cigarettes.
2   CHORUS TWO: Karen moved in with Lu Yan's family. Lu Yan's
3   father was a violinist with the city orchestra. There was
4   always music in the house.
5   LU YAN: *(To AUDIENCE)* For our wedding, Bibi sent us a box
6   filled with books and music tapes. It was like a time
7   capsule from the West. *(With quiet enjoyment, LU YAN and*
8   *KAREN listen to a few bars from Louis Armstrong's version*
9   *of "Ain't Misbehavin'.")* I could eat them up. Every one, this
10   Hemingway. This Truman Capote. This biography of
11   Mahatma Gandhi. *(To KAREN)* Look! Newspaper clippings
12   about the New China, our new economic experiments.
13   KAREN: Our friends from the university come to our
14   apartment. We sift through the box. *(To LU YAN)* This is
15   what Christmas must be like!
16   CHORUS FOUR: Tammy Wynette! Patsy Cline!
17   LU YAN: Mickey Spillane!
18   CHORUS THREE: Jonathan Livingston Seagull. James Michener!
19   CHORUS FOUR: *A Streetcar Named Desire!* The theory of
20   relativity!
21   CHORUS THREE: Dr. Spock's Baby Book!
22   KAREN: Dear Bibi, Lu Yan would like to thank you for the book.
23   *I'm O.K., You're O.K.*
24   CHORUS THREE: New ideas. New dissatisfactions.
25   LU YAN: The more she read, the more Karen grew depressed.
26   CHORUS FOUR: Even though the sun seemed to shine very
27   bright in China.
28   CHORUS THREE: Politically speaking.
29   CHORUS ONE: Summer 1987.
30   KAREN: Dear Bibi, I am a bird in a cage. A beautiful bird with
31   yellow and green and red feathers. I have a great plumage,
32   but no one can see it. I live in a place that is blind to such
33   wonderful colors. There is only grey and blue and green.
34   *(BIBI's MOTHER steps from the CHORUS, is on the*
35   *telephone.)*

1   MOTHER: Bibi? Are you listening to me?

2   BIBI: Winter 1987. Dear Karen, Do you know why I live so far

3   from home? So I don't have to face their disapproval. My

4   sister, my mother. My family.

5   MOTHER: Come home. It's too cold in Connecticut. You do not

6   miss your mother? I miss you. Don't you miss me?

7   BIBI: I like the seasons. I like long red coats and mufflers, ice

8   skating on a real lake. I like snow.

9   MOTHER: You're crazy. Come home. Are you losing weight? Are

10   you drinking that diet tea I sent to you?

11   BIBI: It tastes terrible.

12   MOTHER: Sure it does. That's because it's good for you. Are you

13   warm enough?

14   BIBI: Yes, I'm warm enough. I'm sitting by the fireplace at

15   what's-his-name's apartment.

16   MOTHER: Come home, get rid of what's-his-name. I do not like

17   him. He has a frog face.

18   BIBI: Oh, can we please drop that subject?

19   MOTHER: (*Disgustedly*) Aiiii.

20   BIBI: Mom. (*Beat*) I'm thinking of quitting the newspaper and

21   becoming an actress.

22   MOTHER: Actress! (*In Chinese: You are killing me.*) **Aiii, nay gek**

23   **say aw.** (*BIBI is silent.*) There's no money in it. How you

24   live? How you pay rent? All those actresses, all they ever do

25   is fool around and get divorced. You want to get divorced?

26   BIBI: Mom, I'm not even married yet.

27   MOTHER: See what I mean? If you quit job, I disown you. You

28   are not special enough to be actress.

29   BIBI: Gosh, my stomach hurts. (*A short pause. BIBI composes a*

30   *letter.*) Dear Karen, what's so special about being special?

31   Mother is absolutely right. I'm not special. And damned

32   proud of it. Special is entirely overrated.

33   KAREN: You are joking again, aren't you? (*A short pause*) See?

34   I'm getting good at knowing you.

35   BIBI: Nothing I do pleases my mother. Karen, I'm not

1   overweight, but I'm too fat. I'm not stupid, but I'm not
2   sensible. I've got a job, but I don't have a lady-like
3   profession. I'm a disappointment and I don't know why I
4   am. Maybe . . . maybe she doesn't . . . maybe she doesn't . . .
5   Gosh, my chest hurts.
6   KAREN: Dear Bibi, your chest hurts because you are crying
7   inside. Don't cry inside. Your mother doesn't mean what
8   she says. She is just doing her duty. She's your mother. She
9   wouldn't be a good mother if she didn't say those things.
10   Threaten your children to the straight and narrow, this is
11   written on the list for what it means to be a good mother.
12 BIBI: *(To KAREN)* Ancient Chinese proverb?
13 KAREN: Fortune cookie.
14 BIBI: She means it all right. You watch. If I go to acting school,
15 she'll tell everyone I'm in law school. Just wait and see if
16 she doesn't.
17 KAREN: Bibi, I think you love your mother very much. But
18 maybe you will love her better, if you listen less.
19 BIBI: Well, she can send me all the diet tea in China, I'm still
20 going to drink Coke Classic™. Mothers are overrated.
21 KAREN: I wish my mother were alive to lecture me.
22 CHORUS (ALL): New age, new wave, new roads. New thinkers,
23 new entrees, new hairdos. New buildings, new careers,
24 new lives. Who am I? Where am I going? America, always
25 on the move! Many choices, many roads, many ways to go.
26 Who am I? Where am I? Which way?
27 KAREN: Winter 1987. Dear Bibi, Lu Yan is always telling me
28 what to do. Married life isn't what I thought. His mother
29 tells me how to wash his shirts, how to make a dinner. She
30 complains I do not concentrate, as my head is always
31 spinning in the clouds. She asked me what mischief I am
32 making. I tell her I feel much puzzlement, as I do not
33 know who I am.
34 BIBI: Spring 1988. Dear Karen, I have changed newspapers five
35 times in the past three years. It's easier to move up by

1   moving out, but I'm getting a little tired of moving
2   around. West Coast, East Coast. No place feels like home.
3   Home doesn't even feel like home. Everywhere I go, I ask
4   myself the question, "Who am I?," "How do I fit in?" The
5   answer changes as fast as my address.

6 KAREN: Summer 1988. Dear Bibi, I am a flower that will never
7   open, never to be kissed by a bee. I want to open. I want to
8   feel the sting of freedom. More and more, I feel bitter
9   towards my life and my uselessness. I go to work, I have
10   ideas to improve my job, and no one listens to me. I am a
11   nobody. And I want to be a somebody.

12 BIBI: *(To KAREN)* Do you realize Karen, we've been friends for
13   almost ten years?

14 KAREN: And for ten years, you have not listened to one word I
15   have said.

16 BIBI: I've listened.

17 KAREN: No you haven't. You are not my friend.

18 BIBI: I see.

19 KAREN: No, you do not see. You are too far away. I could be a
20   real friend and see you everyday. You could be a real
21   friend to me, but you refuse. My hand hurts from writing.
22   My dictionary is all torn up.

23 BIBI: Karen, but you are a married woman now.

24 KAREN: I thought my marriage would make a solution, but it
25   doesn't. It is not what I wanted for my life. Bibi, you know
26   my heart. But you won't help me. I want to count for
27   something. I can count for something in California.

28 BIBI: Here or there, your struggle is my struggle. No matter
29   where we are, the struggle is the same. I'm trying not to
30   run away from my problems. Why can't you be happy
31   where you are?

32 KAREN: Why can't you?

33 BIBI: You are so naïve.

34 KAREN: You are so naïve.

35 BIBI: You're one to talk.

1   KAREN: You live in a democracy, the individual can vote. You
2   can count for something.
3   BIBI: What elementary school book did you read that from? Oh
4   sure, Karen, my vote counts – as long as I'm a white male
5   rich business tycoon, which last I looked in the mirror I
6   ain't. Wake up from your dreamland, Karen.
7   KAREN: That's right. You have the luxury to be selfish. To think
8   of only yourself. You live in Paradise, and I live in hell.
9   BIBI: Well Karen, it can be hell living in Paradise.
10 KAREN: I want democracy. Democracy for me. Freedom of
11   speech. Freedom to choose.
12 BIBI: Freedom to be confused. But if you like America so much,
13   come join me in the national pasttime.
14 KAREN: What? Baseball? I like baseball.
15 BIBI: No, I'm talking retail therapy. Let's go shopping.
16 KAREN: I think you must be making a bad joke. Democracy is
17   not the same thing as capitalism.
18 BIBI: Oh, you have the old definition.
19 KAREN: Even then I think the new definition is better than what
20   we have in China. At least you have incentives to strive for a
21   better life. But here whether I work one hour or ten hours,
22   it's all the same. You just don't know what it's like.
23 BIBI: I've read Marx, thank you very much. Can I help it if good
24   ideals are polluted by extremists and dictators? Can I help
25   it if the desire to be fair and equal is completely
26   antithetical to human nature? Health care for everybody.
27   Jobs for everybody. Everyone *equal* under the law.
28   Everyone working towards the greater good. And here's a
29   novel concept – people actually caring about the well-
30   being of other people. In America, we call that welfare,
31   and anyone on it is seen as a slackard and a mooch. In
32   China, and probably in the eyes of God, it's called social
33   responsibility and Charity with a capital C.
34 KAREN: If you think China is so good, you should come and live
35   here. Bibi, I think you must be a Communist at heart.

1   BIBI: I shudder to think what you would do with a credit card.
2   *(Beat)* I can see it now. You'd be mesmerized by our
3   shopping malls. We've got mini malls, gigantic malls, also
4   Rodeo Drive – all linked by a chain of freeways stretching
5   into infinity.
6   KAREN: I don't want to shop.
7   BIBI: I can see you now Karen – at the altar of The Church of
8   Our Lady of Retail kneeling beside me at the cash register
9   as it rings up our sale. Fifty percent off – the most
10   beautiful three words in the English language. Now that's
11   America.
12   KAREN: I do not want to shop.
13   BIBI: Now, that's downright un-American. Forget it Karen,
14   you'll never fit in.
15   KAREN: Somewhere I read that there is a difference between
16   democracy and capitalism.
17   BIBI: And you think I'm naïve. Well in America, we like to
18   think we're a democracy, but we're definitely a nation of
19   shoppers. *(Pause)* Ahhh, I know. You're a K-Mart Girl.
20   *(BIBI's new beau JONATHAN interrupts.)*
21   JONATHAN: Bibi, let's get going, we'll be late.
22   BIBI: Sorry, Karen, I've got to go. *(Pause)* Karen, what do you
23   think of him? Jonathan is very reserved. A damned
24   Yankee blue blood. He says I'm the only person he can
25   really talk to. A real solid person. My opposite in every
26   way. But . . . *(Pause)* he brings out the best in me and it
27   feels right, you know? I'll keep you posted. Love, Bibi.
28   KAREN: *(To AUDIENCE)* What's K-Mart?
29   CHORUS (ALL): Everything happens in the mall. We meet in
30   the mall. We see movies in the mall. We buy presents in
31   the mall. We eat lunch in the mall. We are a nation of
32   shoppers. Attention shoppers. *(BIBI and JONATHAN are in*
33   *the shopping mall. Slides from life in the galleria)*
34   BIBI: You are joking right? Jonathan?
35   JONATHAN: You yourself said I have a rare and seldom seen

1   sense of humor.

2   BIBI: I guess you aren't joking. Let me get this straight. You

3   think I'm too passionate, too adventurous, and too

4   enthusiastic. You think I'm special, so special that you

5   don't deserve someone as special as me. Jonathan, I

6   assure you special is very overrated. Ask my mother.

7   JONATHAN: Let's not talk about it right now, OK? Let's just go

8   to the movie.

9   BIBI: No, no. Permit me a small public scene. It's only our

10   future we're talking here. No Jonathan, you can't drop a

11   bombshell, and then go sit in the dark with a bag of

12   popcorn.

13   JONATHAN: I told you I don't want to do this, make a scene

14   here between the Sears' and the J.C. Penney's.

15   BIBI: I won't cry or shout, if that's what you are afraid of.

16   Besides, the mall is where all of America gets dumped.

17   Latchkey kids graduate from television to the local

18   galleria.

19   JONATHAN: Do you have to be cute all the time? Just stop it,

20   OK? Look, don't get me wrong. I think you are terrific. But

21   it's just . . . well I don't require as much.

22   BIBI: I see.

23   JONATHAN: Since you asked.

24   BIBI: Go on. I know there's more.

25   JONATHAN: It's just too intense for me. You're like a pebble in

26   my still pond. When I'm with you I feel like I'm riding a

27   horse run wild, and I can't get my feet into the stirrups.

28   BIBI: The real issue here. The real issue, Jonathan, is that your

29   mother likes me. You wanted to shock your family, and

30   instead, they embraced me with open arms to your

31   complete dismay. You are a rebel without a cause, and

32   you're about to sacrifice your future for your infantile

33   desire to horrify your mother. I can't change the fact your

34   mother thinks I'm terrific, and I'm not going to join the

35   junior league. If I want to French kiss you at the Quaker

1   meeting, then I might. If I have to change to keep you,
2   then . . . I'm not going to change.
3 JONATHAN: You couldn't even if you tried. You don't know how
4   to be anything less than terrific.
5 BIBI: So essentially, you are dumping me because you prefer
6   less than terrific?
7 JONATHAN: I'll probably regret it later. *(JONATHAN rejoins the*
8   *CHORUS.)*
9 BIBI: Not that it matters, but *(Mouths the words.)* I love you.
10   *(KAREN at home)*
11 KAREN: Winter 1988. Dear Bibi, my nephew asks if you would
12   send him a baseball glove. Also Lu Yan's mother would
13   like the same perfume you sent to me. Oh, by the way, the
14   Madonna tapes must be great, but the tape recorder is
15   broken. Can you send us another one?
16 BIBI: Dear Karen, I just can't afford anything right now. I'm
17   unemployed – again.
18 KAREN: How can you help me, if you don't become a stable,
19   responsible citizen?
20 BIBI: Very funny.
21 KAREN: Did you get fired from your job?
22 BIBI: No, I quit. And I'm glad I did. I had names, addresses,
23   quotes that would curdle your milk. And the paper
24   wouldn't print it. Family paper, they said. We're having an
25   election here Karen, and a black man is on the ballot. I
26   couldn't believe what people told me, and I put it into the
27   story. Quote, "I'd never put a black man in office." Quote:
28   "No nigger is going to run this country." So, I storm in the
29   managing editors' office during a budget meeting.
30   Everybody was there. I said, "Hey what is this?"
31 CHORUS: Calm down, Bibi. What's your complaint?
32 BIBI: How dare you sanitize the news, making it all pretty and
33   clean for public consumption. I strenuously object. *(Beat)*
34   And that's when they said:
35 CHORUS: Hey, it's a family paper.

1   BIBI: And while we're on the subject, what about that story
2   about the Vietnamese girl who was harassed, spat on, with
3   nasty racial epithets carved with a knife on her dormitory
4   door. That was cut, and relegated to page three, inside.
5   Nobody reads page three, inside.
6   CHORUS: Big news day, short of space.
7   BIBI: And what about the follow-up stories I did on racism on
8   college campuses. You buried that story in the zone editions.
9   That was a metro story, with national implications.
10 CHORUS ONE AND TWO: Aren't you being just a little too
11   sensitive?
12 CHORUS THREE AND FOUR: Aren't you being just a little
13   politically correct?
14 BIBI: Go to hell. My editors. They would rather put in a bloody
15   photograph of a local car wreck, than print the truth
16   about racism in America. So, in short, Karen, I quit.
17 KAREN: How lucky you are.
18 BIBI: What do you mean lucky?
19 KAREN: You get to live your own life, your way.
20 BIBI: Sure I'm lucky. I get to fight my battles totally alone and
21   unsupported, both at work and at home. I'm a lone wolf
22   howling, and no one listens except my cat. No, I'm trading
23   in my frustration for a new one. I am going to an acting
24   school where they take your money and teach you how to
25   pursue all the wrong dreams.
26 KAREN: Dreams. I have them too. New ones.
27 BIBI: My mother doesn't support me. The only way to convince
28   her is to make a clean break. Everyone disapproves. My
29   sister is the worst. You . . . on the other hand . . . have a
30   support system – the state, your brother, your husband.
31   You even know who your enemies are and what you are
32   fighting against.
33 KAREN: Perhaps you can swallow your pride. If the support
34   system, the harmony of your family is that important to
35   you, then you should do as they tell you to do.

1 BIBI: Spoken like a true Chinese.

2 KAREN: I am Chinese.

3 BIBI: And I am American. And I will live my own life, my way.

4   *(Beat)* Even if it kills me.

5 KAREN: Bibi, I have been thinking about what you say about

6   America, and I think you are right. I have been running

7   away from myself, my marriage, and my country. *(Beat)* I

8   think the east wind has moved a little to the west, so I

9   think voices of wolves perhaps now may be heard. You

10   see, Bibi, my country is changing and I have a new hope

11   for a better life. And, I no longer wish to come to be an

12   American like you. You are too confused. *(Beat)* But I will

13   always be your friend.

14 BIBI: Say, why don't you come and visit me?

15 KAREN: I don't know. There is much work to do here. I'm going

16   to meetings for the first time. Many meetings.

17 BIBI: Look, why don't you come? You can meet my mother. I'm

18   sure she'd be happy to lecture you too. Go to the consulate.

19   Ask them for a visa.

20 CHORUS ONE: Karen went to the consulate.

21 KAREN: I have a friend in the United States who will vouch for me.

22 CHORUS THREE: Many people are exchanging, visiting from

23   China to the world.

24 KAREN: I told them I wanted to be one of them.

25 CHORUS FOUR: Cultural exchanges. Ballet dancers, playwrights,

26   artists, singers.

27 CHORUS TWO: Scientists, engineers, lawyers, architects,

28   businessmen of all sorts.

29 CHORUS THREE: Bringing computers and cars and Coca Cola

30   and T-shirts.

31 CHORUS ONE: So many people and things and ideas flowing

32   from west to east, east to west. Amazing!

33 KAREN: Since I am neither a student or an important

34   dignitary. I am only an accountant. A very ordinary speck

35   of dust.

1   CHORUS ONE: Karen was refused a visa. No one would tell her
2   why.
3   CHORUS TWO: But it all comes down to money. She didn't have
4   the . . . the diñero, *(Attempting to be hip)* the bread, man.
5   CHORUS THREE: March 1989.
6   LU YAN: Karen, when you write to Bibi, thank her for the
7   Baudelaire. Tell her I love French poetry, and to send
8   more of it.
9   KAREN: All right, I will. Lu Yan, should I tell her about . . . our
10   news?
11   LU YAN: Huh? *(Pause)* Ahhh, yes, yes, yes, yes. Maybe she can
12   come up with a good American name for our boy.
13   KAREN: But what if it's a girl?
14   LU YAN: Then we will try again.
15   KAREN: But we can't do that. I told Aunt Wu, they are already
16   making arrangements for me to have the operation after
17   the baby is born. I too hope it will be a boy. But if it's a girl,
18   I hope you will not be angry with me. *(Beat)* If it's a girl, I
19   think I will name her Bibi.
20   LU YAN: That's a good idea.
21   KAREN: The letter is finished. Come on, we better get going.
22   The students are gathering at the university. And Hu
23   Yaobang is speaking, we don't want to miss it. *(Beat)* Is it
24   considered to be counter-revolutionary to listen to a
25   counter-revolutionary? Lu Yan, I made a joke. You never
26   laugh at my jokes.
27   LU YAN: What if our baby is a girl? It's too distressing. Only one
28   child per family. Karen, how can our life improve? I
29   cannot teach at the university and you cannot quit your
30   job to become a student. We cannot get permission for
31   anything, so what's the point of trying to make
32   improvements? What's the point of going to the meeting?
33   KAREN: You are so funny. Didn't you say yesterday we should
34   be open to new ideas in order for our lives to improve?
35   Wasn't it you who said, we must always have hope.

1   LU YAN: You are right. *(Beat)* Maybe we can talk to Hu Yaobang
2   about this one child per family. I want to be a father of a
3   great many children.
4   KAREN: *(Horrified)* You do?
5   LU YAN: Come on, we'll be late. *(BIBI in New York City, with her*
6   *MOTHER.)*
7   BIBI: Spring 1989. Dear Karen, New York City is a place you
8   should see. I've been living here for six months now and I
9   love it. Recently, my mother came to visit me for the first
10   time since I've been on the East Coast. She *loved* it!
11   MOTHER: It smell!
12   BIBI: She especially loved the efficient and clean public
13   services.
14   MOTHER: It noisy! *(Beat.)* Too many bums!
15   BIBI: She also thought my apartment was very cozy.
16   MOTHER: It so small! How can you live like this! Like a mouse
17   in cage. Noisy all day, all night. How do you sleep?
18   BIBI: Happily, I took mother to see all the sights, including the
19   Statue of Liberty.
20   MOTHER: Yes, I've always wanted to see it. Come on, let's go.
21   *(MOTHER and BIBI on the ferry, at the railing)*
22   BIBI: It's a grey somber day. A bit choppy out. The ferry ride to
23   Liberty Island doesn't take very long, it just seems long
24   when you'd rather be eating lunch at the Russian Tea
25   Room. We get off at Liberty Island, magnificent view of
26   the city. And we join the hundreds of people, from all over
27   the world, as we jostle our way off the ferry and down the
28   walkway. *(MOTHER and BIBI at Liberty Island)*
29   MOTHER: Look! She's so beautiful.
30   BIBI: Mother, are you all right? Hey, where are you going?
31   *(BIBI's MOTHER tries to read the inscription at the base of*
32   *the statue.)*
33   MOTHER: *(Laboring over the words)* Give me your tired, your
34   poor . . .
35   BIBI: *(Overlapping)* . . . poor, your huddled masses, yearning to

1   breathe free. The wretched refuse of your teeming shore.
2   Send these, the homeless, tempest tossed to me: I lift my
3   lamp beside the golden door. *(One by one, the CHORUS*
4   *joins BIBI.)*
5   **CHORUS ONE:** *(Overlapping)* The wretched refuse of your
6   teeming shore. Send these, the homeless, tempest tossed
7   to me. I lift my lamp beside the golden door.
8   **CHORUS TWO:** *(Overlapping)* Send these, the homeless,
9   tempest tossed to me: I lift my lamp beside the gold door.
10   **CHORUS THREE:** *(Overlapping)* I lift my lamp beside the
11   golden door. *(Lights out)*
12
13   *(KAREN at Tiananmen Square)*
14   **KAREN:** *(To AUDIENCE)* **May 1989. Dear Bibi, Here I am – sitting**
15   **in a tent on ChangAn Avenue in Tiananmen Square – do you**
16   **know what this means – it means the Avenue of Eternal**
17   **Peace. I cannot begin to describe – there is this change in the**
18   **air – to be here, surrounded by my comrades – student**
19   **activists and ordinary citizens – men and women, all**
20   **patriots for a new China. I think this is what "pursuit of**
21   **happiness" must be. Bibi, for the first time in my life, I**
22   **believe I can be a somebody, I believe my contribution will**
23   **make a difference. I believe freedom will not grow out of**
24   **theory but out of ourselves. We are fighting for a system that**
25   **will respect the individual. The individual is not dead. The**
26   **government must listen to us. The government will listen to**
27   **us. All we want is a dialog. A conversation. We want an end**
28   **to censorship. We want an end to corruption. We are the**
29   **voices of tomorrow. And our voices will be heard. There is so**
30   **much power to be here together – singing songs, holding**
31   **hands, listening to the speeches of our student leaders.**
32   **CHORUS ONE:** "The Power of the people will prevail."
33   **KAREN:** *(Overlapping)* " . . . People will prevail."
34   **CHORUS TWO:** "To liberate society, we must first liberate
35   ourselves."

1   KAREN: *(Overlapping)* ". . . we must first liberate ourselves."
2   CHORUS THREE: "We must give our lives to the movement."
3   KAREN: Yes. I will give my life to the movement! *(KAREN sings*
4   *the national anthem of the People's Republic of China. BIBI*
5   *at home)*
6   BIBI: May 1989. Dear Karen, I've been watching the television
7   reports. Everybody always asks me how I feel about what
8   is happening in China. I'm so envious of your power – of
9   how you have caused your government, caused the world
10   to take notice. But I am also concerned about your naiveté
11   in striving towards a foreign ideal. I do believe change will
12   come, but it must be at your own pace. I am not sure
13   America is the proper model for the new China that you
14   want. Perhaps you should look to make a Chinese
15   democracy. Please understand that I feel a deep
16   connection to you, but right now, I think that to be a
17   somebody in China is suicide. I don't mean to dampen
18   your spirits, but I am worried. Please, please be careful.
19   *(The CHORUS joins KAREN in singing China's anthem. A*
20   *short pause)*
21   CHORUS ONE: Students. The time is now for freedom. The
22   time is now for democracy. For six weeks, we have felt a
23   jubilation. A celebration of spontaneity.
24   CHORUS TWO: I think we should shave our heads in protest.
25   We should shave our heads like prisoners because our
26   government turned our country into a prison.
27   CHORUS ONE: The time for freedom is now. The time for
28   democracy is now.
29   KAREN: We are lying on the floor. Students on a hunger strike.
30   Most of us are women. We haven't eaten in days, and I will
31   not until I have my freedom.
32   SOLDIER: This is foolishness. Resolutely oppose bourgeois
33   liberalism.
34   CHORUS ONE: I'm sorry, but we disagree completely.
35   CHORUS FOUR: Yes, we disagree completely.

1   CHORUS ONE: The time is now for freedom.

2   KAREN: A clean division between what we want and what the

3   government stands for. A clear break.

4   SOLDIER: Children should not defy their parents. Harmony

5   must be preserved. Resolutely oppose bourgeois

6   liberalism.

7   CHORUS FOUR: Mothers are here.

8   CHORUS TWO: Workers, laborers, doctors.

9   CHORUS ONE: Lawyers, bakers, bricklayers.

10   KAREN: Accountants, teachers, writers, students, children,

11   babies.

12   CHORUS (ALL): We are all here. Will you hear the will of the

13   wolf? Will you let the wolf roam free? We want to be free!

14   SOLDIER: The students gave me food, water. I did not want to

15   hurt them.

16   CHORUS ONE: We heard speeches.

17   CHORUS FOUR: We heard songs.

18   CHORUS TWO: We are like a small plant, tender and young,

19   trying to reach the sunshine.

20   CHORUS FOUR: From this movement, which is a movement

21   across China, free thought will grow, and from free

22   thought a new China will grow.

23   CHORUS TWO: The students erected a thirty-three-foot statue

24   called the Goddess of Democracy.

25   CHORUS ONE: Seven weeks of freedom.

26   KAREN: So this is freedom. How good it is. Seven weeks of

27   freedom.

28   CHORUS (ALL): Summer 1989.

29   SOLDIER: Go home and save your life. This is China. This is not

30   the West. *(Gunfire. The CHORUS and KAREN link arms and*

31   *march toward the AUDIENCE. They move in military*

32   *fashion, stepping up to replace others as they are mowed*

33   *down by tanks.)*

34   KAREN: On June 4, 1989. Tanks, armored personnel carriers

35   and trucks full of troops marched into Tiananmen

1   Square. Many of us linked arms, and tried to stand in their
2   way.
3   SOLDIER: Be a good Chinese and go home. Go home and save
4   your life. This is China. This is not the West. Be a good
5   Chinese and go home.
6   CHORUS ONE: I decided to stay. Ten thousand people decided
7   to stay. A man stood naked on the roof and shouted, "I am
8   who I am. I am me."
9   KAREN: Tanks marched forward and crushed the first row. We
10   marched forward.
11   SOLDIER: Go home and save your life.
12   CHORUS FOUR: Change is coming. March forward!
13   CHORUS TWO: Watch your head. Watch out behind you. March
14   forward!
15   SOLDIER: This is not the West. Be good Chinese and go home.
16   CHORUS ONE: Run! Get out of the way. Get out of the way.
17   KAREN: Run! Get out of the way. Run!
18   CHORUS FOUR: This is the Avenue of Eternal Peace.
19   CHORUS TWO: The Goddess of Democracy is crushed.
20   KAREN: Lu Yan, watch out! Lu Yan!
21   SOLDIER: Troops pouring out of the gate.
22   CHORUS FOUR: The Gate of Heavenly Peace.
23   CHORUS ONE: Bullets riddle the crowd.
24   CHORUS FOUR: Beatings. Bayonets. Bricks. Rocks. Beatings.
25   Bayonets. Bricks. Rocks.
26   KAREN: Lu Yan, where are you?!
27   CHORUS TWO: Blood.
28   KAREN: Blood everywhere.
29   CHORUS: Blood everywhere.
30   SOLDIER: Soldiers, forward. Students, comrades! Be good
31   Chinese and go home. This is China. This is not the West.
32   CHORUS TWO: A black curtain.
33   CHORUS ONE: A black curtain.
34   CHORUS: A black curtain.
35   CHORUS FOUR: Over the entrance.

1 KAREN: A Black curtain.

2 CHORUS FOUR: Blocking the view.

3 CHORUS ONE: Of blood and bodies.

4 CHORUS: A black curtain falls over China.

5 KAREN: Lu Yan? Where are you? Lu Yan.

6 SOLDIER: Be good Chinese and go home.

7 KAREN: The statue fell. Everyone was running.

8 CHORUS TWO: Everyone was falling.

9 CHORUS ONE: Everyone was pushing.

10 CHORUS FOUR: Blood everywhere. Screaming.

11 KAREN: (*Screams.*) You animals! (*Lights out. Slides of the*

12 *Tiananmen Square massacre flash in rapid fire succession*

13 *on a screen. The final image is the famous photograph of the*

14 *lone man standing in front of a line of tanks. BLACK OUT. A*

15 *spotlight on BIBI)*

16 BIBI: On that day, as I watched the news, as world events

17 marched into my living room. For the first time in my life,

18 I knew . . . I felt . . . Chinese. And as days passed, I searched

19 my TV set for reports that might answer my questions and

20 ease my grief. But I saw and heard nothing. (*The CHORUS*

21 *reports.)*

22 CHORUS ONE: And here is the news.

23 CHORUS TWO: According to newspaper and television

24 reports . . .

25 CHORUS THREE: . . . five days after the massacre in

26 Tiananmen Square.

27 CHORUS FOUR: Deng Xioaping congratulated his army troops

28 on a job well done.

29 CHORUS ONE: He did not mention the killings.

30 CHORUS TWO: Leaders of the Democracy Movement were

31 arrested, and many of their supporters were rounded up.

32 CHORUS THREE: Remarkably, some students were able to

33 escape.

34 CHORUS FOUR: A Beijing army general who refused to attack

35 the students was sentenced, eighteen years in prison.

1   Lesser generals were summarily executed.

2   CHORUS ONE: The nineteen-year-old man who stood alone
3   against a column of tanks is missing. The government
4   claims he was never arrested.

5   CHORUS TWO: Statistics on the death toll have been confusing.
6   The Chinese Government says less than 400 people were
7   killed, and only 23 of them were students.

8   CHORUS THREE: But according to unofficial reports, at least
9   5,000 died, and at least 30,000 people were reportedly
10   injured.

11   CHORUS FOUR: The world has turned its attention to other
12   events of the world.

13   CHORUS ONE: Other struggles, other tragedies.

14   CHORUS TWO: And China has begun a policy of selective
15   historical amnesia.

16   CHORUS THREE: And America has begun its habit of selective
17   historical amnesia. *(BIBI at her writing desk)*

18   BIBI: Spring 1990. Dear Karen, where are you? It's been several
19   months since . . . I haven't heard . . . are you and Lu Yan all
20   right? I know you will write to me when it is safe. *(Beat)* I
21   want you to know I haven't forgotten you. I want you to
22   know I am thinking of you and Lu Yan. Somehow, let me
23   know if you are all right. Love, your good friend, Bibi.
24   *(Lights out.)*

25

26   **END OF PLAY**

27

28

29

30

31

32

33

34

35

Yasuko and the Young S-S-Samurai
(A one-act farce)
by Karen Huie

Commentary by Karen Huie

Yasuko and the Young S-S-Samurai by Karen Huie has been performed throughout California. It is a one-act farce about a reluctant samurai trying to convince a dewy-eyed maiden that gutlessness is next to godlessness in a country rife with honor, hara kiri and Hondas. It began when Ms. Huie was asked to write and perform something for Asian Pacific Heritage Week at UCLA. She performed it successfully there and at several other theatres in Los Angeles. Since then, it has been presented successfully by others at other theatres and on radio.

"...best sketch...the piece is humorous and yet layered with a depth of cultural feeling." —*Los Angeles Times*

"It is revealing that the best attempt of the festival, is *Yasuko and the Young S-S-Samurai* by Karen Huie." —*Drama-Logue*

"...provides the most laughs...so the group has sense enough to save the best for last." —*Downtown News*

"...was enormously entertaining...giving the piece a thought-provoking integrity all its own." —*L.A. Life*

Yasuko and the Young S-S-Samurai was so popular, one of the theatres requested a sequel. Ms. Huie has considered making it into a series and will begin with Yasuko and Shinage stealing into San Francisco in the 1850s. Within this format, the author can explore the history of Asians in America in a comedic way.

Karen Huie is an actor/writer who has worked in theatre, film, television and radio. On-stage she won critical acclaim for her portrayal of Madame Mao Tse Tung in *The Chairman's Wife* by Wakako Yamauchi, and co-starred in *Wild Bill*, written and directed by Walter Hill. She was hired to write a sitcom pilot based on her comedy, *Songs of Harmony* for CBS and Castle Rock Entertainment. Currently she is directing a documentary about Chinese-Americans growing up in New York"s Chinatown.

Characters:

It is suggested that the play be performed by two actors. One to portray the male characters and the other, the female characters, to add to the concept of fantasy and parody.

SHINAGE-SAN: The Young Samurai, unafraid to fight for what he believes in — unless it involves pain.

YASUKO IZU: The Young Maiden, a hopeless romantic — even in the face of reality

JIM: The Announcer, Jim Lange-type host

SAMURAI(S) #1, #2, and #3: Mating Game contestants (The Young Samurai, in disguise)

JAPANESE WIFE: Commercial type; concerned

JAPANESE HUSBAND: Straight out of "Shogun"

JAPANESE CRONY: Snoopy next door neighbor

YOUNG BOY: Japanese-American

STATION ANNOUNCER: Speaks in cut time

1 **ACT ONE**

2 **SCENE ONE**

3 *TIME: 1860, Meiji era*

4 *SET: Osaka, Japan; the bedroom of YASUKO IZU which is*

5 *separated from its adjoining chamber by a paper screen. At rise,*

6 *YASUKO IZU, a young Japanese maiden of eighteen, is folding*

7 *clothing as she hums "Sakura." From outside, we hear the distant*

8 *clacking of geta (wooden sandals) growing close, closer. The*

9 *young SAMURAI charges in awhirl. He is Japanese, twenty-one*

10 *and dons a bowler hat and a western style (tail)coat over his*

11 *kimono. He hears YASUKO and anxiously removes his geta.*

12

13 **SAMURAI: Yasuko?** *(Beat)* **Yasuko!!**

14 **YASUAKO: Who is it?**

15 **SAMURAI: Yasuko!** *(Unable to see each other through the paper*

16 *screen, they chase each other's voices along the paper screen*

17 *until they're beside each other.)*

18 **YASUKO: Shinage-san? Is it you?**

19 **SAMURAI: It is I, Shinage!**

20 **YASUKO: Shinage-san!!**

21 **SAMURAI: Yasuko!**

22 **YASUKO: Shinage!**

23 **SAMURAI:** *Ya-chan!*

24 **YASUKO: You miss me?**

25 **SAMURAI:** *Hai.* **Miss you.**

26 **YASUKO: Miss you, too.**

27 **SAMURAI: Think about me?**

28 **YASUKO: Yes.**

29 **SAMURAI: What?**

30 **YASUKO: What?**

31 **SAMURAI: What do you think about me?**

32 **YASUKO: I can't tell you.**

33 **SAMURAI: Tell me...**

34 **YASUKO: No.**

35 **SAMURAI: Come on...**

1 YASUKO: OK, OK. I think about you with your kimono pulled
2   open with sweat glistening on your heaving chest–your
3   sword pointing down with blood dripping drop by drop
4   into a big, red –
5 SAMURAI: Yasuko, can we talk?
6 YASUKO: What, Shinage? You don't want to marry me
7   anymore?
8 SAMURAI: Oh yes I do, Yasuko, more than anything, but about
9   this s-s-samurai thing. I don't want to –
10 YASUKO: Oh, Shinage, don't worry. I know all about the risks
11   and dangers you must face. I'm a samurai's daughter. I
12   understand. Now, why don't you go back home and get
13   some sleep. Tomorrow's a big day for you, no?
14 SAMURAI: (*Shouting*) No! This is no time to sleep!
15 YASUKO: My lord, you'll awaken my family.
16 SAMURAI: This is important! I care not who I disturb.
17 YASUKO: Father sleepwalks with his sword, you know.
18 SAMURAI: I'll try to keep it down. Yasuko, in several more
19   hours, I'm supposed to be sworn in as a s-s-samurai!
20 YASUKO: Why then, aren't you resting in preparation?
21 SAMURAI: S-s-samurai, Yasuko! You know – (*The young*
22   *samurai demonstrates pillaging, sees imaginary enemies, is*
23   *overcome by fear, then commits suicide.*)
24 YASUKO: An honor!
25 SAMURAI: Honor?
26 YASUKO: The courage that it takes to pledge one's life!
27 SAMURAI: Co-co-courage?
28 YASUKO: Fearless in the face of death!
29 SAMURAI: Death.
30 YASUKO: To blossom and wither like the Cherry Blossom. How
31   romantic it all is. (*She sings.*) *Sakura, Sakura, ya yo i no...*
32 SAMURAI: Yasuko...
33 YASUKO: Yes, my lord?
34 SAMURAI: Death...
35 YASUKO: My lord?

1 SAMURAI: ...is not romantic.

2 YASUKO: Oh. Painful, my lord? A savage, shimmering, steel
3   sword slicing –

4 SAMURAI: – my shivering spleen, stomach...scrotal sac!
5   Yasuko, don't let them take me!

6 YASUKO: Shinage-san, you mean you don't want to become a
7   samurai?

8 SAMURAI: I don't want to die!

9 YASUKO: But it's in the Samurai Code, my lord.

10 SAMURAI: Yasuko, I don't have to become a s-s-samurai. I can
11   take on another profession – a scroll maker, a twig
12   bundler – plumber even. Help me, Yasuko!

13 YASUKO: My lord, you put me in a most sorry plight! I want to
14   marry you but you know that father has arranged for
15   three dashing, handsome and courageous men to come to
16   court my hand in marriage the day after tomorrow and I
17   must choose one. I was going to choose you, but if you
18   don't become a samurai –

19 SAMURAI: Look, Ya-chan, forget the s-s-samurai stuff! Run
20   away with me! We can hitch to...

21 YASUKO : I can't! A daughter of a samurai must marry a
22   samurai.

23 SAMURAI: Yasuko, you don't want me to become a s-s-samurai.
24   I wouldn't be home at nights. I'd get blood stains all over
25   my fundoshi – and you know what it's like scrubbing
26   blood out of a white cotton loin cloth!

27 YASUKO: Father insists that I marry a samurai to carry on the
28   tradition of Japan.

29 SAMURAI: Tradition?

30 YASUKO: Become a samurai and I'll carry the tradition on for
31   you...after you're dead...by word of mouth.

32 SAMURAI: Yasuko, it's not practical. Besides, the s-s-samurai
33   tradition is phasing out.

34 YASUKO: Yes, because father says we are raising a country of
35   gutless men.

1 SAMURAI: No, just men who want to keep their guts.

2 YASUKO: Father wants a son who is not afraid to fight for what
3   is his.

4 SAMURAI: That's why I'm fighting for my life! It's mine! It's
5   mine! Yasuko, please. Look, we can run to this...

6 YASUKO: I won't leave my country...my proud heritage! The
7   breadth of Mt. Fuji...the home of Nikon™ cameras...the
8   birthplace of Akira Kurosawa. I *can't* run away with you.

9 SAMURAI: Yasuko, please, we can begin a new life, in a new
10   world!

11 YASUKO: Because you're afraid of death.

12 SAMURAI: No, because I'm in love with living.

13 YASUKO: And when your life is over?

14 SAMURAI: Then I'll die.

15 YASUKO: A coward.

16 SAMURAI: But happy! Please, Yasuko, don't you want to live
17   and die happy with me?

18 YASUKO: Yes, Shinage-san, but I can't disobey my father. I'll
19   have to live miserably with another. I must sleep, for the
20   day after tomorrow, I am to become a samurai's wife.
21   Good night, Shinage. And, good-bye! *(Yasuko falls into a*
22   *heap and quickly cries herself asleep.)*

23 SAMURAI: Yasuko! Yasuko! Ya-chan! How will I ever convince
24   her to choose me? I don't want to become a s-s-samurai.
25   But I can't live without my Ya-chan. I know! I'll persuade
26   her courtiers to go elsewhere and then play all the
27   courtiers myself! She will not be able to see me through
28   this paper screen. That way, no matter who she chooses,
29   I'll surely win. *(The Samurai exits. Fade.)*

30

31

32

33

34

35

1 **ACT ONE**
2 **SCENE TWO**
3 *TIME: Two days later*
4 *SET: The Izu house*
5
6 *At rise, YASUKO is adjusting her kimono and hair as the young*
7 *SAMURAI enters. In his (tail)coat and bowler hat, the young*
8 *SAMURAI assumes the role of the announcer.*
9
10 ANNOUNCER: O-o-ohayo, Ladies and Gentlemen, welcome to
11   the Mating Game, coming to you live from the house of
12   Toshiro and Umeboshi Izu. My name is Jim Hang, The
13   Love Professor, and I'll be your host today as our
14   contestant chooses a mate for life! Sound serious? You
15   betcha! Because if she makes a wrong choice, she'll be
16   stuck for life! So ladies and gentlemen, don't hold back!
17   Let her know if she's headed for danger in today's game of
18   love! And now, let's meet our blushing young maiden. She
19   hails from Osaka, Japan. Daughter of a s-s-samurai and a
20   geisha, she spent most of her free time – alone. Would you
21   join me in welcoming Yasuko Izu! *(Applause)* Welcome,
22   Yasuko!
23 YASUKO: *Arigato gozaimasu.*
24 ANNOUNCER: How are you today, Yasuko?
25 YASUKO: I am fine, thank you.
26 ANNOUNCER: Welcome to the Mating Game.
27 YASUKO: It is with great pleasure that I be here today, and...
28 ANNOUNCER: Well, it's just a pleasure to have you. Are you
29   ready to play the Mating Game?
30 YASUKO: I'm a little frightened, I'm afraid.
31 ANNOUNCER: And for good reason! Because whatever happens
32   in the next fifteen minutes will determine your life
33   forever. Now, if you will take your place, we'll have the
34   fellas come out and say hello to you. Remember! No
35   peeking! Samurai #1, will you say hello to Yasuko? *(The*

1   *persona of Samurai #1 is a female impersonator, Samurai #2*
2   *is a Yakuza gangster and samurai #3 is our own sweet*
3   *Shinage.)*
4   **SAMURAI #1: Please hel-lo, Ya-su-ko!**
5   **ANNOUNCER: Samurai #2?**
6   **SAMURAI #2: *Ohayo,* Yasuko.**
7   **ANNOUNCER: And you, Samurai #3?**
8   **SAMURAI: Hello, Yasuko.**
9   **ANNOUNCER: Nothing like sincerity, is there? And, if all of you**
10   **are ready, Yasuko will begin the questions. Have you got**
11   **them, Yasuko?**
12   **YASUKO: Oh yes, right here. *(She takes out a scroll.)* Samurai #1,**
13   **my mother is a geisha, what does that mean to you?**
14   **SAMURAI #1: Oh, about 3,000 yen a half hour.**
15   **YASUKO: Samurai #2, same question.**
16   **SAMURAI #2: I think I know her. Heh-heh-heh.**
17   **YASUKO: And you, Samurai #3?**
18   **SAMURAI: I would honor her as I would you.**
19   **YASUKO: Oh...Samurai #2, my father is a samurai and would be**
20   **very angry if he found you alone in my company. What**
21   **would you say if he pointed his sword to your chin?**
22   **SAMURAI #2: Mine is bigger.**
23   **YASUKO: And you, #1?**
24   **SAMURAI #1: I saw you once in a movie with Toshiro**
25   **Mifune...you were very good!**
26   **YASUKO: And Samurai #3?**
27   **SAMURAI: I was afraid for your beautiful daughter's safety, my**
28   **lord.**
29   **YASUKO: Oh, I'm sure he'd like that. Samurai #1, if you had just**
30   **one wish...**
31   **ANNOUNCER: Yasuko, if you would just hang onto that**
32   **question, we'll come right back after this!**
33   **JAPANESE WIFE: How many times have you had nagging**
34   **headaches?**
35   **JAPANESE HUSBAND: How many times must I tell you? No**

1   starch in my fundoshi!
2   JAPANESE WIFE: And your head would pound....
3   JAPANESE CRONY: Fish for dinner again, dear?
4   JAPANESE WIFE: And pound....
5   YOUNG BOY: Mommy, what's a Jap?
6   JAPANESE WIFE: And pound. Does life seem like an endless
7   stream of misery? Do you ever wish you were dead? Want
8   the solution? Hara Kiri! The fastest alleviator of pain!
9   Now, never before offered to the general public is this
10   special Hara Kiri kit, with everything you'll need to
11   perform the rite. It's safe, it's fast and more importantly,
12   it's easy. This Hara Kiri blade is absolutely amazing. It
13   never dulls! Cuts tomatoes in a breeze, steaks are never a
14   problem and even after slashing your guts, it still cuts
15   paper! Why prolong your agony? Want the solution? Here's
16   how to order.
17   STATION MAN: Just send your name and address on a 3" x 5"
18   index card with the words, "I want the solution" to: Harry
19   Kerry, P. O. Box 900, Imperial Valley Highway, California,
20   90047 and receive your special Harry Kerry kit.
21   JAPANESE WIFE: That's right! And if you order now, you'll get
22   the name of your choice engraved on the handle. A great
23   gift for friends and family. Why not let them know how
24   you really feel about them by sending them a gift that says
25   it all? Hurry, while the supplies last.
26   ANNOUNCER: Welcome back to the Mating Game with our
27   contestant, Yasuko Izu. Yasuko, are you ready for Round
28   Two?
29   YASUKO: Yes.
30   ANNOUNCER: That's just great. They're all yours.
31   YASUKO: Samurai #2, my father thinks a samurai should give
32   his life fully and wholeheartedly to Japan. How do you feel
33   about that? *(The young samurai confuses the two samurai.)*
34   SAMURAI #1: Sure, if you're a *real* man.
35   YASUKO: Samurai #2?!

1   SAMURAI #2: Oh! *(Readjusting)* **Crime pays much better.**

2   **YASUKO: And you, #3?**

3   **SAMURAI: I would rather give my life to you, whom I love. For**

4   **what I could give to you is worth more than a faceless**

5   **death, − even for my country!**

6   **YASUKO: Shinage-san! You're here! You did it! You became a**

7   **samurai! Oh, Shinage! I knew you would!** *(YASUKO charges*

8   *towards SHINAGE, who keeps things rolling for fear she'll*

9   *find out there's no one else there.)*

10 **ANNOUNCER: No! Don't come over here! Oh! Yasuko, we only**

11   **have time for one more question and I ask that you think**

12   **carefully before you ask it. This may be the one that**

13   **makes your final decision for a Mate for Life!**

14 **YASUKO: Only one more? Oh, um...Samurai #2, give me one**

15   **good reason why I should choose you.**

16 **SAMURAI #2: Ask your mother. Heh-heh-heh.**

17 **YASUKO: #1?**

18 **SAMURAI #1: We could be girlfriends.**

19 **YASUKO: And you, #3?**

20 **SAMURAI: You'll know what I did was right. You won't be**

21   **ashamed of me!**

22 **YASUKO: Shinage, why should I be ashamed of you. Father will**

23   **be so proud!**

24 **SAMURAI: Even if I decided to skip the ceremony?**

25 **YASUKO: Skip the ceremony! You mean you didn't become a**

26   **samurai? Shinage? Shinage!**

27 **ANNOUNCER: And there you have it. Charming and witty**

28   **answers from three eligible s-s-samurai. And now, I ask**

29   **you, Yasuko Izu, who will be the lucky s-s-samurai to get**

30   **your hand? Uh, uh! Take your time. Think about it. You'll**

31   **never get another chance. And now, what we've all been**

32   **waiting for. Yasuko Izu, are you ready to pick the lucky s-**

33   **s-samurai to spend the rest of your life with?**

34 **YASUKO: Yes, I think I am!**

35 **ANNOUNCER: And now, let's see who Yasuko will choose.**

1   Yasuko, will it be...Samurai #1, Samurai #2 or Samurai #3?
2   *(The young samurai acts out the three different samurai,*
3   *encouraging the audience to vote for Samurai #3.)* **Yasuko?**
4   YASUKO: *(Playing along)* **Oh, Jim, they were all so charming and**
5   **witty. But I'm going to have to go with – Samurai #2!**
6   ANNOUNCER: Samurai #2? #2! Yasuko, would you tell us why
7   you picked Samurai #2?
8   YASUKO: Because – because – because he's brave!
9   ANNOUNCER: A very wise choice. Let me tell you about
10   Samurai #2. Samurai #2 is a yakuza – a high-ranking
11   member of the Japanese syndicate. He's killed countless
12   people and instead of getting a tattoo to symbolize his
13   killing spirit, he just had his whole torso painted blood
14   red. When he's not out slaying, he likes to show off his
15   culinary skills cutting sashimi into animal shapes at his
16   restaurant – Ai-kiru-yu. Would you welcome, P.J., "Sleaze"
17   Shigeta!
18   SAMURAI #2: Me? Does that mean I can't see her mother
19   anymore? No! *(The young samurai feigns the suicide of*
20   *Samurai #2.)*
21   ANNOUNCER: I'm terribly sorry Yasuko, Samurai #2 has just
22   committed Hara Kiri. You'll have to pick another.
23   YASUKO: Oh! *(Beat)* Well then, I'll go with Samurai #1.
24   ANNOUNCER: Samurai #1?! Samurai #1 hails from Tokyo, where
25   he is an onagata – female impersonator! Tiring of the
26   formality and rigidity of the Kabuki theatre, he decided to
27   strike out on his own with his cabaret act. Now, nightly on
28   the Ginza he impersonates song birds from all over the
29   world – Dietrich, Piaf, Whitney Houston! Please welcome,
30   Jerry "Ginger" Wakabayashi!
31   SAMURAI #1: I can't marry her! I'm a her! I like hims! *(The*
32   *young samurai feigns a suicide for Samurai #1.)*
33   ANNOUNCER: Oops! There goes another one! Yasuko Izu, I'm
34   sorry that you're having such a terrible "stroke" of luck.
35   Luckily, we have one more samurai left. Samurai #3! Yeah!

1   Samurai #3 hails from your own hometown — Osaka,

2   Japan. He's tall, dark, handsome and very in love with

3   you! Would you welcome Shinage-san!

4   SAMURAI: Yasuko! Yasuko! You chose me!

5   YASUKO: Shinage-san. You tricked me!

6   SAMURAI: But — you haven't heard the prize yet! *(He becomes*

7   *the announcer again.)*

8   ANNOUNCER: Isn't that just wonderful? Don't they make a

9   lovely couple? And now, Yasuko and Shinage, you two

10   lucky people will win the prize we are about to announce.

11   Are you ready? *(No response)* Along with a chaperon, you

12   two are going to spend a year's honeymoon at — Camp

13   Manzanar Springs! Three hundred acres of what was

14   believed to be just barren wasteland is now a resort for the

15   Japanese-American community. Congratulations again,

16   lucky couple, thanks for playing the Mating Game and

17   now if you'll join me in throwing our Mating Game Kiss —

18   *(YASUKO runs over to the adjoining chamber.)*

19   SAMURAI: Yasuko! Wait, please! Yasuko! All right, forget the

20   kiss. It's a stupid idea anyway.

21   YASUKO: Get out of my house!

22   SAMURAI: Not until you listen to me.

23   YASUKO: There's no one here but you!

24   SAMURAI: Yes, but — I did pretty good, didn't I?

25   YASUKO: A Yakuza and an onagata!

26   SAMURAI: Fooled you though, didn't I?

27   YASUKO: You think you're pretty clever, don't you?

28   SAMURAI: Boy, it wasn't easy keeping all those people and

29   voices straight. In Question #2 I thought for sure you knew

30   I was —

31   YASUKO: Never mind! You'd better go now because my

32   courtiers will be here soon.

33   SAMURAI: No they won't.

34   YASUKO: They won't? Why not?

35   SAMURAI: I killed them.

1 YASUKO: Killed my courtiers?

2 SAMURAI: Well, not exactly. I told them you weren't Japanese.

3 YASUKO: What?!

4 SAMURAI: That you were adopted and that you're actually

5   Chinese.

6 YASUKO: And they believed you?

7 SAMURAI: Mmm...not until I told them you had a highly

8   contagious disease.

9 YASUKO: Ugh! What an awful story!

10 SAMURAI: Hey, it worked. But that's all in the past now. I've

11   won you.

12 YASUKO: I won't marry you! You're deceitful, dishonest and —

13 SAMURAI: Debonair?

14 YASUKO: Disturbing, get out!

15 SAMURAI: But Yasuko...

16 YASUKO: Don't —

17 SAMURAI: Ya-chan...

18 YASUKO: Stop it, you're confusing me.

19 SAMURAI: You think you're confused!

20 YASUKO: Just go!

21 SAMURAI: No. I'm not going anywhere. I'm going to wait by

22   your window until you marry me. And you can tell your

23   father I'm just fighting for what belongs to me. Your

24   heart.

25 YASUKO: Then I'll grow old with loneliness.

26 SAMURAI: But I did all this so we can live happily ever after!

27 YASUKO: I can't break the tradition! I can't disobey my father!

28 SAMURAI: Not here, not in Japan.

29 YASUKO: What do you mean?

30 SAMURAI: If we run away to America, we won't have to follow

31   tradition anymore! We can live any way we want to!

32 YASUKO: America! I'm not moving to America. I don't even

33   know where that is!

34 SAMURAI: Well, it's a ways, but, we'll only have to make the trip

35   once.

1　YASUKO: I'm sorry Shinage, I can't turn my back on my
2　　　country.
3　SAMURAI: You'd rather turn your back on me?
4　YASUKO: You leave me no choice.
5　SAMURAI: I'm the choice! You can choose me!
6　YASUKO: Why should I choose you?
7　SAMURAI: Because I'll love you until the days grow dim – or
8　　　until my eyes grow dim, whichever comes foist! *(YASUKO*
9　　　*looks puzzled.)* New York. That's how they talk there. No,
10　　　really! Come on Ya-chan, you love me, don't you? OK,
11　　　maybe I'm rushing things. Why don't you marry me first
12　　　and then later we can work on – You may as well, because
13　　　I'm never gonna go away and then you'll have to explain
14　　　who I am to the next guy –
15　YASUKO: I don't care!
16　SAMURAI: – and the next –
17　YASUKO: I don't care!
18　SAMURAI: And tell them you're not Japanese.
19　YASUKO: All right, all right, you really want my hand?
20　SAMURAI: Only if it comes with the rest of you. *(She pulls out a*
21　　　*knife.)*
22　YASUKO: Then fight for it!
23　SAMURAI: Are you out of your mind? I can't fight you, Yasuko!
24　YASUKO: Why not, because I'm a woman?
25　SAMURAI: Because you're the daughter of a s-s-samurai, you're
26　　　gonna kill me!
27　YASUKO: Fight!
28　SAMURAI: Ya-chan, please, I'm wearing my best kimono.
29　　　*(YASUKO ensues. They fight. He overtakes her. She drops the*
30　　　*sword.)*
31　YASUKO: Shinage-san!
32　SAMURAI: Satisfied?
33　YASUKO: Yes.
34　SAMURAI: What'd you do this for?
35　YASUKO: Just wanted to make sure you could protect us when

1   we move to America.

2   **SAMURAI: You mean you still want to marry me?**

3   **YASUKO: Yes, Shinage.** *(SHINAGE throws down the knife and*

4   *hovers over YASUKO.)*

5   **SAMURAI: Oh, Ya-chan!**

6   **YASUKO: Shinage-san!**

7   **SAMURAI: Ya-chan.**

8   **YASUKO: Shin-chan.** *(Fade out)*

9

10   **END OF PLAY**

11

12

13

14

15

16

17

18

19

20

21

22

23

24

25

26

27

28

29

30

31

32

33

34

35

The China Crisis
by Kipp Erante Cheng

Playwrights will often say that their plays are like their children, and it would be impossible — perhaps unfair — to single out one of them as their favorite or least favorite. I have no such problem with favoritism or lack thereof, especially since I know that many of my plays will ultimately end up as throwaways.

I've always thought that *The China Crisis* was one of those throwaway plays, a little trifle of a classroom exercise. Call it "film noir" lite, I wrote *The China Crisis* for a playwright-director workshop while I was attending Columbia University in 1994. Like most of the plays I was writing at that time, I wrote this play quickly, purposefully trying to maintain and include the nutty sloppiness of a first draft that I tried to pass off as experimenting with form and language. In truth, I wanted to write a play that would be a crowd-pleaser, a simplistic, wacky one-act that would get the audience to laugh and maybe, eventually, get them to come to see (or read) my more "serious" plays. (I was a tortured, grad-school playwright, after all.)

The overwhelmingly positive response I got for the workshop production of the play baffled me. The chairman of the graduate theater program told me that he felt *The China Crisis* was the culmination and synthesis of the kind of satirical writing I was interested in and the articulation of Asian-American identity that seemed so hidden in my previous work. I nodded and thanked him, thinking at the time that he was full of crap.

Shortly after graduate school, there were a few failed attempts at producing *The China Crisis,* along with its companion play *The Fortunate One* — about a guy who writes fortunes for a fortune cookie company, makes a deal with the Devil, then hilarity ensues. But other than the brief flirtation with production, the play ended up sitting on a bookcase in my apartment, collecting dust. In the meantime, I stopped writing plays, started writing plays again, then stopped, started and basically went on a roller coaster ride that became my life as a playwright.

I rediscovered *The China Crisis* after Roger Ellis said he wanted to include the play in an upcoming anthology of multicultural plays. Reading the script nearly four years later, I found that it has maintained the silliness and camp that I knew had always been there. But I also found in it a satirical edge and complexity that I had never seen before. When I re-read the Dragon Lady's speech, "There are things about Chinese people you will never understand," I thought, "Yikes! That's it!" I realized that I may have been unduly harsh in my initial thoughts on *The China Crisis*, and I am thrilled to have it included in this anthology.

Of course, the play could not have made it into this book without the creative input of my director, Ernie Barbarash, my dramaturg, Shirley Fishman, and the original workshop cast: Richard Hlatki, Lisa Ann Li, Julie Oda and Chris Roberts.

Characters:
> **MICKEY FINN,** Private Detective
> **LOLA CHOW-FUN,** Femme Fatale
> **THE DRAGON LADY**
> **MR. LOW FAT**

Setting: The Golden Chopstix Restaurant in Chinatown

Time: Late at night

1 *In black, the plaintive sounds of a solo saxophone. The titles:*
2 *"The China Crisis," followed by "Chinatown," appear on a*
3 *projection screen. Half-light on a street outside of the Golden*
4 *Chopstix Restaurant. The blue and orange glow of neon cuts*
5 *through the dense fog of the night. There is a street light. A*
6 *match is struck, a cigarette lit, then the sound of a man coughing.*
7 *Mickey Finn, Private Investigator, enters. He wears a trench coat,*
8 *a hat, and a dead-pan, tough-guy smirk. He speaks into a hand-*
9 *held tape recorder.*
10
11 FINN: Reminder: Time to quit the smokes. Dolores, remind
12   me to quit the smokes. And get a pound of Java, ground
13   extra fine. And some kitty litter for the cat. *(Beat)* And
14   some flowers for the old lady. *(FINN lights another*
15   *cigarette, then turns to address the audience.)* The name's
16   Finn. Mickey Finn. Private Investigator. I usually do the
17   kind of paper-pushing work that doesn't amount to a hill
18   a beans in a city like New York. Divorce surveillance.
19   Insurance fraud. Cases with simple solutions and happy
20   endings. It was two-thirty in the A.M. I was standing
21   outside of the Golden Chopstix, a sleazy dive in the heart
22   of old Chinatown. Great Hunan egg rolls. But forget the
23   Moo Goo Gai Pan. This was the kind of restaurant that
24   invented the phrase MSG reaction. After a long night of
25   sneaking around in dark alleys and hiding under beds, all
26   a guy wants to do is pick up some Chinese take-out, go
27   back to the flea-bag that he calls home, and listen to some
28   Glenn Gould until the liquor takes hold. Or at least until
29   his girl calls, looking to acquire company. Or until
30   morning comes and everything starts all over again.
31   *(FINN puts out his cigarette.)* Gotta quit these things. Soon.
32   The trouble is, the taste gets under your skin. Every drag
33   reminds you of some girl in a bar, singing a sad song,
34   singing the song as if you're the only chump around. As if
35   she's singing the song just for you. Cigarettes are like

1   **Chinese food. You have one and then half an hour later**
2   **your fingers are itching to get hold of another precious**
3   **coffin nail.** *(Beat)* **I guess that's just the nature of**
4   **addiction.** *(A gong is struck. Then lights change to reveal the*
5   *interior of the restaurant. There is a table with a steaming*
6   *order of Chicken Lo Mein. Next to the table, there is a chalk*
7   *outline of a body and a pair of gold-plated chopsticks on the*
8   *floor. LOLA CHOW-FUN enters. She wears a red silk dress*
9   *and holds out an unlit cigarette.)*
10 **LOLA: Got a light, Big Boy?**
11 **FINN: Vices will be the death of me. I'm trying to quit.**
12 **LOLA: Aren't we all. But then some habits die hard.**
13 **FINN: Especially those habits that give us pleasure.**
14 **LOLA: Those are the best kinds of habits to have. The**
15   **pleasurable ones. At least you can die with a smile on your**
16   **face.**
17 **FINN: Yes. I know what you mean.**
18 **LOLA: How can I help you tonight? Would you like to try some**
19   **of the Three Happiness Beef and Broccoli? It's our special**
20   **today.**
21 **FINN: No thanks, ma'am. I'm just here to pick up a couple of**
22   **your Hunan egg rolls.**
23 **LOLA: Yes, the Hunan egg rolls. They're addictive.**
24 **FINN: And maybe an order of Chicken Lo Mein.**
25 **LOLA: Good choice. What's your name?**
26 **FINN: The name's Finn. Mickey Finn. Private Investigator.**
27 **LOLA: I'm Lola Chow-Fun. But my friends just call me Lola.**
28   **Would you like to be my friend, Mr. Finn?**
29 **FINN: I imagine it's pretty dangerous to be friends with a dame**
30   **like yourself, Lola. A good boy could get into a lot of**
31   **trouble with a bad girl like you.**
32 **LOLA: Well — whatever Lola wants, Lola gets.**
33 **FINN: And what do you want, Lola?**
34 **LOLA: Did you say twelve Hunan egg rolls and an order of Lo**
35   **Mein?**

1   FINN: *(Thinks.)* Yes. That's right.

2   LOLA: I'll see that your order is taken care of.

3   FINN: I'm sure you will. *(LOLA exits into the kitchen. FINN to*

4   *audience)* I was reading her like a book. Trying to get a

5   handle on what this dame wanted from me. Dames always

6   want something. Especially a dame with legs to here and

7   a voice like gravel and too many cigarettes. The kind of

8   voice that could make a very bad boy fall asleep against

9   her breasts like a little baby in his mother's arms. *(LOLA*

10   *re-enters with the food.)*

11 LOLA: Who are you talking to?

12 FINN: Who? Me? I wasn't talking to anyone. It's just an

13   occupational hazard.

14 LOLA: Here's your order. I hope you'll find it satisfying.

15 FINN: Thanks, Lola. *(FINN turns to leave.)*

16 LOLA: Mr. Finn?

17 FINN: Yes?

18 LOLA: I was wondering. Since you were here. And since you do

19   some work in investigations. And since you seem to like

20   our Hunan egg rolls. I wonder if you would be interested

21   in doing a job for me?

22 FINN: What kind of job?

23 LOLA: Never mind. It was silly for me to ask.

24 FINN: *(To audience)* She piques my curiosity, then dismisses me

25   right away. I think I might be in love with this dame.

26 LOLA: It's just...I'm in a particularly sticky situation right now.

27   With the restaurant.

28 FINN: What kind of sticky situation?

29 LOLA: Well...there's been a death here.

30 FINN: Murder at the Golden Chopstix Restaurant? *(There is a*

31   *dramatic musical flourish.)*

32 LOLA: I didn't say murder. I said death.

33 FINN: The only difference between murder and death is who

34   happens to be on the receiving end of the bad news.

35 LOLA: What?

1 FINN: I mean, the only difference between murder and death
2   is what intentions a dame has for a man.
3 LOLA: Like I said, there was no murder.
4 FINN: But there was a death?
5 LOLA: Yes. *(Beat)* It was Low Fat.
6 FINN: Excuse me?
7 LOLA: The deceased. He was Mr. Low Fat. He owned the Cuban-
8   Chinese restaurant up the street.
9 FINN: Yes. El Loco Pagoda Restaurant. I've been there. Terrible
10   service. Good Shrimp Dumplings. Lousy egg rolls.
11 LOLA: I have a tiny little problem with the death of Mr. Low Fat.
12   Low Fat was dining in the restaurant when he bit the
13   giant egg roll. If word gets out, it could be terrible for
14   business.
15 FINN: Low Fat dining at the Golden Chopstix? So you want me
16   to take care of some damage control.
17 LOLA: If you don't mind. Help me dispose of the evidence.
18 FINN: And what's in it for me?
19 LOLA: Your usual fee. Plus expenses. And I could give you all
20   the Hunan egg rolls you want.
21 FINN: Expenses plus the Hunan egg rolls? This sounds too good
22   to be true. What's the catch?
23 LOLA: No catch. *(Beat. Realizes.)* Maybe just one tiny little catch.
24   *(Beat)* I seem to have misplaced the body of Mr. Low Fat.
25 FINN: Misplaced?
26 LOLA: I don't think he just walked away.
27 FINN: And you would like me to find the body?
28 LOLA: If you don't mind. It would help me immensely.
29 FINN: Tell me, Lola. When did the murder occur?
30 LOLA: Like I said, there wasn't a murder. Low Fat just died.
31 FINN: People don't just die. They tend to be led toward their
32   deaths.
33 LOLA: Or they die willingly. With a smile on their face. Any
34   number of things are possible.
35 FINN: Yes, you're right. When did you discover Mr. Low Fat?

1 LOLA: Some time this evening.

2 FINN: And what was your relationship with the deceased?

3 LOLA: Did I mention that the Three Happiness Beef and

4   Broccoli was our special tonight?

5 FINN: Yes. You already told me. *(To audience)* What she didn't

6   tell me was why she would want to kill an old tired slob

7   like Low Fat. Lola Chow-Fun was my number one suspect.

8 LOLA: We were lovers. *(The titles: "Suspect #1.")*

9 FINN: Yes?

10 LOLA: For a short time. Low Fat gave me pleasure. And I gave

11   him dinner. At a discount. He had a weakness for my

12   Hunan egg rolls.

13 FINN: I can see how he could have a weakness for your egg

14   rolls. *(Beat)* And a weakness for dames like you.

15 LOLA: And what kind of dames might that be?

16 FINN: Mysterious dames who keep a lot of secrets.

17 LOLA: I guess that's just part of my Oriental disposition.

18 FINN: I imagine that the Chinese know a lot of secrets about

19   life and death.

20 LOLA: What would you know about the Chinese?

21 FINN: *(In Mandarin)* Rats will know the way of rats.

22 LOLA: I don't speak Chinese.

23 FINN: Rats will know the way of rats. Ancient Chinese proverb.

24 LOLA: I myself have never been to China. *(There is a moment of*

25   *awkward silence.)*

26 FINN: Was there anyone else who might have seen the body of

27   Low Fat? Perhaps other patrons?

28 LOLA: Bing-Bing. Our head busboy. But he took the day off.

29   Said he had to go upstate to see his girl. Thursdays are

30   slow nights at the restaurant. The only other person who

31   was in the restaurant at the time of the murder couldn't

32   possibly know —

33 FINN: Did you say murder? I thought you said there was no

34   murder?

35 LOLA: Just a slip of the tongue. I meant death. Yes. That's what

1   I meant to say. The Dragon Lady might know something.

2 FINN: The Dragon Lady? *(A gong is struck.)*

3 LOLA: Yes. The Dragon Lady. She's our head cook.

4 FINN: And where might The Dragon Lady be right now?

5 LOLA: She's in the kitchen. She's our head cook.

6 FINN: Right. In the kitchen. *(Beat)* What would The Dragon

7   Lady be able to tell us about Low Fat?

8 LOLA: Little. I suppose. Her English. It's fractured. At best.

9 FINN: But she has eyes.

10 LOLA: She had eyes. The accident with the exploding wok.

11   Sesame oil can be lethal. In the right context. Now the

12   Dragon Lady is legally blind. Can't see two inches in front

13   of her. Not without her glasses. *(FINN picks up a pair of*

14   *glasses out of the Lo Mein.)*

15 FINN: *(Checks glasses.)* She's blind as a bat.

16 LOLA: The Dragon Lady only sees what she wants to see. *(A*

17   *gong is struck. THE DRAGON LADY enters, wearing a chef's*

18   *hat and a filthy apron. She squints as she stumbles to the*

19   *table. She carries a steaming wok in her hands.)*

20 THE DRAGON LADY: Ai-ya! Ruined! Peking Scallops and

21   Shrimps ruined!

22 LOLA: Dragon Lady. What are you doing out here?

23 THE DRAGON LADY: We get call. People order delivery. I don't

24   wear glasses. I can't see. I look and look. All over. For

25   glasses. No find anywhere. Ruin food. Ruin Peking

26   Scallops and Shrimps.

27 FINN: Here are your glasses, ma'am. *(THE DRAGON LADY puts*

28   *on her glasses.)*

29 THE DRAGON LADY: Ah so? Who this? Copper?

30 FINN: I'm Mickey Finn. Private Investigator.

31 THE DRAGON LADY: I Dragon Lady. You Copper? I know

32   nothing. I see nothing. I not wear glasses. Blind. I blind

33   without glasses. Tell him. Lola, you tell Copper I blind

34   without glasses.

35 LOLA: She's blind. Without her glasses.

1 FINN: You didn't see anything unusual tonight? Perhaps the
2   body of Low Fat? Do you have any knowledge as to what
3   happened to Mr. Low Fat's body?
4 THE DRAGON LADY: I see nothing.
5 FINN: Would you have any reason to want to see Mr. Low Fat
6   dead, Dragon Lady?
7 THE DRAGON LADY: I never like Low Fat. He want get secret
8   recipe for Hunan egg rolls. He try get recipe from Lola. I
9   not like him. I only cook Hunan egg rolls.
10 LOLA: Our Hunan egg rolls have, shall I say, a secret ingredient.
11 FINN: And that secret would be?
12 THE DRAGON LADY: Ai-ya! Tell you secret and then secret not
13   secret anymore! I not dumb! You stupid man. Who this
14   man?
15 LOLA: He's here to help us find the body of Low Fat.
16 THE DRAGON LADY: *(Innocently)* Why we need find Low Fat's
17   body?
18 LOLA: The body is missing.
19 FINN: *(Thinks.)* A secret recipe. A secret recipe so secret it might
20   be worth killing someone to maintain its secrecy? *(To*
21   *audience)* I was checking out the joint. Looking for clues.
22   One of these women killed Low Fat. To insure that their
23   secret recipe for Hunan egg rolls would remain a secret.
24   But what happened to the body?
25 THE DRAGON LADY: Low Fat want take over egg roll business
26   in New York City. But I cook best egg roll in Tri-State area.
27 FINN: And that's why you killed him. With this pair of gold-
28   plated chopsticks.
29 THE DRAGON LADY: I not hurt anyone.
30 LOLA: We don't need to resort to violence. Besides, I couldn't
31   hurt a fly. Not a tiny little fly. *(LOLA kills a bug.)*
32 FINN: *(To audience)* As I was piecing the clues together, I
33   thought I had the case half-solved. Picture this: During a
34   lovers' quarrel, Lola Chow-Fun stabs her lover — Mr. Low
35   Fat — in self defense, with this pair of gold-plated

1 chopsticks. Then the Dragon Lady entered the scene and
2 became suspect number two. The Dragon Lady had just as
3 much motivation and opportunity to kill Low Fat at the
4 Golden Chopstix. What did she really know? And what did
5 she really see? *(The titles: "Suspect #2." FINN begins to*
6 *interrogate LOLA and THE DRAGON LADY.)* **Where were**
7 you at the time of Low Fat's untimely death? Why haven't
8 the police been notified? Who drew that chalk outline?
9 How did your glasses end up in this particular order of Lo
10 Mein? How many egg rolls did you feed Low Fat before you
11 killed him? Why do I sometimes get two fortunes in my
12 fortune cookies instead of one? What is the chemical
13 structure of Monosodium Glutamate? Why isn't Peking
14 Duck called Beijing Duck after all we've been through? Is
15 the Great Wall really all that great? How do you solve a
16 problem like Maria? How do you catch a cloud and pin it
17 down? What is the cube root of 4069? If a train leaves
18 Boston at 6 pm traveling at a speed of 130 miles per hour,
19 what time does it reach Philadelphia? And for God's sake,
20 why doesn't the Golden Chopstix take reservations?
21 THE DRAGON LADY: I Dragon lady. I cook long time. No see
22 nothing. I no kill. Killing for someone else. Other people's
23 business. I cook Hunan egg rolls for Golden Chopstix
24 Restaurant. That's all. Low Fat, I meet him only once,
25 maybe twice. He come restaurant, come see Lola. But
26 when she not here, Low Fat come talk to me. He sample
27 Hunan egg rolls and say best he ever have. He ask me go
28 work at El Loco Pagoda restaurant, bring secret recipe to
29 his restaurant. I say no, but he push me. He ask for secret
30 ingredient. But I no tell. No price worth selling secret
31 from many generations from China. *(Beat)* There things
32 you not know about Chinese people. *(THE DRAGON LADY*
33 *begins to transform.)* But you think you know. Things you
34 expect. But don't understand. There are things about
35 Chinese people you will never understand. *(THE DRAGON*

1   *LADY has transformed into a beautiful woman.)* **There are**
2   **things about us that you will never be able to get a handle**
3   **on. You can only wonder and hope that maybe one day**
4   **you will be able to get a little closer to what it really**
5   **means to be Chinese. The Golden Chopstix Restaurant is**
6   **filled with the unexpected. Like all Chinese restaurants,**
7   **our restaurant is a place filled with mysteries. There are**
8   **over two hundred choices on the menu alone and if you**
9   **multiply those individual choices with mild, hot, and**
10   **extra hot combinations, your experience at the Golden**
11   **Chopstix Restaurant is practically limitless. Where else**
12   **can you get a plate of noodles, have a cup of coffee, and**
13   **get a slice of New York cheesecake for under five**
14   **dollars?**
15 **LOLA: Only at a Chinese restaurant.**
16 **FINN: That was amazing. How did you do that?**
17 **THE DRAGON LADY: I'm not just here to fry egg rolls. I have a**
18   **brain, too. If I have to fry one more Hunan egg roll, I'll just**
19   **scream!**
20 **FINN: There's nothing wrong with your egg rolls, baby. You're**
21   **beautiful.** *(To audience)* **I think I might be in love with this**
22   **dame. Why do you continue to cook egg rolls if you are so**
23   **unhappy?**
24 **THE DRAGON LADY: My name is The Dragon Lady. What else**
25   **am I supposed to do? It's not like I can take any old job.**
26   **Maybe this was part of my destiny.**
27 **FINN: You could maybe change your name?**
28 **THE DRAGON LADY: And disrespect my family legacy?** *(Beat)*
29   **You think just because I work at this restaurant, I can't do**
30   **anything else? I have dreams, too. One day I'll leave this**
31   **rat-infested hole in the wall. But until that day comes, I'm**
32   **stuck here. In the bowels of New York City. In the armpit**
33   **of Chinatown.**
34 **LOLA: Well. I wouldn't say it's really all that bad.**
35 **THE DRAGON LADY: Are you kidding? We're like animals**

1   trapped in cages. Chinatown is like one of the lowest rings
2   of Hell.
3 LOLA: You think?
4 THE DRAGON LADY: Yes. Of course it is. Lola, don't you realize
5   that there is a great big world out there? There are regions
6   of possibilities just waiting for us to explore and exploit.
7   Picture this: we start small, with this little dive. Then
8   when word starts to get out about our new and improved
9   Hunan egg rolls, we expand into an entire chain of
10   restaurants. We'll build an empire of restaurants all over
11   the world. You think the Golden Arches are something,
12   wait until the world gets a load of the Golden Chopstix!
13 LOLA: Yes. Yes. I can picture it!
14 THE DRAGON LADY: World domination!
15 LOLA: Yes. And I can finally buy that little villa in Spain that
16   I've had my eye on for all of these years.
17 THE DRAGON LADY: You can buy two villas if you want, Lola.
18   *(There is a moment of awkward silence.)*
19 FINN: Yes. Back to the murder of Low Fat.
20 THE DRAGON LADY: Perhaps there was no murder in the first
21   place. Perhaps this was all just a big misunderstanding. I
22   don't see a body. Without a body, it would be difficult to
23   prove there was a murder.
24 FINN: What happened to the body? Where is Mr. Low Fat? Do
25   you have something you need to tell me, Lola? *(LOLA backs*
26   *away from FINN.)* Admit it, Lola. You killed Mr. Low Fat.
27 LOLA: It's not like I stabbed him with a pair of gold-plated
28   chopsticks.
29 THE DRAGON LADY: That would have been too cliché.
30 LOLA: Yes. Too predictable. Who says it's a crime to feed a man
31   Hunan egg rolls? He liked my Hunan egg rolls. I just
32   wanted to satisfy him. *(Beat)* OK. I confess. I was present
33   when Low Fat passed away. I admit I laughed, a little,
34   when he had his heart attack. But I didn't murder the
35   man. Cholesterol is not a murder weapon in this country.

1   At least not yet.

2   FINN: If you saw Mr. Low Fat die, then what happened to his
3   body?

4   THE DRAGON LADY: You're hungry. Let me get you something
5   to eat. *(A cast of fog enters the restaurant. Lights change.*
6   *THE DRAGON LADY enters with a Pu Pu platter.)* You can
7   have the Pu Pu Platter for two. Included with this
8   appetizer set you get a portion of cold sesame noodles,
9   deep-fried chicken wings, shrimp dumplings, either fried
10   or steamed, and several Hunan egg rolls.

11   LOLA: Or you can substitute an additional order of Hunan egg
12   rolls for the shrimp dumplings.

13   THE DRAGON LADY: Our Hunan egg rolls are our biggest
14   sellers. And with good reason.

15   LOLA: Yes. Very good reason.

16   THE DRAGON LADY: They are addictive. People have a bite of
17   our Hunan egg rolls and they keep coming back for more.

18   LOLA: Yes. They come back for more.

19   FINN: Your Hunan egg rolls are good. But are they really that
20   good?

21   THE DRAGON LADY: Have you tried our new and improved
22   recipe?

23   FINN: I don't think so.

24   LOLA: Why don't you have a bite. One bite won't kill you. *(THE*
25   *DRAGON LADY brings out a platter of Hunan egg rolls. FINN*
26   *is mesmerized by the egg rolls.)*

27   FINN: Yes. You're right. One bite won't kill me.

28   THE DRAGON LADY: Now do you see what we mean?

29   FINN: They're delicious. What's in these things?

30   THE DRAGON LADY: Our secret recipe.

31   FINN: It tastes a little bit like chicken.

32   LOLA: Pretty good stuff, huh?

33   FINN: Yes. Delicious. But. All of this MSG is giving me a major
34   headache. Excruciating. I think I might have to sit down.
35   My head is spinning. What's going on? *(Lights change,*

1   *while spooky music begins. MR. LOW FAT, dressed in a suit*
2   *and a Panama hat, appears through a haze of smoke with the*
3   *Giant Menu of Dreams. He doesn't have any feet.)*
4   **MR. LOW FAT: Mickey Finn.**
5   **FINN: Who are you?**
6   **MR. LOW FAT: In life I was called Low Fat. But now they just**
7   **call me the Grand Fromage. Or the Loco Poco from the**
8   **Casa del Pagoda. I have a message for you. From beyond**
9   **the Great Wall. From beyond the Giant Menu of Dreams.**
10 **FINN: What is it?**
11 **MR. LOW FAT: Take a look at the appetizers. In them, you will**
12 **find the truth.**
13 **FINN: The truth to what?**
14 **MR. LOW FAT: The truth to everything.**
15 **FINN: Everything?**
16 **MR. LOW FAT: Everything. You will find out why Hot and Sour**
17 **Soup costs more than the special Wonton Soup. You will**
18 **find out why you get ten chicken wings when you eat in,**
19 **but only eight when you take out. You will find out why**
20 **there is no duck in the duck sauce. And, you will find out**
21 **what is really in the Hunan egg rolls. And why they are so**
22 **addictive.**
23 **FINN: In the menu? I will find these answers in the Giant Menu**
24 **of dreams?**
25 **MR. LOW FAT: Look for the answers in the Menu.**
26 **FINN: Low Fat? How did you die? Was there any foul play**
27 **involved?**
28 **MR. LOW FAT: My weakness for Lola's Hunan egg rolls got the**
29 **best of me. I couldn't resist.** *(Samples some egg rolls.)* **I**
30 **should have listened to my doctor. These things will kill**
31 **you.**
32 **FINN: Do you know what the answer is to low fat dining at**
33 **Chinese restaurants? I need to know.**
34 **MR. LOW FAT: Order the Perpetual Happiness Vegetarian**
35 **Platter. You won't ever go wrong.** *(MR. LOW FAT disappears*

1 *with egg rolls. FINN reads the Giant Menu.)*
2 FINN: There's a typographical error on this menu. Your Hunan
3   egg rolls are misspelled as Human egg rolls.
4 LOLA: Good choice. They're addictive.
5 FINN: Wait a minute. Just wait one minute here. Human egg
6   rolls. Either someone can't spell or someone is playing a
7   sick practical joke on this eating establishment.
8 THE DRAGON LADY: We only cook with the finest ingredients.
9 FINN: *(Thinking.)* Mr. Low Fat's missing body. A spooky visit by
10   his ghost. A platter of Hunan egg rolls. A misspelling on
11   the Giant Menu of Dreams. *(To audience)* I have the case
12   solved!
13 LOLA: Tell us!
14 THE DRAGON LADY: Yes. Tell us! *(Musical flourish)*
15 FINN: Hunan egg rolls are made of people! They're made of
16   people!
17 LOLA: We could have told you that.
18 THE DRAGON LADY: It's right there. On the Giant Menu of
19   Dreams.
20 LOLA: Besides, a girl has to do what a girl has to do to get by
21   these days. To keep up with the competition.
22 FINN: I ate one of those Hunan egg rolls.
23 THE DRAGON LADY: And wasn't it simply delicious?
24 FINN: I'm a Private Detective. I am not a cannibal.
25 THE DRAGON LADY: But it was delicious anyway. In half an
26   hour you'll be craving another Hunan egg roll. You won't
27   be able to get enough. Mr. Low Fat knew the secret
28   ingredient to our Hunan egg rolls. He wanted to find out
29   so badly, so what better poetic justice than Mr. Low Fat
30   becoming the secret ingredient to our Hunan egg rolls?
31 LOLA: Wait a minute. You didn't tell me that you used Low Fat
32   in the egg rolls.
33 THE DRAGON LADY: His body was right there. How could I
34   resist? Come on Lola. Remember the villa in Spain.
35 LOLA: Yes. The villa. Two villas. I guess it's really no big loss.

1   THE DRAGON LADY: And now Low Fat Hunan egg rolls are
2   being delivered to apartments all across Manhattan. And
3   people will become addicted. And they will have to come
4   back for more! And then the cash will start flowing into
5   the restaurant and I can leave this stink-hole! This is only
6   the beginning. Yes! I feel so justified in my actions. As for
7   you Mr. Finn —
8   FINN: I'll just be on my way out. It was nice meeting you two.
9   LOLA: What about your take-out order?
10 FINN: I think I'll take Low Fat's advice and start ordering the
11   vegetarian platter.
12 LOLA: You'll be back.
13 THE DRAGON LADY: You've already had a taste of flesh.
14 LOLA: And you'll have to come back. For more. *(THE DRAGON*
15   *LADY and LOLA disappear in a cloud of smoke. FINN is once*
16   *again on the street.)*
17 FINN: A Chinese restaurant is always more than you think. So
18   the next time you go into a Chinese restaurant, ask them
19   how the beef is and order it without MSG. And don't order
20   the egg rolls. Unless you have a craving for something a
21   little bit different. *(Slow fade of lights on FINN, who takes a*
22   *bite out of a Hunan egg roll. A single spotlight on the plate of*
23   *Lo Mein. Hold for a few beats, then blackout.)*
24
25
26 **END OF PLAY**
27
28
29
30
31
32
33
34
35

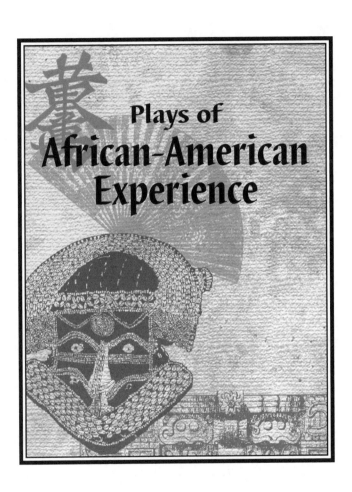

Plays of
African-American
Experience

The Basement at the Bottom at the End of the World
by Nadine Graham

This play faces the issue head-on: Black and White racial conflict, one-on-one, between two characters trapped in a room with no way out. Can they reach mutual understanding? Or will their backgrounds and experience doom them to incessant struggle, with the death of one or both of them the only resolution? Is there some common ground they can discover and share? Some peaceful form of co-existence, if nothing else? A workable compromise for each of them? Or will their cultural biases keep them forever at each other's throats, as the world they know hurtles to its destruction because of cataclysmic forces beyond the characters' control?

Perhaps the play's basic situation — the earth suddenly leaving its orbit to crash into the sun — supplies a metaphor for racial struggle today. There are many who feel that racial conflict is no longer "manageable" in our society, that it's beyond anyone's ability to prevent. Like the two characters here, feeling themselves caught in the grip of forces beyond their control, they struggle to retain whatever shreds of belief from former days might still give them meaningful choices and responses.

But perhaps that's just the playwright's point. Former values, older cultural attitudes and social relationships are no longer useful. New responses are now called for. Daneen and Paul have to first trash their racial stereotypes and then begin all over again if they're to discover some way of living together, of surviving together without killing each other. And they do: they find it in love.

What makes the play most interesting, however, is that the love each character finds for the other is not at all based on sexual attraction. The playwright instead focuses upon each character's *need* for the other in very basic ways: the need for companionship, for sympathy, for help in amusing oneself and feeding oneself and understanding oneself and dealing with one's private regrets and dreams and guilt. And of course, for easing each other's death. Very basic needs indeed. And the poignancy of the drama's final moments can resonate long after the audience leaves the theatre.

Considered in these terms, the play forces its audiences to ask: Does it take a situation this extreme to bring our culturally diverse society together? To end racial conflict and force us all to work together for the common good, the common need?

Nadine Graham wrote this play as a very young author, when she was first enrolled at Tisch School of the Arts in a playwriting class. In October of 1994, *The Basement at the Bottom At the End of the World* won the Young Playwright's Festival in New York City, and received its first production at the Public Theatre.

1 **SCENE ONE**
2
3 *A basement, once neat and orderly, that now looks like someone*
4 *picked it up, threw it on its side and then put it back. Tables and*
5 *large pieces of furniture are knocked over. In one corner some old*
6 *toys have fallen out of a toy chest. Cans of paint have fallen out of*
7 *shelves, books out of boxes, dresses out of drawers, that sort of*
8 *thing. It looks like an earthquake hit it, which it has. There are*
9 *stairs leading up to a top floor we never see and a trapdoor set into*
10 *the ceiling. DANEEN, a seventeen-ish black girl, comes down*
11 *those stairs. She is gripping a white rag doll. She looks around*
12 *warily, her eyes wide and her body tense. Her clothes are ragged*
13 *and ripped up. Her hair is in a ponytail in some effort to tame it,*
14 *but huge wisps keep on breaking free. She slowly starts down the*
15 *steps. A rustle. She stops.*
16
17 **DANEEN: Hello?** *(Silence)* **Hello? Yo, is anybody down here? If you**
18   **down there just tell me and we'll leave.** *(Silence)* **Alright,**
19   **we're coming in. You sure you not down there?** *(Beat)* **OK.**
20
21 *(She walks, a little quicker but still carefully. When she reaches*
22 *the bottom, she looks around once more to make sure no one is*
23 *there. When she is sure, she starts searching frantically. She finds*
24 *an empty can of cherries. She sticks her finger inside to see if she*
25 *can scrounge up some leftover sauce. Suddenly, the door swings*
26 *open. PAUL, a nineteen-ish white guy, comes in. He is holding a*
27 *gun in both hands and pointing it at DANEEN. His clothes are*
28 *about as ragged as hers and he looks dirty.)*
29
30 **PAUL: Freeze!** *(DANEEN instantly drops the can and puts her*
31   *hands up, holding her doll in one.)*
32 **PAUL: Who the hell are you and what are you doing in my**
33   **house? What are you, a looter?**
34 **DANEEN: I didn't know it was your house! I thought it was**
35   **empty.**

1   PAUL: So? Can't a person leave his house for a few months
2   without having to worry about looters? *(He picks up the*
3   *can.)* Look at this. You were eating my cherries. *My*
4   cherries!
5   DANEEN: I didn't eat those.
6   PAUL: I'm supposed to believe that? Look you, just get down on
7   the floor until the police get here. I called them. They're
8   on their way.
9   DANEEN: What do you mean you called them?
10   PAUL: I mean I called them! I picked up the phone and dialed
11   911.
12   DANEEN: The phones don't work.
13   PAUL: Shut up! *(He finds a chair and sits in it. The gun is trained*
14   *on DANEEN's back.)* This is my house you're trying to loot.
15   Not nobody else's. Mine. You try to take MY stuff, loot MY
16   house, this is what you get. After three months I come
17   back, after three months of trekking across this goddamn
18   country by foot, this is what I come back to find. Some
19   goddamn black bitch looting my house. Taking MY stuff.
20   Eating MY cherries! It's bad enough out there, but in MY
21   house, sanity rules. I got on the phone, called the police,
22   and they're gonna take you, and give you a trial, and find
23   you guilty, and they're gonna put you in jail. That's what
24   they do. That's what's sane. Hear that? Do you?
25   DANEEN: Yes. *(Beat. Under breath)* God damn crazy ...
26   PAUL: What did you call me?
27   DANEEN: Goddamn crazy! There are no police, there are no
28   phones, there are no cars, no planes, no nothing! It all
29   shut down months ago! In December, you asshole!
30   PAUL: What do you mean?
31   DANEEN: Haven't you noticed that it's hot? That it's hotter than
32   it usually is in April?
33   PAUL: No.
34   DANEEN: We are all gonna die. And there's nothing the police
35   can do about it.

1   PAUL: That's not the truth.
2   DANEEN: Yeah, that is. So look, you wanta let us go? I can pay. I
3   know where the bank is, we could go in and get some
4   money. Or if you want we can do it. I mean I'll do it, but my
5   sister can't see or hear anything. We were just trying to
6   find some food —
7   PAUL: Your sister?
8   DANEEN: Yea, my sister.
9   PAUL: Where is she?
10 DANEEN: Right there.
11 PAUL: Where?
12 DANEEN: Here. There. Can't you see? *(She motions to the doll.)*
13 PAUL: That's a doll.
14 DANEEN: Yea, she is, isn't she? Don't you get any ideas, she only
15   three.
16 PAUL: That's a white doll.
17 DANEEN: She's light skinned. *(She gets up.)*
18 PAUL: Hey, I didn't say you could get up.
19 DANEEN: You want to hold her? *(She offers him the doll. He*
20   *shies away from it and she takes it back. He starts pacing.)*
21 PAUL: You're crazy.
22 DANEEN: So are you! Weren't you out there? Didn't you see the
23   bodies of all those people who killed themselves? Smell
24   them? Feel the heat?
25 PAUL: It's not that hot.
26 DANEEN: Oh yeah, that's why you're sweating like that and why
27   your sleeves are ripped off.
28 PAUL: At least I don't have a doll for a sister!
29 DANEEN: Leave her out of this!
30 PAUL: I have a gun here, I could blow you into next goddamn
31   week if I wanted to, I could snuff out your life and your
32   doll's just like that! People are supposed to listen to you
33   when you have a gun. It's the rule, it's a law. What the
34   hell's the matter with you? Why aren't you scared? *(She*
35   *gets up.)*

1   DANEEN: You can't shoot me. *(She starts heading for the stairs.)*
2   PAUL: Where are you going?! Get back here!
3   DANEEN: Bye. Have a nice life, what's left of it. *(She is at the*
4   *bottom of the stairs.)*
5   PAUL: I swear to God, if you don't get back here I'm gonna
6   shoot.
7   DANEEN: God doesn't live here anymore. Didn't you hear? The
8   earth's orbit is out of whack. We're crashing into the Sun.
9   *(She is near the top.)*
10 PAUL: Get back down here Now! Or I'll shoot, I swear to God!
11
12 *(She reaches the top. She is about to open the door when*
13 *BLACKOUT. We hear: 1. The loud sound of the gun going off and*
14 *2. The room start to shake. The noise builds up from a little titter*
15 *to something like an earthquake. It is unbearably loud. Crashes*
16 *are heard. The audience should feel their seats moving with the*
17 *vibrations. It almost sounds like the rest of the house is falling on*
18 *them. Which is exactly what it is. Note: the BLACKOUT is merely*
19 *a suggestion. In the YPF production, flashes and drop boxes were*
20 *used.)*
21
22
23 **SCENE TWO**
24
25 *(Lights come up. The basement is even more of a shambles, if*
26 *that's at all possible. PAUL is lying on his back, a bookcase over his*
27 *feet. DANEEN is on the steps, on her stomach. They are both*
28 *unconscious. PAUL slowly regains consciousness.)*
29
30 PAUL: Uhh. *(He struggles with the bookcase. He gets it off and*
31   *tries to walk. He falls down.)* **Hey, Hey, where are you?** *(He*
32   *crawls forward on his arms to where DANEEN is. Tries to*
33   *shake her awake.)* **Hey, hey, get up.**
34
35 *(He turns her over. There is a bloody wound on her shoulder.*

1 *Shock. He stares at it for awhile. Then he walks over to a cabinet*
2 *on its side, finds a First Aid kit, and starts to wrap the wound. He's*
3 *almost done when DANEEN regains consciousness. He stops.)*
4
5 **DANEEN: What are you doing?**
6 **PAUL: Nothing.**
7 **DANEEN: What happened?**
8 **PAUL: I don't know.** *(DANEEN sees the blood on her shoulder.)*
9 **DANEEN: You shot me.**
10 **PAUL: There was some earthquake or volcano or something.**
11 **DANEEN: You shot me!** *(Pause)* **Are we stuck in here?!** *(PAUL*
12   *bangs door.)*
13 **PAUL: There's some...Something's collapsed...I think the**
14   **house...But I can get it —**
15 **DANEEN: Where's my daughter?**
16 **PAUL: Your daughter?**
17 **DANEEN: My daughter. Cianna.**
18 **PAUL: Do you mean the doll?**
19 **DANEEN: I mean my daughter.** *(PAUL hands her the doll and*
20   *goes to try the door again, this time with a stick.)*
21 **PAUL: Calm down!**
22 **DANEEN: If we can't get out we're gonna die in here. I've heard**
23   **stories of people getting trapped. I don't wanna die in**
24   **here! I don't wanna die in some strange white boy's**
25   **basement, I don't!**
26 **PAUL: Calm down! There must be some way of getting out of**
27   **here.**
28 **DANEEN: It's not just me who's gonna die! It's you too, and**
29   **Cianna! I wanta live! I wanna live for my daughter!**
30 **PAUL: Before she was your sister.**
31 **DANEEN: If I do have to die, I don't wanna die here, with you! I**
32   **have to die out there. I have to see the sun and I have to**
33   **yell, "you didn't get me!"** *(Dizzy)* **So far.** *(She collapses. He*
34   *sits her down.)*
35 **PAUL: I'm getting us out of here.** *(He walks away, and tries the*

1   *door again. It still won't open.)*
2   DANEEN: Someone shot someone else and the house fell down.
3   PAUL: Shut up. The house did not fall down. I'm getting us out.
4   DANEEN: *(Under breath, sing-song like)* **Someone shot someone**
5   **and the house fell down, someone shot someone and the**
6   **house fell down —**
7   PAUL: Shut up!
8   DANEEN: No. You can't do anything to me.
9   PAUL: Oh yeah? *(He takes her doll and holds it over his head.)*
10   DANEEN: Give her back!
11   PAUL: I can't do anything to you? You want your goddamn dolly
12   **back? Here take her.** *(He dangles the doll within arms reach*
13   *of her bad arm, knowing full well she can't reach it.)*
14   DANEEN: *(Getting dangerous)* **Give her back. You give her back**
15   **right now you asshole or I'll kill you, I swear to God. Give**
16   **her back!**
17
18   *(She makes a lunge for the doll. PAUL runs away with it. They run*
19   *around in a circle and come to a face off. DANEEN spots*
20   *something on the floor. During the next few lines she slowly*
21   *bends down to pick it up.)*
22
23   DANEEN: How can you be so cruel? She's only a baby!
24   PAUL: I can't do anything to you?
25   DANEEN: Fine. Fine you can. *(Points the gun.)* **Give her back to**
26   **me. Or I'll blow a hole in your chest the size of Delaware.**
27   **I swear!** *(PAUL stops.)*
28   PAUL: That gun doesn't have any more bullets left.
29   DANEEN: Uh huh. Then why'd you stop, huh? You're not sure,
30   are you? You up for a game of Russian Roulette?
31   PAUL: OK, OK. I wasn't gonna hurt her.
32   DANEEN: You lie. That's what you do, you lie. Even when you
33   tell the truth you lie. Sit down! *(PAUL sits. DANEEN gets the*
34   *doll.)* **I should shoot you right now. Get you back for**
35   **shooting me.**

1   PAUL: I didn't —

2   DANEEN: Shut up! You could've killed me. Not like I much care,

3   but still. I don't like death.

4   PAUL: I don't either.

5   DANEEN: Shut up! Did I say you could speak? Did I? *(To doll)*

6   Mommy's back now, don't worry. *(Kisses her.)* Goddamn

7   crazy white boy shooting me.

8   PAUL: I didn't mean to shoot you! The gun went off in my

9   hands.

10 DANEEN: You lie.

11 PAUL: I grazed your shoulder.

12 DANEEN: You're a lousy shot. *(DANEEN gets up and paces.)*

13 PAUL: Can I talk?

14 DANEEN: Nothing else to do.

15 PAUL: What we need to do is survive.

16 DANEEN: If you don't shut up soon you won't.

17 PAUL: You said I could talk.

18 DANEEN: I lied. *(She paces some more.)* OK, talk now. *(PAUL says*

19   *nothing.)* Talk!

20 PAUL: What do you want me to say?

21 DANEEN: I don't care.

22 PAUL: We need food and water.

23 DANEEN: OK.

24 PAUL: We need...we need...a bathroom.

25 DANEEN: Oh God.

26 PAUL: Actually, I need a bathroom. Right now.

27 DANEEN: Can't you hold it?

28 PAUL: Until when?

29 DANEEN: OK, uhh-the back. Go in the back! *(He goes to the back.*

30   *DANEEN follows, gun on him the whole time.)* What's

31   taking you so long?!

32 PAUL: I need something to hold it in!

33

34 *(DANEEN looks for a bucket, but her handicap hinders her. PAUL*

35 *sneaks up behind her and tries to take the gun from her. They*

1   *struggle. It clicks on an empty chamber. DANEEN lets go. PAUL*
2   *looks at it in amazement.)*

3

4   **PAUL: Shit.** *(Click)* **I was right.** *(Click)* **It was empty!** *(He shoots off*
5   *the gun again, only this time it goes off. The bullet ricochets*
6   *off the walls and they both take cover. A tremor shakes the*
7   *basement. When it is over, DANEEN slowly gets up from her*
8   *hiding place, her eyes livid with rage. PAUL picks up the gun*
9   *and empties it. One bullet is left.)* **Look, one bullet left.**
10 **DANEEN: Aarrgghhh!!!!** *(She stalks off, sits in a corner and plays*
11   *with her doll.)*
12 **PAUL: I thought you weren't talking to me.**
13 **DANEEN: Did I say that? No. You are the embodiment of bad**
14   **luck.**
15 **PAUL: Really?** *(He fingers the gun.)* **What if I put this bullet back**
16   **into this gun, walked over there, and shot you? Who'd**
17   **have the bad luck then, eh?**
18 **DANEEN: Go ahead.** *(Lights out.)*

19

20

21 **SCENE THREE**

22

23 *(PAUL is applying hydrogen peroxide to DANEEN's wound. Hard.*
24 *She winces.)*

25

26 **PAUL: You know I don't even know your name. When you die I**
27   **won't be able to give you a proper burial. You'll just be**
28   **"the Crazy Black Girl who looted my house, got trapped in**
29   **the basement and died." The Crazy Black Girl for short.**
30   **CBG for short. Yea, that's it, I'll put CBG on your**
31   **tombstone and bury you in that toy chest over there. You**
32   **and your doll.**
33 **DANEEN: Is that some kind of pitiful attempt to get to know my**
34   **name?**
35 **PAUL: Yeah.**

1   DANEEN: Daneen.

2   PAUL: Daneen?

3   DANEEN: What's yours?

4   PAUL: Paul.

5   DANEEN: That's a really...plain name.

6   PAUL: We all can't be Naneens or Janines or whatever you are.

7   DANEEN: It's Daneen. It happens to be a black name, OK? Have

8   respect.

9   PAUL: Oh, what? For a name?

10 DANEEN: Yes for a name. We happen to put a lot in our names.

11 PAUL: Really?

12 DANEEN: Yeah. There's a lot of black names out there. There's

13   me, Daneen, and Janine — Well, Janine's not really so

14   much black — and Keisha, and Tisha and Miaya — Tisha

15   and Miaya are twins — and Azurdee and Shanta and

16   Dahila and Sewana and, and then they're the boys,

17   Daavon and Jamal and Tupac and Mikel and Nashawn and

18   just...just...just a whole bunch of people.

19 PAUL: OK.

20 DANEEN: So my name isn't so strange.

21 PAUL: OK. *(Pause)* It just seems funny that all of them rhyme.

22 DANEEN: We're a rhyming bunch of people.

23 PAUL: Well, I know a black guy named Robert and a girl named

24   Tiffany. How do you explain them?

25 DANEEN: They're deviants. Anyway, I bet you they say their

26   names differently than white people do. We can do that.

27 PAUL: Do what?

28 DANEEN: Make things ours. Take things that used to be yours and

29   change them to be ours. We're more imaginative that way.

30 PAUL: What do you mean, more imaginative?

31 DANEEN: It takes no imagination to come up with a name like

32   Paul. Sounds like Bob, and Bob's the plainest name I

33   know. *(She pronounces "Bob" scathingly, drawing out the*

34   *"o.")* All your names sound like Bob. Billy. Bob. Paul. Bob.

35   Richard. Bob —

1 PAUL: How does Richard sound like Bob?! And what's so wrong
2   with Bob as a name? I had a friend named Bob.
3 DANEEN: It's boring. It's plain. It's that kind of whitewash
4   name, "Oh, it's Bob again." People named Bob don't get
5   noticed. And all your names sound like Bob! *(Pause)* I
6   think I'm gonna change your name.
7 PAUL: What the hell are you talking about?
8 DANEEN: I think we're gonna call you Mikel. Oh, no, wait
9   Nashawn! I knew a guy named Nashawn —
10 PAUL: No. You're gonna call me Paul. That's my name.
11 DANEEN: Might as well just call you Bob.
12 PAUL: Well there you go. Call me Bob.
13 DANEEN: I don't want to call you Bob.
14 PAUL: You want something to be boring? You want plain?! Fine!
15   I'll be that! Call me Bob.
16 DANEEN: No.
17 PAUL: *Call me Bob.*
18 DANEEN: *I don't want to.* (PAUL *walks away in anger. We hear*
19   *him rumbling around in the back.*) **What're you doing back**
20   **there?!**
21 PAUL: Nothing!
22
23 (DANEEN *sits for awhile, then picks up her doll and starts singing*
24 *"Swing Low, Sweet Chariot," quietly at first, but quickly*
25 *crescendoing to almost the top of her lungs. She's playing with*
26 *her voice, adding whoops and dips where she feels like.*
27 *Melodrama drips from every note. She's starting on a Patti*
28 *Labelle-type riff when PAUL comes out. Note: I don't want*
29 *DANEEN to have a great voice. It should be extremely mediocre,*
30 *nice enough to listen to but nothing to write home about. When*
31 *she sees her attempts are yielding less than their desired effect,*
32 *she changes to "Papa was a Rolling Stone.")*
33
34 DANEEN: "Papa was a rolling stone named Bob," "That's why
35   he named his son Paul Bob," "And his mom's name was

1   Bob," "All those white people named Bob." *(PAUL, behind*
2   *her, starts glowering as DANEEN does a little dance around*
3   *him with the doll.)* **"Papa was a rolling stone"** *(Ad-libbed on*
4   *the offbeat:)* **That's why Paul don't got one,** "Whoever
5   **spread their legs was his home,"** "And when he died, he
6   **didn't...answer the phone."**
7 PAUL: Shut up!!
8 DANEEN: Aww, did I hurt the poor little baby?
9 PAUL: Do you want me to kill you?! Don't you dare speak about
10   my father! Don't you ever open your filthy mouth and say
11   his name again! *(Silence for a beat)*
12 DANEEN: *(Quieter)* I didn't say his name.
13 PAUL: That doesn't matter! I don't want you thinking about
14   him. Your thought sullies his memory.
15 DANEEN: *(A little put off)* What was so great about your father?
16 PAUL: My father went through Korea and Vietnam, fifteen
17   years spent in the defense of this country. My father
18   carried another soldier half a mile through a steaming
19   rain forest, in the rain, lost the use of both his legs, and
20   still managed to support both me and my sister, OK? My
21   father was a wonderful, beautiful man. My father was a
22   hero. And the likes of you are not worthy to touch the
23   ground he walked on. And you are definitely not worthy to
24   slander his name like that. *(Silence for a beat)*
25 DANEEN: Was he named Bob?
26 PAUL: No, he was not named Bob! He was named Conrad.
27 DANEEN: Conrad? That's worse than your name!
28 DANEEN: Tell me more about Conrad. The brave warrior.
29 PAUL: No.
30 DANEEN: Oh, come on. With who else do you have to share the
31   tales of his wonderful exploits? *(PAUL looks at her,*
32   *considering. He seems hesitant.)* They'll die with me. *(She*
33   *crosses her heart and smiles.)* Cross my heart.
34 PAUL: What do you want to know?
35 DANEEN: I don't know. Tell me about that whole tripping

1   through the rain forest bit.
2   PAUL: You mean when he had to carry his wounded friend
3   through the steaming rain forest –
4   DANEEN: Yeah, that whole thing. *(He stops, thinking. DANEEN*
5   *looks at him.)* **Well?**
6   PAUL: I'm remembering! OK. It was the middle of the night. My
7   father's troop was lying in wait for the Viet Cong. Hear the
8   noises of the jungle, the crawling insects, the rattling
9   snakes, the laughing hyenas. Got it? *(DANEEN just gives*
10   *him a look.)* OK. Now, there's one guy, Pete. Pete was real
11   young, real green, real nervous. Dad took him under his
12   wing, kinda. That's set up. OK. So the Viet Cong comes
13   down the road and my father's troop attacks! It was hand
14   to hand, face to face mortal combat. Dad whips through
15   the enemy like a one man armor truck. *(PAUL, in his*
16   *excitement, makes motions.)* **Bang!** But in the end, even a
17   one man armor truck can't beat the odds. Dad had to
18   order a retreat. As he's retreating, he trips, and there was
19   Pete, the green one, under his feet, dying from a wound, a
20   big, huge gash on his leg. And Dad, without even thinking,
21   picks up Pete, throws him over his shoulders, and runs.
22   Fifteen miles to the base he runs, singing "My Wild Irish
23   Rose." Pete sometimes came to and sang the chorus with
24   him. OK. Finally, they can see the base. Dad's about to
25   scream with relief and joy when he hears a gunshot. The
26   Viet Cong followed them all the way! There's no time to
27   lose. He runs and runs and is almost to the base when
28   **BOOM!** He gets shot in the leg! Well, that's it, you think,
29   right, right? No. Because, as he was falling, Dad threw Pete
30   over a barricade and into a trench! Pete was saved! And
31   the other men –
32 DANEEN: The other men.
33 PAUL: The ones who were left behind, they get some grenades,
34   blow up the Viet Cong, drag Dad into the trench and radio
35   for help. And it was raining. Did I tell you it was raining?

1   *(Silence for a beat)*

2   DANEEN: You forgot the land mines. Every good war has land
3   mines.

4   PAUL: You don't believe me?

5   DANEEN: If you're gonna lie, at least make it somewhat
6   plausible!

7   PAUL: That was the truth! It's a matter of military record!

8   DANEEN: Have you ever seen this record?

9   PAUL: Are you saying my father lied to me?!

10   DANEEN: He was either lying to you, or he had a horrible
11   memory. Maybe he was going senile and substituted what
12   really happened with what he had wished happened. Maybe
13   he was a little bit crazy. Off his rocker. Bats in the belfry.

14   PAUL: You're saying he was crazy! You! I'm supposed to believe
15   you?

16   DANEEN: Believe what you want.

17   PAUL: He wasn't lying. *(The lights dim.)*

18

19

20   SCENE FOUR

21

22   *(In the dark)*

23

24   PAUL: I knew it. I knew it, I knew it, I knew it! *(Lights up. PAUL*
25   *has found a trapdoor set into the ground. DANEEN is*
26   *looking over his shoulder.)* See, I knew it. I was right. My
27   father hid all this. There's water down here, everything.
28   *(He reaches into the trapdoor and brings up cans of food.*
29   *DANEEN looks on.)*

30   DANEEN: He didn't tell you where it was?

31   PAUL: If the Russians invaded, they wouldn't be able to squeeze
32   the information out of me. *(DANEEN gives him a look.)*

33   PAUL: Let's see what we got here. *(Picks up a can.)* Beets.

34   DANEEN: Carrots.

35   PAUL: Can of corn!

1   DANEEN: Paul.

2   PAUL: Yeah.

3   DANEEN: If we don't eat any of this stuff soon I'm gonna bite
4   your arm off.

5   PAUL: OK, what we need for this is...a can opener.

6   DANEEN: Don't tell me we don't have a can opener.

7   PAUL: *(Searching frantically)* We do. Shut up, all right! We got
8   food and we're gonna have a can opener.

9   DANEEN: *(Vindictively)* Why don't you just shoot them open?

10   *(PAUL pauses in his search.)*

11   PAUL: I didn't mean to shoot you.

12   DANEEN: You coulda fooled me. *(PAUL ignores her and*
13   *continues with his search.)*

14   DANEEN: Tell me something? Why? *(Beat)* OK, OK, stupid
15   question. How? I know why.

16   PAUL: Listen you, will you shut up about it? Like I couldn't
17   shoot somebody if I needed to. I can! And I did, I did shoot
18   you, I finally started something and I finished it. So get off
19   of it, OK? Leave it alone, it's done.

20   DANEEN: It is not done! It'll be done when I bleed to death! It'll
21   be done when my life is over because you finally wanted to
22   finish something in yours! Well you have finished
23   something. You've finished me.

24   PAUL: You're not dead yet.

25   DANEEN: Oh I'm not? What do you call this? *(She points to her*
26   *shoulder.)* Or this basement? Or the Sun? We are dead, Paul.
27   No hope is left. It's not even a case of "we're dying"
28   anymore, it's a case of "Stick the dirt on them before they
29   rot." We're running around with our heads cut off, refusing
30   to realize that the knife came down. That the farmer came
31   and went for us. Now all he has to do is wait for us to stay
32   still like proper chickens so he can cook our bodies.

33   PAUL: Daneen.

34   DANEEN: Give me my doll. *(He hands it to her. She cuddles it*
35   *with her good arm.)*

1   **PAUL: I'll go look for the can opener.** *(PAUL goes back to looking*
2   *for the opener. Silence for awhile)*
3   **DANEEN:** *(Patting the doll's head)* **You know, I think Cianna needs**
4   **a new dress. She'll be going to school pretty soon and she**
5   **can't just wear the same old ratty dress every day. She also**
6   **needs some new shoes. You ever heard of a little girl going**
7   **to school without shoes? She'll get calluses and her feet will**
8   **bleed. Then she won't be able to wear shoes 'cause she'll**
9   **bleed all over them. She'll bleed in the classroom and**
10   **probably stick to the ground after awhile! And she'll have**
11   **infections. Her feet will turn into big white puss balls that**
12   **pop when you poke them.** *(Pause)* **Are you listening to me?**
13   **PAUL: No.**
14   **DANEEN: Then how did you know I asked you a question?**
15   **PAUL: Whenever something gets to you, you go to that doll.**
16   **DANEEN: So? She is not a doll, she's my niece.**
17   **PAUL: Wasn't she just your daughter?**
18   **DANEEN: Who keeps track of these things?**
19   **PAUL: I wish you would stop making up these wild**
20   **speculations about her life! She's not real!**
21   **DANEEN: What makes you so goddamn sure? You think you're**
22   **real? You and your goddamn gun and your pitiful food.**
23   **She's realer than you!**
24   **PAUL: Maybe you're right. Maybe I'm not real. Maybe I didn't**
25   **really come into this basement and really didn't shoot**
26   **you. Maybe that gunshot wound isn't real.** *(He pokes it.)* **Is**
27   **that real, huh? Is that real?**
28   **DANEEN: AHHH! You bastard!**
29   **PAUL:** *(Pokes her repeatedly.)* **Huh? Is that real? Is that real?!**
30   **DANEEN: Stop it! I'm gonna kill you! Get away from me!** *(She is*
31   *kicking and screaming. She manages to kick him in the*
32   *groin. He doubles over in pain.)*
33   **PAUL: AHHHGH!** *(They both lie in their respective positions,*
34   *panting. PAUL glances at the ground, picking it up in*
35   *wonderment.)* **A can opener.** *(BLACKOUT.)*

1 **SCENE FIVE**

2

3 *(They are sitting at a table. Empty cans are discarded all over. They*

4 *are lying back, full. They look around, then at each other. Silence)*

5

6 **DANEEN: I would have been getting ready for the prom. Me and**

7 **Kevin. I knew my dress too.** *(Pause)* **God, look at me. I don't**

8 **even know why I'm thinking about the prom. There's not**

9 **gonna be no prom for me, boy. I wanted that prom so bad.**

10 **PAUL: It's not anything.**

11 **DANEEN: Why? You went?**

12 **PAUL: Yeah, I went. We all got dressed up and spent a lot of**

13 **money for two hours and that was it. No big thing.**

14 **DANEEN: No big thing! God, you are so stupid!**

15 **PAUL: I guess Melinda had a good time.**

16 **DANEEN: Your date?**

17 **PAUL: Yeah.**

18 **DANEEN: Of course she had a good time. It was the night of her**

19 **life.**

20 **PAUL: You don't know her.**

21 **DANEEN: Who needs to know her? It would have been the night**

22 **of my life. Was there a band?**

23 **PAUL: Yeah.**

24 **DANEEN: What did they play?**

25 **PAUL: I don't know. Songs.**

26 **DANEEN: You're hopeless.** *(He shrugs.)* **You know what song I**

27 **wanted at my prom?**

28 **PAUL: I'm sure you're gonna tell me.**

29 **DANEEN: Always and Forever.**

30 **PAUL: What's that?**

31 **DANEEN: A song. You don't know "Always and Forever"?!**

32 **PAUL: Should I?**

33 **DANEEN:** *(Singing)* **Always and Forever, this moment with you,**

34 **is just like a dream to me, that somehow came true...You**

35 **don't know it?**

1 PAUL: Why should I know it?
2 DANEEN: Everyone I know grew up on that song. How could
3   you not know that song?
4 PAUL: I'm sorry, I don't know the song.
5 DANEEN: You don't know the song...Did you pick her up in a
6   limo?
7 PAUL: Yeah.
8 DANEEN: What kind?
9 PAUL: I don't know. Limos 'R Us or something.
10 DANEEN: More than likely it was a Lincoln. That's what I want,
11   a Lincoln. Did you give her a corsage?
12 PAUL: Yes.
13 DANEEN: And roses?
14 PAUL: Yes.
15 DANEEN: Did they announce your names when you came in?
16 PAUL: Yes.
17 DANEEN: Did you get your picture taken?
18 PAUL: Yes.
19 DANEEN: Did you dance a lot? To slow songs? Did you hold her
20   like the night would never end, and whisper "I love you"
21   in her ear and mean it with all your heart?
22 PAUL: Uh, yeah, I guess.
23 DANEEN: Were you King and Queen, and did you dance with a
24   spotlight on only the two of you, like you were the only
25   two people in the world, to "Always and Forever,", and did
26   you sing it to her off-key but lovingly?
27 PAUL: No, of course not!
28 DANEEN: Say yes.
29 PAUL: No.
30 DANEEN: Say yes.
31 PAUL: We were not King and Queen.
32 DANEEN: Say yes anyway.
33 PAUL: No.
34 DANEEN: Paul! Thank you so much for killing my dream.
35 PAUL: You're welcome.

1   DANEEN: Oh, come on, say it once. Just a little word, yes. What
2   harm is it gonna do? Just a little itty-bitty word —
3   PAUL: Yes.
4   DANEEN: No, it doesn't feel the same. The dream is gone.
5   Shattered. You killed it.
6   PAUL: Sorry.
7   DANEEN: One little thing you couldn't do for me. One little
8   thing.
9   PAUL: Will you stop picking on it? I was feeling good until you
10   started.
11 DANEEN: I just wanted to have a little fantasy, dream a little
12   dream, is that wrong? I just wanted to remember a time
13   everything wasn't so fucked up. But you couldn't help me
14   out. It was just a stupid little word. Y-E-S, three letters, one
15   syllable, but you couldn't do it. *(PAUL rolls his eyes and*
16   *sticks his tongue out at her. She looks at him in shock, then*
17   *sticks hers out too. She makes a face. In the course of making*
18   *a new one PAUL starts to retch. DANEEN's eyes open wide in*
19   *alarm.)* **The bucket, the bucket!** *(PAUL runs to the back*
20   *where the bucket is and gets down on his knees, his back to*
21   *the audience. We hear him vomiting. DANEEN goes to get*
22   *some water.)* I knew we shouldn't have eaten like that, I
23   knew it!
24 PAUL: Please don't give me the runs, please don't give me the
25   runs. *(DANEEN's eyes widen again.)*
26 **DANEEN:** Oh my God. *(PAUL gets up and runs behind a curtain*
27   *put up in a corner.)*
28
29 **INTERLUDE #1**
30
31 *(DANEEN walks over and sits on the steps.)*
32
33 DANEEN: I wonder what it's like out there still. *(Pause)* We are
34   gonna die in here. And we can't do anything about it.
35   We're gonna bake to death. I mean, think about it. *(PAUL*

1   *enters.)* **Think about how pale a roast is when it first goes**
2   **in the oven, and then it turns browner, and browner, and**
3   **the meat starts to cook. And it gets plumper. Are we gonna**
4   **get plumper, Paul? Are we gonna pop out of our skins —**
5   **PAUL: Daneen, stop it.**
6   **DANEEN: It has to happen.**
7   **PAUL: Stop it!** *(Pause)* **I don't feel good.**
8   **DANEEN: I'm scared.**
9   **PAUL: What am I supposed to do about that?**
10   **DANEEN: It's really gonna happen.**
11   **PAUL: But do we have to think about it? More than likely we'll**
12   **kill each other before that anyway.**
13   **DANEEN: How?! There's only one bullet left.**
14   **PAUL: I wasn't serious!**
15   **DANEEN: Well, maybe we should.**
16   **PAUL: What, kill ourselves? Commit suicide?!**
17   **DANEEN: Why not? We're gonna die anyway!**
18   **PAUL: Well, I'm not gonna die like that! What happened to you**
19   **yelling at the sun? Where did that go?**
20   **DANEEN: Do you see a sun down here, Paul? No, all you see are**
21   **these damn four walls and that door that doesn't go**
22   **anywhere! Up there, you knew where your death was,**
23   **approximately when it would get to you, and you could**
24   **face up to it. Down here we're just hiding, waiting for the**
25   **thing to sneak up to us. I don't want to wait.**
26   **PAUL: It's a mortal sin to kill yourself.**
27   **DANEEN: You don't still believe in God!** *(PAUL doesn't say*
28   *anything.)* **Where is He? If God exists, why didn't He save**
29   **us? Where was He when the riots started, when my father**
30   **got shot, huh? Where was He?**
31   **PAUL: I don't know!** *(Pause)* **I'm sorry.**
32   **DANEEN: Yeah, well —**
33   **PAUL: My father got shot too. And my sister.**
34   **DANEEN: Oh.** *(Pause)* **Sorry.** *(Pause. Neither of them know what*
35   *to say.)* **So. How'd yours happen?**

1 PAUL: (*He looks at her, deciding.*) **February 22. After Clinton**
2 **made the last announcement. After TV stopped, right**
3 **before radio did. It was still cool. We were living in this**
4 **house, even though everyone else in the neighborhood**
5 **left. A band of looters were on their way. My father ...We**
6 **weren't gonna leave because he had worked too long for**
7 **this house and he wasn't gonna let it go that easy. So they**
8 **came. They ... shot my father point blank in the face and**
9 **my sister as she was running away. And me, I...I wasn't**
10 **there. I was across the street. Under...under the**
11 **neighbor's porch.**
12 DANEEN: **You were hiding? While they shot** –
13 PAUL: **I had a plan! I was gonna shoot them when they came in,**
14 **shoot their gas tanks so that their cars would blow up.**
15 **Only they didn't come in cars, they came on bikes, and**
16 **there were so many of them...so many** –
17 DANEEN: **Did you shoot any? At all?**
18 PAUL: **I stopped them from raping my sister's body. I shot that**
19 **sick bastard's face off. I got maybe ten of them. The rest**
20 **scattered.**
21 DANEEN: **Oh God, Paul.**
22 PAUL: **I got on a bike and I rode away, I went...south. I lost the**
23 **bike, I think it was in Delaware. So I walked back.**
24 DANEEN: **You came back here to die.**
25 PAUL: **No** – **I** – **No! Yes. But not to kill myself. To be with my**
26 **family.**
27 DANEEN: **Your dead family.**
28 PAUL: **Oh God, shut up.**
29 DANEEN: **Paul.**
30 PAUL: **No! No, shut up!** (*She takes him, puts his head in her lap*
31 *and rocks him.*)
32 DANEEN: **You want to die. So do I.** (*Lights fade to black.*)
33
34
35

1 **SCENE SIX**

2

3 *(DANEEN is dealing out cards. They are sitting at a table playing*

4 *poker with cans of food as playing chips. PAUL is losing badly.)*

5

6 **DANEEN: My sister was ten years older than me. Bitch! Ten**

7 **years older than me, ten years of bitch. She had**

8 **supposedly "found God" but all she found was a**

9 **justification to be more bitchy. Really.**

10 **PAUL: You really don't believe in God, do you?**

11 **DANEEN: I used to.**

12 **PAUL: I did. Do. *(Beat)* Maybe.**

13 **DANEEN: You had better decide quickly. Judgment Day's**

14 **coming up.** *(She looks at her cards, takes a small can of food*

15 *and places it in the middle.)*

16 **PAUL: I see your one and raise you five.** *(Throws small and*

17 *medium sized cans.)*

18 **DANEEN: I see your five and raise you ten.** *(Throws medium and*

19 *large cans. They both drop cards and pick up new ones.)*

20 **PAUL: I — I fold.**

21 **DANEEN: Hah!** *(She gathers the cans in and displays her cards.)*

22 **PAUL: Two pairs!**

23 **DANEEN: You're a very bad player, Paul.**

24 **PAUL: Shut up, OK? Shut up!**

25 **DANEEN: Your food's disappearing.**

26 **PAUL: Deal!** *(She deals again.)*

27 **DANEEN: My mother died when I was four. I don't remember**

28 **that much about her. She had long hair.**

29 **PAUL: How'd she die?**

30 **DANEEN: Car crash.**

31 **PAUL: Oh. Sorry.**

32 **DANEEN: That's OK. I don't really remember much.** *(Pause)*

33 **Funny how we're always saying sorry to each other.**

34 **PAUL: Yeah, well, life sucks. What about your father?**

35 **DANEEN: Daddy? Well he...he...he was...he worked in an office.**

1   PAUL: Oh. What was he like?

2   DANEEN: Normal. Plain, normal guy.

3   PAUL: What was his last name? I mean, what's yours?

4   DANEEN: Brown.

5   PAUL: Brown? What was his first name, Bob? *(DANEEN doesn't*

6   *say anything.)*

7   PAUL: It was?! *(Still nothing.)* It was!

8   DANEEN: Yeah. But don't — *(Paul starts laughing.)*

9   PAUL: You are such a hypocrite! Bob Brown! That's like John Doe!

10 DANEEN: That's right, laugh. I don't care.

11 PAUL: You hate people named Bob because your father's name

12   was Bob? What did he ever do to you?

13 DANEEN: Nothing. That's the whole problem. He was boring.

14 PAUL: You hate white people named Bob 'cause your father was

15   boring?

16 DANEEN: No. Yes. Wait — No, I don't hate white people named

17   Bob. I hate people named Bob. And all white people's

18   names sound like Bob.

19 PAUL: What kind of twisted logic is that?!

20 DANEEN: It's not twisted. It — No one should be named Bob. It's

21   the worst possible thing you can do to your child. People

22   named Bob are like sandpaper. He was a cipher. She died

23   and he canceled himself out. Go to work, come home, go

24   to work, come home — he never even noticed I was there.

25 PAUL: Maybe he couldn't get over his grief.

26 DANEEN: What do you know about it, you and your wonderful

27   important father man saving thousands of lives —

28 PAUL: He didn't save thousands. More like a couple.

29 DANEEN: We don't know how many he saved, do we? For each

30   Viet Cong guy he killed off in those lethal hand to hand,

31   face-to-face mortal combats he had, he might have saved

32   an entire village.

33 PAUL: Don't be cute.

34 DANEEN: Oh, I wouldn't dare be cute to wonderful important

35   father man's son.

1   PAUL: Maybe he did lie a little.

2   DANEEN: A little?

3   PAUL: OK, so maybe he lied a lot.

4   DANEEN: Maybe you lied.

5   PAUL: Maybe someone did.

6   DANEEN: Why?

7   PAUL: Because you were...you were talking about him!

8   DANEEN: I can't talk about people?

9   PAUL: You were making fun of him. You shouldn't have made
10   fun of him.

11 DANEEN: Was he really in the army?

12 PAUL: Really in the army, really had medals, really lost a leg.
13   Real – asshole. But I couldn't let you make fun of him. *(He*
14   *looks at her, kind of lightly.)* You're such a bitch. *(DANEEN*
15   *blows him a kiss.)* Bob Brown. Geez. *(He smiles.)* Buster.
16   Brown. Baby. Brown. Brown Bob.

17 DANEEN: Shut up.

18 PAUL: No. You know, I'm tired of all the black people I know
19   saying snide things under their breath about white people
20   and then refusing to own up to them.

21 DANEEN: What? What snide things?

22 PAUL: We have no rhythm.

23 DANEEN: You don't.

24 PAUL: We do too.

25 DANEEN: No you don't. None of you do. Even when you do you
26   don't. The best of you look funny. Happy?

27 PAUL: No! How about when you patronize us? Pat us on the
28   head and say "Don't worry about it, you're white."

29 DANEEN: When have I ever done that to you?

30 PAUL: Don't tell me it's something you haven't done.

31 DANEEN: Of course it is, but not to you.

32 PAUL: But you've done it.

33 DANEEN: Listen, there are certain ethnic things that only black
34   people know. You can not know them now or ever. They
35   are outside your realm of experience. Inside my skin and

1   not coming out anytime soon.

2   PAUL: You're being evasive.

3   DANEEN: Ya think? Forget about it. *(Pause)*

4   PAUL: You ever wonder about us?

5   DANEEN: No.

6   PAUL: Why not?

7   DANEEN: Television.

8   PAUL: What are the Dozens?

9   DANEEN: No. No, no, no.

10 PAUL: Come on. Who else are you gonna tell?

11 DANEEN: Fine. The Dozens are jokes.

12 PAUL: And —

13 DANEEN: That's it.

14 PAUL: Tell me some.

15 DANEEN: You've never heard any?

16 PAUL: I wanna hear yours.

17 DANEEN: Fine. Your mama's so stupid instead of riding the 4

18   train she rode the 2 train twice. *(PAUL smiles.)* Your mama's

19   so poor she can't pay attention. *(He laughs. She's getting into*

20   *this.)* Your mama's so stupid she put M&Ms in alphabetical

21   order. You're so ugly, when you were born, the doctors

22   slapped your mama. *(He doesn't like this one.)* Your mama's

23   so fat if they gave her an X jacket helicopters would land on

24   her back. Your mama's like an elevator; push the right

25   buttons, she'll go down on you. *(PAUL laughs.)* Do one for me.

26 PAUL: Uh ... Your mama's so poor she can't pay attention.

27   *(DANEEN gives him a look.)*

28 DANEEN: White! White! You are so inexcusably white!

29 PAUL: What? I said the stupid joke!

30 DANEEN: You said it wrong.

31 PAUL: What do you mean I said it wrong?!

32 DANEEN: You just did! I swear, I'm never telling you anything

33   again!

34 PAUL: What did I do? *(She won't speak to him.)* Fine, keep your

35   stupid jokes.

1   DANEEN: That's right, mine. Jokes me and mine understand.
2   *(Pause)* **God, I hate you!**
3   PAUL: Yeah, well —
4   DANEEN: **All you white people!** **All you ever do is investigate**
5   **your little noses where they don't belong, invade, keep**
6   **what you like and dismantle the rest! We were over in**
7   **Africa, we had our blues music, and what did you do?**
8   **Invade, dismantle and leave. And here we are again. I give**
9   **you a taste of the dozens and what do you do? You invade**
10   **and dismantle. You can't leave or else you would.**
11   PAUL: It doesn't matter anymore, does it?
12   DANEEN: **I swear, all you white people know how to do is suck**
13   **the soul out of something till it's as bland as you. Like this**
14   **girl at school. She had dreads. Do you know what dreads**
15   **mean, Paul? Do you?**
16   PAUL: **None of this matters anymore!**
17   DANEEN: **They represent a chosen way of life. That white girl**
18   **had no idea what she had in her head. Dreads are a black**
19   **thing. Only we can do it. It only looks right on our hair.**
20   **How dare she try to be me!**
21   PAUL: **None of this shit matters anymore. The Sun, the world's**
22   **answer to racism, world peace, cancer, dreads, AIDS and**
23   **all the other great ills. Let's just get off it, OK?**
24   **DANEEN: Fine.** *(Pause. She starts, lightly, snapping her fingers.)*
25   PAUL: **Will you stop that?**
26   DANEEN: *(Doing it louder)* **No.** *(He's getting visibly annoyed.)*
27   PAUL: **Stop, that's annoying!**
28   DANEEN: *(Chanting)* **No justice, no peace! No justice, no peace!**
29   *(She gets up, still chanting. He flings her doll at her.)* **Don't**
30   **fling her like that! You might hurt her head!**
31   PAUL: **And of course we all know we can't hurt the goddamn**
32   **dolly's head!**
33   DANEEN: **Oh shut up! You don't know what you're talking**
34   **about! You never know what you're talking about!**
35   PAUL: **And of course you know everything, right?**

1   DANEEN: At least I can tell a real child when I see one and not
2   fling her around like she was a rag doll!
3   PAUL: What the hell's the matter with you?!
4   DANEEN: What the hell's the matter with you?!
5   PAUL: You!
6   **DANEEN: You!** *(DANEEN has a faint spell. Paul has his back to her,*
7   *and so doesn't see.)* **Paul...**
8   PAUL: What?! *(She faints.)*
9
10 **BLACKOUT**
11
12
13 **SCENE SEVEN**
14
15 *(DANEEN is now asleep on a table. She has pillows and blankets.*
16 *PAUL is trying to comfort her. Their lines overlap.)*
17
18 PAUL: Daneen, Daneen, stop!
19 DANEEN: No! No! I didn't want to do, I had to, I couldn't, I know,
20   it was the only way, I know, I know, I'm sorry. I'm sorry,
21   I'm sorry, I'm sorry, *I'm sorry!* *(She wakes up in shock, sees*
22   *PAUL, and clutches the sheet, wary.)*
23 PAUL: Shh. Shh. I had a dream about you. We were on the
24   ocean, me and you. We were in these little pea pod things,
25   on our backs, with our feet dangling over the sides. The
26   wind was blowing us apart. I tried to reach you, I almost
27   touched your hand once, but the stupid pods wouldn't let
28   me stand up and I kept tilting every time I tried to save
29   you. The closer we got the farther we got blown apart. *(She*
30   *is asleep.)* And then, when I couldn't see you anymore, my
31   pod turned over...and I woke up. *(Lights dim. Come back*
32   *up on PAUL watching her as she wakes up.)* **Daneen?**
33 DANEEN: Hmmmm.
34 PAUL: How do you feel?
35 DANEEN: Hot.

1   PAUL: Other than hot.

2   DANEEN: Sick. Why, what happened?

3   PAUL: You fainted.

4   DANEEN: I know that.

5   PAUL: I think your shot is infected.

6   DANEEN: Infected? You mean I'm finally gonna die?

7   PAUL: I don't know.

8   DANEEN: Isn't that nice? Silence for a while.

9   PAUL: Want to eat?

10 DANEEN: No.

11 PAUL: We have — *(DANEEN starts to chuckle to herself.)* **What?**

12 DANEEN: I can't believe I was wrong.

13 PAUL: What?

14 DANEEN: (*Amused*) You shot me. You honest to God shot me.

15 PAUL: Yeah, well, I didn't mean to —

16 DANEEN: You shot me! *(She is now laughing hard.)* I can't

17   believe — I was wrong! I'm — never wrong! But you shot

18   me! And now — I'm gonna die because of you. This is your

19   fault. *(She starts to cough. PAUL comes back over and lays*

20   *her down. She looks at him.)* How? I know people. People

21   like you don't shoot people. I had a feeling you wouldn't

22   shoot.

23 PAUL: I didn't mean —

24 DANEEN: How could you — I guess you're the first person I've

25   ever been wrong about. And now I'm gonna die. That's

26   funny. I would get stuck in a basement with someone I

27   can't read. Do you think you'll care? *(PAUL is silent.)* That

28   means you won't. That's sad. I would like to have someone

29   care when I die.

30 PAUL: (*Quickly handing it to her*) Here's your doll.

31 DANEEN: (*Pure terror*) No! No, no, that's OK, I don't need her!

32   Take her away!

33 PAUL: But it's your doll —

34 DANEEN: I don't want it anymore! Put her away, throw her out!

35 PAUL: OK, OK. What's the matter with you?

1 DANEEN: Nothing.

2 PAUL: Daneen? What do you dream about?

3 DANEEN: I'm tired. I'm going back to sleep.

4 PAUL: No, no, ummm...you need to eat. *(He gets a can of split pea*

5   *soup and shoves it in her face.)* **Come on, eat it.**

6 DANEEN: It's green.

7 PAUL: Oh come on.

8 DANEEN: It's cold and hard and green. What is it, anyway?

9 PAUL: Split pea soup.

10 DANEEN: ILLL!

11 PAUL: You weren't so picky before.

12 DANEEN: Like I knew what I was eating. Anyway, this is split

13   pea soup.

14 PAUL: You've eaten everything else!

15 DANEEN: This is cold split pea soup!

16 PAUL: Daneen, drink it. It's warm enough. The room

17   temperature warmed it. See? *(He places his hand against*

18   *the can.)* **Warm. Drink.** *(DANEEN looks at him for a long*

19   *while.)*

20 DANEEN: Paul, why don't you just kill me?

21 PAUL: Look, I'll drink some. *(Makes motions.)*

22 DANEEN: Paul, I'm serious.

23 PAUL: So am I. You need to drink some soup. Here –

24 DANEEN: I don't want to drink any damn soup! I want to talk to

25   you.

26 PAUL: Then speak sense.

27 DANEEN: I am speaking sense. This is a very sensible thing I'm

28   asking here. I'm gonna die anyway –

29 PAUL: We are not talking about this....

30 DANEEN: Listen! I'm gonna die anyway. Wouldn't it be better in

31   my own hands? You owe this to me.

32 PAUL: I owe you no such thing! How the hell are you gonna tell

33   me I owe somebody something like this!

34 DANEEN: You shot me! You caved the house in so we couldn't

35   get out! You! You, you, you, you, all you!

1   PAUL: No! You're not making me do this! There is no way for
2   you to get me to do this!
3   DANEEN: (*Trying to calm him*) Paul, Paul, Paul –
4   PAUL: (*Overlapping*) No, I won't do it, not in cold blood –
5   DANEEN: You already have! (*Beat*)
6   DANEEN: (*Quieter*) Finish what you started. (*PAUL turns to look
7   at her.*)
8   PAUL: Finish what you started? You know who you sound like?
9   You sound like my father. "Always finish what you start."
10   What – does he want me to kill you? I don't think so. I think
11   he meant for me to nurse you back to health. And now you
12   decide you want to die. Well, you're not going to. I'm gonna
13   do what he wanted. I'm gonna make you well again.
14 DANEEN: I'm not gonna live.
15 PAUL: You will live! You just want me to kill you, so I can be
16   trapped down here with your dead body. You want me to
17   go and get Dad and Cass too? You can all have a big dead
18   body fest. Play bingo. (*Pause*) You don't really want me to
19   kill you, do you Daneen?
20 DANEEN: It'd be easier.
21 PAUL: Easier. You try to shoot someone, you see how easy it is!
22   You are all so stupid. Why the hell are you so quick to die?
23   My father, he could have lived, but said he had his pride.
24   He didn't have pride, he had a death wish! It's his fault, he
25   wanted us all to die! How the hell can you call that pride?!
26 DANEEN: I don't know.
27 PAUL: That wasn't pride!
28 DANEEN: I'm sorry. (*He walks off. Silence. DANEEN studies her
29   hands. She starts speaking almost unconsciously, starting
30   quietly.*) I dream – I dream about my doll. Cianna. She's
31   real, like she always is, only, only she's – she's dripping
32   blood and she has a hanger sticking out of her eye. She
33   says "Why did you do it, mommy? Why did you do it?" She
34   hates me. Because I killed her. With a hanger. But I had to.
35   I couldn't have her here just to die, I couldn't! She hates

1   me. "Why did you do it, mommy? Why?" And I can't
2   answer her, my answers all sound like excuses, all like
3   excuses, like I could have had her if I wanted to, and I
4   couldn't, I know I couldn't. And it was nasty, and bloody,
5   and I bled for days, it was like my soul was leaking out of
6   me, but what else was I supposed to do? No one else was
7   there. It was the only way. I didn't know what else to do,
8   and I couldn't have you, I couldn't, I couldn't, I'm sorry,
9   I'm sorry, I'm sorry, I'm so sorry –! *(She starts screaming.*
10   *PAUL tries to restrain her. Lights dim.)*
11
12
13 **SCENE EIGHT**
14
15 *(Lights up. PAUL is staring at the sleeping DANEEN with gun in*
16 *hand. He takes the gun in one hand and points it at her. It starts to*
17 *shake, so he uses both of his hands. He stands there for a while.*
18 *DANEEN opens her eyes, and sees the gun. She doesn't say a word.)*
19
20 **PAUL: Daneen, I can't. I** – *(Lights dim.)*
21
22
23 **SCENE NINE**
24
25 *(DANEEN is sleeping on the table. PAUL is looking at a sign.*
26 *DANEEN wakes up.)*
27
28 **DANEEN: Paul...** *(PAUL gets up quickly and hides the sign.)*
29 **PAUL: You're awake. How do you feel?**
30 **DANEEN: Paul, you're my only friend, you know that? Only you.**
31 **PAUL: Daneen...**
32 **DANEEN: After everything fell apart, everyone went away.**
33   **You're the only person who stayed.**
34 **PAUL: Daneen** –
35 **DANEEN: I'm tired.**

1 PAUL: I made you a surprise. *(He puts up a sign with the words*
2 *"DANEEN'S PROM" written on it. He has made paper roses*
3 *and paper crowns. Everything looks pitiful: the worse, the*
4 *better.)*
5 DANEEN: It's hot.
6 PAUL: It's what you want most in the world. Look at your
7 surprise!
8 DANEEN: Surprise?
9 PAUL: Look! But you have to stay, you can't go anywhere, you
10 have to stay with me, understand?
11 DANEEN: I'm tired, Paul.
12 PAUL: No, you have to stay up.
13 DANEEN: I'm tired. *(She falls asleep.)*
14 PAUL: I made you a prom, like you wanted. I couldn't get you a
15 band or a Lincoln or a picture, but I could get you some
16 roses. Here, *(He takes them out.)* I made us crowns. We'll be
17 King and Queen, like you wanted. *(She won't respond. He*
18 *starts to shake her. She will not wake up.)* No, Daneen, No!
19 Daneen, wake up! Wake up! *(He shakes her some more, but*
20 *she does not respond. He stops shaking her, stares at her*
21 *and, slowly, kisses her eyelids. He then kisses her, lightly, on*
22 *the mouth.)* Don't go. Daneen, come on? You wouldn't
23 leave me alone, would you? *(Delirious and in a panic, he*
24 *picks up her doll and pushes it at her.)* Look, look, your doll,
25 your doll! *(He takes the doll and places it in the crook of her*
26 *arm. He looks at her pleadingly. His eyes wander to the doll.*
27 *He looks at it, then back to DANEEN.)* The doll, Daneen. The
28 doll, Daneen, the doll... *(To the doll)* Daneen? *(PAUL takes it*
29 *out from under her arm and holds it up, still staring at it, as*
30 *curtain falls.)*
31
32
33 **END OF PLAY**
34
35

The Magic Kingdom

by Louis Felder

Commentary by Louis Felder

The Magic Kingdom is a story about two young people who are about to get married and honeymoon in Disneyland, and they're waiting for the bus. They don't know much about the world outside of their small town or the challenges they will face. They have little money, their dreams are small, but they are in love. As they wait in the small shack of a bus depot, they are already in the Magic Kingdom.

The girl is about eighteen, pretty but not beautiful, white, in high school in the small country town of Elk Valley in central California. The young man is about nineteen, African-American, with the same country accent and manners as the girl; they both grew up in Elk Valley.

The Magic Kingdom is part of a collection of one-act plays called "Going Places" having to do with people moving on or moving out, after which their lives will never be the same. Each one-act features a particular mode of transportation. *The Magic Kingdom* has a bus. Others feature a limousine in *Trumps*, a train in *Jungle Express*, a cruise ship in *Lemonade on the Promenade*, a taxi in *Sparks*, and a plane in *Flight of Fancy*.

These one-acts have been performed individually and as *Going Places* in Los Angeles and in Vermont.

Other full-length plays by Louis Felder are: *Tribune, Far From the Tree, Cold Feet, Hot Set, Timber, Socially Prominent*. Screenplays include: *Rocky Libido in San Francisco, Reach for the Sun*, and *Territory*. He has written and performed comedy for television shows. He is also an actor having appeared in over a hundred television episodes, films and commercials.

1   *TIME: Present*
2   *PLACE: A bus depot in Elk Valley, California.*
3
4   *The "depot" is one room in back of a gas station, with wood walls,*
5   *furnished with only a candy machine, a soft drink machine, and*
6   *four metal folding chairs. On the wall is a hand-lettered sign:*
7   *"Walker Bus Service — Elk Valley to Visalia — 11 am M-F, Return 3*
8   *pm — No staying inside overnight! — Bud Walker, owner — USE*
9   *BATHROOM IN GAS STATION!" A GIRL, white, about eighteen,*
10   *wearing jeans, work boots and a T-shirt is sitting on a chair going*
11   *through her dusty backpack, her only luggage. In her pack, she*
12   *finds a lipstick and uses the candy machine mirror to put some*
13   *on. She can't help smiling to herself and mumbling a top ten love*
14   *song. When she puts the lipstick back in her pack, she removes a*
15   *brown paper bag. She takes out a necklace which is still packaged*
16   *in cardboard and covered with a plastic dome. She puts on a*
17   *string of large imitation pearls in front of the mirror. She hears*
18   *something, and stops singing. She turns to face the door, and*
19   *waits, giggling with anticipation.*
20
21   **THE GIRL: Hey there.** *(A young man enters, about nineteen,*
22   *African-American, with the same rural mannerisms as the*
23   *girl.)*
24   **THE YOUNG MAN: Hey.** *(He swings down his backpack. They*
25   *aren't sure what to do, so they look at each other and laugh,*
26   *and then kiss.)*
27   **THE YOUNG MAN: You all ready?**
28   **THE GIRL: All packed.** *(Laughing at her pack)* **My trousseau.**
29   **THE YOUNG MAN: Your dad give you a ride? I seen his truck.**
30   **THE GIRL: Yep.**
31   **THE YOUNG MAN: What did he say?**
32   **THE GIRL: "Good luck."**
33   **THE YOUNG MAN: Well, that's something.**
34   **THE GIRL: That's nothing. I don't think he cares one way or**
35   **'nother.**

1   THE YOUNG MAN: My dad – he surprised me. Look.

2   THE GIRL: (*Impressed*) Twenty dollars?

3   THE YOUNG MAN: And then he opened a can of Meisterbrau™

4   and we sat outside his trailer and we drank it – together.

5   THE GIRL: Aw, that's nice, honey.

6   THE YOUNG MAN: Yeah. Surprised me, you know?

7   THE GIRL: Sure. That's a nice surprise.

8   THE YOUNG MAN: Yeah. So, that means we now got twenty

9   extra dollars to spend.

10   THE GIRL: Whoo-whoo!

11   THE YOUNG MAN: You want to get something to eat? You

12   hungry?

13   THE GIRL: Are you? I got a sandwich in my pack.

14   THE YOUNG MAN: I ate a burger at the Queen. Hey, you want a

15   candy bar over here or something? Take a look.

16   THE GIRL: We got to save our money.

17   THE YOUNG MAN: Get out, this is our honeymoon. You want

18   some Milk Duds™ or a Coke™? Come on, pick something

19   out.

20   THE GIRL: Oh, my God! Look what they want for the Milk

21   Duds™! At the Sav-On, it's half of that – all your candy

22   bars are half of this here. Oh, this isn't right.

23   THE YOUNG MAN: M & Ms! Get out of here!

24   THE GIRL: What a rip-off.

25   THE YOUNG MAN: Yeah, a rip-off. Yeah – so what! Come on, I'll

26   buy you something, pick it out.

27   THE GIRL: I'm too excited. Aren't you excited?

28   THE YOUNG MAN: That's why I had to eat something.

29   THE GIRL: Well, I can't eat 'cause we're on our way. You hear

30   me, we're going, we're going, we're going!

31   THE YOUNG MAN: We're going!

32   THE GIRL: Oh, this is gonna be so fun.

33   THE YOUNG MAN: Yeah.

34   THE GIRL: What do you want to do first?

35   THE YOUNG MAN: First?

1 THE GIRL: Yeah, first.
2 THE YOUNG MAN: Well, first — we go to Visalia.
3 THE GIRL: (*Laughing, punching him*) **After that!**
4 THE YOUNG MAN: We get married.
5 THE GIRL: (*Laughing, shaking him*) **No. After that!**
6 THE YOUNG MAN: After that, well, we go to the Greyhound™
7   Bus Station —
8 THE GIRL: (*Laughing and playfully attacking him*) **No, you bozo!**
9   **When we get there? What's the very first thing you want to**
10   **do?**
11 THE YOUNG MAN: (*Thinking, then looking at her with*
12   *excitement*) **The Matterhorn Ride!**
13 THE GIRL: Yes! Oh God!
14 THE YOUNG MAN: And then — then, what's the name of that
15   space ride on the rocket ship —
16 THE GIRL: No!
17 THE YOUNG MAN: Yeah.
18 THE GIRL: No, no sir-ee.
19 THE YOUNG MAN: What?
20 THE GIRL: What! What!
21 THE YOUNG MAN: What?
22 THE GIRL: What's the most famous thing in Disneyland®? The
23   thing that's so famous — the whole best thing in the whole
24   Magic Kingdom®? (*The YOUNG MAN shakes his head.*) **We**
25   **talked about it!**
26 THE YOUNG MAN: Adventureland?
27 THE GIRL: (*Exploding with a raspberry laugh, and cracking up*)
28   **Adventureland!!**
29 THE YOUNG MAN: Yeah! I want to take that jungle boat! Deep
30   in the swamps of the jungle. Hey, ain't that a crocodile
31   down there? Watch out! Help, the boat's turning over!
32 THE GIRL: The boat can't turn over, stupid!
33 THE YOUNG MAN: How do you know? You never been there.
34 THE GIRL: You neither. How do you know they got crocodiles?
35 THE YOUNG MAN: I seen it on T.V.

1 THE GIRL: Yeah, well, what I saw on T.V. is the best thing in the
2   whole Magic Kingdom®.
3 THE YOUNG MAN: What's that?
4 THE GIRL: The Parade of Lights.
5 THE YOUNG MAN: Aw.
6 THE GIRL: It's got to be so beautiful! It's a big long parade and
7   everybody's wearing these costumes and they're all lit up
8   with lights at night, and they're like butterflies and fairies –
9 THE YOUNG MAN: (*Laughing*) Fairies. I don't want to see no
10   fairies.
11 THE GIRL: I don't mean that kind. That kind's in Hollywood.
12 THE YOUNG MAN: I don't want to see nothing around Los
13   Angeles, no way.
14 THE GIRL: I wouldn't mind seeing a movie star. Wouldn't that
15   be cool, if we're like walking down Main Street and we see
16   some movie stars maybe, like Tom Cruise, or Julia
17   Roberts, oh I'd give anything to see her.
18 THE YOUNG MAN: I thought you liked Michael J. Fox.
19 THE GIRL: No, he's a shrimpy little bug, I don't want to see him.
20   Who do you want to see?
21 THE YOUNG MAN: You know who I'd like to see in person?
22 THE GIRL: Who? Male or female?
23 THE YOUNG MAN: Female. Just be walking down Main Street
24   and turn the corner and bump right into . . .
25 THE GIRL: I know, I know – Janet Jackson.
26 THE YOUNG MAN: Yeah. You know what I'd say to her?
27 THE GIRL: What?
28 THE YOUNG MAN: (*Thinking, then laughing*) I don't know. (*They*
29   *laugh.*) No, we're staying way away from L.A., nowheres
30   near that city.
31 THE GIRL: Can't afford it anyways.
32 THE YOUNG MAN: All that gang stuff, you don't got to worry,
33   but they see me and I'm wearing the wrong color shirt or
34   hat or something, bang, they drive by and shoot me. No
35   ma'am.

1 THE GIRL: *(Teasing)* You're not afraid, are you?

2 THE YOUNG MAN: I'd be a fool if I wasn't. I couldn't even
3   understand what they're talking about, that gang rap, you
4   know. I got to worry about that.

5 THE GIRL: Not in the Magic Kingdom®. Everybody's just there
6   for a good time, and it's so clean and pretty, and
7   everybody's polite to you, 'cause they just want to be
8   happy too. And you know what? If I could, I'd like to stay
9   in there for the rest of my life.

10 THE YOUNG MAN: Well, we got twenty extra dollars – that's
11   twenty extra we didn't figure on – maybe we can stay for
12   two days maybe, maybe three.

13 THE GIRL: Where? We're not staying in a hotel.

14 THE YOUNG MAN: Unless they make us. Like if they got rules
15   and signs and stuff. *(Using an elaborate word)* Ordinances.

16 THE GIRL: *(Laughing at the word)* Ordinances?

17 THE YOUNG MAN: Yeah, some kind of law that you can't sleep
18   out.

19 THE GIRL: I don't care, we're not staying in a hotel. We got
20   sleeping bags. There's got to be a place.

21 THE YOUNG MAN: Yeah, they got to have a park around or a
22   playground – someplace.

23 THE GIRL: Sure, we'll find a place.

24 THE YOUNG MAN: I know, I can ask a friend of mine works
25   inside the Magic Kingdom®.

26 THE GIRL: Yeah? Who's that? Who do you know?

27 THE YOUNG MAN: Mickey Mouse. *(THE GIRL laughs.)* Or Goofy.
28   If I see Goofy, I'll say: "Hey Goofy, where's me and my wife
29   gonna toss a couple of bags?"

30 THE GIRL: *(imitating Goofy's voice)* Well, gee, I don't know
31   there. You got me. *(They crack up.)*

32 THE YOUNG MAN: We'll find a place.

33 THE GIRL: Yeah. It's gonna be so fun.

34 THE YOUNG MAN: You feeling OK? You OK this morning?

35 THE GIRL: I'm fine. I don't think I'm pregnant. Honest.

1   THE YOUNG MAN: Well, you tell me if you are.

2   THE GIRL: I sort of guess you'd be like the first to know. *(THE*

3   *GIRL hears something, then leaps to her feet.)*

4   THE YOUNG MAN: Hey – is that the bus? The Bus! *(They listen.)*

5   No.

6   THE GIRL: Sounded like it.

7   THE YOUNG MAN: Just a truck pulling in for gas.

8   THE GIRL: I think we got about ten minutes yet. Ten more

9   minutes! Aren't you excited?

10 THE YOUNG MAN: I been to Visalia before.

11 THE GIRL: *(Swatting him happily)* Oh you!

12 THE YOUNG MAN: You haven't.

13 THE GIRL: So? I'm going now.

14 THE YOUNG MAN: I been to Fresno. Twice. Two times.

15 THE GIRL: Can I have your autograph?

16 THE YOUNG MAN: You never been.

17 THE GIRL: So? I hear I don't miss much.

18 THE YOUNG MAN: You know what's in Fresno?

19 THE GIRL: A shopping mall. Did you see it? What was in it?

20 THE YOUNG MAN: In Fresno is the local of the Plumber's Union.

21 THE GIRL: You went there?

22 THE YOUNG MAN: No, but that's where it's at. And someday...

23   someday –

24 THE GIRL: *(Wistfully, his dream, their dream)* I know, honey, I

25   know.

26 THE YOUNG MAN: I'm not staying doing what I'm doing.

27 THE GIRL: You're working good now.

28 THE YOUNG MAN: Construction grunt? Forget that.

29 THE GIRL: You're not going to quit?

30 THE YOUNG MAN: No, I'm not, I'm thinking. If I could work

31   carpenter – on the forms – just do the rough on the

32   foundation forms –

33 THE GIRL: For the concrete.

34 THE YOUNG MAN: Yeah, for the 'crete see, and then maybe

35   work the P.V.C. on the sewer and drains, that's not hard to

1   do, I watched them. They might let me.
2   THE GIRL: Like an apprentice.
3   THE YOUNG MAN: Yeah. Just make myself handy, kinda like let
4   'em show me how, you know.
5   THE GIRL: And if they like you as much as I do —
6   THE YOUNG MAN: I talk to those guys sometimes, union
7   plumbers, some of them are OK, but most of them — real
8   stuck-up. You ought to see 'em come driving on site,
9   Toyota Four By Fours, Dodge Ram Pickups, some of 'em
10   with camper shells on 'em. I seen one of them —
11   THE GIRL: I saw.
12   THE YOUNG MAN: I saw one of them spend nine dollars at the
13   canteen truck one morning, bought himself breakfast,
14   whatever he wanted. Nine dollars!
15   THE GIRL: I'll cook breakfast for you. What do you want?
16   THE YOUNG MAN: And what they're driving maybe is only
17   their second car. They got another car for nighttime and
18   weekends. And you know where they go? On trips. They go
19   camping.
20   THE GIRL: Like us.
21   THE YOUNG MAN: And the Plumber's Union got a resort up by
22   Lake Tahoe I think, for the members.
23   THE GIRL: Just for them?
24   THE YOUNG MAN: Yeah. And they own houses. When you're a
25   plumber — when you're in the Plumbers Union — you can
26   buy a house. *(Pausing to think)* **A Residence.** *(They are quiet*
27   *for a moment, hardly letting themselves dream.)*
28   THE GIRL: It'd sure be nice.
29   THE YOUNG MAN: International Brotherhood of Plumbers.
30   THE GIRL: You got to show them a high school diploma?
31   THE YOUNG MAN: I don't know. I guess.
32   THE GIRL: Maybe you can take an exam or something instead.
33   THE YOUNG MAN: Maybe.
34   THE GIRL: We were going to get a house once, then my mom
35   split.

1   THE YOUNG MAN: My dad's always had the tin can.

2   THE GIRL: But it's all his.

3   THE YOUNG MAN: We got to look for a place, when we get back.

4   THE GIRL: Out by the quarry, there's a trailer park, and if I get

5   work after school —

6   THE YOUNG MAN: At the beauty parlor?

7   THE GIRL: Salon.

8   THE YOUNG MAN: Beauty salon.

9   THE GIRL: I don't think it'd be steady.

10   THE YOUNG MAN: No?

11   THE GIRL: They only need me after school and Saturdays.

12   THE YOUNG MAN: Who sweeps up the rest of the time?

13   THE GIRL: One of the girls; it's not that busy during the week.

14   THE YOUNG MAN: Oh.

15   THE GIRL: But after graduation — and nobody promised — it

16   isn't for sure, but after I graduate, fingers crossed, maybe

17   I can do washes.

18   THE YOUNG MAN: Yeah?

19   THE GIRL: And that means tips, I'm not kidding.

20   THE YOUNG MAN: And if you're good at that, maybe you can do

21   the fancy stuff too, permanents and like that.

22   THE GIRL: I wish. It's kind of fun to think ahead, like we're

23   planning our future.

24   THE YOUNG MAN: If we're both working, you know, two of us

25   bringing home a paycheck, maybe we could buy a car.

26   THE GIRL: Maybe.

27   THE YOUNG MAN: Or a truck.

28   THE GIRL: *(Teasing)* Like my dad's? *(They both laugh.)*

29   THE YOUNG MAN: He drives that car, sounds like he's making

30   popcorn. They're gonna arrest him for pollution.

31   THE GIRL: How they gonna see him behind all that smoke!

32   *(They both cough.)*

33   THE YOUNG MAN: *(Coughing)* Stop! You're under arrest — hey,

34   where'd you go?

35   THE GIRL: He disappeared!

1   THE YOUNG MAN: Behind a cloud of smoke!
2   THE GIRL: Like Batman.
3   THE YOUNG MAN: Batman. Hell, his truck is older than Bud
4   Walker's bus.
5   THE GIRL: Where is that darn bus at?
6   THE YOUNG MAN: Damn, Bud Walker, come on. I don't want to
7   spend my honeymoon in here.
8   THE GIRL: I don't like him, the way he looks at me sometimes
9   when he drives by — gives me this real creepy smile.
10 THE YOUNG MAN: Well, you tell him — no, I'll tell him — you're
11   a married woman now or gonna be, and he better keep his
12   eyes on the road or I'll close them up and he won't see
13   nothing for a week.
14 THE GIRL: Oooh, you big tough guy gonna protect me? Huh?
15   Huh? Tough bozo? Huh? Big tough guy? *(She playfully tries*
16   *to box with him. He fends her off, grabs her hands and spins*
17   *her around to hug her from behind, which she enjoys.)*
18 THE YOUNG MAN: Damn right I'm tough. I got to be to protect
19   my family.
20 THE GIRL: You gonna protect me in the Haunted House?
21 THE YOUNG MAN: The Haunted House, yeah. Oooo, let's go
22   through that at night.
23 THE GIRL: Yeah, after the Parade of Lights. No no, before. I
24   don't want to get scared after. I want to feel nice and warm
25   after seeing it. Oh, this is gonna be so great.
26 THE YOUNG MAN: Yeah. Everything's going to be great.
27   Everything.
28 THE GIRL: Everything.
29 THE YOUNG MAN: You know something? I never been this
30   happy in my life.
31 THE GIRL: Me neither.
32 THE YOUNG MAN: We're lucky, you know?
33 THE GIRL: I know. It scares me.
34 THE YOUNG MAN: What scares you?
35 THE GIRL: Being so happy...with you...right now...right here.

1   *(They sit together, his arm around her. They stare off, to the*
2   *future, and are quiet.)*
3   **THE YOUNG MAN: The Magic Kingdom®.** *(They look at each*
4   *other. She rests her head against his. With nothing more to*
5   *say, they sit quietly and wait for the bus to take them away.*
6   *They are already in the Magic Kingdom.)*
7
8   **END OF PLAY**
9
10
11
12
13
14
15
16
17
18
19
20
21
22
23
24
25
26
27
28
29
30
31
32
33
34
35

Ezigbo, the Spirit Child

An Igbo story as told by Adaora Nzelibe Schmiedl
Dramatized for the stage by Max Bush

Commentary by Adaora Nzelibe Schmiedl, storyteller

Igbo Storytelling

The Igbo tradition of storytelling, while seemingly informal, was very much a part of day-to-day life before the advent of the amenities of modern life and in some families remains a viable form of entertainment. Everyone is a teller and a participant, although some are better tellers than others. The process of telling stories is learned very young. It begins in the kitchen, overseen by the women of the house, as a way to energize and quicken the evening meal process.

In what used to be a primarily agriculture-based community, the evening meal was the most involved and the most substantial, providing sustenance for the daily farming of the land. The women and children of the household would gather to make soup and pound *fou-fou*: grinding and prepping ingredients for *egusi*, *ogbono* or bitter leaf soup, and engaging in the long process of boiling, pounding, re-boiling, and re-pounding the cassava root. This would ensure a meal for that evening as well as for the rest of the week. There was no refrigeration in this tropical climate, so soaking, drying and boiling foods were also a part of the evening chores. While gathered around what sometimes could be a multitude of cooking fires, depending on the size of the family, children were entertained by the mothers, aunts and "*umu-agbogho*" (young unmarried girls) with varied stories. Under the guise of keeping the young children occupied, the adults were also entertaining themselves and keeping the tasks at hand from growing monotonous.

These stories, while having the same roots and learned at similar fires in the past, differed from person to person, family to family and from audience to audience. Even the preparation of the meal could make a difference in the sounds or outcome of the story. For example, if the teller that evening were a large woman her character might seem weightier, both in its characteristic walk as the teller moved to stir the soup and in the verbal description of the character. The teller might know that one of the small children had a tendency to take food that did not belong to him, so the story would be adjusted accordingly. The animal who yesterday was celebrated for his trickery is punished and ridiculed for theft today. In the background, the wood might be wetter than usual and the crackling noise prompts the teller to change her song to include the sound of the wood in the sung response. An Igbo proverb says that a good storyteller comes from a good fire. Most individuals known for their way with words are from families that have a long-standing reputation for the telling of tales. Proper families always eat the evening meal together, so if there is a dearth of storytellers in one generation it is almost guaranteed that the next is just as bad!

In this easy atmosphere of family improvisation, young children are encouraged to tell their own stories. And often after the meal is done and washing-up over, the children sit and practice. At school, during any free time or while taking illicit time out during chores, small or large groups of children can be seen gathered around a young teller honing her/his craft. The next evening they inch closer to telling during "prime time," while the business of a meal goes on around them, knowing that they must be good tellers in order to engage young as well as old.

Most adult tellers are women. Before the young male retains the maturity of a presentable teller, he is banned from the kitchen to do "men" things with the adult men. The women folk have total control over the kitchen and do not tolerate any adult male, even if he grew to manhood in that very kitchen. Often young men find they have chores that can only be accomplished suspiciously close to the kitchen fires.

The old ways are changing. Roads, electricity and migration to the cities have done much to intrude on the evening meal ritual. While the Igbo tradition of storytelling may move outside of the family kitchen and encompass a larger and rapidly expanding community, the stories of an Igbo storyteller are part of her heritage. Their roots begin in the nuclear family tested with early scathing critiques by children from school, church or village and are enriched by life experiences, maturing as the teller matures. These stories can never be stagnant, for each story traces the life-line of the teller.

The Story of Ezigbo

In many third-world countries the infant mortality rate is very high. This was and remains true in Nigeria. For the Igbo, the most prized possession of a family is their children. If a man or a woman does not have children, they have no real stature in the community. So even though for decades many children died young, there was and is no sense of resignation; the death of every child is a tragedy.

I believe that the myth of the *ogbange* is tied to this unwillingness to accept the senseless death of the young. The *ogbange* is a spirit child, born only to die. But there is still hope that with great effort and care the *ogbange* child can sometimes find a permanent home in the human world.

As a young girl in the West African village of Ihiala, I was torn between the western anti-mythical practical realism learned in a Washington, D.C. elementary school and the generations of blind belief that my playmates in Udengwo Primary School represented. Faced by the constant deaths of schoolmates and the repeated community acknowledgment of *ogbange*, I too sought comfort. In turning away from the more rambunctious children playing clapping games in the schoolyard to listen to the more introspective enclaves of child tellers, I began to explore an unfamiliar yet inherited belief. The story of an *ogbange* girl who is born to a chief's wife with certain restrictions as to her upbringing is a common one. The songs, the dialog, the dance and the characters differ from teller to teller. I believe that my telling of this story is influenced by a cultural duality. While my elementary science reader told my classmates and me that the high rate of death for children in the rainforest region of Nigeria was caused by tapeworms, cholera and malaria, I wanted to believe that the loss of fellow pickers of udala and stealers of mango was more than disease. I wanted to believe, as all my classmates did so effortlessly, that the lost children were still playing alongside us in the spirit world. When I first told the story of the girl Ezigbo to my aunt many years ago, it varied from other versions being told because all my attention was focused on the spirit children. I could not take their existence for granted as did most Igbo children. Inside of me there was a core of disbelief that forced the story outwardly, as I told it then, to glorify and beautify the *ogbange* to emphasize my newly donned belief.

As I tell this story to American audiences I allow my confusion over these spirit children to emerge. It is a reaction I feel this audience has the background to share. To prepare them for the *ogbange* I include as much tangible detail of the daily life of the community as I can, yet even in the telling of the most mundane activity, I bring the initial responses of an American girl face-to-face with the reality of life in a small West African village.

I believe that every storyteller has a mixed reaction to forcing a story to paper. Although the adaptation of the story to the stage feels truer to the original tradition, it still remains an uneasy partnership. The teller has told the playwright who tells the actors and technical staff who then tell the audience. This process is strongly evocative of the true form of Igbo storytelling. The stage is the kitchen, and when the story is told, different every night because live theatre can never be stagnant, the listeners take home versions influenced by their own lives and backgrounds.

The uneasiness comes back when I feel a strict form is being forced on the story. A true story told in the Igbo tradition can have no one teller or author. If it remains in the version as told by one particular teller, the story dies with the teller. If it is repeated verbatim by another teller, the story has not grown, so it still dies. In contrast, I also belong to a culture that makes no bones about ownership and possession being building blocks of society. If I am true to one culture I cannot own this or any other story, but I live in the other culture that does not seem to understand the evolution of the story and demands it be owned, labeled and presented neatly with all the other African stories. The *ogbange* are not the only things that confuse me.

Characters:

MOTHER - 32

OKEKE - 11

RIVER

EZIGBO - 10

MEDICINE WOMAN - 45

NGOZI - 10

THREE OGBANJE - They are Forever-Children; child spirits. The literal meaning of *ogbanje* comes from two roots: *Ogba* means to run away from, *nje* means to run to.

TRANSLATOR(S) - Any member(s) of the cast

Casting Notes:

By doubling River and an Ogbanje, and Okeke and an Ogbanje, all roles can be played by 6 females, 1 male. If more than three Ogbanje are cast, 50% should be male.

Running Time:

Approximately one hour.

A tape of all the songs and pronunciations of the Igbo language is available from the author.

1   *TIME: A long time ago.*

2   *PLACE: In Nigeria, West Africa: within an Igbo family compound,*

3   *the bush, and at the riverside.*

4

5   *At rise we see part of the family compound surrounded by a*

6   *thatched mud wall about five feet high and encircled by the bush.*

7   *What we see of the compound is the Mother's cooking hut, the*

8   *family shrine, a tree and a stump.*

9

10 *The household shrine is off in the corner of the compound. It's a*

11 *small hut made of wood, with a thatched roof and a small altar*

12 *that sits in the shrine's opening. Bright cloth, feathers, pots,*

13 *masks, carved figurines, beads, shells, and a dried skin decorate*

14 *the shrine. The ground in front of the shrine is hard-packed mud,*

15 *decorated with geometric chalk drawings.*

16

17 *The cooking-hut is made of bamboo poles that support a square,*

18 *thatched roof. There are no walls. Within it is a stack of firewood*

19 *and three rocks that form a tripod and support an iron pot.*

20 *The DRUMMER(S) straps on a drum, stands and energetically*

21 *drums The Call to the Play.*

22

23 *DRUMMER finishes, the MOTHER enters, crosses to foot of stage*

24 *and addresses the audience directly. She is at once the storyteller*

25 *and a central character in the play. She is followed by the*

26 *TRANSLATOR(S), who will also assume a role(s) in the play. She*

27 *begins animatedly telling the story in Igbo.*

28

29 **MOTHER:** *Oge gara-aga, mgbe ndi mmo na ndi mmadu bi nso,*

30   *n'ala anyi echefugo, onwe otu nwanyi. Nnanyi a bu*

31   *nwunye eze.*

32 **TRANSLATOR:** *(Translating)* **A long time ago, when human**

33   **beings and spirits were still close, in a land we have**

34   **forgotten, there lived a woman.**

35 **MOTHER:** *Eze a nuro otutu nwunye, etu eze kwesi e nu, ma*

1   *nwunye ezizi ya, nke o huru nanya ka-cha cha ndi ozo, a*
2   *mughi nwa.*
3   **TRANS: Now this woman was the wife of a powerful chief – an**
4   ***Eze.* This Eze had many wives, as a powerful chief should**
5   **have, but his first wife, whom he loved above all others,**
6   **had no child.** *(MOTHER picks up palm broom and slowly*
7   *drags/sweeps the compound.)* **During feast days, she**
8   **always took her portion last, because she had no children**
9   **to share her food. The chores of her house that would have**
10   **been done by a child, she does alone.** *(MOTHER moves*
11   *Upstage, still sweeping.)* **This woman could have children,**
12   **yes, she had given birth, but her womb was possessed by**
13   **the spirit of an ogbanje.**
14

15 *(OGBANJE enter playing a version of hide and seek. MOTHER*
16 *doesn't see them, as they seek a place to hide. They wear half-*
17 *masks and are dressed in a form of brilliantly colorful, traditional*
18 *Igbo dance attire. The female Ogbanje wear a strip of bright fabric*
19 *around their breasts, while their skirts are flounced and full —*
20 *petticoat-like. Some wear beads on their ankles and waists. The*
21 *male Ogbanje are bare-breasted and wear shorts of the same*
22 *bright fabric. All of them have drawn geometric designs on their*
23 *bodies with a soft, dark, pencil-like marker.)*
24

25 **TRANS: An Ogbanje is an invisible spirit-child that lives among**
26   **the people. Sometimes this spirit wants to become part of**
27   **the human world, to do the things that human children**
28   **do.** *(EZIGBO, another Ogbanje, enters. She's "it" in the*
29   *game. She is similarly dressed and marked except she adorns*
30   *her ankles and wrists with cowrie shells.)* **But when this**
31   **child is born, it longs for the spirit world and the company**
32   **of its friends.** *(EZIGBO moves closer and closer to a spirit.)*
33   **And, if this longing becomes too strong, it will die, and**
34   **return to the spirit world.** *(The OGBANJE jump out, yell*
35   *and EZIGBO touches them all. DRUMS; they quickly form a*

1 *circle around EZIGBO and dance around her for a short*
2 *time, then dash off, laughing. EZIGBO starts off with them,*
3 *but stops, turns to MOTHER, who now kneels in mourning.*
4 *EZIGBO moves near her.)* **This particular Ogbanje had**
5 **visited the Eze's wife five times – five times it was born to**
6 **this woman as a child – and each time left, leaving**
7 **grieving parents to mourn.**
8
9 *(Third OGBANJE re-enters, holds out her hand to EZIGBO.*
10 *EZIGBO runs to her, takes her hand, and they run off. MOTHER*
11 *focuses on shrine. She does not approach it, however; tending the*
12 *shrine is the Father's responsibility.)*
13
14 **MOTHER:** *(Sings mournfully, without drums)* ***M NA-ACHO***
15 ***NWA M O,***
16 **TRANS: "I am looking for my child."**
17 **MOTHER:** *NWA MU-U NWERE OBIOMA EH-EH-EH,*
18 **TRANS: "My child who had a good heart."**
19 **MOTHER:** *OLEMGBE K'M GA-HU ANYA OZO,*
20 **TRANS: "When will I see my child again?"**
21 **MOTHER:** *ONWU I ME N'ARU.*
22 **TRANS: "Death, you have done me a great wrong."**
23 **MOTHER:** *MA K'O DI BA.*
24 **TRANS: "But I accept."**
25 **MOTHER:** *(Sings.)* *M NA-ACHO NWA M O,*
26 ***NWA MU-U NWERE OBIOMA EH-EH-EH,***
27 ***OLEMGBE K'M GA-HU ANYA OZO,***
28 ***ONWU I ME N'ARU.***
29 ***MA K'O DI BA.***
30 **TRANS: Time moved on. One morning, the chief's wife went to**
31 **the banks of the river to wash her clothes.** *(OKEKE, eight,*
32 *enters river area, playing enthusiastically with a carved toy*
33 *with wheels. MOTHER rises, places her clothes basket on her*
34 *head, moves to the river. OKEKE sees MOTHER coming,*
35 *moves away from her, as she begins washing her clothes on*

1   *a river rock.)* **She watched the children playing, then she**
2   **saw one of her favorite children** –
3   **MOTHER: Okeke!**
4   **TRANS: The youngest son of one of her husband's wives.** *(Exits.)*
5   **MOTHER: Okeke, come, join me here, while I wash my clothes.**
6   *(He gets a running start and crashes his toy into a rock. He*
7   *screams and falls as if he were the toy.)* **How is your mother?**
8   **And what of your sister?** *(He plays dead.)* **Come and show**
9   **me** – **if you are still living among us** – **what you are**
10   **playing with.**
11   **OKEKE:** *(Rising, moving closer, but still keeping distance)* **I need**
12   **some river-sand to make the wheels smooth. That will**
13   **make it go faster. It's going to be the fastest in the village.**
14   **MOTHER: Okeke, there's some sand over here.**
15   **OKEKE: And I found some berries over there that will make**
16   **red paint. I'm going to paint this like fire.**
17   **MOTHER: That will be good. Did you make it?**
18   **OKEKE: I made it myself.**
19   **MOTHER:** *(Stopping washing, moving a step toward him)* **May I**
20   **see it?**
21   **OKEKE:** *(Backing away a step)* **I made it myself and I'm going to**
22   **paint it like fire to make it go faster.** *(He makes it move fast.*
23   *EZIGBO dances on. She immediately sees OKEKE and his*
24   *toy, lays near him, watching closely. She's dying to touch the*
25   *toy and play with it herself.)*
26   **MOTHER: Oh, Okeke, my son, I have something for you.**
27   **OKEKE: What is it?**
28   **MOTHER: Here, come and see what I have for you.** *(From her*
29   *basket she takes out beancake wrapped in a banana leaf.)* **I've**
30   **made some** *akara* – **some beancake,** *(EZIGBO jumps up at*
31   *the sound of akara.)* **and I'd love to share it with you. Come**
32   **closer, come share the** akara **with me.** *(EZIGBO moves to*
33   *MOTHER'S out-stretched hand, almost touches the akara.)*
34   **OKEKE:** *(Moving closer to her)* **You make good akara.** *(EZIGBO*
35   *clearly agrees with this.)*

1 **MOTHER: And this is especially sweet.**

2

3 *(Frustrated, EZIGBO dances away to OKEKE, reaches to touch the*
4 *toy, then dances by. She stops and watches. Second OGBANJE*
5 *enters, moves to EZIGBO, holds her hand.)*

6

7 **OKEKE: You eat some first.**
8 **MOTHER:** *(Takes a small bite.)* **Sweet. Okeke, it is sweet. Share it**
9   **with me; here.** *(She holds it out.)* **You can have this. I have**
10   **more.** *(He hesitantly moves to her, then begins to reach out*
11   *to take it. His inner struggle intensifies.)* **You can take the**
12   **akara and then sit down. I have a story to tell you. You like**
13   **stories, I know, and I will tell you a new one about Mother**
14   **Python and her children.**
15 **OKEKE: I'm sorry, Oldest Wife. But my mother says I can't take**
16   **that from you. Because you have an ogbanje.** *(He runs off.)*
17 **MOTHER: Okeke! Ah! Okeke . . . you, too . . . don't want what I**
18   **give . . .**
19 **EZIGBO:** *(Sadly)* **No.** *(1 & 3 OGBANJE run on, join the others.)*
20 **MOTHER: My child, my ogbanje, I know you are here. But I**
21   **can't see you. I can't hold you.** *(To river)* **It would be better**
22   **to drown than go back to my empty hut.**
23 **EZIGBO: Hah?**

24

25 *(EZIGBO moves toward her, letting go of 2 OGBANJE'S hand.*
26 *Drums for RIVER. The moment the OGBANJE see her, they*
27 *withdraw out of respect for her power. The RIVER is played by an*
28 *unmasked female, with flowing hair, wearing a long skirt tightly*
29 *wrapped around her legs. A long sash is tied around her chest; the*
30 *long ends hang down her back. She dances her words, sensuously,*
31 *beautifully, moving mostly her upper body.)*

32

33 **RIVER: Woman! What can be so wrong?**
34 **MOTHER: River Spirit . . .**
35 **RIVER: Many children die. Mothers grieve. But even without**

1   children, you are a daughter of Igboland . . . Speak.

2   MOTHER: I have no one to help me wash clothes or take meals

3   to my husband's hut. I sleep alone. And in the evening,

4   when the other women gather their children around to

5   tell their stories, I tell my stories to no one.

6   RIVER: You know it is an abomination to the earth to cut any

7   human life short. There will be no place to bury you.

8   MOTHER: You will bury me in your water.

9   RIVER: I will cast you onto the bank and they will throw you in

10   the Evil Forest.

11   MOTHER: You would do that?

12   RIVER: Your life is not just your own. It belongs to your people,

13   your ancestors, to the gods, and to Chukwu, the source of

14   all life.

15   MOTHER: They have left me; my child has left me. I wish to die

16   in your water.

17   RIVER: Go, make a sacrifice to Ani, the Earth Spirit, for

18   speaking such things. Then, go to your hut and seven

19   market weeks from now you will have a child.

20   MOTHER: *Mmu?*

21   EZIGBO: (*Indicating herself*) *Mmu?*

22   1 OGBANJE: Sister?

23   MOTHER: A child . . . (*The OGBANJE are deeply saddened by*

24   *this.*)

25   2 OGBANJE: Sister . . .

26   RIVER: But you must never strike your child. Or the child will

27   remember all the friends left in the spirit world and be

28   overcome with longing for the home left behind. (*EZIGBO*

29   *looks sadly back at the OGBANJE.*) And will leave you alone

30   as you were before.

31   MOTHER: Oh! I will never strike the child! (*DRUMS change*

32   *from the sensuous beat of the river to the celebration*

33   *rhythm of the birth of a child. Sings and dances.*)

34

35

1   ***ERI-MERI-NA-ASUSO***

2   ***ERI-MERI EH-H***

3   ***ERI-MERI NA-ASUSO***

4   ***ERI-MERI EH-H***

5

6   *(While she sings, RIVER exits, the OGBANJE move slowly, sadly*

7   *off. EZIGBO moves to MOTHER, then dances off in a different*

8   *direction.)*

9

10   ***ONWU EGBURU NWANYI N'AFO IME***

11   ***KA O MUTARA YA NWA***

12   ***K'ANYI TA OGBOROKO***

13   ***NNO MANYA NGWO***

14

15   *(Drums continue quietly, MOTHER begins song again, quietly, to*

16   *allow translation to be heard.)*

17

18   **TRANS: "Feasting is sweet."**

19   *(This next is meant to be humorous.)*

20 **WOMAN:** ***ERI-MERI-NA-ASU SO***   **"Every man, even Death,**

21   **would like a wife with a**

22   **pregnant stomach**

23   ***ERI-MERI EH-H***   **To have children for him**

24   ***ERI-MERI-NA-ASUSO***   **Let us eat dried fish**

25   ***ERI-MERI EH-H***   **and drink palm wine!"**

26

27 *(Drums full force. Others enter, join in the song and "Pass the*

28 *Baby" dance. MEDICINE WOMAN dances on with baby wrapped*

29 *in cloth. She presents baby to each child that is dancing, then [if*

30 *there are no other adults] dances to MOTHER, hands her the baby.*

31 *If there are other adults, the baby is passed between them with*

32 *the MOTHER being passed the baby near the end of the song.)*

33

34

35

1   **MOTHER/OTHERS:**

2   *ONWU EGBURU NWANYI N'AFO IME*

3   *KA O MUTARA YA NWA*

4   *K'ANYI TA OGBOROKO*

5   *NNO MANYA NGWO*

6   *ERI-MERI NA-ASU SO*

7   *ERI-MERI EH-H*

8   *ERI-MERI NA-ASUSO*

9   *ERI-MERI EH-H*

10

11 *(The others dance off, leaving MOTHER and BABY, and*

12 *TRANSLATOR.)*

13

14   *ONWU EGBURU NWANYI N'AFO IME*

15   *KA O MUTARA YA NWA*

16   *K'ANYI TA OGBOROKO*

17   *NNO MANYA NGWO.*

18

19 **TRANS: And seven market weeks later, she was blessed with a**

20   **child. And she named the child ...**

21 **MOTHER:** (*Holding baby high*) **Ezigbo, the Good One.**

22 **TRANS**: (*Taking baby*) **And as she grew it became obvious to all**

23   **that her name was fitting. Time moved on. Now she has**

24   **stayed with her Mother for ten years.**

25

26 *(TRANSLATOR exits as EZIGBO, now a thin girl of ten and dressed*

27 *as a human girl [unmasked], enters, sweeping the compound.*

28 *EZIGBO'S hair is typical of ogbanje children; it has not been cut or*

29 *combed and she wears isi-dada, or what we call dreads. Her hair is*

30 *not unkempt, however; it is oiled and hand-combed. [It isn't*

31 *necessary EZIGBO wear dreads, it is preferred.] In contrast to the*

32 *MOTHER, EZIGBO drags broom energetically in large circles.)*

33

34 **EZIGBO: Mama, can you see how straight the lines are?**

35 **MOTHER: Very straight.**

1   **EZIGBO: And how perfect the circles?**

2   **MOTHER:** (*Playfully*) **Oh, Ezigbo, people will come from far**

3   **villages to see your work.**

4   **EZIGBO: But I don't know why I have to sweep every day. The**

5   **sand is so clean. And I don't see any footprints of the**

6   **spirits.**

7   **MOTHER: Don't talk like that when there may be some spirits**

8   **near – slow ones who have not yet left.**

9   **EZIGBO:** (*Stopping sweeping, shaking broom at them*) **Hurry up,**

10   **go away. I don't want to do this work over again.**

11   **MOTHER: And you shouldn't ...**

12   **MOTHER & EZIGBO: talk about things you don't understand.**

13   **EZIGBO: I'm finished. How does it look?**

14   **MOTHER: You missed this spot. The spirits walked here last**

15   **night; I see a footprint.**

16   **EZIGBO:** (*Looking at spot. Quietly, to herself*) **That is your**

17   **footprint.**

18   **MOTHER: They do what they want at night, but we must clean**

19   **them away in the morning because the day is ours. Now**

20   **you are finished.** (*Embracing EZIGBO*) **And, because you**

21   **are Ezigbo the Good One, I have a surprise for you today.**

22

23   *(EZIGBO moves to put broom down near the hut as NGOZI, a*

24   *robust girl about the same age as EZIGBO, sneaks on behind her*

25   *carrying a waterpot under her arm. She puts pot down then*

26   *moves up behind EZIGBO and pinches her sides.)*

27

28   **NGOZI: Ezigbo!** (*EZIGBO starts, NGOZI runs.*)

29   **EZIGBO: Ngozi!** (*Trying to hit her with the broom, EZIGBO*

30   *chases her around the MOTHER.)*

31   **NGOZI:** (*While running away, around MOTHER*) **I saw you first!**

32   **I came all the way up to you –**

33   **EZIGBO: I'll get you –**

34   **NGOZI: – and you did not see me! You didn't see me!**

35   **EZIGBO: I do now!**

1   **MOTHER: Ezigbo** — **Ezigbo, you know you should . . .** *(NGOZI*
2   *squeals, runs off. As EZIGBO runs after her, MOTHER takes*
3   *the broom from EZIGBO.)* **. . . not run like that.**
4
5   *(MOTHER puts broom down, moves to her cooking hut, picks up*
6   *a flat basket of black-eyed peas and chaff. She picks up another*
7   *empty basket, moves out of hut, sets down baskets. She picks up a*
8   *short stool and places it near baskets. EZIGBO runs on, into*
9   *MOTHER'S arms, followed by NGOZI.)*
10
11   **EZIGBO: Mama!** *(NGOZI runs past, slaps EZIGBO on the*
12   *bottom.)* **Ah!** *(EZIGBO now chases NGOZI, catches her, tries*
13   *to slap her bottom. They wrestle.)* **I'm going to get you — I'm**
14   **going to get you — I'm going to get you.**
15   **NGOZI: No, no, no, no! Ezigbo —**
16   **EZIGBO: Yes, Ngozi, yes, yes!**
17   **MOTHER: Eh-eh-eh-eh!** *(NGOZI sits, trying to avoid being hit.)*
18   **EZIGBO: Over! Turn over!**
19   **NGOZI: No, no!** *(EZIGBO turns her over and swats her. NGOZI*
20   *screams.)*
21   **EZIGBO: I got you. I told you I would get you.** *(EZIGBO and*
22   *NGOZI collapse into laughter.)*
23   **MOTHER: You had better not let your father see you running**
24   **and wrestling like a boy.**
25   **EZIGBO: We can run faster than boys. Isn't that true, Ngozi?**
26   *(She coughs.)*
27   **NGOZI: Yes, because we have done it.**
28   **EZIGBO: Even older boys.**
29   **MOTHER: Which of you girls is older?**
30   **NGOZI: I am older.**
31   **EZIGBO: No, I am older.**
32   **NGOZI: I am older.**
33   **MOTHER: If you are older, Ezigbo, you should have more**
34   **sense. Running is dangerous for you. And if you are**
35   **older, Ngozi, you should not help her do these things.**

1   What would your Mother do if she saw you wrestling like
2   a boy?
3   NGOZI: I would not do that near my mother.
4   MOTHER: What would she do?
5   NGOZI: She would make me sit. And then she would say "You
6   will act like a young woman," and then I would laugh and
7   then she would hit me so hard I would feel it for days.
8   MOTHER: Ah!
9   EZIGBO: Yes! Yes, that's what she would do. And so would
10   Mama Nkiru, I have seen her.
11   NGOZI: But Mama Ezigbo, you are much nicer. You never hit
12   Ezigbo and you almost never make her sit so she will
13   laugh at you.
14   MOTHER: Yes . . . yes, that is true, Ngozi, but . . . Look at what I
15   have. *(MOTHER picks up flat basket of black-eyed peas.)* I
16   bought these beans at the market yesterday, and when
17   they are cleaned, I will make akara.
18   NGOZI & EZIGBO: Akara!
19   EZIGBO: Should I go to the river to fetch water?
20   MOTHER: First we must separate the beans from the chaff.
21   Would you like to help me?
22   NGOZI: I will help you, Mama Ezigbo.
23
24   *(MOTHER picks up flat basket, tosses beans and chaff into the air*
25   *and catches them on basket. She does this again, then blows on*
26   *them, blowing the chaff away. She does this rhythmically,*
27   *gracefully, almost like a dance. The CHILDREN pick up beans in*
28   *their hands, watch MOTHER. They then throw beans up, blow, try*
29   *to catch them, and most of the handful falls to the ground.)*
30
31   MOTHER: Perhaps you should pick out the beans with your
32   fingers.
33   EZIGBO: I am sorry, Mama. *(The CHILDREN kneel and pick up*
34   *beans. The OGBANJE run on, move among the people,*
35   *curious about what they are doing. The children will put the*

1   *cleaned beans in the empty basket through the following*
2   *scene.)*
3   **MOTHER: So, it is time that you two stopped running and**
4   **pushing. You are ten years old.** *(The OGBANJE sit together*
5   *a distance from EZIGBO, watching her. During the games*
6   *they move as individuals, but otherwise, the OGBANJE*
7   *move as a single unit. When they are standing or sitting,*
8   *they're in a tight, touching, physically overlapping group.)*
9   **In a year or two you will want to bring home to your family**
10   **a good bride-price.** *(The children look at each other.)*
11   **EZIGBO: Bride-price . . .**
12   **NGOZI: Ezigbo the Bride . . .**
13   **EZIGBO: Of a man.** *(They fall down laughing.)*
14   **MOTHER: That is right. And a young man and his family do not**
15   **want a wife who can run faster than him. There is not a race**
16   **on the wedding day to see who is the fastest. There is . . .**
17   **NGOZI: There is what, Mama Ezigbo?**
18   **MOTHER: There is...***(She smiles.)***...a feast.**
19   **EZIGBO: So a young man wants a Bride who can eat.** *(They*
20   *laugh.)*
21   **NGOZI: If that is true, I will bring a big Bride-price. I can eat a**
22   **lot.** *(She eats a raw bean.)*
23   **EZIGBO: You ate that?**
24   **NGOZI: It was a bean.**
25   **EZIGBO: It was not cooked.**
26   **NGOZI: You eat mangos and they are not cooked.** *(EZIGBO puts*
27   *a bean in her mouth, chews it, finds it tastes bad, then spits*
28   *it out in her hand.)*
29   **EZIGBO: You will eat anything.**
30   **MOTHER: Do not eat those beans. Come, help me.**
31
32   *(OGBANJE singing sadly, quietly, without drums. EZIGBO*
33   *becomes dizzy, faint.)*
34
35

1 OGBANJE: *M NA-ACHO EZIGBO,*

2 *NWA MU-U NWERE* 1 OGBANJE: Here, Sister.

3 *OBIOMA EH-EH-EH*

4 *OLEMGBE K'M GA-HU* 3 OGBANJE: Come back with us.

5 *ANYA OZO, ONWU I ME*

6 *N'ARU.*

7 *MA K'O DI BA.*

8

9 *(EZIGBO rises, feeling faint, moves away from NGOZI and*

10 *MOTHER and toward the OGBANJE.)*

11

12 MOTHER: *(To EZIGBO)* What is it, *Ada? (a pet, affectionate name)*

13 OGBANJE: *(Singing)* "*M NA-ACHO EZIGBO,*

14 EZIGBO: I . . . I feel dizzy.

15 *NWA MU-U NWERE* 2 OGBANJE: Come, Sister,

16 *OBIOMA EH-EH-EH,* you've been gone so long.

17 *OLEMGBE K'M GA-HU* MOTHER: Then you should sit

18 *ANYA OZO . . .* down, not stand up. And you

19 see? You should not run like

20 that. It makes you cough and

21 dizzy.

22 EZIGBO: *(Distantly)* Yes, Mama.

23 *(Mother goes to her, takes her hand.)*

24

25 MOTHER: *(OGBANJE singing trails off.)* Ngozi, bring her the

26 other stool. *(NGOZI gets other stool. 2 OGBANJE rises,*

27 *moves to EZIGBO, stands near her. Warmly, to NGOZI)* And

28 you must help her. Ezigbo has fallen in love with her

29 human family – and you – and wishes never to go home

30 again. She has stayed with us ten years and she wants to

31 stay a long, long time. That is right, isn't it, Ezigbo?

32 EZIGBO: Yes, Mama.

33 MOTHER: So you must help her stay, Ngozi.

34 NGOZI: Yes, Mama Ezigbo.

35

1   *(MOTHER leads EZIGBO back to NGOZI. EZIGBO sits on the*
2   *stool; 2 OGBANJE follows her over and sits behind her. EZIGBO*
3   *hums the song the OGBANJE were singing.)*
4
5   **MOTHER: Why do you sing that mourning song?**
6   **EZIGBO: I don't know.**
7   **MOTHER: There is not a funeral today. There is akara!**
8   **EZIGBO: I am sorry.** *(MOTHER begins chanting an improvised*
9   *song to the rhythm of her throwing the beans into the air.)*
10 **MOTHER: I went to the market, the market, the market. I went**
11   **to the market,**
12 **CHILDREN:** *(It becomes a song and response.)* **the market, the**
13   **market.**
14 **MOTHER: Looking for some cloth.**
15 **CHILD:** *(Cloth is boring)* **some cloth, some cloth.**
16 **MOTHER: Did not find the cloth,**
17 **CHILD:** *(Very boring)* **the cloth, the cloth.**
18 **MOTHER: So I looked for some beans.**
19 **CHILD:** *(Much more interesting)* **some beans, some beans!**
20 **MOTHER: I found some good onions,**
21 **CHILD:** *(Onions make us cry.)* **good onions, good onions.**
22 **MOTHER: with a very big smell.**
23 **CHILD:** *(Smelling the big smell)* **big smell, big smell.**
24 **MOTHER: Then they gave me some pepe.**
25 **CHILD:** *(Pepper; it's hot)* **pepe, pepe.**
26 **MOTHER: Then I remembered crayfish.**
27 **CHILD:** *(I love these!)* **crayfish, crayfish!**
28 **MOTHER: I loaded my basket and carried it home.**
29 **CHILD:** *(Home is also boring.)* **home, home.**
30 **MOTHER: I began to make akara.**
31 **CHILD:** *(The Best!)* **akara, akara!**
32 **MOTHER: I pounded the pepe.**
33 **CHILD:** *(They're hot.)* **the pepe, the pepe.**
34 **MOTHER: I added crayfish.**
35 **CHILD:** *(Love them.)* **crayfish, crayfish!**

1 **MOTHER: I cut up the onion.**
2 **CHILD:** *(Smelly, tears)* **onion, onion.** *(She stops, looks at girls,*
3 *then at the basket.)* **but where are the beans?** *(They chant,*
4 *frantically picking the beans out.)* **the beans, the beans!**
5 **ALL: Where are the beans, the beans, the beans!** *(They laugh as*
6 *MEDICINE WOMAN enters carrying a pot covered with a*
7 *leaf, and a small bowl.)*
8 **MED WOMAN:** *(Saluting them as they are working)* **My**
9 **Daughters, ndeme.**
10
11 *(Means "thank-you." She is thanking them for working. Their*
12 *working is good for everybody. OGBANJE react to MEDICINE*
13 *WOMAN'S entrance, becoming more alert and curious. 2*
14 *OGBANJE rises and returns to others.)*
15
16 **MOTHER & EZIGBO & NGOZI: Oh.**
17 **MOTHER: Nno. Welcome, Mama Nkiru.** *(Mother looks at*
18 *EZIGBO, sees a smudge on her face.)*
19 **MED WOMAN: Ndugi.** *(Meaning:)* **Life to you, my Daughter. Did**
20 **you wake well from the night?**
21 **MOTHER & EZIGBO: Yes.**
22 **NGOZI: I did, too.**
23 **MOTHER:** *(She licks her thumb and wipes smudge off EZIGBO'S*
24 *face. She fixes EZIGBO'S hair)* **How are you?**
25 **MED WOMAN: Fine.**
26 **MOTHER: Have you come to my house, then?**
27 **MED WOMAN:** *(Setting down pot and bowl)* **Yes, I have come.**
28 *(EZIGBO picks up her stool to offer it to MED. WOMAN.)*
29 **MOTHER: As yourself or Ani's messenger?**
30 **MED WOMAN: As your Priestess. Are your people well? Is your**
31 **husband well?** *(MOTHER and DAUGHTER indicate yes.)*
32 **Ngozi, how is your mother?**
33 **NGOZI: Fine, Mama Nkiru.**
34 **MED WOMAN: Tell her I send my greeting.** *(EZIGBO offers the*
35 *stool to MED. WOMAN.)* **Thank you.** *(She sits.)*

1   MOTHER: Since you are here and since it is a good day, let me
2   get some kola nut.
3   EZIGBO: Should I get the kola?
4   MOTHER: I will get it. *(MOTHER exits. NGOZI works with beans.)*
5   NGOZI: Mama Ezigbo is going to make akara.
6   MED WOMAN: Akara . . .
7   NGOZI: My mother never makes it because it takes too many
8   hours and too much work. And she says "I will make it the
9   day you deserve to have it. But on that day, I will probably
10   be long dead." So will I. *(This amuses Medicine Woman.)*
11
12   *(OGBANJE begin singing quietly. Again, EZIGBO becomes dizzy,*
13   *disoriented, and drifts toward the seated OGBANJE. PRIESTESS*
14   *watches her.)*
15
16   OGBANJE: *M NA-ACHO EZIGBO,*
17   *EZIGBO MU-U NWERE* 3 OGBANJE: Here, Sister.
18   *OBIOMA EH-EH-EH,*
19   *OLEMGBE K'M GA-HU* 1 OGBANJE: Come home.
20   *ANYA OZO,*
21   *ONWU I ME N'ARU.*   2 OGBANJE: Come home to us.
22   *MA K'DI BA.*   1 OGBANJE: Home . . .
23
24   MED WOMAN: Ezigbo,
25   what do you hear?
26   EZIGBO: I don't hear anything.
27   *M NA-ACHO EZIGBO,*
28   *EZIGBO MU-U NWERE*
29   *OBIOMA EH-EH-EH,*
30   MED WOMAN: Child, Why do you
31   stand there?
32   *OLEMGBE K'M GA-HU*
33   *ANYA OZO, ONWU I ME N'ARU.*
34   EZIGBO: I feel dizzy. I want . . .
35   I want . . .

1
2   *MA K'O DI BA.*   2 OGBANJE: Sister . . .
3   EZIGBO: I want . . . *(EZIGBO*
4   *coughs.)* something.
5   NGOZI: Why aren't you
6   helping me?
7   1 OGBANJE: Come home.
8   NGOZI: Don't you want akara?
9
10   EZIGBO: Akara! *(This breaks EZIGBO'S reverie and ends the*
11   *OGBANJE'S song.)* That's what I want! It is my favorite food.
12   1 OGBANJE: Sister?
13   *(MOTHER enters with kola in a dish made from a gourd.)*
14   EZIGBO: Mama. *(She moves to her, hugs her. The OGBANJE*
15   *move slowly off.)*
16   MOTHER: What is it, Ezigbo?
17   EZIGBO: You are making akara.
18   MOTHER: Yes, but we have a guest, now. My Mother? *(Holds out*
19   *kola to MED. WOMAN.)*
20   MED WOMAN: *(Passing her horse's tail over gourd)* May the gods
21   bless this kola and bless our conversation. May your
22   husband's god and your household god live in peace. May
23   your child grow taller than all the others. And may Ngozi
24   live healthy and long.
25   EZIGBO: *(Quietly, to NGOZI, while the MED. WOMAN breaks the*
26   *kola)* I will grow taller than you because I am older than
27   you. And I always will be older than you, so I always will be
28   taller than you.
29   NGOZI: But I am older than you.
30   EZIGBO: No, I am older than you.
31   MED WOMAN: Ngozi?
32   NGOZI: But I am older than Ezigbo.
33   MED WOMAN: Ezigbo is older. Come. *(As is tradition, the*
34   *youngest, NGOZI, takes gourd, offers it to MED. WOMAN,*
35   *then MOTHER, then EZIGBO, then takes some herself. She*

1   *then returns gourd to kitchen hut. The two CHILDREN sit by*

2   *the beans and clean them by hand, while MED. WOMAN*

3   *pulls MOTHER aside.)* **Mama Ezigbo, do you watch your**

4   **child? Do you see how she hears things we cannot hear?**

5   **MOTHER: It comes when she is dizzy.**

6   **MED WOMAN: "If you see something dancing on top of the sea,**

7   **you must know there is another something underneath**

8   **the waters playing the tune." I know she is ten years old**

9   **and has stayed this long, but it came to me in the night**

10   **and again, just now − my heart came out just now as I**

11   **watched her − the Ogbanje are calling her. And she is**

12   **listening.**

13   **MOTHER: That is why I asked you to come, today.**

14   **NGOZI:** *(A whisper to EZIGBO)* **You are older than me. You must**

15   **behave as if you are older.**

16

17   *(NGOZI throws a bean at EZIGBO; EZIGBO throws a bean at*

18   *NGOZI. They do this again, then laugh quietly. EZIGBO takes a*

19   *handful of beans and places them on NGOZI'S head. NGOZI*

20   *shakes her head. They try to stifle their laughing.)*

21

22   **MED WOMAN: We are warned. "If a chicken crows at dawn, he**

23   **doesn't crow for nothing."**

24   **MOTHER: I want protection from the Ogbanje.**

25   **MED WOMAN: I will give her my blessing.**

26   **MOTHER: Thank you.**

27   **MED WOMAN: Ezigbo, come here.** *(EZIGBO rises, crosses to them.)*

28   **MOTHER: And I want something more. You understand.**

29   **MED WOMAN: Oh, yes. Ezigbo, go sit down.** *(EZIGBO, confused,*

30   *sits back where she was.)* **I have a drink. I have brought it**

31   **with me. I will give it to her, but then you must pay.** *(With*

32   *real but small enthusiasm)* **It will be strong. For this I have**

33   **to have a goat.**

34   **MOTHER: A goat? I don't have a goat to give. I have a chicken.**

35   **MED WOMAN: For a chicken I will give her my blessing. For the**

1   drink I will need a goat. I went into the bush and found
2   what was necessary; the plants and the tree-bark. This is
3   strong and if you want this you must pay.
4   MOTHER: I don't have a goat to pay you.
5   MED WOMAN: Two chickens and one bag of cowrie shells.
6   MOTHER: And cowrie shells? I can give you two chickens but
7   no cowrie shells.
8   MED WOMAN: For you, my daughter, and my friend. For my
9   blessing and the drink, two chickens.
10   MOTHER: Thank you, Mother. Ezigbo, come here. *(EZIGBO*
11   *rises, crosses to them.)*
12   MED WOMAN: Ah, yes. *(Holding up amulet; it is a small leather*
13   *envelope on a leather string.)* I was hoping to give you this
14   amulet for her to wear; it will always protect her. It is the
15   strongest medicine I have, but you have no goats and no
16   cowrie shells.
17   MOTHER: Ezigbo, go sit down. *(Confused, she sits back down.)*
18   What must you have for that necklace?
19   MED WOMAN: I treated and cured this leather myself. I
20   gathered the charms that are inside. It has the blood of
21   many sacrifices on it. For this you must pay a cow.
22   MOTHER: A cow? My husband would not agree to a cow.
23   MED WOMAN: And a goat.
24   MOTHER: And a goat!
25   MED WOMAN: And a bag of cowrie shells.
26   MOTHER: Ah, Mama Nkiru! She will never wear it! And look at
27   her, so thin. Mother, what can I do? She must have this
28   and I can't give it to her.
29   MED WOMAN: What can you do?
30   MOTHER: I will give you a female goat for that amulet.
31   MED WOMAN: A female goat, yes, and a bag of cowrie shells.
32   MOTHER: Where will I get them? I have no cowrie shells. A goat
33   and another chicken.
34   MED WOMAN: I have chickens. You should know this. You are
35   giving them to me.

1   MOTHER: A goat and a basket of corn.

2   MED WOMAN: A goat and three baskets of fresh corn.

3   MOTHER: A female goat and one basket of fresh corn.

4   MED WOMAN: Two baskets of fresh corn.

5   MOTHER: One.

6   MED WOMAN: Let us not haggle, here, like market women.

7   Look at your daughter. She walks around as if she is in a

8   dream because she is talking with spirits. Two.

9   MOTHER: Yes, two.

10 MED WOMAN: You are a good mother. Ezigbo, come here.

11   *(EZIGBO rises, walks to her, then returns, sits back down*

12   *where she was.)* Ezigbo, I told you to come here. *(EZIGBO*

13   *moves to her. PRIESTESS holds EZIGBO'S head.)* I see what

14   is happening to you, Ezigbo; the spirits follow you, they

15   talk to you; they are calling you. But you do not have to

16   listen to them. *(The PRIESTESS feels the glands in*

17   *EZIGBO'S neck; they are sore and EZIGBO pulls away*

18   *sharply.)*

19 EZIGBO: Ah! I don't listen to them because I can't hear them.

20   *(PRIESTESS again feels her neck, but carefully.)*

21 MED WOMAN: Because they want you to leave us. Open your

22   mouth. *(EZIGBO opens her mouth wide, the MED. WOMAN*

23   *tilts EZIGBO'S head and looks in her mouth.)* I am a mother

24   myself and understand what the death of a child would

25   mean. Your mother would waste away in grief over you. *E*

26   *na nukwa? (She pulls EZIGBO'S ears.)* Do you hear?

27 EZIGBO: Ah! Yes, I hear you.

28 MED WOMAN: You must keep warm, you must not stay in the

29   water too long, you must be careful what you eat and you

30   must listen to your mother. *(She pulls ears again.)*

31 EZIGBO: *(Pained)* But I need my ears if I am to listen to her.

32 MED WOMAN: Now . . . *(She takes up the small bowl, uncovers*

33   *the pot and dips bowl in. She then holds the bowl up to*

34   *EZIGBO'S lips.)* Drink.

35 EZIGBO: What is that?

1   MED WOMAN: Medicine. It will help protect you. The Earth
2   Spirit, Ani, will make your will stronger, to stay with us.
3   EZIGBO: Does it taste good?
4   MED WOMAN: Everything is not akara; it tastes strong, like
5   earth.
6   EZIGBO: I will drink it if it will help me stay with my mother.
7   And Ngozi. I will do whatever you say.
8   MED WOMAN: Drink it all, all at once. *(EZIGBO drinks, starts to*
9   *pull back as drink is bitter.)* All of it! Yes, all of it, Ezigbo.
10   *(EZIGBO tries, only it's very bitter. She shivers in disgust.)*
11 NGOZI: *(With a smile)* Does it taste good, Ezigbo? *(She makes a*
12   *face that resembles Ezigbo's.)*
13 EZIGBO: It tastes like rotten fish. *(NGOZI groans.)* I think Ngozi
14   should drink some because she is my friend.
15 NGOZI: No.
16 EZIGBO: But you will eat anything. You will like it.
17 NGOZI: Not that.
18 MED WOMAN: *(To MOTHER)* You must help her drink a bowl
19   every morning until it is gone.
20 EZIGBO: All of it?
21 NGOZI: Look how much there is!
22 EZIGBO: If I drink all of it I will die from that.
23 MED WOMAN: *(Taking out leather amulet)* And now, Ezigbo –
24 EZIGBO: Do I have to eat that?
25 MED WOMAN: No, you must wear it.
26 EZIGBO: *(Relieved)* Ah. What's in it?
27 MED WOMAN: My most powerful medicine.
28 EZIGBO: Does it smell bad?
29 MED WOMAN: It smells like earth.
30 EZIGBO: *(She smells it expecting the worst. Pleasantly surprised)*
31   No . . . Like . . . the trees after rain.
32 MED WOMAN: *(Putting amulet on EZIGBO; EZIGBO sits on her*
33   *lap.)* In it I have put symbols of our love for you. You must
34   never take this off so you know, and the Ogbanje know
35   that we want you with us. So, when you hear the Ogbanje

1   and you feel their hands on you, you can touch this and
2   remember how many people in the village want you here.
3   Touch this and you will remember how much your
4   mother loves you.
5   **EZIGBO: Thank you. Ngozi** . . . *(She holds it up to NGOZI to see;*
6   *NGOZI begins to reach to touch it.)*
7   **MED WOMAN: I have heard that one touch of that can kill**
8   **someone.** *(NGOZI snaps her hand back.)* **No one else may**
9   **touch it.** *(NGOZI sniffs it and smiles. MED. WOMAN rises,*
10   *faces the shrine, raises her hands.)* **Ogbanje.** *(Drums.)*
11   **Ogbanje!** *(The OGBANJE run on. Drums continue under*
12   *following.)* **See what we have done! Hear what the voice of**
13   **Ani says! And when Ani speaks, what Ogbanje dares not**
14   **listen?** *(To EZIGBO)* **Walk about and show these Ogbanje**
15   **how powerful you are, now. Let them know your will to**
16   **stay is strong.** *(EZIGBO walks around compound, holding*
17   *the amulet.)*
18   **EZIGBO: I am staying. With my mother and my family. And**
19   **Ngozi.** *(The OGBANJE move toward her. One reaches toward*
20   *the amulet, pulls hand back as if shocked. They back away.)* **I**
21   **am getting well. I am getting stronger. I will stay strong. I**
22   **am staying.**
23   **MOTHER: Now you are protected. Now you will stay with me.**
24   *(MOTHER and DAUGHTER embrace.)*
25   **MED WOMAN:** *(To EZIGBO)* **And now you can be first wife, like**
26   **your mother. And have many children.** *(To the OGBANJE.)*
27   **Leave this family. Go. Go!** *(A flourish of drums, as*
28   *OGBANJE exit. End drums.)* **And like this, my work is done.**
29   **EZIGBO:** *Ndeme*; **thank you, Mama Nkiru.** *(MED. WOMAN*
30   *exits.)* **Mother, the Priestess said that I would be a first**
31   **wife. Have you been thinking of someone for me?**
32   **MOTHER: Oh, yes.**
33   **EZIGBO: Who?** *(NGOZI cleans up the beans and replaces stools in*
34   *cooking hut.)*
35   **MOTHER:** *(Fixing EZIGBO'S hair)* **Whatever boy or young man**

1   we choose will be wonderful.

2   **EZIGBO: Who are you thinking of?**

3   **MOTHER: Someone who will be a good farmer, kind to the**

4   **land, and kind to you.**

5   **EZIGBO: It is not Okoli, is it?**

6   **NGOZI: Okoli!**

7   **MOTHER: You know I cannot tell you. Now, Ezigbo, I need**

8   **more water to soak the beans for akara and to cook the**

9   **meal. Take one of our pots and go to the river.**

10   **NGOZI: I have to get water for my mother, too.**

11   **MOTHER:** (*She gets a pot, gives it to EZIGBO.*) **I want you to be**

12   **sure to come back before dark. Because bad things go**

13   **walking in the bush at night.**

14   **EZIGBO: Yes, Mama.**

15   **MOTHER: Go; and do not run so much.**

16

17   (*MOTHER exits. NGOZI picks up her pot, then both girls place a*

18   *cloth on their heads and put the pots on their heads. EZIGBO and*

19   *NGOZI walk the path toward the river.*)

20

21   **NGOZI: I am glad you are staying. Even though you are older.**

22   **EZIGBO: I think I will like you more than my husband.**

23   **NGOZI: Who do you think they are thinking of for you?**

24   **EZIGBO: I hope it is not Okoli.**

25   **NGOZI:** (*The demon himself*) **Okoli!**

26   **EZIGBO: He teases me all the time. "Oh, come here," he calls,**

27   **"Come here, my little wife."**

28   **NGOZI:** (*They stop walking.*) **He says that to you?**

29   **EZIGBO: Whenever there's anyone else around, he does.**

30   **"Come here, my little wife." He smells bad.**

31   **NGOZI: Yes he does. And he spits a lot.** (*That is disgusting.*)

32   **EZIGBO: All the time.** (*She shows how he does it, pretending to spit.*)

33   **Ugh. And he laughs like a pig.** (*She laughs like a pig. NGOZI*

34   *laughs at this, then laughs like a pig as well. EZIGBO laughs for*

35   *real, then snorts again.*) **I will ask the River Spirit to not let it be**

1   **Okoli.** *(They walk. EZIGBO begins to sway her hips.)*

2   **NGOZI: How are you walking?**

3   **EZIGBO:** *(Exaggerating her swaying)* **You would not understand.**

4   **I am older. I understand.**

5   **NGOZI: You are walking like Nkiru when she walks in front of**

6   **boys.**

7   **EZIGBO: Yes! Nkiru walks like this, but only when boys are**

8   **watching!**

9   **NGOZI: That is because she is much older – two years.**

10 **EZIGBO:** *(Even more exaggeration)* **"I am Nkiru. Look at me. See**

11   **how I walk? I am beautiful."**

12 **NGOZI: I can walk like that.** *(They walk and sway together,*

13   *exaggerating their hip movements. They float down the*

14   *path.)* **Do boys like this?**

15 **EZIGBO: No, they think it is funny.**

16 **NGOZI: Why don't they laugh, then?** *(They stop.)*

17 **EZIGBO: They do laugh. After Nkiru has passed by, they look at**

18   **each other and laugh.**

19 **NGOZI: I think they like it.**

20 **EZIGBO: Why?**

21 **NGOZI: Because they like Nkiru. And I know this because when**

22   **they see her coming, they jump on each other and wrestle**

23   **so when she walks by, she will see how strong they are.**

24   *(They walk on.)* **"I am Nkiru."**

25 **EZIGBO: "Nnnkiiirruuu"**

26 **NGOZI: "I am beautiful. Oh, you are such a good wrestler. You**

27   **are so strong.** *(EZIGBO picks up on this, takes pot off her*

28   *head, and begins to walk like a man.)* **Won't you talk to my**

29   **father?"**

30 **EZIGBO:** *(As a man)* **My father and your father will talk.** *(She*

31   *pretends to spit.)*

32 **NGOZI: Ah, Okoli, it is you! I love the way you spit!** *(They gag in*

33   *disgust.)*

34 **EZIGBO: You come over here, my little wife.** *(OKOLI laughs.)*

35 **NGOZI: I love the way you laugh.** *(They laugh like him.)* **And we**

1   will have such wonderful children. *(They become the small*
2   *children, laughing like little pigs.)*
3   NGOZI: *(dropping the game)* **We should marry brothers. Then**
4   **we would be friends and sisters, too.**
5   EZIGBO: **Yes! I will tell my mother and father to look for two**
6   **brothers for us.** *(They proceed to the river. EZIGBO puts her*
7   *pot down, kneels, tests the water.)* **The water is warmer,**
8   **today. Let's bathe.**
9   NGOZI: **You know you should not bathe; you were coughing,**
10   **today.**
11   EZIGBO: **But the water is warmer. Come bathe with me.**
12   NGOZI: **But it is not warm enough. You shouldn't walk back**
13   **wet.**
14   EZIGBO: **It was the River Spirit who first told my mother I was**
15   **going to be born. When I am bathing, I think I hear the**
16   **spirit talking to me.**
17
18 *(NGOZI wipes away the top of the water, dips and fills her pot, but*
19 *EZIGBO loses momentum and sits back on her heels, staring at*
20 *the water.)*
21
22 **NGOZI: Ezigbo?**
23 **EZIGBO: I'm going to stay here a while.**
24 **NGOZI: I cannot. I have to bring my mother the water or she'll**
25   **have a *good* reason to hit me, again.**
26 **EZIGBO: You can go on.**
27 **NGOZI:** *(No one ever does this.)* **You want to stay here alone? Why?**
28 **EZIGBO: Will you tell my mother I stayed by the river and I'll**
29   **come back soon?**
30 **NGOZI: You're not going in the water, are you?**
31 **EZIGBO: I promise I won't go in the water.**
32 **NGOZI: How will you get your pot on your head?** *(She takes*
33   *NGOZI'S pot, NGOZI kneels, EZIGBO helps her place the pot*
34   *on NGOZI'S head. NGOZI rises.)*
35 **EZIGBO: I have done that before.**

1   **NGOZI: Don't stay too long. Your mother needs the water to**
2   **soak the beans for akara.** *(As she goes off)* **"I am**
3   **Nkiiirruuu. I am sooo beautiful."** *(EZIGBO turns to the*
4   *river, sighs. She sits on a rock, looks down one way, then the*
5   *other. To river)*
6   **EZIGBO: Will I have children?** *(Silence)* **Will I grow older and**
7   **have children?** *(Silence)* **Why did you talk to my mother**
8   **and not to me? You have never talked to me. Have I made**
9   **you angry?** *(Silence)* **Biko? Please? Will I marry well? Will I**
10   **have children?** *(No answer. She sings quietly to herself,*
11   *slowly and absentmindedly. She sings both the refrain and*
12   *response.)* ***ONYE GA-AGBA EGWU? E-YOW-YOW-YOW . . .***
13   *(She drifts off. Then she begins again.)* ***ONYE GA-AGBA***
14   ***EGWU. E-YOW . . .*** *(She trails off, then stands and walks to*
15   *the river's edge. She begins song again, setting a rhythmic*
16   *step.)* **Who will dance with me?** ***E-YOW-YOW-YOW. E-YOW-***
17   ***YOW. E-YOW!*** *(Drums. The OGBANJE run on, and, once*
18   *facing EZIGBO in a semi-circle, they "twirl" and become*
19   *visible. This twirl is something that reoccurs and should be*
20   *done with the same drum theme and movements throughout*
21   *play. EZIGBO does not see them as she is looking downriver.*
22   *OGBANJE drums end.)* **Will no one dance with me?**
23
24   *(Drums for song. All sing and dance. EZIGBO dances differently*
25   *to this song than the OGBANJE, who, as usual, move as a group.)*
26
27   **EZIGBO & OGBANJE: *E-YOW-YOW-YOW. E-YOW-YOW. E-YOW!***
28
29   *(EZIGBO turns and sees them. She does not recognize them or*
30   *know who they are, nor is she startled. Rather, she's somewhat*
31   *delighted. OGBANJE form a circle around EZIGBO and they all*
32   *sing and dance.)*
33
34   **EZIGBO: Will no one dance with me?**
35   **OGBANJE: *E-YOW-YOW-YOW. E-YOW-YOW. E-YOW!***

1 EZIGBO: *(Fairly seriously)* **Is there something wrong with me?**
2   **Is my hair too messy? Are my knees way too big?**
3 OGBANJE: *E-YOW-YOW-YOW. E-YOW-YOW. E-YOW!*
4 **1 OGBANJE** *(1 OGBANJE moves into middle, EZIGBO joins the*
5   *circle, and they dance the song, again.)* **Who will dance with**
6   **me?**
7 EZIGBO & OGBANJE: *E-YOW-YOW-YOW. E-YOW-YOW. E-YOW!*
8 **1 OGBANJE: Will no one dance with me?**
9 EZIGBO & OGBANJE: *E-YOW-YOW-YOW. E-YOW-YOW. E-YOW!*
10 **1 OGBANJE:** *(In contrast to EZIGBO'S seriousness during this*
11 *verse, 1 OGBANJE'S rendering is much more comical.)* **Is**
12 **there something wrong with me? Is my hair too messy?**
13 **Are my knees way too big?**
14 OGBANJE & EZIGBO: *E-YOW-YOW-YOW. E-YOW-YOW. E-YOW!*
15 *(Song ends; Drums are quiet.)*
16 EZIGBO: Who are you?
17 OGBANJE: *(Drums; singing and dancing refrain)* *E-YOW-YOW-*
18 *YOW. E-YOW-YOW. E-YOW!* *(They laugh. Drums end.)*
19 EZIGBO: I am Ezigbo, daughter of a chief. What village are you
20 from and who is your family?
21 **2 OGBANJE: A village close to here.** *(The OGBANJE find this*
22 *tricky answer amusing.)*
23 EZIGBO: You knew the song. But I haven't seen dancing like
24 that, before.
25 **1 OGBANJE: We make our own dances. And we make our own**
26 **games.** *(Reaching out, touching EZIGBO'S face)* **And we can**
27 **teach you many new songs, sister.** *(They all move to*
28 *EZIGBO, touch her. Their interest is so intense, she backs up*
29 *until she sits on a rock and they surround her. They are*
30 *especially curious about her clothes, adornments and hair,*
31 *but avoid her amulet.)* **We will play a long time.**
32 **3 OGBANJE: Tell me, Ezigbo, do you like fetching water?**
33 EZIGBO: I must do it. Do you like to fetch water?
34 **2 OGBANJE: That looks like fun, carrying the pot on your head.**
35 EZIGBO: Don't you carry your pots on your head?

1   **3 OGBANJE: We don't work. We only play.**

2   **2 OGBANJE: Do you like to sweep the compound?**

3   **3 OGBANJE: Do you like sweeping more or gathering firewood?**

4   **EZIGBO: I don't like sweeping, I would rather go to the farm**

5   **with the older girls. But I like getting firewood.**

6   **2 OGBANJE: What is it like to eat your mother's akara?**

7   **EZIGBO: Oh, she makes the best akara in the village.**

8   **2 OGBANJE: What is it like?**

9   **EZIGBO: Do you mean the taste? It tastes like . . . akara – the**

10   **best akara. She is making some today and that is why I**

11   **have to be careful with the water, so there is enough to**

12   **soak the beans.**

13   **1 OGBANJE: Who would like to do these chores, eh? We'd rather**

14   **play!** *(Pulling EZIGBO off rock)* **And so would you, sister.**

15   **We all want to play!**

16   **3 OGBANJE: What is that?**

17   **EZIGBO: My amulet.** *(3 OGBANJE reaches out, thinks better of it,*

18   *withdraws her hand.)* **Do you want to smell it? It smells**

19   **good.**

20   **3 OGBANJE***: (Holding out hand)* **May I see it?**

21   **EZIGBO: Oh, I can't take it off.**

22   **3 OGBANJE: Yes you can. It will come off over your head. May I**

23   **see it?**

24   **EZIGBO: I won't take it off. It protects me.** *(3 OGBANJE reaches*

25   *out to take it.)* **I have heard that one touch of this may kill**

26   **someone.** *(3 OGBANJE'S hand snaps back in pain.)* **No one**

27   **may touch it but me. But you can smell it.**

28

29   *(1 and 2 OGBANJE lean, smell it. Seriously repelled, they choke,*

30   *trying to vacate what they've inhaled, back away repulsed.)*

31

32   **1 & 2 OGBANJE: Ah!**

33   **EZIGBO:** *(Assuming they are playing, she laughs.)* **Oh, I see you**

34   **like it. So do I.** *(She smells it, reacts like they did, coughing*

35   *and shaking her head.)* **You said you make your own games.**

1   **Will you teach me one?**

2   **3 OGBANJE: Watch and when you understand, join us.**

3   **1 OGBANJE: Animal game!**

4   **3 OGBANJE: Animal game!**

5   **1 OGBANJE: First!**

6   **2 & 3 OGBANJE: First! First!**

7   **1 OGBANJE: I am first this time!**

8   **2 OGBANJE: Second!**

9

10   *(They form a semi-circle, facing audience. EZIGBO, intrigued,*

11   *watches them, as the Animal Game begins. DRUMS may*

12   *accompany game. [More description at end of text]. The character*

13   *on Stage Right of the semi-circle — 1 OGBANJE — moves out from*

14   *the group and becomes an animal, both physically and vocally [an*

15   *eagle]. Once he has fully assumed the animal and expressed it as*

16   *well as he can, the person who is now Stage Right in the semi-*

17   *circle moves out, becomes an animal and challenges the first*

18   *player [a tiger]. The two animals challenge each other, attempting*

19   *to be fiercer, stronger, more powerful and frightening than the*

20   *other. They do not physically engage each other; it is a show of*

21   *force. The watching players make comments on the struggle,*

22   *cheering and voicing support for excellent representations of an*

23   *animal, and of particularly dynamic moves. Soon, one or the*

24   *other of the animals backs down [the eagle]. Once he has turned*

25   *and moved away, he returns to human form, returns to the end of*

26   *the line and the winner of the face-off celebrates [in the style of*

27   *the animal she is playing, a tiger]. Then the next player comes out*

28   *of group as a monkey and challenges the winner of the first*

29   *confrontation [the tiger]. During that confrontation, the monkey*

30   *appears stronger than the tiger, the tiger turns and runs. Then the*

31   *player drops the tiger [comments on the struggle], and moves to*

32   *the end of the line, while the monkey celebrates by leaping about,*

33   *screeching like a monkey. EZIGBO joins in the game after the first*

34   *two or three players have gone. As soon as she does, the OGBANJE*

35   *move her to first in line. MOTHER, carrying wooden bowls and a*

1   *long wooden spoon, and TRANSLATOR enter. The game*
2   *continues under narration.)*
3
4   **MOTHER:** *Ezigbo we soro ndi ogbanje*
5   *gwuba-eguu, anwu we nna.*
6   **TRANSLATOR: Ezigbo followed the children and played until**
7   **the sun left the sky.**
8
9   *(TRANSLATOR exits. MOTHER moves to cooking hut and works*
10 *on preparing the evening meal. She stirs the soup with a long*
11 *wooden spoon. EZIGBO goes out as a lion and challenges. We*
12 *should see that she is adept at the game. During the challenge,*
13 *when EZIGBO isn't looking, 2 OGBANJE takes EZIGBO'S pot off.*
14 *EZIGBO wins her challenge and when she turns to celebrate, the*
15 *OGBANJE run off. Drums end. She is suddenly alone, growling*
16 *and rearing like a lion, celebrating her victory. She sees she's*
17 *alone, stops playing.)*
18
19 **EZIGBO: Where . . . where did you . . . I won! I scared you all and**
20   **you ran home! I won! Home** − *(She notices darkness*
21   *descending on her. Sounds of the night begin to be heard.)*
22   **Oh! Water** . . . *(She goes to get her pot.)* **Where** . . . ? **Where**
23   **did I. . .?** *(She searches.)* **Our pot! I put it there. I put it here**
24   **. . . Our pot . . . Where. . .?** *(EZIGBO looks up, sees how dark*
25   *it is. She looks one more time, then begins to walk the path*
26   *to the compound.)*
27 **MOTHER:** *(Moving from fire, looking out into the night)* **Ezigbo** . . .
28   *(MOTHER sets out the two low stools, a large bowl of foo-foo*
29   *and two soup bowls, one for her and one for EZIGBO.*
30   *EZIGBO emerges from the bush. Greatly relieved.)* **Ezigbo!**
31 **EZIGBO: Mama.**
32 **MOTHER: Are you hurt?**
33 **EZIGBO: No.**
34 **MOTHER: Where have you been?**
35 **EZIGBO: I was playing with some new friends by the river and**

1   we played a game and it was getting dark —

2 MOTHER: You must come home before dark, otherwise I worry

3   too much.

4 EZIGBO: Yes, Mama, I know, but —

5 MOTHER: Because you do not stay away like this. You always do

6   what I ask. How do you feel?

7 EZIGBO: Fine.

8 MOTHER: You weren't sick?

9 EZIGBO: No, I was playing.

10 MOTHER: Ah, you are here. Not hurt and not sick. You are here.

11   Ah. Where is the water?

12 EZIGBO: I lost the pot.

13 MOTHER: What?

14 EZIGBO: I looked and looked for it but I couldn't find it.

15 MOTHER: You lost it?

16 EZIGBO: Yes, Mama.

17 MOTHER: You are one of the best children, Ezigbo, but you are

18   the first child to lose a pot in any village, anywhere.

19 EZIGBO: I am?

20 MOTHER: You will find it, tomorrow. Come, I borrowed some

21   water from Mama Okeke and made the meal. *(They move*

22   *to stools.)*

23 EZIGBO: It is ready?

24 MOTHER: I set it out. Sit down.

25 EZIGBO: I have to bring food to Father.

26 MOTHER: I had to take food to your father.

27 EZIGBO: I will take it!

28 MOTHER: You were gone too long.

29 EZIGBO: No.

30 MOTHER: He asked me where you were. I had to make up a

31   story. Do not make me do this again.

32 EZIGBO: I am sorry.

33 MOTHER: Sit.

34

35 *(Both sit on short stools. There is one bowl of foo-foo and two*

1 *bowls of soup placed between them. They eat only with their right*
2 *hands. Each picks up foo-foo, delicately roll it in their fingertips.*
3 *MOTHER dips hers in the soup and eats. EZIGBO dips hers, but*
4 *stops before she eats, holds her food.)*
5
6 **EZIGBO: Will I have children?** *(The question catches MOTHER off-*
7 *guard; she hesitates.)* **Will I grow older and have children?**
8 **MOTHER: Yes.**
9 **EZIGBO: I asked the River but She wouldn't answer me. She**
10 **has never answered me. Have I made Her angry, too?**
11 **MOTHER: Maybe She does not know. But I know. You will be**
12 **first wife and have many children.**
13 **EZIGBO: Will they . . . will they be Ogbanje?**
14 **MOTHER: No one can know that.**
15 **EZIGBO:** *(After a moment)* **I hope they are like Ngozi. Not like**
16 **me.** *(EZIGBO stands, looks into the night, lost in thought.)*
17 **MOTHER: What are you thinking, Ada?**
18 **EZIGBO: About Ngozi's sister Nkechi. Why didn't you let me go**
19 **to her funeral? And Okafo's funeral and Uche's funeral**
20 **and —**
21 **MOTHER: Many children die; there are too many funerals for**
22 **children in Igboland.**
23 **EZIGBO: Ngozi was allowed to go. Nkiru went. Why couldn't I go?**
24 **MOTHER: I do not want you to think so much of death.** *(Short*
25 *silence)*
26 **EZIGBO: Do you?**
27 **MOTHER: Death is for me to think of, Ada. Not you.**
28 **EZIGBO: I do not know how to not think of it. I have always**
29 **thought of it. It is always around me. I must think of it or**
30 **it will come.**
31 **MOTHER: Think of how much there is here for you.** *(Short silence)*
32 **EZIGBO: I want to stay. I want to stay.** *(She sits, eats.)*
33 **MOTHER: Yes, you think of staying.** *(They eat in silence. They*
34 *dip the foo-foo into the soup and swallow without chewing.*
35 *They delicately lick their fingertips. EZIGBO looks at*

1   *MOTHER'S bowl.)* **You may have that.**

2   **EZIGBO: What?**

3   **MOTHER: I see you looking at that piece of meat.**

4   **EZIGBO: I wasn't looking at that piece of meat.**

5   **MOTHER: You know what happens to children who eat too**
6   **much meat? They grow up to be thieves.**

7   **EZIGBO: I know, but I wasn't looking at it. I was looking at that**
8   **big piece of okra under it.**

9   **MOTHER:** *(Picking it out, putting it in EZIGBO'S mouth)* **Eat. It**
10   **will keep you strong. But do not tell Ngozi you ate my**
11   **meat. Or her Mother will be over here again, complaining**
12   **about how I spoil you.**

13   **EZIGBO: I won't tell Ngozi, if you won't tell her I lost my pot.**
14   **Because then her mother will be over here, again,**
15   **complaining about how strange I am.**

16   **MOTHER: I won't tell her.**

17   **EZIGBO: Then, when her mother comes here to complain, she**
18   **can complain about something else, like, Ngozi eating all**
19   **the food in the hut, again.** *(She dips her foo-foo, eats. Her*
20   *MOTHER smiles at her.)*

21   **MOTHER:** *(Turns to audience. EZIGBO rises, takes food and*
22   *bowls to cooking hut.)* **Mgbe chi furo. Mama Ezigbo zi nna-**
23   **gu ozi; echu-mmir; ha ga-anu, na mmiri ha ya-esi nri.**

24   **TRANSLATOR: When morning came, Mama Ezigbo called her**
25   **daughter.**

26   **MOTHER: Ezigbo.**

27   **EZIGBO: Yes, Mama.**

28   **MOTHER: There is no drinking water in the hut. Please go to**
29   **the river and return as fast as you can, so that we may**
30   **prepare the meal.**

31   **EZIGBO: Yes, Mama.** *(NGOZI sneaks on, carrying her pot.)*

32   **MOTHER: And look for our other pot by the river.** *(She moves to*
33   *get the other pot.)*

34   **EZIGBO: I see you, Ngozi!**

35   **NGOZI: I saw you first, Ezigbo!**

1   **MOTHER:** (*Quietly, so the approaching NGOZI can't hear*) **This is**
2   **the last one we have.** (*Putting pot on Ezigbo's head*)
3   **EZIGBO:** (*Quietly*) **Nothing will happen to this pot.**
4   **NGOZI: Good morning, Mama Ezigbo. How are the beans?**
5   **MOTHER: They are soaking.**
6   **NGOZI: When will the akara be finished?**
7   **MOTHER: Tomorrow.**
8   **NGOZI: Tomorrow?** (*EZIGBO starts down path to the river.*
9   *NGOZI, pot on her head, hurries to follow her.*)
10 **MOTHER: Stay on the path – and come right back!**
11 **EZIGBO:** (*To herself, as she hurries down path*) **I will go and be**
12   **back so fast Mama will forget about last night.**
13 **NGOZI: Wait. Wait!** (*EZIGBO speeds up.*) **Oh, I see. But it isn't a**
14   **fair race because I didn't know we were racing and you did.**
15   **And you started ahead of me . . . like a boy.** (*To herself*) **I will**
16   **still be first to the river.** (*She speeds up; they race. EZIGBO*
17   *sees her getting closer, squeals and speeds up more.*)
18 **1 OGBANJE:** (*Off*) **Ezigbo . . .**
19 **2 OGBANJE:** (*Off*) **Ezigbo . . .** (*EZIGBO slows down, suddenly*
20   *dizzy and out of breath.*)
21 **3 OGBANJE:** (*Off*) **Sister . . .**
22 **2 OGBANJE:** (*Off*) **Come play with us . . .**
23 **NGOZI:** (*She moves ahead.*) **Ah!** (*They come into the river*
24   *clearing; NGOZI jumps on rock.*) **I won! Even though you**
25   **started first, I won!**
26 **EZIGBO: You won. You were faster.** (*EZIGBO quickly puts pot*
27   *down, sits on rock, pulls her knees up and puts her head*
28   *down.*)
29 **NGOZI: Even though you are older, I won.** (*Sees EZIGBO is*
30   *distressed, moves off rock.*) **But you slowed down. Why?**
31   **Were you dizzy?** (*No answer*) **You were dizzy.**
32 **EZIGBO: I am all right, now. I always feel better by the river.**
33   (*She looks around for her new friends.*)
34 **NGOZI: It was not a fair race so it was not a race. No one won.**
35   **We will walk back slowly.** (*She kneels. The OGBANJE run*

1   on, invisible to everyone. EZIGBO senses their presence.)

2 **NGOZI: Ezigbo, what do you hear?**

3 **EZIGBO: Nothing.**

4 **2 OGBANJE**: *(Whispered)* **Sister . . .** *(EZIGBO coughs.)*

5 **NGOZI: You are still dizzy.**

6 **EZIGBO: No.**

7 **NGOZI: Then fill your pot.** *(NGOZI fills her pot. The OGBANJE*

8   *wait in the background.)*

9 **EZIGBO: You can go, Ngozi, I will come soon.**

10 **NGOZI: You shouldn't be here alone when you are sick.**

11 **EZIGBO: But I feel better, now.**

12 **NGOZI: What do you do here alone?**

13 **EZIGBO: Talk to the river.**

14 **NGOZI: Yesterday you stayed here until after dark. I know this**

15   **because your mother came looking for you.**

16 **EZIGBO: Ngozi, go on.**

17 **NGOZI: There are bad things that walk about at night. They**

18   **will find you.**

19 **EZIGBO: The sun is still high in the sky.**

20 **NGOZI:** *(Standing)* **Your mother will be angry. I heard her say**

21   **come right back. She will ask where you are.**

22 **EZIGBO: Tell her where I am.**

23 **NGOZI: Then she will be angry at me. She does not hit you but**

24   **she will hit me if I leave you here alone and you come**

25   **home after dark, again.**

26 **EZIGBO:** *(Standing)* **She will not hit you. She has never hit you.**

27 **NGOZI: You know you should come with me! Fill your pot and**

28   **come back!**

29 **EZIGBO: I want to be alone!**

30 **NGOZI: Stop acting like an ogbanje!**

31 **EZIGBO: I am an ogbanje!** *(Silence, quieter)* **I am an ogbanje.**

32 **NGOZI:** *(Much softer)* **Then you should come with me so you are**

33   **all right. And not act so strange.**

34 **EZIGBO: I have an amulet to protect me. I am safe.**

35

313

1   *(She takes NGOZI'S pot, NGOZI kneels, EZIGBO helps her place*
2   *the pot on NGOZI'S head. NGOZI rises, starts off.)*
3
4   **NGOZI: Ogbanje.**
5
6   *(She exits. EZIGBO looks for her friends, doesn't see them. She*
7   *turns to the river bank. Drums. The OGBANJE "twirl" and*
8   *become visible. Drums end.)*
9
10   **EZIGBO: Our other pot . . . I put it right here, I know I did. But**
11   **. . .** *(She looks for the other pot. OGBANJE charge her.)*
12   **OGBANJE: Ezigbo, Ezigbo, play with us! Play with us!**
13   **EZIGBO: No —**
14   **OGBANJE: The animal game! Play the animal game!**
15   **EZIGBO: Not the animal game, again, I won that game**
16   **yesterday. You ran away.**
17   *(Simultaneously)*
18   **3 OGBANJE: Dance with us!**
19   **1 OGBANJE: Oh, yes, dance, dance.**
20   **2 OGBANJE: Dance. You haven't danced with us.**
21   **EZIGBO: No — No. I must go back and give my mother her**
22   **water. My mother was angry at me because I played too**
23   **long yesterday.**
24   **1 OGBANJE: Angry?**
25   **EZIGBO: Yes.**
26   **1 OGBANJE: What did she say?**
27   **3 OGBANJE: What did she do?**
28   **EZIGBO: She said I was the only child in any village anywhere to**
29   **lose a pot. And she had to take my father his food. After I**
30   **have given her the water, I will come back and play with you.**
31   **2 OGBANJE: Oh, but Ezigbo, look, we have a new dancing game.**
32   **3 OGBANJE: We know you love dancing games.**
33   **1 OGBANJE: Look at this one.**
34   **OGBANJE: Dancing game! Dancing game!**
35   **EZIGBO: I have to go home with water so —**

1   **3 OGBANJE: The sun is still high in the sky. There's plenty of**
2   **time.**
3   **2 OGBANJE: Play with us for a small, small time, and then you**
4   **can go back.**
5   **1 OGBANJE: Remember how much fun we had when we played**
6   **the animal game?**
7   **EZIGBO: Yes, but –**
8   **1 OGBANJE: This is more fun. It's a dancing game. We know**
9   **you love to dance.**
10   **OGBANJE: Dancing game! Dancing game!**
11
12   *(They break into the dancing game. EZIGBO moves to river,*
13   *kneels to fill her pot with water but stops, watches the game. They*
14   *play the dancing game accompanied by drums. [More description*
15   *at end of text.])*
16
17   **SINGER:** *(Dancing)* **Nobody can dance like this.** *(She holds out*
18   *her arms, falls back, is caught by others.)*
19   **CHORUS: AY, A – LIKE THIS!** *(On "this", the others throw dancer*
20   *back up and on her feet and she dances and sings.)*
21   **SINGER: Nobody can dance like me.** *(She holds out her arms,*
22   *falls back, is caught by others.)*
23   **CHORUS: AY, A – LIKE ME!** *(On "me", the others throw dancer*
24   *back up and on her feet and she dances and sings.)*
25   **SINGER: Like a man. Like a woman.** *(She holds out her arms,*
26   *falls back, is caught by others.)*
27   **CHORUS: AY, A – LIKE A WOMAN!** *(On "woman", the others*
28   *throw dancer back up and on her feet and she dances like a*
29   *woman and sings.)*
30   **SINGER: Like a woman. Like a man.** *(She holds out her arms,*
31   *falls back, is caught by others.)*
32   **CHORUS: AY, A – LIKE A MAN!**
33
34   *(On "man", the others throw dancer back up and on her feet and*
35   *she dances like a man and sings. Everyone dances during the*

1   *following. The next player dances to the front becoming the*
2   *singer, the first singer dances back into others.)*
3
4   **ALL**: *(dancing, moving into next position)*
5   *TA MBO MBO, MBO MBO TA.*
6   *MBO MBO, MBO MBO TA.*
7   *MBO MBO, MBO MBO TA.*
8   **2 SINGER:** *(dancing)* **Nobody can dance like me.** *(Falls.)*
9   **CHORUS: AY, A – LIKE THIS!** *(Throw.)*
10   **2 SINGER:** *(dancing)* **Nobody can dance like me.** *(Falls.)*
11   **CHORUS: AY, A – LIKE ME!** *(Throw.)*
12   **2 SINGER**: *(dancing)* **Like a man. Like a woman.** *(Falls.)*
13   **CHORUS: AY, A – LIKE A WOMAN** *(Falls.)*
14   **2 SINGER**: *(dancing)* **Like a woman. Like a man.** *(Falls.)*
15   **CHORUS: AY, A – LIKE A MAN!** *(Throw.)*
16   **ALL**: *(dancing, moving into next position)*
17   *TA MBO MBO, MBO MBO TA.*
18   *MBO MBO, MBO MBO TA.*
19   *MBO MBO, MBO MBO TA.*
20
21   *(EZIGBO joins the game after the second singer finishes. EZIGBO*
22   *is fourth or fifth to be the singer. She is an adept player of this*
23   *game as well. Lights fade during the later part of the game.*
24   *Drums, twirl theme. While EZIGBO sings, after her turn, the*
25   *OGBANJE "twirl" the opposite direction they use to appear, and*
26   *they disappear to EZIGBO.)*
27
28   **EZIGBO:** *MBO MBO, MBO MBO TA.*
29   *MBO MBO, MBO MBO TA. (The OGBANJE withdraw into*
30   *the night, but not out of sight of the audience. Drums are*
31   *suddenly silent. We hear the night-sounds of the bush.)*
32   *MBO MBO, MBO MBO TA.* **Where . . . where did – Why do**
33   **you do that? . . . Our pot!** *(She runs to it, picks it up.)* **Here!**
34   *(Relieved.)* **Mother, it is here.** *(She looks skyward.)* **Oh.** *(She*
35   *moves to river, kneels, wipes top of water, dips her pot. She*

1 *places the cloth on her head, then struggles to put pot on her*
2 *head, then starts off down the path home.)* **There is still**
3 **light. I can still see.** *(The OGBANJE dance after her, making*
4 *quiet, ominous sounds of the night. They move in surging*
5 *waves, then fall back, only to move up on her again. When*
6 *they near her, EZIGBO senses danger and tries to hurry.*
7 *Down the path, 1 OGBANJE lays on its back and puts out its*
8 *arm. EZIGBO approaches, trips, the pot begins to fall. 2*
9 *OGBANJE catches it, carries it off.)* **No! No, no!** *(EZIGBO*
10 *frantically tries to find the pot by feeling with her hands. 1*
11 *and 3 OGBANJE remain, continuing to make quiet sounds of*
12 *the night.)* **It didn't break. I didn't hear it break. Where is**
13 **it? It must be here! . . . Not our second pot . . .** *(MOTHER,*
14 *NGOZI and MEDICINE WOMAN enter variously and move*
15 *to the cooking hut.)*
16 **MED WOMAN: I could not find her. Have you seen her?**
17 **NGOZI: No one has seen her.**
18 **MOTHER: She said she would come home before dark.**
19 **NGOZI: Maybe she is just late.**
20 **MED WOMAN: And she plays just as a disobedient child plays.**
21 *(EZIGBO gives up feeling for the pot, rises and walks toward*
22 *home. OGBANJE follow her.)*
23 **MOTHER: She always does what she says.**
24 **MED WOMAN: Some children change and that is all it is.**
25 **MOTHER: Then I do not like this change.**
26 **1 OGBANJE: Sister . . .**
27 **3 OGBANJE: Ezigbo ...** *(3 OGBANJE grabs EZIGBO, who frantically*
28 *pulls away and runs into compound. OGBANJE exit.)*
29 **EZIGBO: Mama!**
30 **MOTHER: Ezigbo!**
31 **EZIGBO: They were following me —**
32 **MOTHER: Who was following you?** *(While MOTHER tries to*
33 *calm her, MED. WOMAN looks into the night to see if there*
34 *is anything there. Frightened, NGOZI stays next to MED.*
35 *WOMAN.)*

1   EZIGBO: They were trying to hurt me —

2   MOTHER: Who?

3   EZIGBO: I couldn't see — *(She hears a noise, screams in fear.)* **Aahh!**

4   MOTHER: What? Why are you screaming?

5   EZIGBO: They're out there!

6   MOTHER: Who? What happened!

7   EZIGBO: I don't know! There are noises —

8   MOTHER: Yes, there are noises. If you came back before dark
9   there would be no noises. Where were you?

10 EZIGBO: Playing at the river, but —

11 MOTHER: Ezigbo, what is it! You have never given me any
12   trouble before. Why now?

13 EZIGBO: I met some new children and they were teaching me
14   dancing games and I forgot to see what time it is and then
15   I forgot . . .

16 MOTHER: You have so many friends here in the compound.
17   When I send you on an errand to fetch the water, come
18   back with it and then go play.

19 EZIGBO: That is what I said but then they wanted me to play.

20 MOTHER: Where is our pot?

21 EZIGBO: I heard noises and I started to run and it fell off my
22   head and I couldn't find it in the dark.

23 MOTHER: *(She glances at MED. WOMAN. Strongly.)* When I tell
24   you to do something, I don't want to hear any excuses! You
25   will do it and come back with it finished!

26 EZIGBO: Yes, Mama.

27 MOTHER: And you will not tell me one thing and then do
28   another! You said you would be back before dark and you
29   were not!

30 EZIGBO: Yes, Mama.

31 MOTHER: Now we will have to eat our food without water. And
32   tonight, again, you cannot bring food to your father.

33 MED WOMAN: Ezigbo, come here. *(EZIGBO moves to her.)*
34   When you were born I was sorry for your mother; I was
35   angry at you.

1   EZIGBO: Angry at me?

2   MED WOMAN: Yes, for coming back again. Nothing good will
3   come of this child, I said. She is Ogbanje, she will find a
4   way to leave her mother. But I was wrong. You are Ezigbo,
5   the Good One. Your mother's joy, a beautiful, human
6   child. Do you know this?

7   EZIGBO: Yes, My Mother.

8   MED WOMAN: I know this. Now, what noises did you hear in
9   the bush?

10 EZIGBO: Animal noises; and some like children.

11 MED WOMAN: And did they call your name?

12 EZIGBO: I think so. *(Takes EZIGBO'S head, feels the glands in*
13   *her neck. EZIGBO exhibits no pain.)*

14 MED WOMAN: Were you dizzy?

15 EZIGBO: No.

16 NGOZI: She was dizzy by the river.

17 EZIGBO: But that was a long time ago.

18 MED WOMAN: Did you take your amulet off?

19 EZIGBO: No, never. *(PRIESTESS holds out EZIGBO'S hair in her*
20   *hands. She lets it fall, holds it out again, examining it.)*

21 MED WOMAN: What were you playing by the river?

22 EZIGBO: Dancing games.

23 MED WOMAN: And did you know these children?

24 EZIGBO: I met them yesterday. They are from another
25   village.

26 MED WOMAN: Were there others from our village who saw
27   these children?

28 EZIGBO: No.

29 MED WOMAN: Show me your hands. *(She holds out her hands.*
30   *MED. WOMAN feels EZIGBO'S hands, paying special*
31   *attention to her nails.)* Show me your feet. *(EZIGBO sits*
32   *down, lifts her feet. MED. WOMAN looks at the bottom of*
33   *each of them.)*

34 MOTHER: What is it?

35 MED WOMAN: *(Holding a foot)* What is this? *(She rubs the*

1   *bottom of EZIGBO'S foot with her finger, EZIGBO squirms,*
2   *laughs.)* **Ezigbo, I can find nothing wrong with you. You are**
3   **healthy and strong. And you have big feet.** *(She throws foot.)*
4 **EZIGBO:** *(Stands.)* **That is why I can run faster than boys.** *(She*
5   *runs around the compound, ending up next to NGOZI.)*
6 **MED WOMAN: If these children come to you again, you must**
7   **use your big feet and run home fast to your mother.**
8 **EZIGBO: I will.** *(Upset, NGOZI moves away from her.)* **Ngozi?**
9 **MOTHER:** *(Pulling MED. WOMAN aside)* **So you believe it was**
10   **the Ogbanje she played with by the river?**
11 **MED WOMAN: Ogbanje? Hah. I don't know why Ani would**
12   **allow it. Probably they were children from another village**
13   **and she played too long and came home late.**
14 **MOTHER: Thank you, Mother.**
15 **MED WOMAN:** *(To all)* **It is time for food. Let us eat well.** *(To*
16   *EZIGBO)* **Ka chi fo, may the morning come.** *(She exits.*
17   *NGOZI begins to move off. MOTHER sees and hears the*
18   *following.)*
19 **EZIGBO: Ngozi?**
20 **NGOZI:** *(Turning back to EZIGBO, genuinely hurt)* **You told me**
21   **you would be back before dark, and you were not. I asked**
22   **you what you were doing by the river and you said talking**
23   **to the river spirit. You did not tell me you were playing**
24   **with friends from another village. You played with them**
25   **all day yesterday and today.**
26 **EZIGBO: You said you could not stay.**
27 **NGOZI: I would have stayed if you had told me you had new**
28   **friends to play with.**
29 **EZIGBO: But you said your mother would hit you.**
30 **NGOZI: Yes, she would hit me, but you knew I would have**
31   **stayed with you, anyway. You chose not to tell me because**
32   **you did not want me to play with you.** *(She exits.)*
33 **EZIGBO: Ngozi?**
34 **MOTHER: Come eat . . . even though we must fight with our**
35   **food to go down without water.**

1   **EZIGBO:** I'm sorry.

2   **MOTHER:** (*Much softer*) **I know. I know, Ezigbo.** (*They walk*

3   *toward hut. MOTHER turns to audience.*) **N ubosi soro**

4   **anyasi ahu. Mama Ezigbo gboro nwa ya, si ya bia-nso.**

5   **TRANSLATOR:** On the day that followed that night, the Mother

6   called her daughter close.

7   **MOTHER:** Ezigbo.

8   **EZIGBO:** Yes, Mama.

9   **MOTHER:** We need water to drink and to cook. Should I fetch

10   the water myself?

11   **EZIGBO:** No, no. Everyone will laugh at me if you go, because

12   they will think I cannot even get water from the river for

13   my mother.

14   **MOTHER:** I will go, then I know it will be done.

15   **EZIGBO:** No; no one will call me The Good One again. It is my

16   chore. I will go.

17   **MOTHER:** (*Getting a painted, highly decorated pot*) I borrowed a

18   pot from one of the other wives because we have no more

19   waterpots in the hut. Now this belongs to Mama Okeke, it is

20   their favorite pot, so please bring it back in one piece, eh?

21   **EZIGBO:** Yes, Mama.

22   **MOTHER:** We've had a peaceful life, here, with no troubles

23   with the other wives. As First Wife it is our responsibility

24   we live in peace.

25   **EZIGBO:** I know.

26   **MOTHER:** Wait for Ngozi, then go.

27   **EZIGBO:** I'm not going to wait for the other girls. I'll go now and

28   I will be back so fast you will not even know I am gone.

29

30   (*EZIGBO takes up the pot and walks down the path with grim*

31   *determination. Drums. 1 OGBANJE appears behind EZIGBO,*

32   *dancing to drums, twirls, making itself visible to EZIGBO.*

33   *EZIGBO turns back, sees the OGBANJE following her, then walks*

34   *on with determination. 2nd OGBANJE dances on ahead of*

35   *EZIGBO, twirls, dances ahead of her. 3rd OGBANJE dances on*

1 *ahead of her, twirls, appears to EZIGBO. As the OGBANJE dance*
2 *down the path in synchronized movements, EZIGBO tries to pass*
3 *them, but they block her way. The group enters the river clearing.*
4 *The drum finishes the song, the OGBANJE jump toward EZIGBO,*
5 *cutting her off and 3 OGBANJE quickly takes pot from EZIGBO'S*
6 *head.)*
7
8 **EZIGBO:** (*Simultaneously exploding*) **No, no, give that back, no,**
9   **no, no, give me Mama Okeke's pot!**
10 **OGBANJE: Play with us, dancing game, dancing game!**
11 **EZIGBO: Can't you see I am fetching water for my mother? I**
12   **have to bring it back now.** (*She takes pot back from the*
13   *OGBANJE.*) **I have to bring her the water, now.**
14 **3 OGBANJE: How is your mother?**
15 **EZIGBO:** (*She goes to the river, dips the pot.*) **Angry. I did not**
16   **bring any food to my father again last night. And we had to**
17   **fight with our food to go down without water. She was**
18   **going to fetch the water herself, that is how angry she is.**
19   (*OGBANJE react at this. EZIGBO carefully places pot on her*
20   *head.*) **I am not playing with you. I am going back, now.**
21
22 (*She starts off. The OGBANJE circle her, speak in her ear. EZIGBO*
23 *walks determinedly, but they turn her around, confuse her.*)
24
25 **1 OGBANJE: Ezigbo, there is plenty of time before the sun goes**
26   **down.**
27 **2 OGBANJE: See? The sun is still high in the sky.**
28 **1 OGBANJE: We want to play with you. We miss you.**
29 **EZIGBO: You always run away.**
30 **3 OGBANJE: Stay with us.**
31 **1 OGBANJE**: (*Pulling her*) **Play with us.**
32 **EZIGBO:** (*Afraid her pot will fall*) **Don't! No! The pot will break!**
33   (*She holds it with both hands. THEY pull her further off*
34   *path.*)
35 **3 OGBANJE: We have new games —**

1 2 OGBANJE: New dancing games, new clapping games.

2 OGBANJE: Clapping games! Do you like clapping games? *(THEY*

3 *let her go and begin a clapping rhythm. EZIGBO walks*

4 *further off the path. Lights begin a long fade into evening.)*

5 *AI-EH-AI-EH! (Clap-clap) AI-EH-AI-EH! (Clap-clap) AI-EH-AI-*

6 *EH! (Clap-clap) AI-EH-AI —*

7 EZIGBO: No, no, I can't play with you!

8 2 OGBANJE: There is plenty of time.

9 EZIGBO: We have to prepare the evening meal.

10 2 OGBANJE: You don't have to eat. You can stay and play.

11 EZIGBO: No, Mama — My Mother is waiting for me. *(They each*

12 *pull her in a different direction.)*

13 3 OGBANJE: This way —

14 1 OGBANJE: This way —

15 2 OGBANJE: This way.

16 1 OGBANJE: No, this way. *(Drums, twirl theme. As each*

17 *OGBANJE says her name, they "twirl", disappear to*

18 *EZIGBO.)*

19 1 OGBANJE: Ezigbo —

20 2 OGBANJE: Ezigbo —

21 3 OGBANJE: Ezigbo —

22 OGBANJE: *(Whispered)* Sister . . . *(They crouch together. In the*

23 *quiet, EZIGBO regains her balance.)*

24 EZIGBO: Gone. Good. *(She looks for path, doesn't see it.)* Where

25 . . . where is the path? *(Night noises begin to be heard. She*

26 *moves one way, then the other.)* Where's the path? . . .This

27 way? *(She walks one way, stops.)* No. There? *(She walks*

28 another way.)* No. *(She looks up.)* Darker. *(She clenches her*

29 *amulet, then smells it.)* Medicine Woman and Mother and

30 Ngozi, all the people of Igboland and Ani, the Earth Spirit

31 are here with me. *(She smells it, again, clenches it.)* I am

32 staying. *(To the bush)* I am staying. *(She begins to walk.)*

33 Just walk and you will find the way. *(She sees the path.)* Ah!

34 The path. You see? This way! *(She moves quickly down*

35 *path. The OGBANJE charge her, screeching and howling like*

1   *animals of the night. Sharp drum sound effects of the night-*
2   *bush. In the darkening night, the OGBANJE circle her, put*
3   *their hands on her, grab her, push her, pull her. she reacts,*
4   *pulls away, holding onto her pot. They release EZIGBO and*
5   *she moves down the path, then THEY surge at her again,*
6   *screeching and grabbing. 1 OGBANJE takes pot, passes it to 3*
7   *OGBANJE who passes it to 2 OGBANJE.)* **No!** *(2 OGBANJE*
8   *throws the pot down and it smashes. Drums end.)* **Ah!**
9   *(EZIGBO kneels, picks up some large pieces, begins to cry.)*
10   **Mama . . .**
11 **1 OGBANJE:** *(Quietly)* **Amulet . . .**
12 **3 OGBANJE:** *(Quietly)* **Amulet . . .**
13
14 *(3 OGBANJE comes up behind her, tries to take hold of the leather*
15 *string on the back of EZIGBO'S neck, but is burned. 1 OGBANJE*
16 *tries to take off amulet, but is burned. EZIGBO starts off down the*
17 *path in sadness, carrying pieces of the pot. The OGBANJE follow*
18 *her. MOTHER appears near hut, waiting angrily for EZIGBO.*
19 *She's followed by MED. WOMAN and NGOZI. EZIGBO enters the*
20 *compound.)*
21
22 **MOTHER:** *(Angrily)* **Ezigbo.**
23 **EZIGBO: Mama.**
24 **MOTHER: Where is Mama Okeke's pot?**
25 **EZIGBO: It broke.**
26 **MOTHER: What did I tell you?**
27 **EZIGBO: But I didn't play with my friends. I got lost and I**
28   **couldn't find the path —**
29 **MOTHER: You know the way! You go to the river every day!**
30   **How many times do I have to tell you the same thing! I told**
31   **you to come home before dark. And you said you would.**
32 **EZIGBO: I tried but they wouldn't let me. I didn't play and I**
33   **filled the pot with water and —**
34 **MOTHER: And you have broken Mama Okeke's favorite pot**
35   **after I promised her you wouldn't.**

1   EZIGBO: The pot got caught on something and broke.

2   *(The next two speeches are delivered simultaneously.)*

3   MOTHER: And still we have no water. Three times! Ezigbo –

4   don't you – listen to me. Listen to me, Ezigbo – no, no –

5   EZIGBO: Mama, it felt like somebody took it off my head –

6   Mama, no, listen to me, no, no – *(MOTHER lightly slaps*

7   *EZIGBO. MOTHER, in horror, starts to go to EZIGBO, who*

8   *pulls away, holding her face.)*

9   MOTHER: Ezigbo . . .

10 EZIGBO: No.

11 MOTHER: *(Horrified)* But I didn't mean . . . *(Again the MOTHER*

12   *goes for her, again EZIGBO backs away.)* Ezigbo?

13 EZIGBO: I thought you would never . . . *(She coughs.)*

14 MOTHER: I am sorry, Ezigbo. I am sorry.

15 1 OGBANJE: Sister . . .

16 EZIGBO: *(She begins to faint.)* Oh . . .

17 MOTHER: Ezigbo? *(MOTHER moves to her.)*

18 EZIGBO: I cannot . . . Mama. *(EZIGBO collapses into MOTHER'S*

19   *arms.)*

20 MOTHER: Ezigbo! Mother, help her. I will give you anything

21   you ask. *(SHE lays EZIGBO down, EZIGBO'S head on her*

22   *knee.)*

23 MED WOMAN: What can I do?

24 MOTHER: Keep her with us. Make her will to stay stronger. Call

25   on the spirits to heal her!

26 MED WOMAN: I cannot insult the River Spirit by asking her to

27   change her laws. She has spoken.

28 MOTHER: But I did not mean to strike her.

29 MED WOMAN: You should know it is much more than that, my

30   Daughter. The spirits want her, they have called and called

31   her, and she has listened. She was dancing with the

32   Ogbanje at the riverside. Now they are calling her home.

33 MOTHER: River Spirit, please, do not take her from me! I will –

34 MED WOMAN: Woman, do not dare to call the River Spirit

35   yourself! She will strike you in anger!

1   1 OGBANJE: Sister . . . *(EZIGBO hears this, stirs.)*

2   **MOTHER:** *(Suddenly hopeful)* **Ezigbo?**

3   **OGBANJE: Sister?** *(EZIGBO slowly sits up.)*

4   **MOTHER: She is still here. Are you — Ezigbo — how do you feel?**

5   **Are you — Ezigbo?** *(EZIGBO rises.)*

6   **2 OGBANJE**: *(The OGBANJE begin to come into focus.)* **Sister?**

7   **EZIGBO: Sister?** *(EZIGBO now sees the OGBANJE, moves to*

8   *them. She reaches for them, touches them.)* **Sister.**

9   **MOTHER: No, no, no. Mother, please!**

10   **MED WOMAN: You were blessed. She was with you ten**

11   **wonderful years. You are more of a family with the other**

12   **wives and children. And no one can say you did not have a**

13   **child. We will still call you Mama Ezigbo.**

14   **MOTHER: Ngozi, speak to her.** *(i.e., Ezigbo)*

15   **NGOZI:** *(To Ezigbo)* **I would have helped you. Why didn't you let**

16   **me help you? You sent me away. You do not have to go. You**

17   **can stay and we will marry brothers so we can be friends**

18   **and sisters.**

19   **EZIGBO:** *(standing among the Ogbanje)* **Ngozi . . . strong and**

20   **healthy . . . you will live long. My friend.**

21   **MED. WOMAN: Take comfort, Mama Ezigbo, she is Ogbanje.**

22   **She will always be around you, playing. And for her, there**

23   **is joy: she is going home.**

24   **MOTHER:** *(EZIGBO backs away from OGBANJE, turns to*

25   *MOTHER.)* **Stay, you can stay, I know you can stay, Ada.**

26   **Please. You are the Good One.**

27   **EZIGBO: Mama . . . You are The Good One.** *(Stands alone, sings,*

28   *without drums, directly to the Mother. MOTHER groans and*

29   *cries.)*

30   *EWO NNE ME O*   **MOTHER: No, no, no, no, no . . .**

31   *UDU M A LAPU KWAM O.*

32   **OGBANJE:** *(Singing)* *UDU*

33   **EZIGBO:** *EWO NNA MA O*   **MOTHER: Ezigbo . . .**

34   *UDU M A LAPU KWAM O.*

35   **OGBANJE:** *UDU*

1   **EZIGBO:** *UDU M JI ECHUBE MMIRI*
2   *MA M ' EGBU YA NATA.*
3   **OGBANJE:** *UDU*
4   **EZIGBO:** *UDU M JI ECHUBE MMIRI*
5   *MA M EGBU YA NATA.*
6   **OGBANJE:** *UDU*
7   **EZIGBO:** *O M NA-AGBA O?*
8   **OGBANJE:** *UDU*
9   **EZIGBO:** *O M NA-AGBA O?*
10 **OGBANJE:** *UDU*
11 **EZIGBO:** (Repeats. *She walks up to* MOTHER, *taking off her*
12   *amulet.)* *EWO NNE ME*
13   *O UDU'M A LAPU KWAM O.*
14 **OGBANJE:** *UDU*
15 **EZIGBO:** *EWO NNA MA O*
16   *UDU M A LAPU KWAM O.*
17 **OGBANJE:** *UDU*
18
19 *(EZIGBO lets amulet fall to the ground. Sadly, SHE touches*
20 *MOTHER'S face, her MOTHER desperately embraces her.)*
21
22 **EZIGBO:** *UDU M JI ECHUBE MMIRI*
23   *MA M EGBU YA NATA.* (EZIGBO *pulls away from*
24   MOTHER.)
25 **OGBANJE:** *UDU*
26 **EZIGBO:** *UDU M JI ECHUBE MMIRI*
27   *MA M'EGBU YA NATA.*
28
29 *(EZIGBO moves to OGBANJE and they enfold her. SHE turns and*
30 *continues singing directly to her Mother.)*
31
32 **OGBANJE:** *UDU*
33 **EZIGBO:** *O M NA-AGBA O?*
34 **OGBANJE:** *UDU*
35 **EZIGBO:** *O M NA-AGBA O?*

1   **OGBANJE:** *UDU*

2   **EZIGBO & OGBANJE:** *ANYI GA-AGRA NA-AGBA EWO*

3   *ANYI GA-AGBA NA-AGBA AH-AH*

4   *ANYI GA-AGBA NA-AGBA EWO*

5   *ANYI GA-AGBA NA-AGBA AH-AH*

6   **TRANSLATOR:** (*As OGBANJE repeat this last part of the song*

7   *quietly*) **We will run to leave.**

8   **All of us must leave in haste.**

9   **Oh, my father,**

10   **Oh, my mother,**

11   **Farewell.** (*OGBANJE lead EZIGBO center.*)

12   **EZIGBO:** (*Sings over*

13   **OGBANJE:** *ANYI GA-AGBA NA-AGBA EWO*   *them*)

14   *ANYI GA-AGBA NA-AGBA AH-AH*   *EWO, EWO, EWO, EWO*

15   *ANYI GA-AGBA NA-AGBA EWO*   *EWO NNA M O*

16   *ANYI GA-AGBA NA-AGBA AH-AH*   *EWO NNA M O*

17   *UDU.*

18

19   (*Song ends. Drums. OGBANJE form a circle around EZIGBO. The*

20   *OGBANJE do an Igbo Celebration Dance around EZIGBO. Drums*

21   *are energetic, the dance exuberant, full of color and joy. The*

22   *OGBANJE welcome EZIGBO, invite her to join them. Half-way*

23   *through the dance, EZIGBO begins to join in their movements. By*

24   *three quarters she is dancing ecstatically and in complete*

25   *synchronization with them. In the end, the OGBANJE, one after*

26   *the other, dance off. EZIGBO dances after them without looking*

27   *back. DRUMS end. Mother turns to audience.*)

28

29   **MOTHER:** (*Narrates*) **Etua ka akwukwo m si we kwusi.**

30   **TRANSLATOR: And this is how my story ends.**

31

32   (*Dim out.*)

33

34   **END OF PLAY**

35

ANIMAL GAME.
Instructions for playing the animal game:

This is a competitive game; each "animal" is seeking to overpower the other in a confrontation. However, there is no wrestling, kicking, biting, etc.

Keep the game moving; it should go fast. Once a player has been beaten, the next challenger should come in before the count of four, while the winner is still celebrating. Challenges are delivered immediately.

Players who are watching should comment and react throughout.

The animals should be played to the others watching the game, to impress them as well as the challenger. Fierceness is strong, but so is excellent physicalization and vocalization of an animal. This close representation can be considered by the group in their judgments about a confrontation.

If a player comes in as a challenger and loses that challenge, he/she is out of the game and must sit and watch.

Some indigenous animals to choose from: monkey, lion, hippo, eagle, vulture, parrot, python, tiger, lizard, turtle, human, rat, chicken, goat.

DANCING GAME.
Some suggestions for playing the dancing game:

This is a show-off game, showing how well each player can dance. Each player should relish his/her turn and strut what they have, playing to everybody who is watching. High energy, lots of movement, lots of fun.

During the TA MBO MBO TA section, the SINGER really gets down, as this is the climax of her turn.

The song and therefore the game have a strong rhythm; the movement, like any dance, should stay within rhythm.

Players dance like a man when they sing "MAN" in the song, and then like a woman when they sing "WOMAN" in the song. Each player should play their Man and Woman differently from every other player.

When SINGER is thrown, she should be thrown as high as possible. The SINGER should also help by jumping when she is thrown. And the SINGER should come up dancing, beginning before she lands.

The catching and throwing players move up behind the SINGER after they throw him. The SINGER should concentrate on dancing and trust that the catchers will be there. But the SINGER *must open his arms so he can be caught.*

Takunda

A Play Using Authentic Shona Folk Tales and Songs

by Charles Smith

Commentary by Charles Smith

Takunda was first presented by Victory Gardens Theater and Body Politic Theatre as part of the Great Chicago Playwrights Exposition (Play Expo) from June 18 through July 19, 1987. An early draft, titled *Tales of South Africa*, was presented by Imaginary Theatre Company, the touring theatre for young audiences of the Repertory Theatre of St. Louis, in February, 1987. This version of *Takunda* was first published by Theatre Communications Group as part of its "Plays in Process" series.

Charles Smith is a member of New Dramatists as is Playwright-in-Residence at Victory Gardens Theater in Chicago which has produced the world premieres of his plays *The Sutherland, Freefall, Jelly Belly, Takunda,* and *Cane.* Both *Freefall* and *Jelly Belly* have also been produced off-Broadway. His other work includes *Black Star Line* which was commissioned and produced by the Goodman Theatre; *City of Gold* which was commissioned and produced by Seattle Rep; *Les Trois Dumas,* commissioned by the Indiana Repertory Theatre; and *Golden Leaf Rag Time Blues* which was workshopped for the HBO New Writers Project. Mr. Smith is a native of Chicago who teaches playwriting at Ohio University.

1   *(A woman is heard singing Off-stage. It is TAKUNDA. She is*
2   *singing the bird song.)*
3
4
5   **TAKUNDA:** *(Off)*
6   ***Rimwe zuva ndiri ndega***
7   ***Ndichi funga zvangu***
8   ***Ndiani aindi chengeta***
9   ***Ndichiri kaduku***
10   *(Her voice is joined by those of the OTHERS in the cast.)*
11   **ALL:** *(Off)*
12   ***Ndivo baba vangu chete***
13   ***Rudo rwavo rwaka komba***
14   ***Pamwe vese na mai***
15   ***Nhasi ndova tenda***
16
17   *(Lights slowly come up on a bare stage. TAKUNDA enters carrying*
18   *a pile of books tied with a leather strap. As she sings, She is slowly*
19   *joined On-stage by the other actors.)*
20
21   **TAKUNDA:**
22   ***Kana ndazo tambudzika***
23   ***Ndichisina shamwari***
24   ***Ndika funga baba vangu***
25   ***Ndino wona zororo***
26   **OTHERS:**
27   ***Ndivo baba vangu chete***
28   ***Rudo rwavo rwaka komba***
29   ***Pamwe vese na mai***
30   ***Nhasi ndova tenda***
31   **WOMAN/CHIPO:** ***Taku! Takunda! Chimbo mira!*** **Wait up!**
32   *(TAKUNDA ignores CHIPO and begins to leave as CHIPO,*
33   *carrying a similar armful of books, runs and catches her,*
34   *grabbing her by the arm.)* **Takunda!** ***Iwe! Indava so, man?***
35   **TAKUNDA:** ***Hapana zvangu.***

333

1   WOMAN/CHIPO: *Indava kusandi mirira?*

2   TAKUNDA: *Ah! Iwe.*

3   WOMAN/CHIPO: Takunda! What's the matter with you?

4   TAKUNDA: I have to get home.

5   WOMAN/CHIPO: Didn't you hear me calling you?

6   TAKUNDA: I heard you.

7   WOMAN/CHIPO: So why didn't you wait?

8   TAKUNDA: I told you.

9   WOMAN/CHIPO: Fungi's looking for you.

10   TAKUNDA: So?

11   WOMAN/CHIPO: So?

12   TAKUNDA: I don't have time for Fungi.

13   WOMAN/CHIPO: Takunda. What's this I hear?

14   TAKUNDA: I don't even like Fungi.

15   WOMAN/CHIPO: He's with a friend.

16   TAKUNDA: Please, Chipo. I have to get home. Talk to him for

17   me. Tell him.

18   WOMAN/CHIPO: You talk to him.

19   TAKUNDA: I can't. I have to go. *(TAKUNDA turns to leave as*

20   *young FUNGI and his FRIEND are heard singing Off-stage.)*

21   MAN 2/FUNGI: *(Off) Sarura wako . . .*

22   MAN 2/FUNGI and MAN 1/FRIEND: *(Off) Kadeya deya nendoro*

23   *chena.*

24   MAN 2/FUNGI: *(Off) Sarura wako . . .*

25   BOTH: *(Off) Kadeya deya nendore chena. (FUNGI and his*

26   *FRIEND enter. The two BOYS clap their hands to the rhythm*

27   *of the song and begin to taunt the girls with their*

28   *movements. CHIPO is obviously enjoying the attention*

29   *while TAKUNDA makes a vain attempt to ignore it all.)*

30   MAN 2/FUNGI: Choose the one you love. . .

31   BOTH: *Kadeya deya nendore chena.*

32   MAN 2/FUNGI: Choose the one you like. . .

33   BOTH: *Kadeya deya nendore chena. (CHIPO joins the two boys*

34   *in song as TAKUNDA continues to try to ignore them. As*

35   *FUNGI sings, HE points to TAKUNDA.)*

1 MAN 2/FUNGI:? *Wangu mutema. . .*

2 ALL THREE: *Kadeya deya nendore chena.*

3 MAN 2/FUNGI: Mine runs real fast. . .

4 ALL THREE: *Kadeya deya nendoro chena.*

5 MAN 2/FUNGI: She wins all the races. . .

6 ALL THREE: *Kadeya deya nendoro chena.*

7 MAN 2/FUNGI: *Sarura wako. . .*

8 ALL THREE: Place a *chuma* around her neck. *(They stop singing*

9   *and clapping.)*

10 MAN 2/FUNGI: I waited for you in the yard.

11 TAKUNDA: I had to get home.

12 MAN 2/FUNGI: Didn't you get my note?

13 TAKUNDA: I got it.

14 MAN 2/FUNGI: And?

15 TAKUNDA: And I told you. I have to get home. *(FUNGI removes*

16   *a string of beads from around his neck as CHIPO and the*

17   *FRIEND giggle. FUNGI cautiously approaches TAKUNDA,*

18   *who has her back to him HE carefully places the beads*

19   *around her neck. TAKUNDA smiles, then turns. WOMAN*

20   *steps away and becomes TAKUNDA's MOTHER.)*

21 WOMAN/MOTHER: Taku! Takunda! *(TAKUNDA jumps, the*

22   *FRIEND runs off.)*

23 MAN 2/FUNGI: I'll meet you here. Tomorrow. Same time.

24 WOMAN/MOTHER: Takunda! *Uri kupi,* Takunda!

25 TAKUNDA: *Ndiri kuno!*

26 WOMAN/MOTHER: Takunda!

27 TAKUNDA: I'm coming!

28 MAN 2/FUNGI: Tomorrow, Takunda!

29 TAKUNDA: OK! Tomorrow! *(FUNGI and TAKUNDA part. SHE*

30   *moves to her MOTHER.)*

31 WOMAN/MOTHER: Takunda! What takes you so long to come

32   home from school?

33 TAKUNDA: Nothing.

34 WOMAN/MOTHER: Nothing delays you for an entire half hour?

35 TAKUNDA: I was with Chipo.

1   WOMAN/MOTHER: Chipo?

2   TAKUNDA: Yes, Momma.

3   WOMAN/MOTHER: And did Chipo give you that *chuma* to

4   wear? *(TAKUNDA quickly removes the beads.)* **You be quick**

5   **when I want you to come home from school. Other days**

6   **you can be tardy, but not today.**

7   TAKUNDA: Tomorrow?

8   WOMAN/MOTHER: Yes, tomorrow you can stay late, but today

9   I need you here.

10 TAKUNDA: Are those tea cakes I smell?

11 WOMAN/MOTHER: Moyra cooked those tea cakes for the

12   meeting tonight, so don't you touch them. And don't

13   disturb your father. He's inside, working.

14 TAKUNDA: Yes, Momma.

15 WOMAN/MOTHER: Now tell me, what did you learn in school

16   today?

17 TAKUNDA: I learned some English words.

18 WOMAN/MOTHER: English?

19 TAKUNDA: I learned how to say, "I beg your pardon."

20 WOMAN MOTHER: What kind of school is this?

21 TAKUNDA: It's an expression. Like, "Pardon me."

22 WOMAN/MOTHER: "Pardon me," I know. But this begging, it's

23   not good for a girl.

24 TAKUNDA: Momma. . .

25 WOMAN/MOTHER: This boy, you meet him in school?

26 TAKUNDA: What boy?

27 WOMAN/MOTHER: The boy who gave you the *chuma,*

28   Takunda.

29 TAKUNDA: He's in one of my classes.

30 WOMAN/MOTHER: Is he Shona?

31 TAKUNDA: Momma!

32 WOMAN/MOTHER: Is he?

33 TAKUNDA: No.

34 WOMAN/MOTHER: I thought so.

35 TAKUNDA: But it's OK, Momma. I like him.

1   WOMAN/MOTHER: I've given the yardboy the day off so I want
2   you to get the broom, come out here and sweep the yard.
3   TAKUNDA: Mama. . .
4   WOMAN/MOTHER: When you are finished you can begin
5   inside, I have to go buy some firewood. And remember,
6   don't disturb your father.
7   TAKUNDA: Yes, Mum.
8   WOMAN/MOTHER: This boy, what's his name?
9   TAKUNDA: Fungi.
10 WOMAN/MOTHER: Don't you think this Fungi would be hurt if
11   he knew you weren't wearing his *chuma*? *(TAKUNDA*
12   *smiles, replaces the beads.)* Now, I know how many tea
13   cakes there are, young lady. I've counted them. You keep
14   away from them or when I get back, I'll burn your butt!
15   *(WOMAN leaves, joining MAN 1 and 2.)*
16 TAKUNDA: I love tea cakes. *(SHE finds the tea cakes and prepares*
17   *to eat one. SHE hears a noise.)* Baba? Is that you? Baba?
18   *(WOMAN and MAN 1 and 2 enter as POLICE.)*
19 MAN 2/POLICE: Alfred Chikomba. Where is he?
20 MAN 1/POLICE: Is he your father, child?
21 MAN 2/POLICE: Is Alfred Chikomba your father? *(Beat)* The
22   child's obviously a deaf-mute.
23 MAN 1/POLICE: Check the house. *(WOMAN and MAN 2 begin to*
24   *leave.)*
25 TAKUNDA: There's no one here!
26 MAN 1/POLICE: So the child is not a deaf-mute.
27 MAN 2/POLICE: But she may be a liar.
28 MAN 1/POLICE: Check inside. *(WOMAN and MAN 2 leave.)*
29 TAKUNDA: He's not here! No one's here. My mother, father, no
30   one.
31 MAN 1/POLICE: It is not your mother we're interested in, child.
32   It's your father. Where is he?
33 TAKUNDA: Why?
34 MAN 1/POLICE: We want to ask him a few questions, that's all.
35   Now where is he?

1   TAKUNDA: Questions about what?

2   MAN 1/POLICE: Inquisitive little girl, aren't you?

3   TAKUNDA: My father's not here.

4   MAN 1/POLICE: We want to ask him about the burglar. Surely
5   you've heard about the burglar here in the area, and your
6   father is such an important man, we want to ask him if he
7   can help us catch that rascal who has been breaking into
8   people's homes.

9   TAKUNDA: I told you, he isn't here. Come back tomorrow. You
10   can see him then. *(MAN 2/POLICE reenters.)*

11   MAN 2/POLICE: We have him, lieutenant. He was inside. *(HE*
12   *leaves.)*

13   MAN 1/POLICE: Splendid.

14   TAKUNDA: No.

15   MAN 1/POLICE: Your father is under arrest for holding illegal
16   meetings. We're taking him to the district station for
17   questioning.

18   TAKUNDA: No! *(TAKUNDA screams, runs and attacks MAN*
19   *1/POLICE. SHE pounds his back, HE pushes her away, SHE*
20   *charges him again. HE turns and slaps her, knocking her to*
21   *the ground. WOMAN/MOTHER moves to TAKUNDA and*
22   *comforts her.)*

23   MAN 2/GIBSON: *(Entering)* I told you this would happen. It was
24   just a matter of time.

25   WOMAN/MOTHER: Please Gibson. The last thing we need is
26   your philosophizing.

27   MAN 2/GIBSON: He should have kept his mouth shut. He didn't
28   have to go around agitating.

29   WOMAN/MOTHER: Will you just shut up.

30   MAN 2/GIBSON: What are we supposed to do now? Answer me
31   that. How are we supposed to live?

32   WOMAN/MOTHER: You make it sound like he isn't coming back.

33   MAN 2/GIBSON: You think he is?

34   WOMAN/MOTHER: They only took him for questioning.

35   MAN 2/GIBSON: Questioning.

1 WOMAN/MOTHER: Will you shut your fat mouth!

2 TAKUNDA: What are they going to do to Baba?

3 WOMAN/MOTHER: Nothing. They only want to ask him some
4   questions.

5 MAN 2/GIBSON: Questions.

6 WOMAN/MOTHER: Gibson!

7 MAN 2/GIBSON: Stop lying to the child.

8 WOMAN/MOTHER: Those meetings were not illegal. They
9   cannot hold Alfred.

10 MAN 2/GIBSON: The Rhodesian police can do whatever they
11   want.

12 WOMAN/MOTHER: You should have more respect for your
13   brother than this.

14 MAN 2/GIBSON: My brother and the entire Musangano are
15   troublemakers.

16 WOMAN/MOTHER: Your brother and the Musangano helped
17   you get a work permit.

18 MAN 2/GIBSON: What good is a work permit with no work?
19   Anyone can get a work permit. I didn't need the
20   Musangano for that. Any *kabenzi* can get a work permit.
21   But work, now that's a different matter. Can the
22   Musangano get me work? Can the Musangano give me
23   money to send home to my family? No. The Musangano has
24   caused me nothing but heartache since I've been here.

25 WOMAN/MOTHER: Then perhaps you should have stayed in
26   the township.

27 MAN 2/GIBSON: Perhaps I should have. *(MAN 1/VENDOR*
28   *enters, pushing a small cart.)*

29 MAN 1/VENDOR: *Mbambaira!* Get your hot *Mbambaira!* Makes
30   your tongue laugh and your tummy dance! Yams, little
31   girl? Would you like a nice hot yam?

32 TAKUNDA: I hate yams.

33 MAN 1/VENDOR: But at a price like this, you can afford to
34   change your tastes. Fifty cents. Best price in town.

35 TAKUNDA: Get away from me.

1   MAN 1/VENDOR: I'm sure a rich little girl like you's got fifty
2   cents.
3   TAKUNDA: I'm not rich.
4   MAN 1/VENDOR: Come now. You can't fool SaMuchena. Girl
5   like you, wears those high-fashion Boer clothes. Your
6   father must have a lot of money.
7   TAKUNDA: You know nothing about my father.
8   MAN 1/VENDOR: He must work for. . .what? The government?
9   TAKUNDA: He's a doctor, for your information.
10   MAN 1/VENDOR: A doctor? Well. That means you must live,
11   where? Harari?
12   TAKUNDA: Kuma Beatrice.
13   MAN 1/VENDOR: Kuma Beatrice. So your family employs a
14   servant.
15   TAKUNDA: Three servants. A houseboy, yardboy, and cook.
16   MAN 1/VENDOR: Then you are a rich little girl. Help poor
17   SaMuchena. Buy a yam.
18   TAKUNDA: Leave me alone.
19   MAN 1/VENDOR: Makes your tongue laugh and your tummy
20   dance.
21   TAKUNDA: Get away from me! You are disgusting. *(VENDOR*
22   *leaves. TAKUNDA moves to WOMAN/GOGO who sits*
23   *grinding peanuts.)*
24   WOMAN/GOGO: Takunda?
25   TAKUNDA: Yes, Gogo.
26   WOMAN/GOGO: Well. What brings you all the way here?
27   Where's your mother?
28   TAKUNDA: She's at home, Gogo.
29   WOMAN/GOGO: And you come here alone? What's happened?
30   TAKUNDA: They arrested Baba. *(The rhythm of GOGO's*
31   *grinding is broken, but only for a second. Pause. SHE*
32   *continues grinding.)* This afternoon. They took him to the
33   district station for questioning.
34   WOMAN/GOGO: It was bound to happen sooner or later.
35   TAKUNDA: That's what Uncle Gibson said.

1   WOMAN/GOGO: Your mother, how is she?

2   TAKUNDA: When I left, she was crying.

3   WOMAN/GOGO: And your mother's daughter?

4   TAKUNDA: She went to the bush to visit with her grandmother.

5   WOMAN/GOGO: But her grandmother is an old woman. What
6   can an old woman do?

7   TAKUNDA: I don't know. I think my mother's daughter is afraid.

8   WOMAN/GOGO: Did I ever tell you about Nyarai and the
9   leopard? *(MAN 1 and 2 enter.)* Nyarai lived west of the
10   Great City of Zimbabwe hundreds of years ago, before the
11   white winds moved south from Cairo. Nyarai loved
12   nothing more than to go into the bush to gather fruits
13   from the different trees he would find, a practice Nyarai's
14   father disapproved of.

15   MAN 1/NYARAI's FATHER: Nyarai. You mustn't go out into the
16   bush so far. There are animals out there, Nyarai. Animals
17   which can hurt you.

18   MAN 2/NYARAI: What type of animals, Baba?

19   MAN 1/NYARAI'S FATHER: Leopards. If one sees you alone, it
20   will eat you.

21   WOMAN/GOGO: Unfortunately, this warning did not deter
22   Nyarai for one day he went out into the bush much farther
23   than he had ever gone before. Suddenly, he heard a noise.
24   *(NYARAI stops, listens.)* Not ten meters from him, Nyarai
25   saw the largest, the fiercest-looking gazelle he had ever
26   seen in his life.

27   MAN 2/NYARAI: A leopard!

28   WOMAN/GOGO: The poor gazelle was more frightened of
29   Nyarai than Nyarai was of the gazelle. So they both stood,
30   frozen, staring at each other for what seemed like hours.
31   Finally, Nyarai couldn't stand it any longer and decided to
32   take positive action.

33   MAN 2/NYARAI *(Trembling)* Please Mr. Leopard, don't eat me.

34   WOMAN/GOGO: This frightened the poor gazelle so much that
35   he jumped, and with a loud —

1   MAN 1: Cooo!
2   WOMAN/GOGO: The gazelle was gone. Nyarai promptly ran in
3   the opposite direction and did not stop running until he
4   had made it back to his village.
5   MAN 2/NYARAI: Baba! Baba! You should have seen it! It was the
6   largest leopard I had ever seen in my life. We looked at
7   each other – this far away! *(He holds out his hands.)*
8   MAN 1/NYARAI'S FATHER: And you escaped!
9   MAN 2/NYARAI: I escaped, Baba, with my life.
10 WOMAN/GOGO: Nyarai's father promptly told the chief and all
11   the elders of his son's adventure and there was a
12   celebration to praise Nyarai's brush with death. That
13   night, around the fire, with the entire village in
14   attendance, the chief made Nyarai a hero.
15 MAN 1/CHIEF: Because, Nyarai, you have displayed courage in
16   the face of grave danger, and because you have displayed
17   bravery fitting that of a warrior, I, Chief Mangwende,
18   award you the title of honorary Shona Warrior. *(NYARAI*
19   *bows.)* Now tell us, Nyarai. . . what happened! What did
20   this fierce leopard look like?
21 MAN 2/NYARAI: Oh, Chief! He was a large one.
22 MAN 1/CHIEF: *(To the others)* Did you hear that! He was large!
23 MAN 2/NYARAI: *(Holding his hand up over his head)* Very large!
24 MAN 1/CHIEF: *(Pauses for a moment, thinks.)* A leopard that
25   stood taller than a man? He was a large one.
26 MAN 2/NYARAI: Oh yes! He was big and brown.
27 MAN 1/CHIEF: A brown leopard?
28 MAN 2/NYARAI: With a white underbelly. And horns. Mean-
29   looking horns that came out to here!
30 MAN 1/CHIEF: And tell me, brave Nyarai. What sort of sound
31   did this fierce brown leopard with the white underbelly
32   and horns make?
33 MAN 2/NYARAI: Oh, Chief. A most horrible sound. He looked at
34   me and said, coooo! Cooo!
35 WOMAN/GOGO: With this, the entire village started to laugh.

1   MAN 2/NYARAI: What's wrong? Why is everyone laughing?

2   MAN 1/CHIEF: Dear Nyarai, dear boy. That was no leopard you

3   saw. What you saw was a frightened gazelle.

4   TAKUNDA: So what does this have to do with my father?

5   WOMAN/GOGO: It's one of my favorites. Like it?

6   TAKUNDA: I came to you for help, Gogo.

7   WOMAN/GOGO: Then you didn't like the story.

8   TAKUNDA: I liked it but it had nothing to do with my father.

9   WOMAN/GOGO: Did you think of your father as I told it?

10 TAKUNDA: No.

11 WOMAN/GOGO: Then it served its purpose. Takunda, child.

12   These eyes of mine have witnessed many things. They've

13   seen my father and his father killed along with thousands

14   of other Shona warriors while trying to fight British guns

15   with spears. These eyes watched as my mother was beaten

16   until she could no longer move. They cried as my brothers

17   were taken away, one by one, and tortured, their bodies

18   dumped like a load of garbage at the edge of the *musha,*

19   and now you tell me my son has been taken away. With all

20   of this pain, all of the bloodshed and death, you should be

21   happy, my child, to spend a little time away, to enjoy a

22   simple story.

23 MAN 1/VENDOR: (*Entering*) *Mbambaira!* Get your hot

24   *Mbambaira!* Makes your tongue laugh and your tummy

25   dance! Ah! It's my friend. Tell me, little one. Have you

26   changed your mind about the *mbambaira?*

27 TAKUNDA: No!

28 MAN 1/VENDOR: Then perhaps I could interest you in some

29   firewood. I have a special today. Five cents a stick. Buy two

30   sticks, get one free.

31 TAKUNDA: Don't you have anything better to do? Than to sell

32   yams and firewood?

33 MAN 1/VENDOR: What do you propose I do? Join the

34   Musangano perhaps?

35 TAKUNDA: That would be something.

1   **MAN 1/VENDOR:** Or better yet, I could get a gun and wage
2   warfare. Join the boys in the bush and fight for
3   independence.
4   **TAKUNDA:** It would show you have courage.
5   **MAN 1/VENDOR:** It takes courage in times like these to laugh.
6   To sing a song and sell firewood when it would be much
7   easier to pick up a gun and fight.
8   **TAKUNDA:** Laughing and selling firewood is for the chicken-
9   hearted.
10   **MAN 1/VENDOR:** But that's where you're wrong, little one.
11   Anyone can pound a table and talk about rebellion. It's the
12   fashionable thing to do nowadays. But to laugh, to sing a
13   song while bearing your burden, to sell firewood in a place
14   of darkness and have hope, now that takes courage.
15   **TAKUNDA:** You are a coward.
16   **MAN 1/VENDOR:** And you, my dear, are a brat! *(TAKUNDA*
17   *moves to her MOTHER.)*
18   **WOMAN/MOTHER:** The first thing we must do is find another
19   place for the meetings.
20   **MAN 2/GIBSON:** Are you crazy?
21   **WOMAN/MOTHER:** They'll be watching the house. To meet
22   here would be too dangerous.
23   **MAN 2/GIBSON:** Forget the meetings altogether. Haven't they
24   caused enough trouble?
25   **WOMAN/MOTHER:** We mustn't let my husband's arrest deter us
26   from meeting. That's what they want to do, to frighten us.
27   **MAN 2/GIBSON:** Well they have succeeded with this Joe. Forget
28   those bloody meetings. At least until it cools down.
29   **WOMAN/MOTHER:** I refuse to allow the Rhodesian police to
30   intimidate me.
31   **MAN 2/GIBSON:** And what about me? What happens when they
32   return?
33   **WOMAN/MOTHER:** They will not return.
34   **MAN 2/GIBSON:** How can you be so sure?
35   **WOMAN/MOTHER:** That's not the way they operate. If they

1   wanted you, they would have taken you. But they're not

2   worried about you.

3 MAN 2/GIBSON: I am Alfred's brother.

4 WOMAN/MOTHER: And you think that makes you important?

5 MAN 2/GIBSON: Important enough to blacklist me.

6 WOMAN/MOTHER: Gibson.

7 MAN 2/GIBSON: It's true. Every day I stand in line at the

8   unemployment exchange. A job comes up for a driver,

9   they give me the address, me and another man go for the

10   job. The man who does the hiring, he looks at my card. He

11   says, "Ah, I see you are a member of the ZANU party." Are

12   you related to Alfred Chikomba?" I say, "Yes, Baz, he and I

13   are brothers." The man smiles, then gives the job to the

14   other man.

15 WOMAN/MOTHER: I don't believe that.

16 MAN 2/GIBSON: It's true. I'm out of work because of Alfred. I

17   can't bring my family here because of Alfred and if I stay,

18   I may be arrested because of him.

19 MAN 1/SHINGAI: I went down to the station. They said they

20   were holding him for questioning.

21 WOMAN/MOTHER: Did they say when they were to release

22   him? *(SHINGAI shakes his head no.)*

23 TAKUNDA: They're not going to release Baba?

24 WOMAN/ MOTHER: They'll release him, Taku.

25 MAN 1/SHINGAI: I think I know what the police were after.

26 MAN 2/GIBSON: What?

27 MAN 1/SHINGAI: The roster. Where is it?

28 MAN 2/GIBSON: What roster?

29 MAN 1/SHINGAI: The roster with the names of the others who

30   attended the meetings. Where is it?

31 MAN 2/GIBSON: I know nothing about a roster.

32 MAN 1/SHINGAI: Please, Gibson. Now is not the time to be coy.

33   The police will be back. Now give me the roster.

34 MAN 2/GIBSON: I don't know what you're talking about.

35 MAN 1/SHINGAI: You're Alfred's brother.

1 MAN 2/GIBSON: So? You think he confides in me?

2 MAN 1/SHINGAI: Alfred knew he was to be arrested. I seriously
3   doubt if he failed to make arrangements.

4 MAN 2/GIBSON: Well he didn't make those arrangements with
5   me.

6 MAN 1/SHINGAI: That roster is the property of this chapter of
7   the Musangano and while Alfred is in jail, I am in charge.
8   Failure to turn it over could bring you much more trouble
9   than I know you're willing to face.

10 MAN 1/GIBSON: And I'm telling you I know nothing about your
11   bloody roster. Alfred does not trust me. He tells me nothing
12   about his political activities and that suits me just fine.

13 MAN 1/SHINGAI: *Brati* shit, man!

14 WOMAN/MOTHER: He's telling the truth, Shingai. Alfred does
15   not trust him.

16 MAN 1/SHINGAI: A man does not trust his own brother? Alfred
17   assured me he would make arrangements. If not with his
18   brother, then who?

19 WOMAN/MOTHER: Me.

20 MAN 1/SHINGAI: You? His wife? He trusted his wife over his
21   brother?

22 WOMAN/MOTHER: Stranger things have been known to
23   happen.

24 MAN 2/GIBSON: There, you see? You're like a dog, Shingai,
25   always barking up the wrong tree. *(He leaves.)*

26 MAN 1/SHINGAI: So. Where is it?

27 WOMAN/MOTHER: Hidden.

28 MAN 1/SHINGAI: Hidden where? *(Pause)* Sarah, Alfred may
29   have trusted you, but you're still a woman and women
30   have no place in the struggle. Now give me the roster. I'll
31   need it to contact the others.

32 WOMAN/MOTHER: I'll contact the others.

33 MAN 1/SHINGAI: You're a woman.

34 WOMAN/MOTHER: That will not prevent me from contacting
35   the others.

1　MAN 1/SHINGAI: You have no right to keep that roster and no
2　　right to refuse me.
3　WOMAN/MOTHER: Alfred told me that if anything happened
4　　to him, not to give the roster to anyone.
5　MAN 1/SHINGAI: I don't believe this. It's like a joke. Like a
6　　bloody nightmare. OK. You want to act like an
7　　Englishwoman and play these games. . .fine. However, I
8　　hope you are willing to accept the consequences when this
9　　entire thing explodes. The blood of others will be on your
10　　hands. *(He leaves.)*
11　WOMAN/MOTHER: Taku?
12　TAKUNDA: Momma?
13　WOMAN/MOTHER: You think I should have given it to him?
14　TAKUNDA: I don't know.
15　WOMAN/MOTHER: I don't know, either. So much is happening
16　　so fast.
17　TAKUNDA: You ever hear the story of Nyarai and the leopard?
18　WOMAN/MOTHER: No.
19　TAKUNDA: Many years ago,, in a village west of the Great City
20　　of Zimbabwe, lived a boy named Nyarai who loved
21　　nothing more than to go into the bush to gather fruits
22　　from the different trees he would find, a practice Nyarai's
23　　father disapproved of. *(She walks away from*
24　　*WOMAN/MOTHER and begins to sing.)* **Sarura wako**
25　　**kadeya deya nendoro chena.** *(She stops and listens.)* **Sarura**
26　　**wako. . .** *(WOMAN/CHIPO joins in.)*
27　TAKUNDA and WOMAN/CHIPO: *(Singing)* **Kadeya deya**
28　　**nendoro chena.** *(TAKUNDA and CHIPO stop and listen for a*
29　　*response.)*
30　TAKUNDA: **Sarura wako. . .**
31　BOTH: **Kadeya deya nendoro chena.**
32　TAKUNDA: So. Where do you think he is?
33　WOMAN/CHIPO: He's here somewhere. I'm sure of it.
34　TAKUNDA: *(Singing)* **Sarura wako. . .**
35　BOTH: **Kadeya deya nendoro chena.** *(MAN 2/FUNGI appears.)*

347

1   TAKUNDA: There you are. I thought for a moment you had
2   forgotten.
3   MAN 2/FUNGI: I had not forgotten.
4   TAKUNDA: You took so long to get here. Perhaps I've changed
5   my mind.
6   MAN 2/FUNGI: Takunda, I must speak with you.
7   TAKUNDA: You want to carry me off to some secret place?
8   MAN 2/FUNGI: Please. *(THEY move away from WOMAN/CHIPO*
9   *as she starts to sing the "Sarura wako" song under the*
10   *following scene.)* Takunda. . .the *chuma*, I need it back.
11   TAKUNDA: Oh? You no longer think I'm pretty? Or have you
12   found another *musikana*?
13   MAN 2/FUNGI: There's another *chuma* I want to give you. But
14   that one, I need it back.
15   TAKUNDA: What's this?
16   MAN 2/FUNGI: Please, Takunda. The other one is much larger,
17   prettier.
18   TAKUNDA: Well. You bring me the other *chuma* and I'll return
19   this one. *(MAN 1 appears as FUNGI's FRIEND.)*
20   WOMAN/CHIPO: *(As she sees the FRIEND)* What's this?
21   MAN 1/FRIEND: Fungi! You get it?
22   MAN 2/FUNGI: Please Takunda. You don't understand.
23   MAN 1/FRIEND: Fungi!
24   MAN 2/FUNGI: *(To FRIEND)* **Ahhh, iwe kani!** *(To TAKUNDA.)*
25   Takunda, please!
26   WOMAN/CHIPO: Takunda?
27   MAN 2/FUNGI: The other one is much prettier.
28   MAN 1/FRIEND: Will you get it and let's go!
29   MAN 2/FUNGI: Give me that one. Come on. I'll give you the
30   other one. Tomorrow. *(TAKUNDA begins to remove the*
31   chuma.)
32   TAKUNDA: Tomorrow?
33   MAN 2/FUNGI: I promise you.
34   WOMAN/CHIPO: Takunda? What's going on?
35   MAN 1/FRIEND: Get it!

1 **WOMAN/CHIPO:** Takunda! *(TAKUNDA hands the* chuma *to*
2   *FUNGI.)*
3 **MAN 2/FUNGI:** I'm sorry.
4 **MAN 1/FRIEND:** Sorry Ferrari, let's get out of here. *(FUNGI and*
5   *his FRIEND leave.)*
6 **WOMAN/CHIPO:** Damn it!
7 **TAKUNDA:** Chipo?
8 **WOMAN/CHIPO:** Come on.
9 **TAKUNDA:** What happened?
10 **WOMAN/CHIPO:** Just come with me, will you?
11 **TAKUNDA:** Where? Chipo? Where are we going? Chipo? *(They*
12   *walk to another part of the stage.)* What place is this?
13 **WOMAN/CHIPO:** It's my secret place. My *bako.* I come here
14   sometimes to be alone.
15 **TAKUNDA:** So why are we here?
16 **WOMAN/CHIPO:** I thought maybe you needed a place to be alone.
17 **TAKUNDA:** What happened with Fungi?
18 **WOMAN/CHIPO:** Takunda, they say your father was arrested.
19 **TAKUNDA:** So?
20 **WOMAN/CHIPO:** So was he?
21 **TAKUNDA:** They took him for questioning.
22 **WOMAN/CHIPO:** When?
23 **TAKUNDA:** Yesterday.
24 **WOMAN/CHIPO:** Takunda. . .why didn't you tell me?
25 **TAKUNDA:** I haven't had the chance.
26 **WOMAN/CHIPO:** Everybody in school has been talking about it.
27 **TAKUNDA:** I don't know why. They're going to release him.
28 **WOMAN/CHIPO:** Takunda, you should have told me!
29 **TAKUNDA:** When? I haven't seen you. When was I supposed to
30   tell you?
31 **WOMAN/CHIPO:** I don't know.
32 **TAKUNDA:** Anyway, what's the big deal? I told you, they're
33   going to release him.
34 **WOMAN/CHIPO:** When?
35 **TAKUNDA:** Soon.

1   WOMAN/CHIPO: Did they say that, Takunda?

2   TAKUNDA: Not in those words. But they're going to release him.

3   WOMAN/CHIPO: I hope so.

4   TAKUNDA: What's this with Fungi? You think that's the reason

5   he took his *chuma* back?

6   WOMAN/CHIPO: I don't know.

7   TAKUNDA: Because of my father?

8   WOMAN/CHIPO: You can't try to figure boys out. You'll go mad

9   like SaMuchena the Vendor.

10   TAKUNDA: He's afraid. Afraid because my father was arrested.

11   WOMAN/CHIPO: Will you forget about Fungi! He's *kabenzi*. A

12   baboon. If he cared about you, he wouldn't let something

13   like this deter him. He's a jellyfish, Takunda. A weak,

14   spineless jellyfish.

15   TAKUNDA: He said he wanted to give me another *chuma*. One

16   much larger, and prettier.

17   WOMAN/CHIPO: Well, if I were you, I wouldn't hold my breath.

18   TAKUNDA: God. He's a jellyfish.

19   WOMAN/CHIPO: I could have told you that a long time ago.

20   *(Pause)*

21   TAKUNDA: This is a good secret place you have here.

22   WOMAN/CHIPO: Thank you.

23   TAKUNDA: You can see out, but no one can see in.

24   WOMAN/CHIPO: You can come back if you like. Whenever you

25   want. We both can come. We can meet here and talk. . .

26   TAKUNDA: You and I?

27   WOMAN/CHIPO: If you want.

28   TAKUNDA: I wouldn't want anyone else here.

29   WOMAN/CHIPO: Whatever you want.

30   TAKUNDA: Can we have a signal?

31   WOMAN/CHIPO: A what?

32   TAKUNDA: A signal, so we'll know when to meet.

33   WOMAN/CHIPO: We don't need a signal.

34   TAKUNDA: This is so close, you'll probably hear it over the

35   entire area. How about this? Coooo! Coooo!

1   WOMAN/CHIPO: You sound like a frightened gazelle.

2   TAKUNDA: That's the idea. If you hear it, that means I'm here

3   and you're to come immediately. And if I hear it, I'll come.

4   Try it. Coooo!

5   WOMAN/CHIPO: I'm not doing that. It's stupid.

6   TAKUNDA: Come on, Chipo. Coooo!

7   WOMAN/CHIPO: Coo.

8   TAKUNDA: You can do better than that! Coooo!

9   WOMAN/CHIPO: Coo.

10   TAKUNDA: Coooo!

11   WOMAN/CHIPO: Coooo!

12   TAKUNDA: That's it. Coooo!

13   WOMAN/CHIPO: Coooo!

14   TAKUNDA: Good. Whenever we want to meet, we'll give the

15   signal.

16   WOMAN/CHIPO: No matter what time?

17   TAKUNDA: No matter what time. Day or night. Deal?

18   WOMAN/CHIPO: Deal.

19   TAKUNDA: Jellyfish.

20   WOMAN/CHIPO: Damn jellyfish.

21   TAKUNDA: Chipo?

22   WOMAN/CHIPO: Yeah?

23   TAKUNDA: Are you afraid?

24   WOMAN/CHIPO: Afraid of what?

25   TAKUNDA: The police.

26   WOMAN/CHIPO: Don't make me laugh.

27   TAKUNDA: You're not afraid of the police?

28   WOMAN/CHIPO: I wish Mapurisa would try to bother me. I'd

29   give them what for and why.

30   TAKUNDA: No!

31   WOMAN/CHIPO: Yes! I'd fight them with my fists and with my

32   feet.

33   TAKUNDA: Chipo!

34   WOMAN/CHIPO: I'd kick them in their *machende.*

35   TAKUNDA: (*Grabbing her crotch*) Oooooooooh!

1   WOMAN/CHIPO: And then pluck out their eyes!

2   TAKUNDA: (*Grabbing her eyes*) Ooooooooo!

3   WOMAN/CHIPO: One thing you have to learn about me,
4   Takunda. I am afraid of no one.

5   MAN 2/FATHER'S VOICE: Chipo! *Uri kupi!*

6   WOMAN/CHIPO: Oh God, except my father!

7   MAN 2/FATHER'S VOICE: Chipo!

8   WOMAN/CHIPO: I've got to go or he's going to kill me.

9   TAKUNDA: I'll see you tomorrow, Chipo.

10   MAN 2/FATHER'S VOICE: Chipo!

11   WOMAN/CHIPO: OK. Tomorrow! (*CHIPO runs off.*)

12   TAKUNDA: And I shall go home to see my father. (*TAKUNDA
13   moves to MAN 2 who has his back to her.*) **Baba?** (*MAN 2 turns.
14   HE is packing a suitcase.*) Uncle Gibson. Is Baba home?

15   MAN 2/GIBSON: No he's not. And he's not likely to come home
16   either.

17   TAKUNDA: What are you doing? Are you leaving?

18   MAN 2/GIBSON: Tell your mother I'll contact her the first
19   chance I get.

20   TAKUNDA: Momma!

21   MAN 2/GIBSON: Don't call her now!

22   TAKUNDA: Uncle Gibson's leaving!

23   MAN 2/GIBSON: Shut up!

24   TAKUNDA: Momma! (*WOMAN/MOTHER enters.*)

25   WOMAN/MOTHER: Gibson?

26   MAN 2/GIBSON: I'm sorry Sarah, but I have no choice.

27   WOMAN/MOTHER: Is this how you show your gratitude? By
28   leaving?

29   MAN 2/GIBSON: Don't talk to me about gratitude. Gratitude
30   has not gotten me a job and gratitude will not bring my
31   family here. I have a wife, Sarah. I have two children. I
32   must provide for them any way I can. Everything else
33   becomes secondary.

34   WOMAN/MOTHER: How is leaving going to help you provide
35   for your family?

1   MAN 2/GIBSON: I'm going *kumusha*. Back to the village.

2   WOMAN/MOTHER: And do what, Gibson? There are no jobs

3   there. There's no money.

4   MAN 2/GIBSON: I don't plan to stay there.

5   WOMAN/MOTHER: Exactly what do you plan to do?

6   MAN 2/GIBSON: I'm bringing my family here.

7   WOMAN/MOTHER: To this flat?

8   MAN 2/GIBSON: I know of another flat, not far from here. We

9   will live there.

10 WOMAN/MOTHER: But how, Gibson? By what means do you

11   plan to accomplish all of this? You don't have money.

12 MAN 2/GIBSON: I have my ways.

13 WOMAN/MOTHER: You need money! You need money to

14   transport a family from the village to here. And you need

15   money to let a flat.

16 MAN 2/GIBSON: I have money.

17 WOMAN/MOTHER: Where'd you get it?

18 MAN 2/GIBSON: What are you now? The police? You must

19   know where everything comes from?

20 WOMAN/MOTHER: I want to know where you got the money.

21 MAN 2/GIBSON: You're worse than Mapurisa. *(MAN 1 enters as*

22   *SHINGAI.)*

23 MAN 1/SHINGAI: I'd like to hear the answer to that myself,

24   Gibson. Where'd you get the money?

25 MAN 2/GIBSON: None of your bloody business, that's where.

26   You people have caused me enough heartache.

27 MAN 1/SHINGAI: I'm sorry about the roster, I was mistaken.

28 MAN 2/GIBSON: You're always mistaken.

29 MAN 1/SHINGAI: I'm sorry, but we need to know where you got

30   the money.

31 MAN 2/GIBSON: Why?

32 WOMAN/MOTHER: There's been talk, Gibson.

33 MAN 1/SHINGAI: About an informant.

34 MAN 2/GIBSON: There's always talk about an informant. What

35   does it have to do with me?

1 WOMAN/MOTHER: We suspect that the informant was
2   someone close to Alfred.
3 MAN 2/GIBSON: You suspect it was me, is that it?
4 MAN 1/SHINGAI: All we need to know is where you got the
5   money.
6 MAN 2/GIBSON: I'm not the person you should be worried
7   about. Once Alfred gives the police the names of the
8   others, there'll be more raids, more arrests. That's what
9   you should be worried about.
10 WOMAN/MOTHER: My husband is not the subject here. The
11   subject is you.
12 MAN 1/SHINGAI: And where you got the money.
13 MAN 2/GIBSON: Am I on trial? Is that it?
14 MAN 1/SHINGAI: We cannot allow you to leave until you tell us.
15 MAN 2/GIBSON: A friend of mine owed money. A while back, I
16   made him a loan. He just repaid it. Satisfied?
17 WOMAN/MOTHER: Why haven't you mentioned it before now?
18 MAN 1/SHINGAI: What's his name?
19 MAN 2/GIBSON: You don't know him. He's not from this area.
20 MAN 1/SHINGAI: I want to know his name and I want to know
21   where he lives.
22 MAN 2/GIBSON: Why?
23 MAN 1/SHINGAI: To contact him. To check your story.
24 MAN 2/GIBSON: This is absurd. I don't have to answer to you.
25 MAN 1/SHINGAI: You will answer. One way or the other. People
26   are getting edgy. They're afraid. There's an informant
27   here somewhere and people are anxious to know who it is.
28   I wonder what would happen if they found out it was you?
29 MAN 2/GIBSON: Why must you do this to me? Alfred brought
30   this trouble upon himself. All I ever wanted to do was to
31   provide for my family. To live like a normal human being.
32   To be happy.
33 MAN 1/SHINGAI: Then stop your lying and tell us the truth.
34   Where'd you get the money?
35 MAN 2/GIBSON: I'm not the informant.

1 WOMAN/MOTHER: Then where'd you get the money?

2 MAN 2/GIBSON: Send the child away.

3 WOMAN/MOTHER: The child stays. It was her father who was

4   arrested. She has a right to know.

5 MAN 2/GIBSON: I didn't get the money by informing.

6 WOMAN/MOTHER: The child stays. *(Pause)*

7 MAN 2/GIBSON: There's a thief. He's been working the houses

8   in the area. I've been working with him.

9 WOMAN/MOTHER: You are the burglar?

10 MAN 2/GIBSON: I am not the burglar. Someone else does the

11   actual stealing. All I do is watch and give a signal if

12   someone comes.

13 WOMAN/MOTHER: But you have stolen from your own people.

14 MAN 2/GIBSON: It wasn't me who did the stealing! It was

15   someone else!

16 WOMAN/MOTHER: But you are the accomplice.

17 MAN 2/GIBSON: What else was I supposed to do? I'd rather

18   work but they won't allow it. I apply for a work permit,

19   they tell me I must first find work. I look for work, they tell

20   me I must have a work permit. I do what I can with what

21   they give me and what they give me is nothing. Perhaps

22   you can suggest a better way for me to make a living.

23 WOMAN/MOTHER: You didn't have to steal. You have food and

24   a place to live.

25 MAN 2/GIBSON: But I also have a family. Can't you understand

26   that? I have a wife, I have a son, I have a daughter. My

27   daughter is Takunda's age. Your cousin, Taku, your cousin

28   you've never even met. She's exactly like you, only she

29   attends a school at which they teach her nothing. For this

30   nothing, she has to walk six kilometers a day. When she

31   comes home, there are no chairs or tables, no fine

32   tapestries to sit on. There's one large room, empty except

33   for a clay pot and a plow. With the plow, she helps her

34   mother try to make seeds sprout in the sand and when the

35   seeds don't sprout, the pot remains empty. So yes, I'm the

1   burglar. I've stolen radios from people who have
2   refrigerators full of food. But I am not the informant. You
3   will have to search elsewhere for him.
4   WOMAN/MOTHER: I'm ashamed for you, Gibson.
5   MAN 2/GIBSON: Keep your pity, I don't want it. If you want to
6   give me something, give me money.
7   MAN 1/SHINGAI: You said you were leaving. Go.
8   MAN 2/GIBSON: If you were wise, you'd leave also. Both of you.
9   It's going to heat up around here when they get through to
10   your husband.
11 WOMAN/MOTHER: My husband is not an informant.
12 MAN 2/GIBSON: I never said he was. But you know as well as I
13   do what they're going to do to him, if they haven't already
14   done it. No man can survive that. I don't care how strong
15   he is. *(MAN 2/GIBSON moves off.)*
16 WOMAN/MOTHER: Alfred will never inform.
17 MAN 1/SHINGAI: We can't be too sure. Where's the roster?
18 WOMAN/MOTHER: Hidden inside my grandmother's *calabash.*
19 MAN 1 SHINGAI: Give it to me.
20 WOMAN/MOTHER: No.
21 MAN 1/SHINGAI: They'll be back, Sarah, looking for it. Give it
22   to me so I can keep it.
23 WOMAN/MOTHER: Alfred told me to give it to no one.
24 MAN 1/SHINGAI: You're being stupid, woman. Don't you
25   realize that Alfred is probably talking to the police at this
26   moment, telling them everything they want to know?
27 WOMAN/MOTHER: He will tell them nothing!
28 MAN 1/SHINGAI: For his sake, you better hope he tells them
29   everything, because that's the only way you will ever see
30   him again. Now give me the roster.
31 WOMAN/MOTHER: I'm sorry, Shingai, but I think you should
32   leave. You're no longer welcomed here.
33 TAKUNDA: *(Moving off)* Cooo! Cooo! *(She pauses, waits for*
34   *response.)* Coooo! Coooo!
35 WOMAN/CHIPO: Taku?

1 TAKUNDA: Over here. What happened to you in school today?

2 WOMAN/CHIPO: My parents wouldn't let me go.

3 TAKUNDA: Why not?

4 WOMAN/CHIPO: They said it was too dangerous.

5 TAKUNDA: Dangerous?

6 WOMAN/CHIPO: They're afraid of a police raid. They say that
7   some students are running off and joining the boys in the
8   bush.

9 TAKUNDA: That's silly.

10 WOMAN/CHIPO: Hey, if it gets me out of English lessons, it's
11   OK with me.

12 TAKUNDA: I saw Fungi today.

13 WOMAN/CHIPO: And what did Mr. Jellyfish have to say for
14   himself?

15 TAKUNDA: Nothing. He was with his friend. He pretended as if
16   he didn't see me.

17 WOMAN/CHIPO: Jellyfish.

18 TAKUNDA: You know what I think? I think Fungi gave his
19   *chuma* to his friend. *(CHIPO laughs, covers her mouth.)* It
20   wouldn't surprise me. They're together all the time.

21 WOMAN/CHIPO: And that would explain everything.

22 TAKUNDA: Wouldn't surprise me one bit.

23 WOMAN/CHIPO: Has your father been released?

24 TAKUNDA: No.

25 WOMAN/CHIPO: It's been three days now.

26 TAKUNDA: I know how long it's been.

27 WOMAN/CHIPO: Aren't you worried?

28 TAKUNDA: No. My mother says they have no basis for his
29   retention. She says they now have to wait for the most
30   opportune time to minimize political embarrassment.

31 WOMAN/CHIPO: My father says the shit's going to hit the fan
32   soon.

33 TAKUNDA: What does he mean, the shit's going to hit the fan?

34 WOMAN/CHIPO: Once the police get the names of the others
35   who attended the meetings.

1 TAKUNDA: But my father is the only one with those names.

2 WOMAN/CHIPO: Ah, Takunda. Surely he'll give them to them.

3 TAKUNDA: But he won't.

4 WOMAN/CHIPO: Takunda ... you don't know what they do to
5   people.

6 TAKUNDA: I don't care what they do to people. My father is
7   strong.

8 WOMAN/CHIPO: And my father says they'll get it out of him,
9   one way or the other. And when they do, look out buddy
10   boy.

11 TAKUNDA: What's this you're talking? You're just like all the
12   rest of them. Like Fungi and Uncle Gibson. You're afraid.

13 WOMAN/CHIPO: I'm not afraid, Takunda.

14 TAKUNDA: You don't come to school anymore, I don't see you
15   or talk to you, you're afraid.

16 WOMAN/CHIPO: I'm not afraid. I'm here now, aren't I?

17 TAKUNDA: Now. Here in your secret place. Your big-time secret
18   place where no one can see us. That's why you brought me
19   here, isn't it? You want to be my friend but you don't want
20   anyone to know. So you bring me here to your secret place.
21   Your big-time, nowhere, secret place.

22 WOMAN/CHIPO: I brought you here because I wanted to share
23   it with you, I never brought anyone here before. Not David
24   when he gave me his *chuma*, not my brothers or sister, no
25   one. I feel good when I'm here. I wanted you to feel the
26   same way. I'm sorry. *(She leaves.)*

27 MAN 1/VENDOR: *Mbambaira!* Get your hot *mbambaira!* Makes
28   your tongue laugh and your tummy dance. *(He sees*
29   *TAKUNDA.)* What do you want?

30 TAKUNDA: A yam, please.

31 MAN 1/VENDOR: That'll be fifty cents.

32 TAKUNDA: I don't have fifty cents.

33 MAN 1/VENDOR: Then how do you expect to get a yam?

34 TAKUNDA: Can I pay you next week?

35 MAN 1/VENDOR: Sure. No problem. You pay me next week, you

1   get a yam next week. You want a yam now, you pay me fifty

2   cents.

3 TAKUNDA: But I don't have fifty cents.

4 MAN 1/VENDOR: Then go about your way. This isn't some

5   Soviet institution. *Mbambaira!* Get your hot *mbambaira!*

6   *(TAKUNDA starts to leave.)* Wait. Come here. You're not

7   giving me some line of *hokum?* You really don't have fifty

8   cents?

9 TAKUNDA: No.

10 MAN 1/VENDOR: What happened? That rich papa of yours cut

11   off your allowance?

12 TAKUNDA: No.

13 MAN 1/VENDOR: And why aren't you in school? You quit or

14   something?

15 TAKUNDA: No.

16 MAN 1/VENDOR: Is that the only word in your vocabulary? No?

17 TAKUNDA: No.

18 MAN 1/VENDOR: *Iwe!* Look, if I give you one of these nice hot

19   yams, what day you going to pay me?

20 TAKUNDA: What day you want me to pay you?

21 MAN 1/VENDOR: The day you get the money.

22 TAKUNDA: Sunday?

23 MAN 1/VENDOR: You going to have fifty cents come Sunday?

24 TAKUNDA: I'll get it.

25 MAN 1/VENDOR: And you'll bring it here and give it to me?

26 TAKUNDA: If you give me a yam.

27 MAN 1/VENDOR: You're not going to turn British on me, are you?

28 TAKUNDA: No. I'll keep my word.

29 MAN 1/VENDOR: It takes courage to be a vendor in times like

30   these. More courage than it takes to stand on a stump and

31   philosophize. Here. I will look for you Sunday.

32 TAKUNDA: Thank you.

33 MAN 1/VENDOR: Now go. Enjoy your yam. It was purchased on

34   the account of kindness. *(TAKUNDA moves to WOMAN/*

35   *GOGO.)*

1 WOMAN/GOGO: Taku?

2 TAKUNDA: Gogo.

3 WOMAN/GOGO: What news?

4 TAKUNDA: None good.

5 WOMAN/GOGO: Then my son has not been released.

6 TAKUNDA: No.

7 WOMAN/GOGO: But that is good news. It means he is still alive.

8 TAKUNDA: Uncle Gibson has left.

9 WOMAN/GOGO: That's not surprising. Rabbits usually run

10   when there's a noise in the bush.

11 TAKUNDA: He went *kumusha* for his wife and children. He's

12   bringing them to the city.

13 WOMAN/GOGO: Gibson has money?

14 TAKUNDA: Yes, Gogo.

15 WOMAN/GOGO: He's been stealing again?

16 TAKUNDA: He got it from a friend. A debt the friend repaid.

17 WOMAN/GOGO: You never lied to me before, Taku. Why lie to

18   me now? *(Pause. TAKUNDA lowers her head.)* How is my

19   son's wife?

20 TAKUNDA: She is well.

21 WOMAN/GOGO: And my son's daughter?

22 TAKUNDA: She is well, also.

23 WOMAN/GOGO: Then why did she come all the way here to

24   visit an old woman?

25 TAKUNDA: No reason. Just to visit.

26 WOMAN/GOGO: I went to the market today. Do you know what

27   I saw?

28 TAKUNDA: No, Gogo. What did you see?

29 WOMAN/GOGO: I saw an old man, much older than myself. He

30   was on his way to the market also. On his back, he carried

31   a large, awkward bundle of sticks. It made him walk with

32   his chest close to the ground. As I passed, he was forced to

33   stop and readjust his burden before continuing his

34   journey. Now tell me. Why have you come?

35 TAKUNDA: There is talk.

1   WOMAN/GOGO: There will always be talk.

2   TAKUNDA: This talk is about Baba.

3   WOMAN/GOGO: Remember I told you about Nyarai and how
4   his leopard became a gazelle? The morning after the
5   celebration, the chief's dagger disappeared. It was a
6   beautiful dagger, the chief's favorite. The chief let it be
7   known that if the dagger was returned immediately, no
8   one would suffer consequences, but if the dagger was not
9   returned, the person who took it would be beheaded. The
10   dagger was not returned and the entire village began to
11   speculate on who could have taken it.

12   MAN 1: I know I didn't take it so it must have been you!

13   MAN 2: I didn't take it. I was with my wife at the time, a fact she
14   will swear to. It wasn't me, so it must have been you!

15   WOMAN/GOGO: That's when Tambo Muvimi came back from
16   his hunt.

17   MAN 1 and 2: Tambo Muvimi!

18   MAN 1: It must have been him! Why else does he leave so early
19   in the morning?

20   MAN 2: And return so late at night? Because he doesn't want
21   anyone to notice him, that's why!

22   MAN 1: And notice how he never speaks to anyone? He has to be
23   the guilty party.

24   MAN 2: I have an idea!

25   MAN 1: What?

26   MAN 2: In the morning, you and I will go to his hut.

27   MAN 1: I'm listening. . .

28   MAN 2: We will confront Tambo Muvimi with what we know,
29   then beat him until he tells us where he has hidden the
30   dagger.

31   MAN 1: Yes?

32   MAN 2: Then you and I will return it to the chief.

33   MAN 1: Yes?

34   MAN 2: We will be heroes and collect a fat reward.

35   MAN 1: Yes, I like it. Good idea.

1 WOMAN/GOGO: But the next morning, when they went to
2   Tambo Muvimi's hut, Tambo Muvimi was already gone.
3 MAN 2: Dammit! We slept too late. Why didn't you wake me?
4 MAN 1: You were supposed to wake me!
5 MAN 2: We have to tell the chief.
6 MAN 1: No, let's wait and find the dagger ourselves. The reward
7   will be larger!
8 MAN 2: I say we tell him.
9 MAN 1: No!
10 MAN 2: We must!
11 MAN 1: Try and you'll get the beating of your life.
12 MAN 2: By who? You and that ox you have for a wife?
13 MAN 1: Ox!
14 MAN 2: That's right. She's an ox! A big, fat ox!
15 MAN 1: I'm warning you!
16 WOMAN/GOGO: That's when the chief found his dagger. It was
17   in its sheath, inside his hut, right where he had left it. He
18   had put it there and forgotten it. Guess what they said
19   about Tambo Muvimi then?
20 MAN 2: Look how industrious he is, rising so early every
21   morning to go hunting.
22 MAN 1: And persistent. He doesn't return until late at night.
23 MAN 2: And notice how he keeps to himself and never speaks
24   to anyone else? I've never seen a man so modest.
25 MAN 1: Persistent.
26 MAN 2: And industrious.
27 WOMAN/GOGO: You see, Taku, in times of crisis, a man's
28   virtues are turned into faults.
29 TAKUNDA: Only his virtues?
30 WOMAN/GOGO: Only his virtues. If a man has no virtues, in times
31   of crisis, he is ignored like a fly on a man's arm is ignored
32   when that man is stalking a leopard. The more virtuous the
33   man, the more faults they will find in times of crisis. Now tell
34   me, what faults have they found with my son?
35 TAKUNDA: They are afraid he will inform.

1   WOMAN/GOGO: One thing you can be sure about your father,
2   Takunda. He will never inform.
3   TAKUNDA: *(Moving off)* Cooo! Coooo! Chipo? Chipo! Come on,
4   Chipo. Please, I'm sorry. Coooo! Cooo! Cooo! *(MAN 2 enters*
5   *as FUNGI.)* Fungi! What are you doing here?
6   MAN 2/FUNGI: I heard a noise. What are you doing here in this
7   place in the dark?
8   TAKUNDA: Nothing. Go away.
9   MAN 2/FUNGI: You were calling Chipo?
10   TAKUNDA: I was calling no one. Now go.
11   MAN 2/FUNGI: I heard you, Taku.
12   TAKUNDA: Your ears must've been playing tricks on you.
13   MAN 2/FUNGI: I know you don't like me, Taku.
14   TAKUNDA: How could you guess?
15   MAN 2/FUNGI: I'm sorry about what happened.
16   TAKUNDA: Just go away, Fungi, please.
17   MAN 2/FUNGI: I want you to know that it was not my choice. It
18   was my father's decision.
19   TAKUNDA: And is it your father who makes you look past me at
20   school?
21   MAN 2/FUNGI: I look past you because you look at me with
22   knives in your eyes.
23   TAKUNDA: How do you expect me to look at you? After you lie?
24   After you make a fool of me in front of Chipo and your
25   friends.
26   MAN 2/FUNGI: I'm sorry. I told you, it was my father.
27   TAKUNDA: Then perhaps it is your father I should be talking to
28   instead of you. *(FUNGI produces the* chuma *and offers it to*
29   *TAKUNDA.)*
30   MAN 2/FUNGI: Here.
31   TAKUNDA: What you expect me to do with that?
32   MAN 2/FUNGI: You want it?
33   TAKUNDA: You said you were going to give me another one.
34   MAN 2/FUNGI: This is all I have. But it comes from my heart.
35   I'd like you to wear it.

1   TAKUNDA: For how long, Fungi? Until your friend tells you
2   otherwise?

3   MAN 2/FUNGI: I won't take it back. I promise.

4   TAKUNDA: Yeah, right.

5   MAN 2/FUNGI: I swear to you, Takunda.

6   TAKUNDA: You willing to apologize to me?

7   MAN 2/FUNGI: Yes. I apologize. I'm sorry.

8   TAKUNDA: You willing to apologize in front of Chipo and your
9   friends at school?

10 MAN 2/FUNGI: In front of the entire world, if necessary.

11 TAKUNDA: In front of your father?

12 MAN 2/FUNGI: Takunda. . .

13 TAKUNDA: Are you willing to apologize to me in front of your
14   father?

15 MAN 2/FUNGI: You know I can't do that.

16 TAKUNDA: Then I can't take your *chuma*.

17 MAN 2/FUNGI: Not in front of my father.

18 TAKUNDA: Just go, Fungi.

19 MAN 2/FUNGI: Please, Taku.

20 TAKUNDA: Go!

21 MAN 2/FUNGI: If you're waiting for Chipo, you're wasting your
22   time. She's gone.

23 TAKUNDA: What?

24 MAN 2/FUNGI: She came home, her family had packed, then
25   they fled. Apparently they are afraid of much the same
26   thing my father is.

27 WOMAN/MOTHER: Taku? Takunda! Where have you been,
28   child? I've been worried sick about you!

29 TAKUNDA: I was out walking.

30 WOMAN/MOTHER: Takunda, it's late.

31 TAKUNDA: I was walking. Why are all the lights out?

32 WOMAN/MOTHER: Don't ask questions. Just come inside, keep
33   quiet!

34 TAKUNDA: I need fifty cents, Momma.

35 WOMAN/MOTHER: For what?

1   TAKUNDA: For school.

2   WOMAN/MOTHER: Takunda, you know there's no money in

3   the house. Did you see anyone while you were out there?

4   TAKUNDA: Anyone like who?

5   WOMAN/MOTHER: People. Did you see any people around the

6   house?

7   TAKUNDA: No. Can we turn the lights on?

8   WOMAN/MOTHER: Leave the lights as they are.

9   TAKUNDA: How did the windows get broken?

10   WOMAN/MOTHER: Children. They were throwing stones.

11   TAKUNDA: They broke all the windows?

12   WOMAN/MOTHER: You ask too many questions for a little girl.

13   Come here. Sit by me. I want you to hold me.

14   TAKUNDA: Baba has not been released?

15   WOMAN/MOTHER: No.

16   TAKUNDA: And Uncle Gibson is gone?

17   WOMAN/MOTHER: He's gone. And our workers have not

18   returned. The houseboy, the yardboy, even Moyra.

19   TAKUNDA: Momma? I went to see Gogo. She told me another

20   story.

21   WOMAN/MOTHER: Shhh! Did you hear something?

22   TAKUNDA: No.

23   WOMAN/MOTHER: Shhh! *(She listens.)* Someone's coming.

24   TAKUNDA: I didn't hear anything. *(There is the sound of*

25   *pounding on the door.)*

26   WOMAN/MOTHER: Just keep quiet. They'll go away.

27   TAKUNDA: Who is it, Momma?

28   WOMAN/MOTHER: Keep quiet!

29   MAN 1/POLICE: Come on missis. Open the door. We know

30   you're in there.

31   TAKUNDA: It's the police. *(MOTHER goes to open the door.)* No,

32   Momma! Don't open it.

33   WOMAN/MOTHER: What took you so long! They were pelting

34   the house with stones.

35   MAN 1/POLICE: Who was pelting the house?

1   WOMAN/MOTHER: I don't know. People from the area.

2   MAN 2/POLICE: We have no report of pelting.

3   WOMAN/MOTHER: Well you can see for yourself they were
4   here. Just look at the house.

5   MAN 2/POLICE: Missis, we have no report about pelting.

6   WOMAN/MOTHER: Then why are you here?

7   MAN 1/POLICE: We've come about your husband.

8   MAN 2/POLICE: Alfred Chikomba.

9   WOMAN/MOTHER: Is he all right?

10   MAN 1/POLICE: He's fine. He's in the best of health.

11   MAN 2/POLICE: And spirit.

12   MAN 1/POLICE: He's cooperating wonderfully.

13   WOMAN/MOTHER: Then he's to be released?

14   MAN 1/POLICE: Perhaps. It depends.

15   WOMAN/MOTHER: On what?

16   MAN 1/POLICE: On what happens here. You see, we need his
17   papers.

18   WOMAN/MOTHER: What papers? He has no papers.

19   MAN 1/POLICE: Come now. A man like Alfred. Surely he kept
20   transcripts of the meetings held here.

21   WOMAN/MOTHER: Those meetings were not illegal.

22   MAN 1/POLICE: No one suggested they were. What we're
23   interested in are the transcripts.

24   MAN 2/POLICE: And roster. We want the roster of others who
25   attended.

26   WOMAN/MOTHER: There are no rosters, or transcripts.

27   MAN 1/POLICE: Please, missis. The night can be very long. Give
28   us what we want and we may even release your husband.

29   WOMAN/MOTHER: But I'm telling you it doesn't exist. You can
30   look for yourself if you'd like.

31   MAN 1/POLICE: We may end up doing just that.

32   MAN 2/POLICE: Where are your father's papers, child?

33   TAKUNDA: He has no papers.

34   MAN 2/POLICE: You might as well give them to us. He's already
35   given us all the information we want. He's given us names

1   of people who attended the meetings, so you're protecting

2   no one by continuing this charade.

3   WOMAN/MOTHER: If he's already given you this information,

4   why are you here?

5   MAN 1/POLICE: We merely want to confirm it, that's all. We want

6   to make sure he has not incriminated anyone unjustly.

7   MAN 2/POLICE: So give us the roster and we'll be on our way.

8   WOMAN/MOTHER: I've told you. There is no roster.

9   MAN 2/POLICE: Pardon me, missis, but you're a lying bitch.

10   MAN 1/POLICE: He's already told us it existed.

11   WOMAN/MOTHER: Then he should have told you where it was

12   because I don't know.

13   MAN 1/POLICE: I'll make you a deal. Instead of tiring ourselves

14   by ripping this shanty apart, we'll look in only one place.

15   If the roster is there, you go to jail. If the roster is not

16   there, we release your husband. Sound fair?

17   *(WOMAN/MOTHER nods her head. He turns to MAN 2.)*

18   What do you think?

19   MAN 2/POLICE: I think we have to make our only guess a good

20   one.

21   MAN 1/POLICE: Any ideas?

22   MAN 2/POLICE: I suggest we look inside the *calabash*. *(MAN*

23   *1/POLICE picks up the* calabash *and smashes it on the floor.)*

24   MAN 1/POLICE: Where is it!

25   WOMAN/MOTHER: Please! I'm telling you, it doesn't exist.

26   MAN 1/POLICE: Fine. Have it your way. Come on. *(POLICE*

27   *begin to leave.)*

28   WOMAN/MOTHER: Wait. My husband. When will he be

29   released?

30   MAN 1/POLICE: What husband? What are you talking about?

31   WOMAN/MOTHER: You said you would release him.

32   MAN 1/POLICE: Who is your husband again?

33   WOMAN/MOTHER: Alfred Chikomba.

34   MAN 1/POLICE: Piet? We don't have Alfred Chikomba in

35   custody, do we?

1 MAN 2/POLICE: Not that I can recall.

2 MAN 1/POLICE: Must be another district.

3 MAN 2/POLICE: Or perhaps he ran off.

4 MAN 1/POLICE: That happens a lot you know. Black men, run
5   off, desert their families and their families blame the
6   police for their disappearance. I'll tell you, it's a sad state
7   of affairs.

8 WOMAN/MOTHER: Please. We don't have the roster.

9 MAN 1/POLICE: And we, missis, don't have your husband.

10   *(POLICE leave.)*

11 WOMAN/MOTHER: Shingai.

12 TAKUNDA: What?

13 WOMAN/MOTHER: It was Shingai. He's the informant. Don't
14   you see? I told Shingai I put the roster inside the *calabash.*

15 TAKUNDA: Why didn't you give it to them?

16 WOMAN/MOTHER: It wouldn't have done any good.

17 TAKUNDA: They would've released Baba.

18 WOMAN/MOTHER: No.

19 TAKUNDA: That's what they said.

20 WOMAN/MOTHER: The only thing you can be sure of when the
21   police speak is that they are lying, Takunda. We have to
22   leave here. We have to go.

23 TAKUNDA: Go where?

24 WOMAN/MOTHER: *Kumusha.* To live with my mother.

25 TAKUNDA: But that's too far, Momma.

26 WOMAN/MOTHER: We have no choice, Takunda. Don't you
27   see? As long as your father is in jail, people in this area will
28   shun us. They will be afraid to speak with us or be seen
29   with us for fear of association. Even if your father was
30   released tonight, things would not get any better. They
31   would get worse. People will wonder why he was released.
32   They will say that he informed for his freedom. Either
33   way, we have to go.

34 TAKUNDA: I want to stay. I want to be here when Baba comes
35   home.

1 **WOMAN/MOTHER: Takunda, child, there is a possibility that**
2   **your father may never come home.** *(There is a sharp sound,*
3   *like a stone hitting a metal roof. She freezes, listens.)* **They're**
4   **back.**
5 **TAKUNDA: What is it?**
6 **WOMAN/MOTHER: Come!** *(WOMAN/MOTHER grabs TAKUNDA*
7   *and pushes her to a corner. Both crouch down as the pelting*
8   *begins. It continues for a few seconds as the two hold each*
9   *other in the dark. Finally the sounds end. Silence. The two*
10   *do not move.)*
11 **TAKUNDA: Sometimes at night, I dream that Baba has been**
12   **released. I dream that I am sitting in the front of the**
13   **house with Fungi and I am wearing his** *chuma.* **Then, up**
14   **the walk, I see Baba. He is wearing his brown derby and is**
15   **carrying his silver-tipped walking stick. The cane taps on**
16   **the sidewalk as he approaches. Then suddenly, he is there.**
17   **He sweeps me up in his arms and hugs me. . .he calls me**
18   **his little girl. I tell him how much I missed him and he**
19   **says that he'll never leave me again.**
20 **MAN 1/VENDOR:** *(Entering)* **Well, what's this I see? Is it my**
21   **friend, the brat? Yes, but it is. Tell me, my friend, do you**
22   **have fifty cents for SaMuchena?**
23 **TAKUNDA: Well. . .no.**
24 **MAN 1/VENDOR: I figured as much. Dealing with you is a**
25   **losing proposition.**
26 **TAKUNDA: But I'll get it for you.**
27 **MAN 1/VENDOR: When?**
28 **TAKUNDA: Tomorrow?**
29 **MAN 1/VENDOR: But the debt is due today.**
30 **TAKUNDA: I'll have it tomorrow.**
31 **MAN 1/VENDOR: And what makes tomorrow different from**
32   **today?**
33 **TAKUNDA: It is the day I'll pay you your debt.**
34 **MAN 1/VENDOR: Well, then I guess I'll have to live for tomorrow.**
35 **TAKUNDA: May I have another yam?**

1   MAN 1/VENDOR: What's this? Once was not enough? You must
2   take me for two?
3   TAKUNDA: I told you. I'll pay you tomorrow.
4   MAN 1/VENDOR: You haven't paid me for today.
5   TAKUNDA: Then forget it. I'll take my business elsewhere.
6   MAN 1/VENDOR: Come here. What is it with you? What's
7   happened?
8   TAKUNDA: Nothing.
9   MAN 1/VENDOR: Don't tell SaMuchena nothing. My mother
10   did not raise a fool.
11 TAKUNDA: You going to give me a yam or not?
12 MAN 1/VENDOR: I'll make you a deal.
13 TAKUNDA: No deals. The police make deals.
14 MAN 1/VENDOR: Do I look like the police to you? OK, I tell you
15   what. I have a proposition for you.
16 TAKUNDA: And what's that?
17 MAN 1/VENDOR: You do work for me, I'll give you a yam.
18 TAKUNDA: What kind of work?
19 MAN 1/VENDOR: What kind of work do you do?
20 TAKUNDA: What kind of work do you want?
21 MAN 1/VENDOR: Well, you could sell yams. Or, you could carry
22   my bundle. You said yourself it was easy.
23 TAKUNDA: I'll carry the bundle.
24 MAN 1/VENDOR: It's heavy.
25 TAKUNDA: I'll carry it. (*TAKUNDA picks up the bundle, takes a*
26   *couple of steps, VENDOR takes a couple of steps. TAKUNDA*
27   *takes a couple more steps, VENDOR watches her, amused.*)
28   How much further?
29 MAN 1/VENDOR: (*Laughing*) Far enough, little one. And for
30   such a monumental event, here is your yam.
31 TAKUNDA: Thank you.
32 MAN 1/VENDOR: Don't thank me, little one. You earned every
33   bit of it. (*VENDOR laughs, TAKUNDA hungrily bites into the*
34   *yam and eats it.*)
35 WOMAN/GOGO: Taku?

1 TAKUNDA: No news. Momma says we have to leave.

2 WOMAN/GOGO: To go where?

3 TAKUNDA: Back to her homeland.

4 WOMAN/GOGO: Your mother is right, child. The people in
5   your area will turn against you. You have to go.

6 TAKUNDA: And what happens when Baba is released? How will
7   he find us?

8 WOMAN/GOGO: If he is released, he'll go to the flat. If the flat
9   is empty, he'll come here. If I'm still here, I'll tell him
10   where you are. But you have to understand, Takunda,
11   there's a chance that your father may never be released.

12 TAKUNDA: But also a chance that he will be, isn't there?

13 WOMAN/GOGO: Yes, but it's a slim chance.

14 TAKUNDA: Then I'll wait.

15 WOMAN/GOGO: Where? You can't stay here with me. This area
16   in which the government has required me to live is worse
17   than the area delegated as your mother's homeland. The
18   soil here yields barely enough to keep an old woman alive.
19   And then it has to be cajoled and threatened.

20 TAKUNDA: I'll stay in the city.

21 WOMAN/GOGO: How?

22 TAKUNDA: I'll manage.

23 WOMAN/GOGO: You might have to manage for quite a long
24   time, Taku. Each day they keep your father, the chances
25   against his release multiply by ten.

26 TAKUNDA: But a chance still remains.

27 WOMAN/GOGO: Yes. There remains a chance. When you look
28   at the moon, what do you see?

29 TAKUNDA: A woman, carrying wood.

30 WOMAN/GOGO: Do you know how she got there?

31 TAKUNDA: No.

32 WOMAN/GOGO: Remember Tambo Muvimi who was accused
33   of stealing the dagger of the chief? Well Tambo Muvimi
34   took a wife and her name was Sekai. From this union,
35   they had a son, Panashe. Panashe possessed his father's

1   strength and his mother's compassion. So gifted was he
2   that the gods decided to make him one of their own. So
3   while Tambo hunted and Sekai collected wood, the gods
4   came down and took the boy away. Sekai, whose
5   responsibility it was to care for the child, discovered him
6   gone, and with the wood she had collected still on her
7   back, she went into the bush to search for the child.
8   Unable to see him, she took a handful of dust and threw it
9   into the sky and that became the moon. Then she climbed
10   onto the moon so that she could see the entire earth and
11   search for her son. That was quite a long time ago,
12   Takunda, and she's still up there, carrying that wood and
13   searching the earth for her son. Now there still remains a
14   chance that she will see him. The chance remains that he
15   will return one day, wearing his brown derby and
16   carrying his silver-tipped walking stick. *(MAN 1 dons a*
17   *brown derby and picks up a silver-tipped walking stick. He*
18   *taps the stick on the ground.)*
19 TAKUNDA: Baba? *(MAN 1 taps the stick.)* Is that you? Baba?
20 MAN 1/ALFRED: Takunda.
21 TAKUNDA: Baba! *(She runs up, hugs MAN 1.)*
22 MAN 1/ALFRED: Takunda, child, what's wrong?
23 TAKUNDA: Baba! I was so scared!
24 MAN 1/ALFRED: Of what?
25 TAKUNDA: I was afraid that they wouldn't release you.
26 MAN 1/ALFRED: Come now. You know I could never leave you.
27 TAKUNDA: Momma left. She had to go *kumusha.* But I waited,
28   Baba. I waited for you.
29 MAN 1/ALFRED: That's good, Takunda. I'm proud of you.
30 TAKUNDA: I waited.
31 MAN 1/ALFRED: Come. . .let's not make a scene here. We have
32   lots to catch up on. But first, we have to find your mother
33   and bring her home. Then, you can tell me everything that
34   happened while I was gone.
35 TAKUNDA: Yes, Baba. So much has happened.

1   MAN 1/ALFRED: Come. Let's find your mother. *(As THEY are*
2   *about to leave, MAN 2 enters as POLICE.)*
3   MAN 2/POLICE: Excuse me.
4   MAN 1/ALFRED: Yes?
5   MAN 2/POLICE: Alfred Chikomba. Where is he? *(MAN 1*
6   *removes his derby.)*
7   TAKUNDA: Baba?
8   MAN 2/POLICE: Where is your father, child?
9   MAN 1/POLICE: The child is obviously a deaf-mute. Check
10   inside. We want to ask him questions, about the burglar.
11 MAN 2/POLICE: Where is your father, child?
12 MAN 1/POLICE: Is Alfred Chikomba your father? *(MAN 1*
13   *laughs, TAKUNDA backs away.)*
14 WOMAN/MOTHER: *(Entering)* Taku? Takunda!
15 TAKUNDA: Baba?
16 WOMAN/MOTHER: Wake up, child. Wake up. Come. It's time to
17   go.
18 TAKUNDA: He's gone.
19 WOMAN/MOTHER: Come. We must leave before the sun comes
20   up.
21 TAKUNDA: No, Momma. I don't want to go.
22 WOMAN/MOTHER: We have no choice. Come.
23 TAKUNDA: I can stay here in the city. I can manage. I won't be
24   any worse off than if I went to the homeland.
25 WOMAN/MOTHER: But you know nothing about the city.
26 TAKUNDA: I'm learning. And somebody has to be here when
27   Baba's released. Somebody has to stay.
28 WOMAN/MOTHER: Well it won't be you. You're just a child.
29   Come, get ready. It's time to go.
30 TAKUNDA: No, Momma. I can't. I'm sorry.
31 WOMAN/MOTHER: So, my little girl thinks she is no longer a
32   child. She thinks she is a woman.
33 TAKUNDA: Momma, please.
34 WOMAN/MOTHER: You don't know what you're letting
35   yourself in for.

1   TAKUNDA: I know that someone has to remain here and wait
2   for Baba, no matter how long it takes.
3   WOMAN/MOTHER: You know how to get to *kumusha?*
4   TAKUNDA: Yes.
5   WOMAN/MOTHER: I'll be there waiting for you.
6   TAKUNDA: And I will be there as soon as Baba is released.
7   MAN 1/VENDOR: *Mbambaira!* Hot *mbambaira! (MAN 2 appears*
8   *as FUNGI.)*
9   TAKUNDA: Fungi!
10 MAN 1/VENDOR: Makes your tongue laugh and your tummy
11   dance. *(FUNGI places the* chuma *around TAKUNDA's neck*
12   *as VENDOR watches.)*
13 MAN 2/FUNGI: This is for you. You wear it. I'm leaving.
14 TAKUNDA: To go where?
15 MAN 2/FUNGI: To the bush. I'm joining the boys. I'm going to
16   fight, Takunda. *(FUNGI exits. Pause.)*
17 MAN 1/VENDOR: It takes courage in times like these. Yam?
18 TAKUNDA: I can't pay you.
19 MAN 1/VENDOR: But you can work. You can learn how to carry
20   this bundle. *(He sets down the bundle. TAKUNDA picks it*
21   *up.)* You must not try to carry it all at once. Or not all
22   alone, either. Sometimes, I will help you. You will learn
23   that it is no easy task. You must learn how to stop and
24   readjust your load before continuing your journey. But
25   most of all, you must learn how to laugh and you must
26   learn how to sing. *(VENDOR leaves. As TAKUNDA carries*
27   *the load, She begins to sing. Her song begins as a mournful*
28   *one, but slowly builds into a celebration as her voice is*
29   *joined by those of the OTHERS in the cast.)*
30 TAKUNDA:
31   *Rimwe zuva ndiri ndega*
32   *Ndichi funga zvangu*
33   *Ndiani aindi chengeta*
34   *Ndichiri kaduku*
35

1 **ALL:**
2   *Ndivo baba vangu chete*
3   *Rudo rwavo rwaka komba*
4   *Pamwe vese na mai*
5   *Nhasi ndova tenda*
6 **TAKUNDA:**
7   *Kana ndazo tambudzika*
8   *Ndichisina shamwari*
9   *Ndika funga baba vangu*
10   *Ndino wona zororo*
11 **ALL:**
12   *Ndivo baba vangu chete*
13   *Rudo rwavo rwaka komba*
14   *Pamwe vese na mai*
15   *Nhasi ndova tenda*
16
17 **END OF PLAY**
18
19
20
21
22
23
24
25
26
27
28
29
30
31
32
33
34
35

Credits

376

About the Editor

Roger Ellis earned his M.A. in English and Drama from the University of Santa Clara, and his Ph.D. in Dramatic Art from the University of California at Berkeley. During that time he was also guest stage director for several colleges and universities. He has authored or edited eight books in theatre, plus numerous articles, essays and short stories. In 1991 he initiated an ethnic theatre program at Grand Valley State University in Michigan, creating guest artist residencies and staging plays celebrating cultural diversity. In addition, he has been director of the University's Shakespeare Festival since 1993. He has worked professionally as actor or director with various Michigan and California theatres and has served as President of the Theatre Alliance of Michigan for the past six years. He is currently a Professor of Theatre at Grand Valley State University.

Order Form

TM

Meriwether Publishing Ltd.
PO Box 7710
Colorado Springs CO 80933-7710
Phone: 800-937-5297 Fax: 719-594-9916
Website: www.meriwether.com

Please send me the following books:

_____ **Multicultural Theatre II #BK-B223**   **$19.95**
          edited by Roger Ellis
          Contemporary Hispanic, Asian, and African-American plays

_____ **Multicultural Theatre #BK-B205**   **$17.95**
          edited by Roger Ellis
          Scenes and monologs by multicultural writers

_____ **New International Plays for Young**
          Audiences #BK-B257   **$19.95**
          edited by Roger Ellis
          Plays of cultural conflict

_____ **International Plays for Young**
          Audiences #BK-B240   **$16.95**
          edited by Roger Ellis
          Contemporary works from leading playwrights

_____ **Scenes and Monologs from the Best**
          New Plays #BK-B140   **$15.95**
          edited by Roger Ellis
          An anthology of new American plays

_____ **Audition Monologs for Student Actors**
          #BK-B232   **$15.95**
          edited by Roger Ellis
          Selections from contemporary plays

_____ **Audition Monologs for Student Actors II**
          #BK-B249   **$15.95**
          edited by Roger Ellis
          Selections from contemporary plays

These and other fine Meriwether Publishing books are available at your local bookstore or direct from the publisher. Prices subject to change without notice. Check our website or call for current prices.

Name: _____ e-mail: _____

Organization name: _____

Address: _____

City: _____ State: _____

Zip: _____ Phone: _____

❑ **Check enclosed**

❑ **Visa / MasterCard / Discover #** _____

Signature: _____   *Expiration*
          (required for credit card orders)   *date:* _____

Colorado residents: Please add 3% sales tax.
Shipping: Include $3.95 for the first book and 75¢ for each additional book ordered.

❑ *Please send me a copy of your complete catalog of books and plays.*